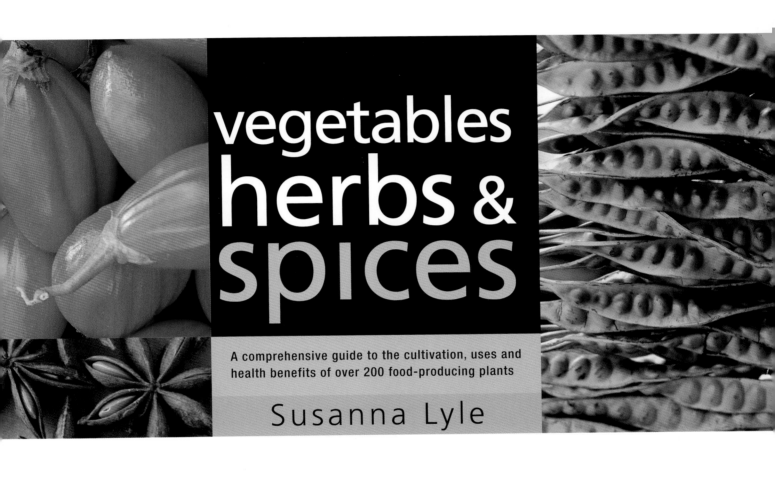

vegetables
herbs &
spices

A comprehensive guide to the cultivation, uses and
health benefits of over 200 food-producing plants

Susanna Lyle

F

FRANCES LINCOLN LIMITED
PUBLISHERS

Frances Lincoln Limited
4 Torriano Mews
Torriano Avenue
London NW5 2RZ
www.franceslincoln.com

Vegetables Herbs and Spices
By Susanna Lyle
Copyright © David Bateman Ltd, 2009
Text copyright © Susanna Lyle, 2009

Susanna Lyle asserts her right to be identified as the author of this work.

First Frances Lincoln edition: 2009

British Library Cataloguing in Publication Data
A catalogue record for this book is available from the British Library

ISBN 13: 978-0-7112-2963-1

Book design: Jag Creative
Typesetting: Book NZ
Illustrations: Errol McLeary
Printed in China through Colorcraft Ltd., Hong Kong

9 8 7 6 5 4 3 2 1

ACKNOWLEDGEMENTS

I would like to thank the following for generously providing images:

Tatiana and Mike at Top Tropicals Nursery in Florida (http://www.toptropicals.com/index.htm) for the following images: *Eryngium foetidum*, *Lablab purpureus*, *Moringa oleifera*, and *Xanthosoma robusta*.

Alistair Grinbergs (Australian Antarctic Division © Commonwealth of Australia) for the kerguelen cabbage image (Atlas Cove, Heard Island).

I am grateful to many friends for sharing information and ideas.

Thanks to Wendy Laurenson for ploughing her way through all the text, and to Caroline List and Tracey Borgfeldt at David Bateman Ltd for all their input and bringing this project to fruition.

PLANT FAMILIES

The majority of edible plant species are members of relatively few plant families. Below, the main species described in this book are listed according to the family they belong to. As you read through the individual species descriptions, the similarity between members of the same family is often apparent.

FAMILY	SPECIES	PLANT NAME
Acoraceae	Acorus calamus	Calamus
Agaricaceae	Agaricus spp.	Mushrooms
Agavaceae (syn. Lilaceae)	Camassia quamash	Quamash
Aizoaceae	Tetragonia tetragonioides	New Zealand spinach (Warrigal greens)
Alismataceae	Sagittaria latifolia	Duck potato (syn. wapato)
	Sagittaria sagittifolia	Arrowhead
	Sagittaria trifolia	Chinese arrowroot
Alliaceae (formerly Liliaceae)	Allium ampeloprasum	Leek, elephant garlic, Babbington's leek, kurrat
	Allium ascalonicum	Shallots
	Allium cepa	Onion
	Allium cepa aggregatum	Potato onion
	Allium cepa proliferum	Tree onion
	Allium fistulosum	Spring onions (scallions)
	Allium sativum	Garlic
	Allium schoenoprasum	Chives
	Allium tuberosum	Garlic chives
	Allium ursinam	Ramsons
Amaranthaceae	Amaranth caudatus	Amaranth
	Celosia argentea	Celosia
Apiaceae (Umbeliferae)	Anethum graveolens	Dill
	Angelica archangelica	Angelica
	Anthriscus cerefolium	Chervil
	Apium graveolens	Celery, celeriac
Apiaceae	Arracacia xanthorrhiza	Arracacha
	Carum carvi	Caraway
	Coriandrum sativum	Coriander (cilantro)

FAMILY	SPECIES	PLANT NAME
Apiaceae	Cryptotaenia japonica	Mitsuba
	Cuminum cyminum	Cumin
	Daucus carota sativus	Carrot
	Eryngium foetidum	Mexican coriander
	Ferula assa-foetida	Asafoetida
	Foeniculum vulgaris	Fennel, Sicilian fennel, Florence fennel
	Levisticum officinale	Lovage
	Levisticum scoticum	Scottish lovage
	Lomatium cous	Biscuit root
	Myrrhis odorata	Cicely
	Pastinaca sativa	Parsnip
	Perideridia gairdneri	Yampah
	Petroselinum crispum	Parsley: French and curled, Cilician parsley, Hamburg parsley
	Pimpinella anisum	Anise
	Sium sisarum sisarum	Skirret
	Smyrnium olusatrum	Alexanders
	Trachyspermum ammi	Ajowan
Aquifoliaceae	Ilex kaushu	Ku ding cha
	Ilex paraguariensis	Maté tea
Araceae	Alocasia spp.	Taro-like spp.
	Amorphophallus spp.	Elephant foot yam
	Colocasia esculenta	Taro
	Cyrtosperma spp.	Giant swamp taro
	Xanthosoma atrovirens	Yautia
	Xanthosoma spp.	Tannia, giant golden taro, giant elephant ear

FAMILY	SPECIES	PLANT NAME
Araceae (continued)	*Xanthosoma violaceum*	Blue taro
Araliaceae	*Aralia nudicaulis*	Wild sarsaparilla
	Aralia racemosa	American spikehead
Ascomycetes	*Morchella* spp.	Morels
	Ustilago maydis	Huitlacoche
Asparagaceae (Lilaceae)	*Asparagus officinalis*	Asparagus
Asteraceae (formerly Compositae)	*Anthemis arvensis*	Corn chamomile
	Anthemis nobilis	Chamomile
	Anthemis tinctoria	Ox-eye chamomile
	Arctium lappa	Great burdock
	Arctium minus	Wild burdock
	Artemisia dracunculus	Tarragon
	Calendula officinalis	Calendula (pot marigold)
	Carthamus tinctorius	Safflower
	Chrysanthemum balsamita	Costmary
	Chrysanthemum leucanthemum	Ox-eye daisy
	Chrysanthemum spp.	Chrysanthemums
	Cichorium endivia	Endive
	Cichorium intybus	Chicory (witloof, radicchio)
	Cynara cardunculus	Cardoon
	Cynara scolymus	Globe artichoke
	Glebionis coronaria	Chrysanthemum, edible
	Helianthus tuberosus	Jerusalem artichoke
	Helichrysum italicum	Curry plant
	Lactuca sativa	Lettuce
	Lactuca sativa asparagina	Celtuce
	Matricaria chamomilla	German chamomile
	Matricaria matricarioides	Rayless chamomile
	Scolymus grandiflorus	Large-flowered golden thistle
	Scolymus hispanicus	Common golden thistle

FAMILY	SPECIES	PLANT NAME
Asteraceae (continued)	*Scolymus maculatus*	Spotted golden thistle
	Scorzonera hispanica	Scorzonera
	Silybum marianum	Milk thistle
	Smallanthus sonchifolia	Yacón
	Taraxacum officinale	Dandelion
	Tragopogon spp.	Salsify
Basellaceae	*Basella alba*	Malabar spinach
	Ullucus tuberosus	Ulluco
Bixaceae	*Bixa orellana*	Annatto
Boraginaceae	*Borago officinalis*	Borage
Brassicaceae (formerly Cruciferae)	*Alliaria petiolata*	Garlic mustard
	Armoracia rusticana	Horseradish
	Barbarea verna,	Landcress
	Brassica campestris	Field mustard
	Brassica hirta	White mustard
	Brassica juncea	Indian mustard
	Brassica napobrassica	Swede
	Brassica napus napus	Rape
	Brassica narinosa	Misome
	Brassica nigra	Black mustard
	Brassica oleracea acephala	Collards, kale
	Brassica oleracea alboglabra	Kai lan
	Brassica oleracea botrytis	Cauliflower
	Brassica oleracea capitata	Cabbage
	Brassica oleracea caulo-rapa	Kohlrabi
	Brassica oleracea gemmifera	Brussels sprouts
	Brassica oleracea italica	Broccoli
	Brassica rapa	Turnip
	Brassica rapa parachinensis	Choi sum
	Brassica rapa pekinensis	Chinese cabbage

tubers need to be carefully removed, often with a section of the stem, to ensure that they have one or more of these buds. Left to establish on their own, these species form large clumps of tubers, with older tubers dying off.

PLANT TYPES

TEMPERATE PLANTS

Temperate plants can be divided into cold- and warm-temperate types. Cold-temperate species can tolerate long, cold winters with temperatures below ~10°C, with many species tolerating temperatures down to ~30°C and colder. They usually cannot tolerate intense heat. Warm-temperate plants can withstand cold winter temperatures, but not excessively so. They may be damaged by temperatures below ~8°C. They can tolerate frosts, but not for extended periods. The division between warm- and cold-temperate plants is often referred to in this book.

Most temperate plants need a period of winter chilling to initiate flowering and leaf growth in spring: if it is not cold enough for long enough, flower buds may open unevenly or not at all. In contrast, if the plant species comes into blossom too early, then there is a risk of frost damage. Cold-temperate species usually need long periods of winter chill, so do not grow well in warmer areas. Warm-temperate species, however, are more adaptable, needing less winter chill, and can grow in a wide band around the middle latitudes, though they are more susceptible to late winter frosts.

In temperate areas, it is possible to grow more frost-tender species as long as they are given extra protection and a sunny location. Avoid hollows that may become frost pockets in winter. Cold air sinks, and there is often a difference in the degrees of frost that can develop between the bottom of a valley and the ridge above it. Growing plants in a container, and moving these into a glasshouse or conservatory in winter, can be another way to overcome cold winters.

In general, blossom and leaves are the most vulnerable to cold damage, followed by younger stems. If these are damaged, many species will grow back from older wood, so give time in spring for this to happen before discarding any frost-damaged plants.

SUBTROPICAL AND TROPICAL PLANTS

A subtropical climate is generally classified as having cooler winters, but no or only light frosts. Temperatures below ~4°C usually cause some damage to the plant. It is only moderately or barely cold in winter, and the summers may be humid or dry. In these regions, it is also possible to grow a number of tropical species, though obtaining a long-enough growing season often determines if a species can produce a mature crop. In warmer climates, although a lack of winter chill limits the growth of some temperate species, there are many exciting warm-temperate and subtropical plants to explore instead.

There is an overlap between subtropical and tropical species; however, tropical species cannot tolerate temperatures near freezing, and can seldom grow, and almost never flower or fruit in warm-temperate regions.

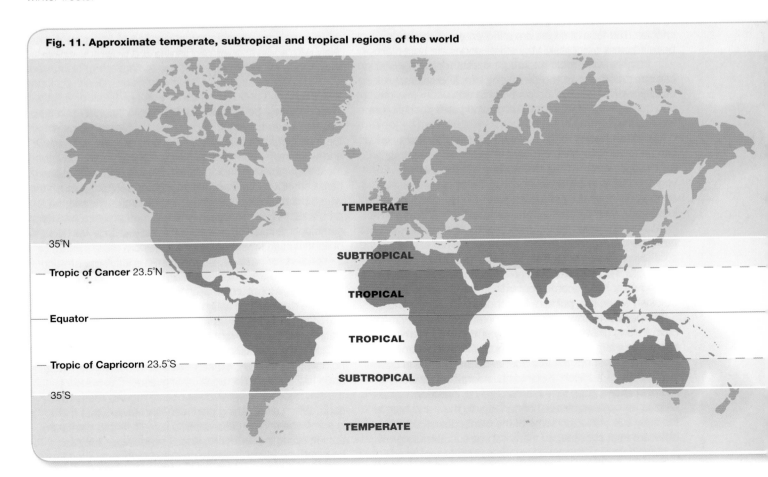

Fig. 11. Approximate temperate, subtropical and tropical regions of the world

35°N

TEMPERATE

SUBTROPICAL

— Tropic of Cancer 23.5°N —

TROPICAL

— Equator —

TROPICAL

— Tropic of Capricorn 23.5°S —

SUBTROPICAL

35°S

TEMPERATE

Fig. 12. Nutrient availability at different pH

Relationship between soil pH and plant-nutrient availability, with the wider the bar, the greater the availability

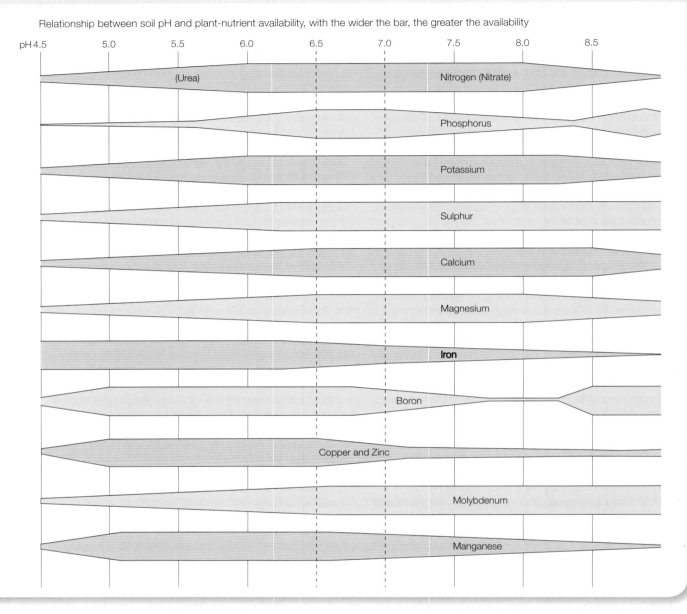

the soil, the greater the pH is above 7. The majority of vegetable and seed species prefer a pH that ranges from 5.7–7.0, somewhat slightly acid to neutral. Plants have adapted to differing pH conditions, not because of the concentration of hydrogen ions, but because of the effect of the soil minerals, some of which are nutrients but also some that are heavy metals, with the latter reaching toxic concentrations at certain pH levels. For example, aluminium and iron become much more soluble and available at more acid pH levels. Although plants take up and use iron as a nutrient, they do not need aluminium: too much aluminium is toxic to plants and can kill them. In addition, many other metals become more available at acid pH levels, e.g. manganese, copper, zinc. Figure 12 shows the availability of the main nutrients at different pH values. It can be seen that at more acidic pH values most nutrients, such as potassium, phosphate, nitrogen and molybdenum, become

less available to the plant. This does not mean that they are not in the soil, but that they are chemically locked up and unavailable. Also note that bacteria do not like acid soil.

At more alkaline or higher pH values, nutrients, such as phosphate, iron, manganese and zinc become unavailable. Iron deficiency is common in alkaline soils, causing iron chlorosis, with leaves becoming yellowish (due to lack of chlorophyll) as iron is necessary in the pathway that produces sugars during photosynthesis (as is magnesium). Application to the leaves of a liquid containing the various micronutrients can overcome this, as can the addition of acidic organic matter, such as sulphate-based fertilisers, to the soil. At acid pH values plants can also suffer various nutrient deficiencies, but these can be simply remedied by the addition of lime to raise pH, rather than the addition of more nutrients, which can result in more problems than it cures.

Neutralising pH

It is easier to make a soil more alkaline than to make it more acidic for planting alkaline- or acid-loving species, respectively. The application of lime, in its various forms, is an easy and controllable way of increasing pH. This can be purchased in farm shops or garden centres, but the addition of crushed shells or chalk will also work, although it tends to take longer for added materials to make a soil more acidic. If planting long-term acid-loving plants, it is a good idea to mix peat or pine needles into the soil, though bear in mind that pine needles also inhibit germination of seeds and growth of seedlings.

The usual method of lowering pH, however, is by adding sulphur. Flowers of sulphur is pure sulphate and is available in most garden centres. It can have an irritating effect on human skin as well as to plant roots, if in close contact with them: historically, it was known as brimstone! Specific bacteria in the soil convert it to sulphuric acid, though this process can take several weeks. It is, by far, the strongest soil acidifier, and should be used cautiously, if at all. However, gardeners sometimes use flowers of sulphur to deter certain pests (e.g. red-spider mite) and bacteria either on or around plants. It has also long been used as an efficient fungicide, particularly on fruit trees.

For acidifying the soil, it is usually better and safer to use ammonium-nitrogen plus a sulphur fertiliser. In some situations, a liquid sulphate (e.g. ammonium thiosulphate) can be applied to crops for a quicker response to cure iron-deficient chlorosis, caused by alkaline pH. Ammonium sulphate is generally thought to be the most effective soil acidifiers: phosphates may also be added to the mix. The addition of just acidic nitrogenous urea also acts as a soil acidifier.

The application of stronger acidifiers needs to be done judiciously, as excess sulphur is difficult to neutralise or remove. As mentioned, flowers of sulphur is by far the strongest, and only minimal amounts are needed to change pH. However, ammonium sulphate and sulphate-coated urea are also powerful compounds (about eight times less powerful than flowers of sulphur) and should also be applied in moderation. In contrast, the sulphate salts, such as potassium sulphate, calcium sulphate (gypsum), magnesium sulphate (Epsom salts) are much gentler acidifiers, with the addition of gypsum also helping to break up heavy clay soils. These salts are more commonly added as plant fertilisers rather than as soil acidifiers, in fact, those containing calcium or magnesium have a negligible effect on changing soil pH. Aluminium sulphate is also sometimes used to lower pH, but does not add any other nutrients, and is a stronger compound. It is often used around camellias and rhododendrons.

NUTRIENTS AND THEIR DEFICIENCY SYMPTOMS

Below are brief descriptions of the main plant nutrients.

Nitrogen (N)

Nitrogen is a somewhat different nutrient to most others because of its dependence on bacteria (see Symbiosis on p. 27). It is essential for plant and animal growth, and is needed for protein and enzyme formation, as well as for the formation of DNA and RNA. It is also related to nutrient uptake: a deficiency of nitrogen can result in poor uptake of other essential nutrients. It is a mobile nutrient within plants, and deficiencies show up first in older leaves.

Most plants take up nitrogen as nitrate (e.g. NO_3); this form of nitrogen is much more available in neutral to alkaline soils. However, nitrate and nitrite are very easily leached from soil, and are better added as well-rotted manure or blood and bone, which are released more slowly. Excess nitrate is rapidly transported down to the groundwater and into rivers and lakes and causes environmental problems (eutrophication).

Some plant species have evolved to grow in acid soils, and are often found in colder climates where peat-like soils are prevalent. In acid conditions, nitrate is not available; instead, plants use ammonia (NH_4, or urea) as their nitrogen source. Although needing less chemical energy to be formed, it is still obtained indirectly from plants via organic breakdown products. Also, like nitrates, it is easily leached and lost from the soil.

Nitrogen increases leaf area and growth, and gives plants a rich green colour; however, too much nitrogen results in lush, thin-leaved foliage that is more susceptible to pathogen attack, drought and frost. In many root, seed and fruit crops excess nitrogen encourages copious leaf growth, but reduces yields of other parts of the plant: many species actually form more fruits/seeds and larger storage organs if mineral nutrition is somewhat compromised, particularly of nitrogen. However, a more severe and prolonged deficiency of nitrogen results in pale-green to yellow leaves with poor growth. Plants are usually much smaller than normal and leaves die more rapidly. Apart from fertiliser, well-rotted manure, blood and bone, and crop rotation with legumes are all good sources of nitrogen.

Potassium (K)

This is a mobile nutrient within the plant: it is needed for transport, is important in fruit and seed formation, and in photosynthesis. It is involved in cell permeability and increases disease resistance. It is fairly mobile within the plant, and older leaves are affected first when potassium is deficient. Symptoms show up as pale, irregular yellow patches around leaf margins and between leaf veins, turning to pale brown-black patches, and leaves can become cupped. Levels of potassium in soils are often quite high, but it tends to be locked up within soil minerals. Any available potassium is fairly easily leached from the soil and so deficiencies can be fairly common, particularly in lighter sandy soils. Wood ash can also be a source of potassium, as can well-rotted manure and compost.

Phosphate (P)

In the plant, this nutrient is part of the cell nucleus and is needed for producing biochemical energy and cell division and is particularly necessary at root and shoot tips where active growth is occurring. It is also involved in opening of stomata. It is not very mobile within the plant, so deficiencies show up in newer leaves, but can be difficult to detect. A dull, mauve-grey-green colour in new leaves is often an indicator, and plants are smaller and older leaves turn yellow. Deficiencies also affect leaf and seed production, and lead to poor root growth. In the soil, this nutrient is again not very mobile and readily forms a range of complex molecules with organic matter and soil particles: this makes phosphate largely unavailable to plants at both high and low pH values (see Mycorrhiza, on p. 28), even though it is present. Because it is also not easily leached, deficiencies are usually a result of unsuitable pH rather than a shortage within the soil.

Calcium (Ca)

Plants need calcium for tissues that are actively dividing, such as the growing tips of plants and roots, but also in cell walls. It can be in short supply in some soils (e.g. those derived from granitic-type igneous rocks and in acid soils), though it can be easily supplied as limestone or dolomite (with magnesium). If calcium-deficient, the younger leaves are affected first. Symptoms can show as terminal bud death, with distortion and necrosis (death) of young leaves, and root tips may become soft, pulpy and swollen.

Magnesium (Mg)

Magnesium is needed by chlorophyll molecules, which trap light energy in photosynthesis: a shortage results in pale leaves. It is also involved with phosphate use and often accumulates in plants that have seeds rich in oil. Deficiencies affect older leaves first. Often visible as interveinal chlorosis, with persistent green-leaf margins, plus yellow patches and brown, dead areas, although you can sometimes get brilliant orange, red or purple tints. Magnesium can be in short supply in many soils, particularly those that are acidic, and is often not as available as calcium. It can be added as dolomite and is included in many general fertilisers. Dolomite is a type of crushed rock and although a little more expensive than ordinary limestone, it is a good remedy as it provides both calcium and magnesium.

Sulphur (S)

Needed for protein and enzyme formation by the plant and is involved in photosynthesis. It is also a component of certain vitamins. Deficiencies show in younger leaves first, identifiable by being smaller, pale green-yellow, with shortened internodes. Leaf veins become chlorotic. However, this nutrient is fairly mobile in the soil and while it can be leached, it does not generally become deficient. In many countries there is no shortage of soil sulphur due to emissions from cars and industry; deficiencies are also unlikely near coastal or volcanic regions. It can be easily added as gypsum if needed.

Micronutrients

These are needed by plants, but only in small amounts. Specific deficiencies are often difficult to confirm, short of doing a leaf analysis. Unfortunately, several diseases can cause similar discolouration to leaves, and symptoms also tend to vary between species. However, if suspected, a pH test is a good starting point: subsequent alteration of soil pH solves the majority of deficiency problems, as does addition of well-rotted manure. Deficiencies can also be treated by using a general fertiliser that includes the micronutrients or they can be added by applying chelates to the leaves. Although the latter can be effectively absorbed through the leaves, they should only be applied at low concentrations as some species are susceptible to leaf burn.

Boron (B): Boron is involved with carbohydrate regulation, and is needed for protein synthesis. It is also crucial for the process of flower fertilisation (pollen germination and growth) and for seed formation: thus, one of the deficiency symptoms is premature flower drop before fertilisation. A deficiency can also result in poor water uptake by the plant. Younger leaves are affected first. They are often light green-yellow at base, misshapen, thick, brittle and small, with dieback of the terminal bud. Cracks and splits occur in leaf and main stems and root tips become enlarged. Deficiency can also cause heart rot in beets and various brassica root crops. It may be deficient in some soils, particularly alkaline and sandy soils, but because plants only need a little, toxicities can also easily occur, so any application needs care. Neutralising the soil pH increases the availability of boron.

Chlorine (Cl): This nutrient is only needed in small amounts. Deficiency results in poor water control and wilting, as well as leaf chlorosis. It seems to work with nitrate within the plant, with greater tissue chlorine resulting in greater disease (particularly fungal) resistance; conversely, higher nitrate levels lead to increased disease. It is now known that plants need more chlorine than was once thought, and although shortages are uncommon and are very unlikely near the coast, they are more possible towards the centres of large continents.

Cobalt (Co): Needed for fixing nitrogen, so is particularly necessary for leguminous species. Soil deficiencies affect livestock, leading to a lack of B12. Availability of cobalt to plant uptake decreases as soils become more alkaline, therefore neutralising pH can remedy the problem.

Copper (Cu): Copper is needed in photosynthesis, respiration and for the usage of iron. Deficiencies sometimes, but not always, show as chlorotic leaves, particularly when they are younger (as it is not very mobile within the plant), poor pollination (therefore poor seed formation) and reduced production of plant hormones. Leaves also become rolled or curled, and emerging leaves are often trapped within older ones. Copper becomes increasingly unavailable to plants in sandy and alkaline soils, so neutralising pH can remedy deficiencies. In very organic-rich soils it can also become unavailable as it forms complex, chemically linked material that is resistant to breakdown, though it is released as the soils begin to weather.

Iron (Fe): There is lots of iron in the soil and it just needs to be available to the plant at the right pH. For example, if planted in more acidic soils many brassica species are likely to suffer from pale chlorotic leaves. These plants are unable to take up adequate available iron and, because iron is needed indirectly for photosynthesis and because it is not very mobile, the younger leaves are affected first. They become pale and stunted, though leaf veins remain darker green. Foliar applications remedy this problem rather than adding iron to the soil, where it is likely to become unavailable again. Alternately, neutralise the soil pH by adding either limestone or sulphur fertilisers (e.g. Epsom salts, see pH on p.33).

Manganese (Mn): This is needed in certain enzyme reactions, the formation and activity of chloroplasts, for

and reduces histamine levels. Can be used to synthesise cysteine. *Sources:* nuts and seeds.

Phenylalanine: Used by the brain to produce norepinephrine, a neurotransmitter, and so promotes alertness and vitality; is also said to elevate mood, decrease pain, and aid memory and learning. Is related to appetite control. Can increase blood pressure in hypotension. Precursor of adrenaline and noradrenaline. Also used to reduce symptoms of arthritis, menstrual cramps, migraines, obesity, Parkinson's disease and schizophrenia. Tyrosine can partially substitute for phenylalanine. *Sources:* nuts, avocado, brown rice, legumes, soy, corn.

Threonine: Needed to maintain proper protein balance in the body; important in the formation of collagen, elastin and tooth enamel. Involved in fat metabolism, and helps prevent the build-up of fat in the liver. Works with phenylalanine to elevate mood. Deficiency may be associated with irritability in children. Involved with the manufacture of adrenaline, and is a precursor of thyroid hormone. *Sources:* whole cereals, nuts, pulses, leafy vegetables.

Tryptophan: Involved in neuronal activity. Produces serotonin, which induces sleep, helps reduce anxiety and depression, and stabilises mood. Improves immune-system functioning and enhances the release of growth hormones. May be involved with blood-clotting mechanisms. *Sources:* pumpkin seeds, brown rice, legumes, peanuts.

Valine: Involved in muscle metabolism and co-ordination, tissue repair and regulates protein turnover. Used as an energy source by muscle tissue. May promote mental vigour, calm emotions and be helpful in treating liver and gall bladder disease. *Sources:* sesame seeds, legumes, peanuts, soy.

Note that most of the above are also found in eggs, dairy products, meat and fish.

Gluten

Gluten is a general name for types of protein-type compounds found in the starchy endosperm of wheat and other cereal grains. It is a sticky, elastic compound that gives bread its open texture, which grains lacking glutens are unable to emulate. It is usually broken down to amino acids; however, some people are unable to properly digest gluten proteins, and are said to have coeliac (also known as celiac) disease (or wheat, rye and barley intolerance). Over time, this disease impairs the ability of the gut to absorb other foods. Gluten is composed of prolamines and glutelins, and it is the prolamine, gliadin that seems to cause this problem, with the body producing antibodies against it. Wheat has the highest amount of gliadin. Several other cereals also contain fairly high quantities of prolamines, though do not contain gliadin, e.g. barley, millet, rye, corn and sorghum. In contrast, oats contain much less prolamine. However, several types of grains do not contain these compounds and are safe to eat, e.g. quinoa, rice, potato, amaranth, buckwheat. Coeliac disease can be life threatening; however, very few people have this condition (1:300 of the population).

In contrast, many more people suffer from non-coeliac wheat sensitivity. This disorder is quite different to coeliac disease. It is caused by difficulty in digesting various compounds within wheat, and can develop as people get older. It is not an allergy. It may be associated with symptoms such as bloating, tiredness, constipation/diarrhoea and intestinal cramps. Some think that many cases remain undiagnosed; others believe that many falsely diagnose themselves with this condition. Professionals may recommend that, if you suspect this disorder, you try a wheat-free diet for three weeks to assess its effects.

Lectins

Lectins are a type of protein found in many grains and seeds, e.g. wheat, but particularly in legumes, e.g. kidney beans. They are a glycoprotein, which can cause cells to stick or clump together, especially red blood cells, to result in various cellular alterations. Thus, they are toxic and can inhibit growth. However, lectins are important in blood typing (ABO) and have also been used in alternative cancer treatments. For beans, particularly red kidney beans, prolonged cooking and discarding the water they are soaked and cooked in, removes almost all lectins.

SUGARS, CARBOHYDRATES AND FIBRE

Complex carbohydrates are readily broken down to simpler carbohydrates and sugars when digested. The size and complexity of the carbohydrate determines how long it takes to be digested. Sugars and simple carbohydrates are absorbed much more rapidly during digestion and, thus, cause more rapid rises in blood-sugar level compared with slow-release, larger-sized carbohydrates. It is thought that, apart from concerns about obesity, the rapid absorption of refined foods, such as sugar and refined carbohydrates, can lead, in the longer term, to hormonal imbalances connected with glucose control. The glycaemic index (GI) gives an indication of how long it takes for carbohydrates to be broken down and used by the body. It gives a numerical value to the speed at which carbohydrates and sugars increase blood-glucose level: the higher the food's number, the faster it is broken down during digestion to increase blood-glucose level. Foods with lower scores are generally higher in dietary fibre. Foods that are broken down more slowly, to give energy over a longer period, are more beneficial than quick-energy foods, such as sugar, unless a quick burst of energy is needed. Most vegetables, cereals and seeds have low GI numbers: however, refined products, such as white flour and rice, which have had their outer fibre-rich husk and aleurone layer removed, have a higher GI. Conversely, foods that contain proteins and fats slow down the absorption of carbohydrates; hence, seeds, nuts and legumes have low GI numbers; they are considered a good food source and provide nutrients and energy over a long time period.

Fibre

Fibre can be divided into two main types: insoluble and soluble forms.

Insoluble fibre: As its name suggests, insoluble fibre is not digested by the gut; instead, it acts like a sponge, absorbing many times its own weight of water. Swollen, it binds around other waste food products, and helps their passage through the gut. Thus, the passage of stools is easier, constipation and haemorrhoids are relieved, and the risk of more serious diseases, such as diverticular disease and bowel cancer, are reduced. Insoluble fibre does not significantly increase the gut-bacterial population, nor does it affect blood-cholesterol levels, but it does inactivate intestinal toxins, inhibit the adhesion of pathogenic bacteria to the gut wall, reduce excess permeability of the intestines, and is linked with decreased risks of colon and breast cancer. Fibre-rich diets have been shown to significantly reduce the incidence of gallstones: this may be partly due to insoluble fibre reducing the secretion of bile acids (excess bile is thought to contribute to their formation). Wheat bran and whole grains, as well as the skins of many fruits, vegetables and seeds, are rich sources of insoluble fibre.

Soluble fibre: Is also excellent for the digestive process, but also absorbs cholesterol; a very good form of soluble fibre is oats. Soluble fibre is broken down as it passes though the gut to form a gel that can trap cholesterol-like substances and then eliminate them before they are absorbed into the blood system. This reduced absorption of cholesterol is thought to lessen the risk of heart disease. Studies have found that people who eat a high-fibre diet have lower total cholesterol levels. Classified within soluble fibre are the pectins (common in many fruits), gums (such as guar), betaglucans, some hemicellulose compounds and inulin. Soluble fibre is found in many whole grains, legumes, brown rice, and some seeds, green vegetables and fruits.

It is thought to be beneficial to those with diabetes as it helps control blood-sugar levels. It reduces the amount of glucose absorbed into the body and delays gastric emptying, thus smoothing out blood-sugar-level peaks and troughs (known as the post-prandial rise in blood sugar). The delay in gastric emptying means that people feel fuller for longer after a meal, thus helping prevent overeating. Diets low in fibre cause sudden increases in blood sugar, which initiates the secretion of insulin from the pancreas. Because habitual peaks and troughs in blood-sugar-level are thought to initiate type II diabetes, adequate soluble fibre within the diet is thought to reduce this disease. This disease also more than doubles the risk of stroke and heart disease.

Soluble fibre binds with bile acids, compounds that are necessary for the digestion of fats and are manufactured by the liver from cholesterol. The complexed bile acids are then treated as waste and removed from the circulation, so do not make it back to the liver. The liver then uses additional cholesterol to make new bile acids, thus taking more cholesterol out of the system. In addition, soluble fibre is 'food' for the 'good' bacteria within the large intestine. They partially ferment it to form short-chain fatty acids. Of these, butyric acid is important in the continual renewal and replacement of cells within the large intestine, it indirectly helps maintain the health of the colon, and may reduce the incidence of rectal and colon cancers: the number one cancer killer. Two other fatty acids produced by gut bacteria are propionic and acetic acids: both are used as energy sources by liver and muscle cells. In addition, propionic acid inhibits enzymes that produce cholesterol in the liver; thus, it may add to the cholesterol-lowering properties of fibre. A further benefit is that the increased population of 'good' gut bacteria reduces the number and survival of pathogenic bacteria in the gut. It is recommended that the diet include ~30 g of insoluble and soluble fibre a day.

Inulin and oligofructose: Inulin is a soluble fibre found in many plants, but is particularly abundant within plants from the Asteraceae (sunflower) family, e.g. Jerusalem artichoke, chicory, dandelion. Also known as fructo-oligosaccharides and as 'prebiotics', inulin is not actually metabolised in the mouth, stomach or small intestines; instead, it is only fermented by the microflora within the colon. There it stimulates the growth of further 'good' gut bacteria (e.g. *Lactobacilli* and *Bifidobacteria*), which benefit the digestive system. The 'good' bacteria stimulate the immune system, aid absorption of calcium and magnesium, and promote the synthesis of B vitamins. It can reduce constipation and suppresses the production of 'bad' bacteria in the colon, which can act as toxins or carcinogens. Because it is not digested, inulin does not result in weight gain, and is suitable for consumption by diabetics: inulin does not affect blood glucose, does not stimulate insulin secretion or affect glucagon secretion. Inulin and oligofructose also reduce serum-triglyceride and cholesterol levels, with significant improvements seen in humans in a short time. Medically, inulin and oligofructose may be used synergistically with beneficial live 'good' bacteria (probiotics, e.g. in yoghurt) to promote intestinal health.

Most commercially produced inulin and the sweeter oligofructose are either made from sucrose or are extracted from chicory roots. They are used worldwide in processed foods as a fat replacement: they improve the texture and taste of fat-free foods, plus adding to the food's fibre content. They have no peculiar flavours and can be added to foods without thickening them. They give foods the impression of sweetness and creaminess without the addition of calories. Oligofructose has a smooth, sweet flavour, is very soluble, and is widely used in low-fat yoghurt and other similar products.

On the negative side, high doses of inulin can cause gastrointestinal complaints such as flatulence and bloating, as those who have eaten too many Jerusalem artichokes can confirm.

FATS

Not all fats are bad. In fact, fats are important in the diet and are a source of the essential vitamins A, D, E and K, with seeds and nuts being an excellent source of many unsaturated fats. About 95% of body fat is in the form of triglycerides, which are classified as simple fats. Triglycerides can be either saturated fatty acids, where all the sites are filled with hydrogen ions (it is saturated with hydrogen) or unsaturated fatty acids, where only some of the sites are filled by hydrogen, and these are liquid at room temperature. The types of fats are outlined as follows:

Unsaturated fats

These are found primarily in seeds, nuts, seafoods and fish, and come in two main types: polyunsaturated and monounsaturated. They differ in the ease that they are broken down inside the body.

Polyunsaturated fats: These have multiple double bonds within their structure, and as the number of these bonds determines their liquidity, these fats remain soluble, even at low temperatures. Unfortunately, the more double bonds a fatty acid has, the greater its susceptibility to becoming rancid. However, combined with vitamin E, this rate of deterioration is reduced. Most polyunsaturated fats can be made within the body from other precursors; exceptions are alpha-linolenic acid (a type of omega-3 essential fatty acid) and linoleic acid (an omega-6 essential fatty acid) — essential fatty acids which have to be taken in within the diet. They are needed as precursors for the formation of other fatty acids, and are used to make several compounds (e.g. eicosanoids) that are involved with increasing or reducing inflammation, affecting mood and behaviour, modulating cellular communication, and affecting DNA activity.

1 *Omega-3 essential fatty acids* (e.g. alpha-linolenic acid). These are easily broken down in the body and are used in many metabolic processes. The human body cannot synthesise omega-3 fatty acids from scratch; however, most can be synthesised from the simple-structured alpha-linolenic acid. Therefore, alpha-linolenic acid must be obtained from food and is, therefore, classified as an essential fatty acid. It has three double bonds, though other omega-3s can have more (e.g. eicosapentaenoic acid has five). A lot of interest and research indicates that omega-3 fatty acids can reduce the risk of arterial disease. They can decrease amounts of 'bad' cholesterol (low-density lipids [LDL]; see p. 48); decrease the tendency of blood platelets to clot together; discourage narrowing of arteries, and increase the production of an anti-clotting agent. The main source of omega-3 fatty acids are from flax, but also nuts, seeds, spirulina, green vegetables, fish and soybeans. They are also vitally important within cell membranes.

2 *Omega-6 essential fatty acids* (e.g. linoleic acid, gamma-linolenic acid [an isomer of alpha linolenic acid], arachidonic acid). These are easily broken down and used throughout the body. They are liquid at room temperature, and are found particularly in borage oil, but also in spirulina and vegetable, seed and nut oils. They are thought to lower both high-density lipids (HDL) ('good') and LDL ('bad') cholesterol. Omega-6 fatty acids include linoleic acid (with two double bonds), an essential fatty acid that needs to be sourced through plants. It is found in corn, sunflowers, sesame and pumpkin seeds. Consuming foods rich in linoleic acid has been shown to lower total cholesterol and to reduce LDL and triglycerides by 2–10% in 16 weeks compared with a control group. Linoleic acid is converted to arachidonic acid, which is a crucial component in the production of a number of hormones that have many functions within the body as well as in the functioning of blood platelets; however, it is also associated with inflammatory responses.

Research has found that the balance between omega-3 and omega-6 fatty acids is important: a lack of omega-3 fatty acids in the diet (which there often is in Western diets) leads to several inflammation-related diseases, and possibly some types of psychiatric illness. Increased dietary omega-3 fatty acids is thought to reduce cardiovascular disease, hypertension and possibly also protect against rheumatoid arthritis. In contrast to the anti-inflammatory activity of omega-3 fatty acids, some omega-6 fatty acids act as pro-inflammatories in response to injuries, allergies and infections. Omega-3s are thought to partially replace the excess concentration of omega-6, inflammation-promoting arachidonic acid in cell membranes. However, omega-6

gamma-linolenic acid works as an anti-inflammatory, and may also have tumour and metastasis-suppressing properties, and is also being trialled for use in treatment of HIV. In summary, a balance of these two essential fatty acids is needed, but because today's diets often have a greater proportion of omega-6, there is strong evidence that increasing intake of omega-3 fatty acids reduces the incidence of several serious diseases, largely initiated through inflammatory responses. It is suggested that more than one part of omega-3 to four parts of omega-6 fatty acids should be included in the diet: at present many diets have ratios of 1:10–30 parts of omega-3 to omega-6, respectively. In addition to oily fish, linseed, perilla, chia, purslane and kiwi fruit are very good sources of omega-3.

Lecithin: an emulsifier found in several foods, such as soy, sesame seeds, sunflower seeds, dandelion, Andean lupin, linseed and eggs. A key component of every cell membrane in the body, it is a mix of glycolipids, triglycerides, and phospholipids. It is particularly important for cell membranes within the brain. It keeps membranes supple and protects cells from oxidation. It is often used in a purified form for medicinal purposes and as a food supplement. Although it can be manufactured within the body, it is also popularly added to the diet. As a food, it is often used as an emulsifier in products, such as chocolate and margarine, to prevent the individual components from separating. Medicinally, plant-based lecithins have been shown to reduce cholesterol and triglyceride levels in the blood.

Monounsaturated fats: These types of fat (e.g. omega-9 fatty acids, oleic acid, palmitoleic acid) have only one double bond and are less liable to become rancid and oxidise compared with polyunsaturated fats. However, they have a higher melting temperature than polyunsaturates, but lower than those of saturated fats. They are liquid at room temperature. Good sources are found in many oils, e.g. olive, almond, canola, avocado, peanut, pecan, cashew, filbert and macadamia oils, and they are easily broken down. They may help lower total blood cholesterol level; as well as lowering LDL ('bad') cholesterol levels. It is thought that monounsaturated fatty acids should be a good proportion of the fats eaten. People in the Mediterranean consume large amounts of oleic acid, found in olives, and have very low rates of heart disease and cancer.

Saturated fats

This group can be divided into two types: long-chain and medium-length saturated fats. The former, as their name suggest, are composed of longer chains of carbon atoms. They have no double bonds and are saturated with hydrogen ions. Both types are usually solid at room temperature and are found in many animal and dairy products, as well as tropical oils, such as coconut and palm oil. Their lack of double bonds and saturation with hydrogen ions makes these fats very stable: they are much more resistant to becoming rancid.

Although both types are saturated fats, they are absorbed and dealt with quite differently by the body. Due to their smaller size, medium-chain fats can be absorbed directly from the small intestine, either intact or following simple hydrolysis. From there, they are transported directly to the liver. In the liver, they can be simply converted to energy (by mitochondria). In contrast, long-chain fats need to be extensively broken down and then treated with pancreatic enzymes or bile in the intestines before they are absorbed and transported, via the lymphatic system to the main blood circulation, which distributes them to various tissues and organs of the body, including fat layers and the liver. In the liver, they need to go through various biochemical cycles before they can be used for energy by the mitochondria. Due to the easier digestion and metabolism of medium-chain fats, these are better utilised by those with disorders of the pancreas, liver, digestive and lymph system. They have also been suggested to have some anti-cancer effects and to even help with weight loss, as they are not transported to the tissues in the same way as long-chain fats. Medium-chain saturated acids, such as lauric acid (dodecanoic acid), found in large amounts in *Cuphea*, coconut and palm oil, although previously receiving bad press, are now being reconsidered for their health benefits. Lauric acid is also thought to have good antimicrobial properties. Myristic acid, slightly longer than lauric acid, is found in nutmeg and mace, as well as in coconut and palm oils.

In the diet, long-chain fatty acids may cause total blood-cholesterol level to rise, and may also be implicated in the occurrence of some types of cancer. An example is stearic acid, which is also the principal constituent of hydrogenated fats and oils.

Trans fats

These fats do not occur naturally, but are produced artificially and are chemically altered to form straight bonds that can stack well, but also readily form plaques (clots). They are often labelled as hydrogenated or partially hydrogenated. They are bad news for health. They raise LDL cholesterol and may also lower HDLs. They are intermediate in consistency between unsaturated and saturated fats. They are popular in the food-processing industry because they prolong the life of fatty foods as, otherwise, these can become rancid with age. They were used in a wide range of processed foods, such as cakes, biscuits, pizzas, crisps, dips, margarine, salad dressings and many more, but due to worries about their health effects their inclusion is now being significantly reduced. There has been increasing evidence that these fats are as, or more, harmful than saturated fats. High quantities have also been implicated in the occurrence of cancer.

Cholesterol

Cholesterol is not a true fat, but is a lipid-like, waxy substance. It is needed by the body for many metabolic processes, including being a major component of cell membranes, and for the synthesis of steroids and bile salts. Although some cholesterol is obtained through the dietary intake of dairy products, meat, eggs and fish, much is also produced by the liver, and the amount produced is determined by the type of fat that is eaten. Interestingly, because dietary cholesterol is derived from the cell membranes of animals, plants do not contain cholesterol. It is the amount of cholesterol that the body produces that can cause problems. And, saturated fats, which are at high levels within dairy products and fatty meats, can encourage the production of excess cholesterol. Most seeds and nuts contain larger ratios of unsaturated fats, which do not have this effect.

Cholesterol needs to be attached to a protein to enable it to travel around the body. The liver thus forms two main types of lipoprotein: low density lipoproteins (LDL) and high density lipoproteins (HDL). Both are needed and are essential to maintain good health.

- LDL contains 60–70% cholesterol. It enables the transport of cholesterol from the liver around the body to cells throughout the body, including smooth muscle, which is what arteries are composed of. This cholesterol, in excess, can initiate the formation of deposits in arteries and, as a consequence, can result in increased risk of heart disease.
- HDL contains 20–30% cholesterol. It transports cholesterol away from the tissues and back to the liver where it is recycled or eliminated. Greater quantities of HDL, compared to LDLs, lowers the risk of heart disease.

Although high levels of blood cholesterol need to be monitored, of more importance is the ratio between LDL/HDL, with a ratio of less than 1 being very low and excellent, with a very low risk of heart disease; ratios more than 3.5 should be treated with some concern. In addition, LDL levels should be less than 130 mg/dL and HDL levels should be more than 40 mg/dL.

MINERALS

Inorganic substances make up only 4% of the body's weight, most of it found in bones, yet they are crucial to many biological processes. Minerals, such as calcium and phosphates are essential for building bones. Others, often termed micronutrients, are only needed in tiny amounts, and although their full role in the body is sometimes not clearly known, a deficiency can result in serious disease. Iodine is an example of an essential micronutrient.

Most minerals are adequately provided for in a balanced diet, although deficiencies can arise in regions where the uptake by plants may be insufficient due to the lack of a particular mineral in the rocks and soil, e.g. zinc and selenium. However, this occurs less often nowadays as food is frequently transported from one region to another. If growing most of your own food, it is worth checking if particular micronutrients are limited in your area, and so can be added to make up any deficit.

Below is a summary of the main essential macro- and micro-minerals. Note though that quantities of these found in a particular species can vary considerably according to soil type, growth rate, variety and other factors.

VITAMINS

Vitamin A (carotenoids)

An antioxidant. Men need ~5000 international units (IU) (1000 mg) and women ~4000 IU (800 mg) of vitamin A per day. However, vitamin A is fat soluble and can be stored in the body for a long period: its storage is so effective, the body can last without additional vitamin A for a couple of years without suffering deficiency. Needs bile salts and fat to be absorbed from the gut.

Carotenoids are a group of compounds that give fruits and vegetables their vibrant orange, yellow and green colours. Beta-carotene, lycopene, lutein and zeaxanthin are all different types of carotenoids. Not all carotenoids (e.g. lycopene, lutein) are converted to vitamin A, though

ESSENTIAL MINERALS NEEDED FOR LIFE

Abbreviations:
RDA: Recommended daily allowance.
M/F/C: male/female/child

Mineral	Uses	Sources
Calcium	The most abundant cation (positively charged mineral ion) in the body: essential for bones, teeth. A little is stored in other parts of the body, with levels controlled by two hormones. Needs vitamin D for its absorption. Needed for blood clotting, several cellular activities, muscle and nerve activities.	Dairy, eggs, shellfish, green vegetables. Acidic foods, such as citrus help its absorption; calcium oxalates (e.g. found in spinach) and excess magnesium reduce its absorption. RDA: M/F 1200 mg; C ~600 mg.
Copper	Needed, with iron, to synthesise haemoglobin. Part of enzymes needed in the formation of collagen (structural, bone producing) and melanin pigments, and needed for formation of capillaries. Important in tissue healing. Works with the antioxidant enzyme, superoxide dismutase. Also involved with the biochemical release of energy.	Whole grains, eggs, beans, nuts, beets, spinach, asparagus, chocolate, potatoes, fish. High levels of zinc or vitamin C in the diet can inhibit copper absorption. RDA: ~900 mg.
Fluorine	Found in bones and teeth, but it is not known if it is essential to the diet. Said to improve tooth strength and reduce carries and to help prevent osteoporosis: controversy over its addition to water.	Fish, tea; small amounts found in most foods, but is probably not an essential mineral.
Iodine	Essential for the production of the thyroid hormone, which regulates metabolic rate, including growth rate and development. 60% of iodine is stored within the thyroid, the remainder is found in blood, muscles and the ovary.	Seafoods, seaweeds, vegetables grown near the coast. Also good amounts in many brassica species, peanuts, cassava and soybeans. Also found in exhaust fumes and in sterilising chemicals: thus, excess of iodine is more of a risk these days than a deficiency. RDA: ~150 mg.
Iron	Iron is an intrinsic part of haemoglobin, giving it its red colour, and is crucial for carrying oxygen. Also needed indirectly in the formation of ATP (adenosine tri-phosphate). Found in muscle, the liver, spleen and in enzymes. Needed for neurotransmitter synthesis and function, for liver detoxification, antimicrobial properties, synthesis of DNA, collagen and bile acids. Too little causes anaemia, but too much may cause cancer due to its ability to form oxygen radicals.	Pumpkin seeds, oily fish, seeds, sweet potato, spinach, meats, shellfish, eggs, legumes, green nuts, some vegetables. In the diet, comes in two main forms: non-haeme iron and haeme, each with different absorption rates. All iron in plants and ~60% from animal sources is the non-haeme type. This type is absorbed more slowly and only partially. It is also dependent on the presence of other substances such as fibre and vitamin C. Therefore, its absorption is improved by eating foods rich in vitamin C. Haeme iron is more rapidly and easily absorbed, and less total iron needs to be eaten. Inclusion of acid foods (e.g. citrus, tomatoes) significantly increases iron absorption, and is reduced by high-calcium foods, cationic minerals, oxalates (e.g. as found in spinach), tannic acid (e.g. tea, coffee) and phytates. RDA 8–15 mg.
Magnesium	Found in bone and soft tissues. Needed for muscle contraction, nervous-impulse transmission, energy metabolism and bone mineralisation. A part of ~300 enzymes. Involved in fatty-acid and protein synthesis, and glucose metabolism. Important in regulation of calcium/magnesium balance. Involved in ATP metabolism and is a potent vasodilator. Deficiency linked to diabetes, high cholesterol, spasms of blood vessels.	Nuts, whole grains (however, processing removes much magnesium), pumpkin seeds, green vegetables, legumes (particularly soy), chocolate, seafoods. RDA: 300–400 mg.
Manganese	Needed for many bodily processes: haemoglobin synthesis, urea formation, bone formation, reproduction, growth, linked to insulin release, helps protect cells from damage. Important in many enzymes.	Wheatgerm, whole grains, green vegetables, nuts, seeds, oysters, sweet potatoes, pumpkin seeds, tofu, chocolate, tea. RDA: ~2 mg.
Phosphorus	The most abundant anion in the body, with almost as much phosphate as calcium in bones and teeth. Tremendously important mineral: also vital for making the energy carrying molecules of the body (ATP: adenosine tri-phosphate). Needed by most cells in the body. Also important in buffering the pH of blood. Needed for muscle and nerve functioning. Component of many enzymes, plus DNA and RNA. Levels controlled by two hormones.	Dairy, meats, seeds, nuts. Well absorbed from foods. Although rich in beans, peas, cereals and nuts, often occurs as phytate or inositol phosphate, which is difficult to digest. However, the enzyme phytase, found in yeast and gut bacteria, can help break these down. Elevated serum phosphate can inhibit activation of vitamin D, which, in turn is necessary for calcium absorption. RDA: M/F ~700–1000 mg.
Potassium	Crucial cation in transmission of nerve impulses and muscle contraction. It is the main charged cation within cells: it is vital for maintaining fluid and electrolyte balance within cells (sodium is the main electrolyte outside cells). Linked with lowering blood pressure. Helps release energy from protein, fat and carbohydrates during metabolism.	Most abundant in fruit and vegetables. Particularly rich in beans, potatoes, sweet potato, squash, pumpkin, tomatoes, greens, dried apricots and bananas. Much is lost through cooking. RDA: 2000 mg.

(continued on next page)

grow in sandy soils but does not grow well in heavier clay soils. Grows best in slightly acidic to slightly alkaline soils: pH 6–8. Once established, okra is relatively drought tolerant, though grows better with regular moisture. It is not at all tolerant of waterlogging.

Pot culture: Their ornamental flower and general appearance makes okra a good vegetable to grow in pots on a deck or patio. In thoroughfares, select hairless varieties.

Planting/propagation: Can get two crops a year in warmer climates. Sow seed, 1–2 cm deep, in warm, moist, but free-draining compost. If the compost isn't warm, germination is poor and seeds tend to rot. Soaking the seeds in warm water for ~24 hours before sowing increases the rate and speed of germination. Allow good air circulation, as young seedlings can succumb to fungal rots, such as damping off. Germination can occur in a few days, but may take longer (3–4 weeks) in cooler climates. Seeds are best sown in individual pots so that, when transplanted, they are disturbed as little as possible. Plant seedlings out in their final position once all risk of frost or cold has passed, and the soil has warmed up, or the seeds can be sown straight outside in warm or subtropical climates. Okra are usually planted in rows with ~30 cm between plants. Minimise weed competition, particularly when young. Mulching with organic matter

or plastic around the plants helps keep the soil warm, retains moisture and reduces weed competition. This is of particular benefit in cooler regions.

Pruning: Plants often form suckers, which also form pods, though some growers believe that suckers take away energy from the main plant and so remove them. Growers sometimes remove one out of every three of the leaves formed when the blossom appears, preferably those leaves towards the centre of the plant, to increase and prolong the okra-pod harvest.

Pests and diseases: Stinkbugs and other beetles can attack the pods and leaves. Aphids and the caterpillar larvae from a number of moths and butterflies can also damage the leaves. Nematodes can be a problem in sandy soils. Fungal blights may also sometimes occur.

Food
Very young okra can be eaten fresh in salads, but it is more usually added to curries, soups and stews, or is fried, often coated in breadcrumbs. Okra can be pickled, steamed or stir-fried. It has a mucilaginous, mild taste, and goes well with vegetables such as tomatoes, onion and eggplant, as well as with shellfish. It readily acts as a thickener in dishes. In India it is commonly known as 'bindi', or as 'bamia' in the Middle East. Okra is used to make the famous Cajun and Creole gumbo dish, popular in the southern states of the United States and the Caribbean. It is best to cook okra in stainless-steel pans, as other metals may cause the okra to turn black in colour. In the Mediterranean, the pods are often soaked in vinegar or lemon overnight to remove some of their 'slimy' quality. The mature seeds can be dried, and are sometimes used as a coffee substitute or ground to make a flour, often added to wheat to give a nutty taste.

Nutrition/medicinal
It contains reasonable amounts of protein and virtually no fat. Most protein is found within the seeds, and has a good balance of amino acids, except for those that contain sulphur. Therefore, can be mixed with foods such as cereals, rice and sorghum, to form a food that contains all the essential amino acids. Okra is rich in soluble fibre, which is proven to lower cholesterol levels, as well as being good for the digestive tract by encouraging the growth of

'good' populations of gut bacteria. It also has high levels of insoluble fibre, important in keeping the bowel regular and healthy, and is thought to reduce the incidence of bowel cancer. Has good quantities of vitamin C (~20 mg/100 g) and vitamin K (~55 µg: ~65% of the RDA), as well as the B vitamins, particularly folate, thiamine and B6. Okra is rich in carotenoids, particularly in lutein, which can significantly slow the progression of age-related macular degeneration and cataracts, and protects against heart disease. Okra is high in manganese, with some magnesium, potassium, calcium, iron and phosphates, and it is rich in antioxidants. The soluble mucilaginous fibres within okra are excellent for the digestive tract. In particular, they almost totally inhibit the adhesion of bacteria, i.e. *Helicobacter pylori*, to the stomach wall. This bacteria is one of the main initiators of stomach ulcers. The mucilage has been used externally on wounds and cuts.

Ornamental
Okra makes a good ornamental addition to the annual flower bed, plus it produces food. The variety 'Red Burgundy' has striking red stems and pods, contrasting with bright green leaves.

Other uses
The stems contain a fibre that can be used in paper and textiles.

uses

Acorus calamus
Calamus (common sweet flag, cinnamon sedge, gladdon, myrtle flag, myrtle sedge, sweet cane, sweet myrtle, sweet root, sweet rush, sweet sedge)
ACORACEAE

A common plant found in wetlands in many parts of the world, it is a monocot species and is within the arum family, with the *Acorus* genus containing only 2–3 species. Although it has a similar common name, it is not closely related to yellow flag, which is a type of iris. Calamus has aromatic foliage and rhizomes, and has been used as a food, as well as a psychotropic drug. It is thought to be native to India, but has now become naturalised across Europe (including Britain), up to Russia, Siberia and northern Asia Minor, eastwards to China and Japan, and southwards to Sri Lanka and Burma. It is also found in North America. People from central Asia have used it for at least 2000 years. It was used by the ancient Egyptians and was revered by the Greeks. It has been considered a symbol of love, lust and affection, and in Japan it was a symbol of the Samurai's bravery, presumably due to its lance-shaped leaves. Its aromatic properties have made it a useful strewing herb. It was introduced into North America in the 16th century, and became popular with the indigenous Indians. It is thought they spread and planted this species in different waterways where it became a popular food for musk-rats, with its common name, calamus, being an Indian word for musk-rat. Calamus has an interesting history of usage, and research has shown it to have many potential medicinal benefits — but also a few negatives.

DESCRIPTION

A perennial monocotyledonous species, forming tall clumps of leaves from rhizomes. Leaves grow to 1–1.5 m tall, and spread 0.6–1 m. Leaves and flower stems die back in autumn and the plant over-winters as storage rhizomes. In many locations, the plants either do not produce flowers or, if they do, do not produce fertile seed. Plants spread almost exclusively by vegetative rhizome spread (see below).

Leaves: Its smooth, hairless leaves are 0.6–1 m long, lanceolate (2–4 cm wide) and typically monocotyledonous, with stomata on both sides and the leaf blade being held almost vertical. The leaf margins are often crinkled and wavy. In addition, this species can be distinguished from other similar species by its leaf vein. Calamus has a prominent midrib vein, which isn't always central, and narrower, less prominent, secondary longitudinal veins.

Flowers: Forms a long, tightly packed spike that projects upwards three-quarters of the way up the stem, as occurs in sedges. This consists of many tiny insignificant, greeny-yellow flowers. Flowering parts are in threes. Although the plant produces flowers, it almost always does not produce viable seed, unless it is diploid. Many plants have triploid, tetraploid and hexaploid forms. Flowers are borne from late spring into summer, with seeds (if fertile) ripening in late summer. Pollination is by wind and insects.

Roots: Forms a compact, dense system of rhizomes after a few years' growth in wet soil. The inner tissue of the rhizome is aromatic, spongy and white, with pore spaces for the transport of oxygen from leaves to rhizomes and roots. The rhizomes have short, stout roots growing off these, which absorb nutrients and moisture.

Harvest/storage: The rhizomes of 2–3-year-old plants are harvested at the end of the growing season, or during the winter. Roots harvested from plants older than 3–4 years become tough and unpleasant to eat. If roots are not used fresh, they can be dried, which is said to improve their sweetness and flavour, though may also concentrate compounds such as asarone (see below). Can be stored for several weeks up to a few months.

CULTIVATION

Location: Can grow in either full sun or light shade. Fairly wind hardy, and can be grown near the coast, though is not tolerant of very brackish water.

Temperature: Plants are cold hardy and will survive freezing temperatures because the underground storage rhizomes are said to tolerate temperatures as low as −25°C. Plants will tolerate heat, as long as they have moisture.

Soil/water/nutrients: Grows best in river-valley soils, which are sandy yet rich in organic matter. Will grow well in silty or muddy soils, but does need regular moisture.

Food

The leaves and rhizomes, when crushed, have a pleasant, warm, citrus–cinnamon-like aroma. The rhizomes have been used to make candy by boiling them in water for ~60 minutes until reduced to a syrup. Reportedly, it can be peeled and eaten raw. It is used as a vegetable, and can be roasted or boiled. The dried rhizomes are used as a flavouring and as a substitute for spices such as cinnamon and nutmeg. The young shoots can be cooked and eaten as a vegetable, and are used as a sweet flavouring. They can be added to salads. The young flowers are said to have a sweet flavour. The essential oil can flavour alcoholic drinks, particularly liqueurs. However, see Warning notes below, particularly if the roots or leaves have a bitter flavour.

Nutrition/medicinal

Historically, this species has been used in Asia and by the Arabs as an aphrodisiac. It has an historic and current use within Ayurvedic medicine. In North America, it was a stimulant for indigenous people, with the rhizome used as a hallucinogen for shamanic rituals. The fresh rhizomes contain ~1–4% essential oil, which is fragrant and is rich in asarone. This compound causes hallucinogens in large quantities, and has tranquillising and antibiotic activities. Historically, this species has been used to treat a wide range of conditions, including as a stimulant, for digestive ailments, to regulate menstruation, an analgesic, a sedative and to reduce fevers. The plant is used topically to treat skin eruptions, rheumatic pains and neuralgia. A large amount of research has been done on this species and a few of the findings are as follows. Calamus has been shown to have antidiabetic properties, to have a protective effect against some forms of kidney disease, to have significant anti-fungal activity, to reduce intestinal spasms and so reduce gastrointestinal disorders such as colic pain and diarrhoea (though large amounts have been said to cause vomiting). It has activity against multiple-resistant *Staphylococcus aureus*, has neuroprotective properties and has high antioxidant activity. **Warning:** Other studies have shown that large amounts of calamus, fed to rats, can act as a carcinogen. This was thought to exist in all calamus types, but research has shown that diploid plants do not contain this compound, triploids contain a little, and tetraploid and hexaploid types contain large amounts. This may be a reason for the often conflicting reports on the safety of this species. Tetraploid and hexaploid types are more often found in Asia, whereas the diploid form is found more often in North America and Europe (though some triploid forms occur in Europe). However, the use of calamus has been discouraged in many countries because of its possible carcinogenic effects. Products from this plant were banned from 1968 as food additives and medicines by the US Food and Drug Administration. Calamus is reported to possibly cause hypertensive reactions if taken with monoamine oxidase inhibitors. It should not be eaten during pregnancy as it may cause miscarriage.

Ornamental

Makes a good ornamental plant around larger pools or water features, though its roots may need to be contained within a wire mesh container to control its spread. There are attractive ornamental variegated varieties.

Other uses

The leaves can be used for a range of uses from making hats, mats and baskets to being pulped to make paper, and for thatching. The essential oil from the rhizome and leaves has been used in perfumery and in incense. This oil has insect-repellent and insecticidal properties.

As with many wetland species, this plant can probably be grown in ordinary soil, but will grow much better in flooded or continually wet soils, where its short roots can more readily obtain nutrients and moisture. Plant easily tolerates anaerobic soils, and is able to get oxygen for root growth via its leaves and spongy rhizomes. However, it does not grow well in sites that have rapid and variable water-level changes.

Pot culture: Containers are a good way to grow this species. If there is no water feature close by, plant rhizomes in a barrel or container of soil and coarse sand and then flood with water. Plant rhizome sections in moist soil within the container. As these begin to form shoots, progressively flood the container as the leaves grow. Keep the soil wet to saturated.

Planting/propagation: *Seed:* If seed is available, this is best sown fresh on moist compost and barely covered with fine soil. Keep moist to very moist, lightly shaded and warm. Germination takes ~14 days. Prick-out seedlings and grow-on in a sand/compost mix with pots standing in water, or watered every day, for about a year until large enough to plant out. *Cuttings:* Sections of young, healthy rhizome are the easiest, quickest and most reliable way to propagate this species. Bury the sections, which should include several healthy buds, in moist, gritty compost to root and form shoots. Keep the soil moist and warm. Rhizome cuttings are best made in early spring, just before growth normally commences, though can be done at other times of the year. This method has a good success rate and plants can be planted out within a few weeks. Space rhizomes ~0.3–0.5 m apart.

Pruning: Old stems can be tidied away if required, but it may be best to leave these to naturally decay and add organic matter to the area.

Pests and diseases: Few problems reported.

Agaricus spp. (*A. bisporus, A. campestris*)

Mushrooms (champignon, portobella)

AGARICACEAE

Mushrooms are fungi, and have a growth form quite different from plants. They have no chlorophyll, and instead of flowers and seeds, their mode of reproduction is by forming fruiting bodies, which produce spores. Mushrooms and toadstools form the familiar stipe (stalk) and cap, with gills on the under surface and these are mostly classified as Basidiomycetes. There are many other types of fungi, including the familiar bluish fungal mould that appears on bread after a few days. The mycelium (a type of root) of these have ramified through the dough, and we are only aware of this when their tiny fruiting bodies erupt, en masse, on the surface of the bread. All fungi produce mycelium (also known as hyphae). These consist of long, multi-nucleated cells that wind their way through the medium they are growing in, be it soil, bread, plant tissue or people's feet. The fruiting bodies appear only after an adequate amount of mycelium has formed, and after they get the right cues from the environment.

Historically, many species of fungi have been used for food, medicinally, and for psychedelic and ritualistic purposes. Much experimentation has gone on over the millennia, some resulting in death, but more often in a delicious meal, and sometimes a psychedelic high. Many different species of fungi have been traditionally utilised from the wild, particularly in Asia and Europe. However, harvesting fungi from the wild can be risky as the inexperienced may mistakenly pick specimens such as the *Aminitas*, which include the death cap and the destroying angel. These species do live up to their names, but are fairly easily identified. If harvesting from the wild, consider searching out a fungal foray to attend. These are invaluable in enabling positive identifications and to help spot many of the delicious species, which are easily overlooked by the inexperienced.

The fruiting bodies of several fungi are edible and delicious, among which are the *Agaricus* species, and in particular *A. bisporus*, which has become the main species of fungi grown worldwide. The species *A. campestris* is the common field mushroom and is often found growing wild. If harvesting these, check that the gills are pink and that the stalk does not have a bulbous base. Young *Amanita* species can look similar. Mushrooms can be grown quite easily, given the right environmental conditions. In addition, there are many other wild delicious fungi, e.g. morel, puffball, ink caps, truffles, chanterelle, shitake, and a number of these fungi are cultivated commercially, particularly in Asia, e.g. shitake, enoki, maitake, oyster. Perhaps try growing your own.

DESCRIPTION

Mushrooms consist of mycelium, a collective term for many long cells (hyphae) that form a sort of root system and are the main permanent part of the fungus. They are not easily visible to the naked eye, but their huge surface area takes up nutrients and moisture from the media in which they grow. Once the mycelium has matured, changes in temperature and moisture status of the soil stimulate the formation of the fruiting body: the familiar mushroom. This consists of a stipe (stalk) and a white cap. As this matures, it changes from being rounded and opens to expose pinkish gills below, which turn dark chocolate brown as they mature. (Avoid any fungus with white gills.) The gills later produce minute spores, which can be readily picked up in air currents and carried far and wide. These then go on to 'germinate' into a new fungus. It is estimated that a mature mushroom can produce ~15 billion spores! In Basidiomycetes, reproduction is sexual, with both male and female parts within the same fruiting body.

Harvest/storage: After inoculation, it takes ~3 weeks for the mycelium to become established and then a further ~4 weeks for the mushrooms to appear. They can be picked as button mushrooms, or left to open. The latter are tastier, but do not keep as well. Mushrooms are harvested by cutting the stipe at soil level. Pulling up the mushrooms damages the mycelium and may reduce future crops. It is best to harvest a few regularly rather than leaving them and harvesting larger amounts in one session. If the following environmental conditions are maintained, the mycelium should continue producing mushrooms for ~6 months.

CULTIVATION

Location/temperature: Mushrooms need a darkish cellar, garage, shed or cupboard that has an even temperature and is free of draughts. (It does not have to be pitch black.) For the mushroom-forming stage, they need a stable temperature of ~14°C, day and night, and a humidity of ~85%. If these conditions can be met, then a good mushroom crop is likely. Mushrooms are usually grown through the winter months, where cooler temperatures and high humidity are easier to maintain.

Planting/propagation (soil/water/nutrients): Kits can be purchased (often only in winter months), which provide the container and the growing medium already inoculated with the mushroom spores. Simply add a little more organic matter and some moisture for the mushrooms to start growing. Alternately, you can prepare your own media. A tray or wooden box, or similar, can be filled with an organic-matter-rich compost.As fungi do not photosynthesise, they need to obtain all of their nutrients, including their carbon, from the media. Therefore, the presence of well-rotted organic matter and straw is important. Straw with fresh manure within it is ideal, i.e. from horses, goats or free-range chickens.

Commercially, spent corn cobs are often used. The compost is prepared by maturing it for a week or two before inoculation by keeping it moist, warm and regularly turned to allow aerobic decomposition. When ready, the mix has a pleasant sweet smell and is a crumbly brown consistency. This then needs to be heated to ~70°C to kill any existing pathogens. To achieve this, stack the compost within a bin for the centre to heat up, but allow aeration from the sides. This takes ~2 weeks, depending on external temperature. A little gypsum is often added to the compost mix to stabilise pH and to improve its texture and aeration properties. Mushrooms need nutrients, particularly nitrogen, and these are supplied via the manure.

To inoculate, the spores (known as spawn) can be bought from various suppliers (several are listed on the internet). Small pieces, ~1.5 cm diameter, are inserted to ~5 cm depth within the prepared compost. Space ~20 cm apart. Initially, it is best to keep the trays as dark as possible, and give them a warmer temperature of ~20°C for the first three weeks while the mycelium is growing.

During this time, keep the compost moist, but not too wet. Once the hyphae have grown to meet each other, the temperature is lowered to ~14°C, and a ~2.5-cm layer of good-quality soil is placed over the compost. Keep the soil surface just moist, not wet.

A cloth placed over the trays helps maintain humidity, keeps them dark and protects them from draughts. After another three weeks, the first button heads start to appear, and in a further 10 days, the first crops are ready to harvest.

Pests and diseases: Commercially, several fungal diseases that attack mushrooms are problematic. However, for home growing on a small scale, these are less likely, particularly if moisture and temperature levels are maintained. Also try to use 'clean' compost, and remove any diseased or damaged mushrooms to reduce the spread of infection. Avoiding unnecessary contamination is important during cultivation.

Food

Mushrooms can be prepared in a multitude of ways and are included within many styles of cuisine. Cooks generally just lightly wash or wipe mushrooms before usage. They do not need peeling. Button mushrooms can be eaten raw, finely chopped and added to salads or sauces. Mushrooms are often diced and lightly fried with butter and garlic, or are grilled with cheese in, e.g. pizzas, or they make delicious soup. They are served with fish, meats or with other vegetables, and are wonderful in many Mediterranean recipes and in Asian soups and stir-fries. Mushrooms are often dried for storage, which intensifies their flavour.

Nutrition/medicinal

Cooked mushrooms contain ~8% protein, including leucine and lysine. They contain no fat, and are unusual in that, unlike plants, they do have some vitamin D. They contain useful amounts of the B vitamins, particularly niacin and riboflavin, with some folate and pantothenic acid. They contain good quantities of the antioxidant selenium, and have some potassium, copper and phosphorus. Oyster mushrooms contain more protein (~10%) and more of the B vitamins. They have higher quantities of minerals, including iron, though have less selenium. Recent research has shown that a species of *Agaricus* (*A. blazei*, Brazilian sun mushroom) and a bracket fungus (*Ganoderma lucidum*, rei-shi) can reduce the incidence of septicaemia caused by some multi-antibiotic-resistant bacteria and may inhibit the growth and spread of some tumours. This latter species has been used to treat diabetes, hyperlipidaemia, arteriosclerosis and chronic hepatitis. **Warning:** If harvesting from the field, get good identification. If in doubt, do not eat.

Other uses

Used compost is excellent on the garden as a soil improver.

Allium ampeloprasum porrum
(syn. *A. porrum*)
Leek
ALLIACEAE (SYN. LILACEAE)

Elephant garlic (*Allium ampeloprasum ampeloprasum*), Babbington's leek (*A. ampeloprasum babingtonii*), kurrat (*A. ampeloprasum kurrat*)

Relatives: onion, spring onion, chives, garlic

Members of the same family as the onion and garlic, these monocotyledonous plants are more distantly related to the lilies. The original wild species, *Allium ampeloprasum*, is the broad-leaved wild leek. From this plant, many subspecies have been selected for various uses and these have been divided into three main groups: the *porrum* group, which includes the leeks; *ampeloprasum*, which includes elephant garlic, which have large, mild-tasting garlic-like cloves; and the *kurrat* group, named after a small plant grown mostly in the Middle East.

The leek probably originated from regions around the Mediterranean, where it was used by the Egyptians and then the Greeks and Romans. There are records of the use of the wild leek dating back to 4000 BC. The modern culinary leek is still popular in these regions, but also in northern Europe, the United Kingdom, the Middle East and Northern Africa. It is a valued vegetable in the United Kingdom, and is the national emblem of Wales. It is said that before the Welsh went into battle with the Saxons, in about AD 640, they adorned their hats with leeks from a nearby garden. They subsequently went on to beat the Saxons and from there it became the traditional plant worn on St David's Day. Cold hardy, it is usually grown to provide a tasty vegetable throughout the winter months.

DESCRIPTION

Although the leek is a biennial that produces leaves in the first year, and flowers and seeds in the second, it is usually grown as an annual. It is a monocot with no true stem, but unlike most other members of this family, it does not form a true bulb in the first year. It does, however, form small corm-like growths around the main stem in its second year. The leek forms a dense sheath of leaves, with mature plants being ~40 ~70 cm tall, with 2–5-cm diameter stems. There are many varieties, which are often divided into two main groups: those that are planted in early spring to give a summer/autumn crop, and those planted in autumn to give a winter/spring/summer crop. The spring-sown plants tend to be somewhat smaller in size, have a milder flavour and can be harvested sooner. Any leek shown to have a quick maturity time is usually a summer-type leek. Autumn-sown varieties usually need a longer period to mature, but are considered by many leek connoisseurs to have a stronger and better flavour. Some popular winter leeks include 'American Flag', which has good disease resistance and a good flavour, 'Carentian Giant', a very cold-hardy European leek with large stems, and 'Winter Giant', with a good flavour and large stems. When selecting seed, check how long they need to mature and what season they should be sown in.

Leaves: Long, thin, strap shaped, grey-green if exposed to light, white to pale yellow-green if blanched. They are sheathed closely and concentrically around a central region, each progressively, directly opposite the other. It does not have a true central stem as such, instead younger leaves emerge progressively from the plant's apex, finally culminating in the production of a stiff, tall, flower stem. Leaf veins run longitudinally along the leaf. As the plant gets older, the upper sections of the leaves above the soil level splay open, 180° apart, to catch the sunlight. The base is usually buried in the soil to blanch it and keep it compact. This is the part of the plant that is particularly valued for its delicate flavour.

Flowers: Attractive, spherical flowerheads ~8 cm diameter, on long, often >1 m tall, cylindrical flower stalks. The head is composed of many white (sometimes slightly purplish or pinkish), six-petalled, star-shaped flowers that radiate outwards to form a globe. Pollination is by bees and insects.

Harvest/storage: Leeks can be harvested over a long period, though young, tender leeks are the most delicious. However, they can be harvested right up until the centre of the 'stem' starts to become woody, which is a sign that the flower stem is forming. At this stage, the stems become hard and lose their flavour. They take 12–22 weeks to be ready for harvest, depending on the variety, and autumn-sown plants take longer. To harvest, carefully dig up the plants by placing the fork beneath the roots, as pulling the leeks up can damage or break the stem. Leeks can be stored for a couple of weeks in a polythene bag in the fridge, or they can be left in the soil during winter until needed. Cooked leeks can only be kept for a couple of days before they begin to deteriorate.

Roots: Fairly shallow, though the soil is mounded around the plants as they grow, so mechanical cultivation to remove weeds is feasible, but avoid damaging the stems.

CULTIVATION
Fairly easy.

Location: They prefer a site in full sun, though will grow in partial shade. They can be grown close to the coast and are relatively wind hardy.

Temperature: They grow better in cool-temperate climates, and most varieties are very frost hardy. Most can withstand the cold of winter, and are often grown as a late autumn crop that lasts through winter, with young plants then separated out in spring to form a summer crop. However, some varieties are more tolerant of warmth, e.g. 'Irish eyes', 'King Richard', 'Lancelot and 'Sherwood', and may even be able to grow in regions such as Florida.

Soil/water/nutrients: Leeks grow much better within a good-quality, nutrient-rich loam. They benefit from organic matter or well-rotted manure being incorporated into the soil before planting. Leeks grow best with regular moisture, though can tolerate short periods of dryness. Extended drought, however, results in a woody, thin stem. Leeks can grow in a variety of soil textures from quite sandy to moderately heavy clay but they do not tolerate waterlogging. They are best with a slightly acidic to neutral pH: 5.5–6.5 as they do not like alkaline soils.

Pot culture: They could be grown in pots if short of space, and could make an interesting display with marigolds or nasturtiums.

Planting/propagation: The seeds can be planted either outside, in rows, at ~1 cm depth to grow into seedlings, or they may be sown inside in trays. Sow thinly as germination is usually good and takes ~14–21 days. Seed is best sown fresh, but can be kept for ~4 years and still be viable. If the seed is sown *in situ*, with seedlings thinned as they grow, it is difficult to mound around the plants to blanch them. Leeks transplant well, and gardeners usually dig up the seedlings when ~20–30 cm tall (after ~10 weeks for spring-sown) and then space these in either pre-prepared trenches (~15 cm deep) at ~15 cm intervals, or insert plants into separate holes dug with a trowel. The former method is good if the soil is loose to begin with, though plants are more likely to flop over until established. The seedling transplants should be watered regularly until established. As the plants mature, the soil is periodically piled against the base of the stem to blanch it and keep it compact. Over time, bury stems to 10–15 cm depth. Soil can be further mounded up around the plants as they mature. Try to prevent soil falling down between the leaves as this results in unwanted grit during food preparation.

Pests and diseases: Leeks have fewer problems than onions, though may be susceptible to the same problems as other *Allium* species. In wet soils or if grown too closely together, they can suffer from various fungal conditions. As with most other vegetables, leeks benefit from being placed in a different site annually, and should not be grown in soil that have recently had other *Allium* species in it.

Food
It is almost inevitable that some soil will be trapped between the leaves. The leeks can be sliced part-way down and then washed to remove this. Some cooks discard all of the green leaves, using only the blanched part of the stem, while others enjoy the green leaves and discard only the older leaves. Young leeks can be diced finely and added to salads instead of onion to give a more subtle, delicate flavour. They can be lightly steamed and served with a dab of butter and black pepper, or they can be sliced and added to stir-fries, or braised with tomato, garlic and bacon. Traditionally, leeks are lightly boiled and used as a vegetable to accompany roasts. If over-boiled they lose their flavour and become slimy so they are best eaten while still a little crisp. They can be added to soups and stews, or they make a tasty bake with sweet potato or potato with cheese. They can be fried instead of onions to get a more subtle flavour and are good finely sliced and gently sweated rather than being fried at a higher heat. Use in quiches and pies, and also as an ingredient in stocks, along with carrots and celery. They are an important ingredient in the French cold soup, vichyssoise, along with potatoes, cream and chicken stock.

Nutrition/medicinal
Leeks contain a little fibre and protein and virtually no fat. They have good quantities of vitamins A and K, with a small amount of vitamin C. They contain several of the B vitamins, particularly folate and B6, plus good amounts of manganese and iron, with some magnesium, potassium, calcium and copper. Note, that these nutrient levels are obtained from the blanched stem, so it is very likely that the greener leaves will be richer in many of the above. The antioxidant and antiproliferative effects of flavonoids within the *Allium* species are being researched for their ability to help prevent cancers, particularly prostate and colon. Similarly, like other *Allium* species, leeks can reduce the levels of LDL and total cholesterol. It has many of the properties of medicinal garlic, but to a lesser extent.

Ornamental
Leeks aren't regarded as an ornamental, but their symmetrical leaves look good contrasting with fine-leaved plants, or bright flowers. Try planting a few among the flower border, or plant a mix of carrots and leeks. The French variety, 'Blue Solaise' has striking blue leaves that turn violet in autumn. It looks great against green or red foliage.

Elephant garlic (Russian garlic), *Allium ampeloprasum ampeloprasum.* Often thought to be a type of garlic, it is, in fact, more closely related to the leek. It produces very large bulbs consisting of a few large, white-skinned, yellowish fleshed cloves that look like garlic, but are much larger, and their taste is much milder. They can be used as garlic, and do not seem to leave a strong smell on the breath, but neither do they have the same excellent medicinal properties as garlic. As they are milder, they are often used in recipes where garlic is too strong, e.g. mayonnaise or salads. Also used in stir-fries, pizzas and pasta. Its leaves are broad and long, and are edible, as are the young flowers. The harvested cloves store well; often longer than garlic. As with garlic, the main bulb forms in the first year, and smaller corms are formed around this in following years. After a few years, the plant forms an attractive clump of flowering heads with several basal cloves. The flowerheads are spherical and are typically *Allium*-like. The plants look good in a flower border. A few cloves can be easily separated and these will readily form new separate plants, which is the usual method of propagation (does not grow well from seed). Grows well in somewhat warmer climates but not so well in regions that have hard frosts. Would make a good pot plant in colder regions where extra warmth could be given if needed.

Babbington's leek, *Allium ampeloprasum babingtonii.* A rare plant found locally in the United Kingdom, often by the coast. It is similar to the cultivated leek, but its flowers are mauvish. It can grow tall (>1 m), and has long, narrow, edible leaves. Like garlic, the flowers produce bulbils, which can be planted and will form a new plant and a basal bulb within the first year. Other bulbs are formed in subsequent years. These can be used as a mild form of garlic and will readily form new plants.

Kurrat (Egyptian leek, Levant garlic), *Allium ampeloprasum kurrat.* Originating from the Middle East, its leaves are popularly used as a flavouring. Has largish, edible bulbs and purplish flowers.

Allium cepa
Onion
ALLIACEAE

Shallots (*A. ascalonicum*), potato onion (*Allium cepa aggregatum* (syn. *A. solanium*)), tree onion (Egyptian onion, walking onion, winter onion) (*A. cepa proliferum* (syn. *A. viviparum*)), spring onions (welsh onions) (*A. fistulosum*)

Relatives: chives, leeks, garlic

These species have been appreciated and used in culinary dishes and medicinally for thousands of years. The onion probably originates from Central Asia. Evidence has been found for its use in Middle Eastern, Bronze-age settlements in ~5000 BC, and onion recipes have been discovered that were written in Babylon. The Egyptians may have been the first to cultivate onions as they were known to have widely appreciated them. Onion is also mentioned in the Bible. The Romans, who grew a wide range of foods, obviously appreciated the onion, and introduced it into several European regions. Historically, in India, , they were considered impure, and only those of low caste ate them. It was not until Muslims in more recent times introduced them into various culinary dishes that their popularity increased hugely. Now, many Indian recipes use onions as a main ingredient, particularly in northern India. The Chinese were dubious of them, and anyone who had eaten onions was not allowed to live inside the town. Today, there are hundreds of varieties that vary in flavour and strength from almost sweet (ideal for salads), to eye-wateringly hot.

DESCRIPTION

A monocotyledonous, biennial plant that grows leaves and a storage organ within the first year, and flowers and sets seed within the second. Plants grow to 30–50 cm tall, with leaves growing from a central crown. They do not form a true stem.

Leaves: Long, cylindrical and hollow, with a pointed tip, juicy and edible. Also see Roots, below.

Flowers: Attractive, mostly whitish, spherical flowerheads formed from many small individual flowers radiating out from a central region. Are both male and female and are pollinated by bees and insects.

Harvest/storage: Sets (forced onion seedlings that have formed a small bulb) take ~10 weeks until they form good-sized onions, though they can be harvested before this as large 'spring onions' (though these are not true spring onions: see below). Seed takes ~5 months to mature. When the bulb is mature, and the present

Food

Probably used in more types and styles of cuisine than any other vegetable, and by most people around the world. If not treated with fungicides, the seeds can be sprouted, and are tasty and nutritious. Red onions and sweet onions are sweeter and less hot, so are more commonly used raw or only lightly cooked, whereas the common golden-brown onions are usually cooked further in curries, etc. Onions, in general can be finely chopped in sauces, salads, mayonnaise, dips. They can be stir-fried, roasted and caramelised with other vegetables, and used in many ways, including the famous French onion soup. They can be boiled to make a white onion soup (often given in convalescence), or simply fried and added to burgers, hot dogs, etc. Frying makes them sweeter and reduces their hotness. Onion is a main ingredient in many styles of spicy curry pastes and a wide variety of Asian recipes. It makes a wonderful mix with good-quality cheddar cheese, fresh crusty bread and a glass of good ale – the traditional English ploughman's lunch. Onions go wonderfully with small, sweet tomatoes. They can be sliced and added to other vegetables, such as eggplant, courgette, tomato and garlic to make delicious ratatouilles. They can be added to stews and gravies. If the onions are to be baked, roasted or steamed, leave the outer skins on as these impart a nutty flavour. Sweet onions have even been used in desserts. Onions can be dried and ground to make a powder that is used as a flavouring.

Nutrition/medicinal

Ordinary and sweet onion bulbs contain a little protein and their carbohydrates are largely in the form of sugars, particularly glucose, but also fructose and sucrose. Has reasonable quantities of vitamin C (~10 mg/100 g) and of the B vitamins, particularly of B6 and folate, with some thiamine. Has good amounts of manganese and some potassium, phosphate, magnesium and calcium. Onions and garlic contain S-alk(en)yl cysteine sulfoxides. These, on injury, are broken down by enzymes (alliinases) to produce their well-known aromas and flavours (allinins). These compounds, thiosulfonates and propanethial-S-oxide, are further decomposed to produce of various detoxifying enzymes, such as glutathione-S-transferase and quinone reductase, and have been shown to prevent the formation and multiplication of a number of cancers, including stomach, breast, prostate, colon and endometrium cancer.

Onions have anti-bacterial properties which have been utilised for thousands of years to treat a wide range of infections, including colds, coughs, flu, and to cleanse the blood. Onions, particularly red onions, are very rich in the antioxidants anthocyanins and flavonols, especially quercetin. These have been shown to be effective in reducing the occurrence of cardiovascular disease. They lower levels of blood triacylglycerols and reduce blood pressure, but also promote and increase the number of white blood cells, particularly lymphocytes, thus improving the immune system. Onions have anti-inflammatory properties which have been used to help heal wounds.

Warning: The bulb releases its strong, eye-stinging properties only when it is injured. The vapour from a cut onion, which contains sulphur-based compounds, mixes with moisture from the eye to form weak sulphuric acid, which stings. Some onion varieties have greater quantities of these compounds than others. The eye duct in response produces copious tears to wash this away. Not removing the root base of the onion reduces this effect somewhat, as can peeling onions under a tap or under water. Breathing through the mouth, rather than the nose, may reduce stinging. In large amounts, onion, in any form, can be seriously toxic to dogs and cats. Also, all members of the *Allium* family (if >25% dry matter) can be toxic to cattle.

Ornamental

Onions could be planted in the flower bed as an interesting contrast-foliage plant.

Other uses

The outer papery skins of brown onions make a traditional and effective brown dye for fabrics.

---

season's leaves begin to turn brown and die back, they can be lifted for storage. Do this when the weather is dry as damp onions easily rot. They are best left in the sun for a day or two before being hung in strings or stored in well-aerated, cool containers. They can then be kept for several months. If temperatures become warm, onions are likely to sprout.

Roots: Chunky, white, emanating off from the base of the onion bulb. Their chunkiness has made them an easy dissecting material for biology students to study root structures. Take care with mechanical cultivation as it can injure these short roots or the bulb. The bulb is, more strictly, a basal swollen stem, where next year's white leaves are tightly packed together and they are composed of storage compounds. In spring, the centre leaves shoot and emerge first. The spherical sheathing nature of the leaves is evident in the pattern of rings when the onion is cut in half horizontally. Around the 'leaves' is the familiar papery protective outer layer, which varies in colour with variety. It is often a golden-tan colour but can be white or red. Large, brown-skinned English onions, such as 'Craig Exhibition' and the German 'Stuttgart Keeper' store well, are more cold tolerant and have moderate heat. Spanish onions can be hotter, but also sweeter. Red-skinned onions have a milder, sweeter flavour.

CULTIVATION

Location: Onions grow best in full sun — lots of light, and a long day length is needed to form a good-sized bulb. Bulb size is more about exposure to light than maturity of the plant. However, varieties have been selected that can grow in shorter days (i.e. 14 hours or less). They are not very wind hardy.

Temperature: Can grow from cool- to warm-temperate climates. Once established, or if planted as sets, they are tolerant of frosts.

Soil/water/nutrients: Grow best in a nutrient-rich, loamy soil. The soil should be loosened well before planting, particularly if it contains any clay, because onions struggle to form good bulbs in compacted soil. Organic matter mixed in with the soil during preparation is beneficial, as is a sprinkle of wood ash on the soil around the plants. Do not use coal ash, as this is too acidic and often contains high quantities of heavy metals. A sprinkle of limestone within the soil helps growth. Onions need some moisture, but too much makes them watery and their storage time is reduced. Conversely, not enough moisture can lead to multiple bulbs.

Pot culture: It is possible to grow these in pots, perhaps with annual flowers or a vegetable, such as carrot, which has contrasting, fine leaves.

Planting/propagation: Can be started off from seed in spring or, in warmer regions, in autumn, to grow slowly during winter. Alternately, garden centres often sell onion sets in spring to get a head start. These are forced onion seedlings that have formed a small bulb. *Seed:* Although it takes longer to get harvestable onions, a much wider choice of variety occurs than with sets. Sow thinly at 0.5–1 cm depth, in rows. Because onions need ~5 months until harvest, start seeds off early in spring. Keep moist and warm. Germination takes ~14 days. Seed only remains viable for about 12 months and is best sown as fresh as possible. Fresh seed has good germination rates: a little seed can go a long way. Can be thinned to ~20 cm apart. Surplus seedlings can be replanted elsewhere or can be used like spring onions. Can be grown closer than 20 cm apart, but then the risk of disease, particularly fungal rots, is increased. Keep young plants weed free, as they do not grow well with competition. *Sets:* Sets are small onion bulbs, and these reduce the time and maintenance needed for their cultivation. They are inserted with a dibber or stick to a depth of quarter to half that of the bulb. Sets are usually sown in early spring in cool-temperate climates, but in warmer temperate regions that don't have hard frosts, they can be sown in autumn and will do some growing over winter. Note, though, that some bird species love to pull sets out of the ground, so firm down the soil around them. If this is a problem, place netting temporarily over the sets until they have rooted. Weeds can quickly compete with onion sets.

Pests and diseases: Generally not too many problems, though onion maggots can attack bulbs. They are particularly attracted to young onions and onion sets, and to the white-bulbed varieties, less so to the brown onion, and least to the red varieties. A fine layer of sand or ash around the base of onion plants helps deter them. Thrips can damage the leaves, sometimes so much so that the bulb fails to develop properly. These are most prevalent in hot, dry weather. Rotation of the onion family in different soils each year reduces the incidence of many pest and disease problems, as does planting them among plants from quite other families, e.g. legumes or brassicas, or in a flower bed.

OTHER SPECIES

Shallots (eschallot), *Allium ascalonicum.* Similar to onions, but smaller, and sweeter in taste. They form several smaller bulbs (compared with the onion's single large bulb) by the end of the season, and are a biennial. Historically, they have been popular in cuisine around the Mediterranean regions, particularly in France, and their sweeter, milder taste is valued in salads, soups and a wide range of dishes. They are often used for pickling, and most 'pickled onions' are actually shallots. They are more fiddly to peel and prepare than onions, but their greater delicacy of flavour is highly valued, particularly by the French. They can be used raw, in e.g. mayonnaise, dips, salads, sandwiches, or only lightly cooked. Their leaves grow to ~50 cm tall, and a few can be picked during the season and used like chives. Like onions, they need a long growing season to form a good harvest of bulbs. These are pulled as the leaves begin to die back in autumn. Unlike onions or spring onions, shallots seldom flower and are usually grown from sets. The harvested bulbs do not store for as long as onions. They have attractive rounded heads of many small whitish flowers. The roots are fairly shallow, so care is needed with cultivation. Could be easily grown in pots. Sets can be planted during winter in warmer areas, or in early spring in colder places. Being smaller, they can be spaced closer than onions at ~10–15 cm apart. Pests and diseases are the same as for 'Onion' above.

Potato onion, *Allium cepa aggregatum* (syn. *A. solanium).* An older variety of onion that is a hybrid between the common onion and spring onion, also known as a multiplier onion as it can only be grown vegetatively. It forms one or more largish (5–8 cm diameter) bulbs that have a golden-tan papery skin and white inner storage tissue. They can be harvested 2–3 months before the ordinary onion, making them a useful addition to the garden. They have a good-quality, sweeter taste than the common onion, and are used thinly sliced in salads, sandwiches, in yoghurt dips or are added to dishes that do not need much cooking. Has similar health benefits to the onion, and its leaves are rich in vitamin A, C and K. This species seldom flowers, and does not set seed but instead it multiplies by the vegetative spread of its bulbs. Can be planted in autumn, though is more usually planted in early spring, in small groups or in rows. Do not totally bury the bulbs, but allow about a third to remain above the soil surface. Once harvested, the bulbs store quite well in a dry, cool, dark place. A similar species is the French shallot (griselle), though this is a separate species (*A. oschaninii*) that grows wild in Asia.

Tree onion (Egyptian onion, walking onion, winter onion, perpetual onion), *Allium cepa proliferum* (syn. *A. viviparum).* An older, perennial variety, which, as its name suggests, forms a tall plant: ~60 cm. Instead of forming basal bulbs, it is grown for its edible bulblets, which form after the flowers on the flower stem. In the wild, after these have formed, the stalks droop downwards until the bulbils touch the soil, where they root to form new plants — hence its common name 'walking onion'. New stems bend downwards and root to 'walk' in their spread from the mother plant. If picked from the plant, these bulbils readily form new plants, or can be eaten. They are often pickled. For cultivation, the bulblets can be pushed into soil in autumn or early spring. They will form leaves in the first year, and then flower and form bulblets in the second. The plants are not invasive and can be left to 'walk' and supply a continual supply of bulblets. In this way, they don't need replanting each year, and a stand can continue for many years. The leaves can be harvested and used like spring onions or chives, though have a stronger but richer onion taste so a little goes a long way. Once harvested, the bulblets have good keeping qualities. They are good planted in clumps and are ornamental. They benefit from the addition of an organic-matter mulch, to provide additional nutrients and to protect plants from heavy frosts; however, once established, plants are surprisingly cold hardy and will tolerate freezing temperatures.

Spring onions (welsh onions, green onions, scallions, bunching onions), *Allium fistulosum.*
Known by a number of common names, and confusingly, some of these are used for other similar onion species. Also, the name 'welsh' has nothing to do with Wales, instead it means 'foreign' in German; and this species is more likely to originate from Siberia or Eastern Asia. It is a similar, but smaller close relative of the onion; however, it does not form a storage bulb. Its hollow leaves are more delicate than those of the onion. Its white flowerheads are smaller, and have a more flattened rounded shape. It is highly valued in a wide range of culinary dishes, usually chopped and only lightly cooked, if at all. Popular in Japanese, Chinese and Asian recipes, as well as in Mediterranean foods, it has traditionally been used in salads in the West. Not as hot as onions, spring onions are an excellent way to add flavour to many foods from meats, poultry and fish to salads, curries, soups and savoury tarts. They are richer in nutrients than the common onion, with more vitamin C (~20 mg/100 g) and vitamin A (~1000 I.U.), good levels of folate, and loads of vitamin K (>200 µg; ~250% of the RDA). They are easy to grow and take up virtually no room. A short row of spring onions will fit into the smallest garden, or they could be grown in pots on the window sill. The seed is usually sown sparsely in rows and covered with ~1 cm of fine soil. The spring onions can be thinned as they grow, and harvested during the season as needed. They benefit from weed control. Grow them in clumps as an ornamental alongside broad-leaved plants and leave a few to form flowers. The variety 'Crimson Forest' has beautiful crimson-coloured bulbs, with the colour forming alternate rings within the bulb. 'Red Bunching' has striking red stem bases.

Allium sativum
Garlic
ALLIACEAE (LILIACEAE)

Similar species: ramsons (bear's garlic) (*Allium ursinam*), chives (*Allium schoenoprasum*), garlic chives (*Allium tuberosum*), garlic mustard (hedge garlic, jack-by-the-hedge) (*Alliaria petiolata*)

Relatives: leek, onion, chives

A relative of onion and leeks, along with about 500 other *Allium* species, garlic is thought to have its origins in Central Asia. It could have been used in Neolithic times, and has almost certainly been used for thousands of years in virtually every civilisation known, including ancient India, Egypt, Rome, China and Japan. Garlic has medicinal value in treating a wide range of complaints, and has long been appreciated as a unique and delicious flavouring that is added to a multitude of recipes. Historically, the nobility often dismissed it due to its pungent smell, and the Buddhists and Jains also rejected it believing it to be a stimulant. Today, garlic is grown around the world, particularly in China and Asia, but also in India and Europe. It is fairly easy to grow, given the right soil conditions and some heat. It takes up very little space, and has a long history of use as a companion species to deter certain plant pests and diseases. Its less powerful relative, ransoms, grows wild in the deciduous bluebell woods of Europe and the United Kingdom, and its leaves make a milder substitute.

Angelica archangelica
Angelica (wild celery, wild parsley, European angelica)
APIACEAE (UMBELIFERAE)
Dong quai (dang gui) (*Angelica sinensis*)
Relatives: parsley, coriander, celery, carrot, parsnip, dill

Angelica, an often undervalued and little-cultivated plant, has many culinary and medicinal uses. Although there are about 40 species of *Angelica*, of these *A. archangelica* is the species usually most valued and cultivated for its culinary properties. Several other *Angelica* species have important medicinal properties, and have been used widely by the Chinese for thousands of years. *A. archangelica* is native to Europe, and is often found growing wild along roadsides in ditches. It has long been grown and valued across Europe, but particularly in eastern and northern Europe, where its flavour is valued in many types of food and drinks. It is happy growing in the colder regions of northern Europe, and is grown and utilised in Sweden, Iceland, Norway and Lapland. In some areas it has been used for hundreds to thousands of years. It is a popular plant in the south of France, where it is cultivated for usage in confectionery and is sometimes combined with Juniper berries. It can now be found naturalised in North America, and may be found in the gardens of many temperate-climate countries. A very useful plant, its roots, stems, leaves and seeds can all be used in savoury dishes as well as desserts, plus it can be added to liqueurs and it makes a good flavouring. It is fairly easy to grow, has an interesting form, and large attractive flowers. There is uncertainty concerning the origin of its unusual name, though several possibilities have been suggested. The name 'angelica' may be derived from the plant's association with important Christian personages. It may be linked to the springtime Annunciation festival. The plant may have revealed itself in an angel's dream as a cure for the plague, or it may be called 'angelica' because it is found blooming on the day of Michael the Archangel.

DESCRIPTION

Often grown as an annual, but can be grown as a biennial, or a perennial if its flowers are removed. When in flower, it can grow 1.5–2.5 m tall. Has ridged, erect, light green stems. Two other similar angelica species are *A. atropurpurea* (masterwort, American angelica), sometimes used as *A. archangelica*, but its flavour is more acidic, and *A. sylvestris* (wild angelica), which is valued more for its extractable yellow dye. Often found growing wild in the United Kingdom, wild angelica grows 0.6–1.5 m tall, has reddish purple hollow stems, and whitish flowers. Take great care if gathering *Angelica* species from the wild, as there are several similar, very toxic species (e.g. hemlock, water dropwort).

Leaves: Leaves are aromatic when lightly crushed, and are similar in shape to those of parsnip. They are deeply indented and light green. Leaves are divided into three lobes, and these again into threes, with each lobe having finely toothed margins.

Flowers: Distinctive of this species is the large, showy, membranous bract that covers the big flower. This peels back, as the flower opens, to reveal a large yellow-green flower head, which consists of many tiny flowers arranged in an umbel that measures ~8 cm in diameter. Flowers are borne from late spring into summer. Removal of flowerheads in the first year prevents the plant from dying in the first season. Plants can then continue to grow for

a further year, or for several years. However, once the plant has flowered it dies. Flowers contain both male and female parts, and can self-fertilise. Popular with insects for pollination, and also, possibly, with bees.

Fruit/seeds: Although often called seeds, the flower produces small dry fruits called schizocarps, which consist of two carpels, with each carpel containing a single seed. The indehiscent fruits are flat on one side, convex on the other, ~0.3 cm long, and are ribbed. Aromatic when crushed.

Roots: It forms long, fleshy, large, yellowish, storage taproots, which are often forked. They may exude a resin when first cut, and have an appealing musk-like aroma.

Harvest/storage: Leaves can be harvested when required during the season. The main stems are usually cut in late spring/early summer, while side shoots can be cut in mid summer. The stems should be still tender. The umbel heads, with their fruits, are harvested when they turn from green to yellow in autumn. If left too long, then the fruits can drop and be lost. The harvested umbels are placed on cloth, in a shaded but aerated place, to dry. Once dry, the fruits can be easily pulled or thrashed from the stalks, and light crushing splits the fruits into their two carpel halves. These should be stored in a cool, dark, airtight container. Roots can be harvested in the plant's first autumn and winter. They can be sliced and dried for storage. They retain their fragrance, and have an aromatic, pleasant,

Food

All parts of this plant can be used: roots, leaves, seeds and stems. It is most popularly associated with confectionery, with its stem being cut into pieces and candied. It is used in cakes and as decoration on desserts. The stem is used in liqueurs. It can be eaten fresh as a substitute for celery, though any tough fibres are best removed. The roots can be washed and then eaten raw, like carrots, in salads, or can be lightly boiled, and served with black pepper and butter. They can be roasted, perhaps with other vegetables. A tea can be made from the fresh leaves or crushed roots. The leaves can be added to soups, stews, pies and vegetable dishes, and are used as a garnish.

The roots and leaves may be cooked with rhubarb or apple to reduce the acidity of the latter. The seeds can be used in the same types of food as the leaves, though should be crushed first to release their flavours. Commercially, the seeds are used in various liqueurs such as Vermouth and Chartreuse. An essential oil can be extracted from the plant, but only in small amounts, and so is costly. It is used as a flavouring and medicinally.

Nutrition/medicinal

The plant is rich in antioxidants and contains many medicinally useful compounds. It is particularly rich in coumarins. Angelica leaves contain ~1% essential oil, valeric acid, angelic acid, sugar and angelicin, a resin that has been historically used to stimulate the lungs and skin. Recent research has found that the essential oil, extracted by steam distillation from the fruits, has cytotoxic properties against various cancer cells, with furanocoumarins accounting for most of its antiproliferative activity. These compounds have a liver-protective function. The fruits are rich in furanocoumarins. However, other as yet unidentified compounds within the leaves have anticancer properties.

Extracts from angelica have significant anti-ulcerogenic activity, and reduce acid output, increase the secretion of mucilage-type substances that protect the lining of the gut, plus other biochemical activities, and give relief comparable to that of certain pharmaceutical products. Its protective effects are hypothesised to be partly due to its flavonoid content and its free-radical-scavenging properties. The essential oil from this species has been shown to induce physical relaxation, to reduce aggressive behaviour, and could be used in anxiety-related disorders.

Historically, the leaves, stem and seeds have been used to treat such chest complaints as coughs, colds and pleurisy, but also used as a tonic, to treat heart disease, to remove phlegm, as a stimulant, as well as to treat colic and rheumatism. The stems and leaves have local anaesthetic properties, and are useful chewed for a toothache.

Angelica is believed to stimulate blood flow to the peripheral parts of the body, and has been used to treat poor circulation. Angelica balsam can be obtained from the roots using alcohol. This has a dark brown colour and contains angelica oil, angelica wax and angelicin. **Warning:** Skin contact with furocoumarins, particularly in combination with sunlight, can cause dermatitis-like reactions in some people.

Ornamental

Angelica looks good planted towards the back of a herbaceous border, with its showy flowers and yellow-green foliage.

Other uses

The dried leaves can be added to potpourri. The essential oil is used in perfumes, soap and shampoo.

somewhat musky flavour. Older roots often become diseased and somewhat woody.

CULTIVATION

Fairly easy.

Location: Prefers a semi-shaded spot and can even grow under moderately shady trees. Do not plant in full sun.

Temperature: Prefers a cool-temperate climate, and is found growing wild in middle and northern European countries. Becomes dormant in winter and is then fully cold hardy. Grows best at summer temperatures of between 7°C and 20°C.

Soil/water/nutrients: Grows best in nutrient-rich loams; incorporate organic matter or well-rotted manure before planting. Can grow in more sandy soils, but benefits from the addition of organic matter. Can grow in fairly heavy clay soils. Needs regular moisture to thrive. Can even grow in wet soils, as long as they do not become anaerobic. A mulch is very beneficial for this species to help retain moisture, add nutrients and reduce weed competition, to which it is susceptible. Prefers acid to neutral soils with a pH 5–7.

Pot culture: Could be grown in deep pots, with a moderately heavy soil, with regular moisture and placed in a light shade.

Planting/propagation: Seed: The seed loses most of its viability within ~12 months, so fresh seed is best. Store seed in a fridge until needed. Can sow seed in spring, but is often sown fresh, in late summer to early autumn, so that seedlings can be planted out the following spring. Germination is slow and takes 21–35 days. Seed germinates better if given a period of 2–3 weeks chilling in a fridge before sowing. Sow in trays and give some warmth and moisture, but light is needed to initiate germination, so do not cover the seeds with soil: just press them gently into a fine soil. If grown inside, grow seedlings on and plant out the following spring. Handle young seedlings carefully as their long taproots are easily damaged and may not recover. Seed can be sown *in situ* outside, but needs to be sown in rows as it has fairly slow germination, and seedlings can be easily overtaken by weeds. Plants are planted or thinned to ~50 cm apart, or wider if grown as an ornamental. Weed control is important. *Cuttings:* Roots can be divided in autumn or spring to form new plants, or offshoots can be removed from the base, but seed-grown plants are said to be of better quality.

Pests and diseases: Very few problems.

OTHER SPECIES

Dong quai (dang gui), *Angelica sinensis.* Although not a culinary herb, this species has a very long history of usage for treatment of women's complaints, particularly for the relief of menopause symptoms, but also to regulate menstruation and relieve menstrual pains. It contains significant amounts of phyto-oestrogens. It is used to treat fatigue and high blood pressure, and is often taken by women as a tonic. Dang gui is very unusual in that it is one of the few plant species reported to contain good amounts of the B vitamin, B12, which is crucial in curing some forms of anaemia. It is believed to have liver-protecting and antibacterial properties. It originates from northern China, and is a cold-hardy (down to ~5°C) perennial, growing to ~80 cm tall.

Anthemis nobilis (syn. *Chamaemelum nobile*)

English chamomile (Roman chamomile, camomile, ground apple, corn chamomile)

ASTERACEAE (COMPOSITAE)

Ox-eye chamomile (yellow chamomile) (*Anthemis tinctoria*); corn chamomile (*A. arvensis*)

Similar species: German chamomile (*Matricaria chamomilla* (syn. *M. recutita*)) rayless chamomile (pineapple weed) (*Matricaria matricarioides*); curry plant (straw plant) (*Helichrysum italicum* (syn. *H. angustifolium*)).

Relatives: globe artichoke, lettuce, chicory, sunflower, thistles

A herb that is well known, usually for the soothing tea that is made from the dried flowers. The chamomile species described here first are those from the *Anthemis* genus, and include English chamomile and ox-eye chamomile, with English chamomile considered the most popular and fragrant chamomile. The name chamomile is believed to be derived from 'kamai', which is Greek meaning 'on the ground', and 'melon', which is Greek for apple and refers to its aroma. *Anthemis* species are often grown as ornamentals, particularly on paths or as a lawn, where the fragrance released from light foot traffic is delightful. This usage goes back at least to the Middle Ages, and in Britain there was a rhyme that went: 'Like a camomile bed, the more it is trodden, the more it will spread'. *Anthemis* species were long valued by the English, particularly the aristocracy, who planted them profusely around their stately homes. English chamomile is native to Europe and Britain, though the Egyptians valued its fragrance and therapeutic aspects, and used it as a strewing herb. It is now often found in grasslands, wasteland and around gardens across Europe, but also in parts of North America where it has become naturalised. English chamomile is often grouped together with German (or Hungarian) chamomile, which is used in very similar ways, though the latter is from a different genus (see below), and is a larger, coarser, erect plant.

DESCRIPTION

The *Anthemis* chamomiles are prostrate, creeping perennials, with their leaves growing to only 15–25 cm in size. Their main stems, or runners, readily root from the leaf nodes, and send up lateral branches that usually produce flowers. It spreads vegetatively via these runners as well as by seed. Ox-eye chamomile is a larger, more erect plant, 20–40 cm tall, and the undersides of its leaves are grey and woolly. The leaves of corn chamomile are less fragrant than other *Anthemis* species, and this species is an annual.

Leaves: The feathery, alternate, finely dissected, mid-green leaves are downy, and have a sweet, apple-like fragrance when lightly crushed. The plant has a mossy texture and appearance.

Flowers: Many tiny flowers cluster together to form a central golden-yellow disc. This is surrounded by white petal-like rays, with the whole forming a flowerhead

Food

The rhizomes, as its name 'wild sarsaparilla' suggests, can be used instead of sarsaparilla to make root beer, and can be mixed with other ingredients such as ginger, allspice, licorice. They are boiled to extract a red-brown fluid, which is used in the beer. It is added to candies and confectionery. The rhizomes can be roasted or baked, and eaten as a vegetable. It has a warm, aromatic, sweet flavour, though some do not rate this flavour highly; however, it is filling and appeases hunger when little else is available.

A pleasant-flavoured tea is made from the ground rhizome. The young shoots can be lightly steamed and eaten as a vegetable. The fruits are edible, with a sweet but spicy flavour, and are used in conserves, jellies and to make a wine.

Nutrition/medicinal

Rich in fibre. Historically, this species has been used to treat heart pain, as an antiseptic, for digestive problems and to ease sore throats. The rhizomes have been used to increase sweating and, thus, they were believed to stimulate and detoxify the body of various maladies. It has been used as a poultice to treat rheumatism, sores, burns, itchy skin, ulcers, swellings and skin problems such as eczema. A tea made from the rhizomes was used as a cough treatment.

A Canadian study has found that extracts from this species have anticancer properties and could be developed into selective anticancer products, which have few side effects and low cost.

Ornamental

Could be grown as an ornamental in shady borders or under trees. Has attractive white, delicate flowers followed by dark-coloured fruits.

DESCRIPTION

A small perennial shrub, growing 0.3–0.6 m tall, with a ~0.4 m spread, and separate flower stems. The stems die back at the end of the season and the plant over-winters as storage rhizomes. Over time, plants form a thick mat of rhizomes.

Leaves: Each leaf stalk (30–60 cm tall) divides into three stems and each of these bears a leaf, divided into 3–5 leaflets. Leaves are oval to cordate, mid-green, have thin, pointed tips, with lightly toothed margins.

Flowers: Tiny, simple, five-petalled, but forming a pretty, greeny-white, radiating sphere containing 12–30 flowers. Looks similar to those from the *Allium* genus. The flowerheads are borne on their own stems, separate from the leaves, however, they can be missed as they are often obscured by the leaves. Each flower has both male and female parts. Flowers are borne from early to mid summer. Not all plants produce flowers. Pollination is by bees, particularly bumblebees and solitary bees.

Fruits/seeds: Small, rounded, shiny, purple-black berries, ~0.6 cm diameter, ripening in late summer to early autumn. *En masse*, they are attractive and eye-catching. Each berry contains ~5 small seeds.

Roots: Forms long, creeping, yellowy-brown, aromatic rhizomes, which grow horizontally at 3–12 cm below the soil surface. These are filled with spongy tissue. Off these, grow longish tough feeder and water-gathering roots.

Harvest/storage: The fruits can be harvested when ripe, in early autumn. The rhizomes are harvested at the end of the season. It is better to take just the older rhizomes, leaving the younger to form a future crop. Can be used fresh, but are more usually dried for later use.

CULTIVATION

Location: Grows best in light to heavier shade, and does not tolerate strong winds.

Temperature: A cold-hardy species once established, tolerating temperatures down to ~–35°C; will tolerate some summer heat, if grown in shade.

Soil/water/nutrients: Likes regular moisture, though is not too fussy about soil type, and plants will grow in low-nutrient stoney soils becoming hardier as a result. However, they will grow larger and better in deeper loams, and appreciate the addition of organic matter. They are not drought hardy, though it is possible they could tolerate short periods of waterlogging.

Pot culture: Its small size makes this species ideal for cultivation in pots. Can be placed in a shady place and enjoyed for its flowers and clusters of dark purple berries. Use fairly good-quality soil and keep the soil moist, though not waterlogged. Replenish soil every couple of years.

Planting/propagation: *Seed:* The seed is best sown when fresh, in a cold frame to allow it to have 3–4 months of chilling. Give purchased seed a similar treatment by placing in a fridge for a few weeks before sowing. Sow the seed thinly and just cover with moist, warm compost. Germination can be slow, taking 4–16 weeks, and germination rate can be poor (only ~35%). Ideally, the seed germinates much better, and much more reliably, if it has passed through the gut of a black bear (up to 93% germination). Prick-out seedlings and grow-on in light shade for a year or two before planting out in spring. *Cuttings:* Plants produce offsets from rhizomes around the main plant; these can be removed and potted up in early spring. Sections of roots can be taken in autumn, and inserted upside-down in sand outside, to over-winter. In spring, they are planted right-way up in pots with moist, warm compost to start growth. Both methods of vegetative propagation give good results. Space new plants at least 0.5 m apart. Plants will form a dense matt of rhizomes after a few years, if not harvested before.

Pests and diseases: Few pest or disease problems reported, though the rhizomes are said to be enjoyed by wild rabbits.

SIMILAR SPECIES

American spikehead (spiceberry, Indian root, old man's root), *Aralia racemosa*. A similar species to wild sarsaparilla, and found in similar regions of North America, this species is used like wild sarsaparilla. A taller more branched plant, growing to 1–2 m high, it has similarly shaped, but much larger leaves. The small, greenish flowers are arranged in numerous clusters, and are borne from mid to late summer. Its berries are reddish brown or dark purple. The rhizomes are chunkier and have prominent stem scars. Their aroma and flavour are stronger than that of *A. nudicaulis*. The rhizomes have similar medicinal properties and are used in various homeopathic remedies.

Arctium lappa
Burdock (great burdock, gobo, Takinogawa)
ASTERACEAE (COMPOSITAE)

Similar species: Great burdock (syn. Japanese burdock) (*Arctium lappa*), wild burdock (*A. minus*)

Relatives: Jerusalem artichoke, chicory, dandelion, sunflower, chrysanthemum

Burdock is often considered a weed. Its fruits, with hooked hairs, readily attach themselves to passing animals for dispersal. It grows wild in Europe, Asia and North America. Although usually undervalued and dismissed, varieties have been selected by the Japanese for their edible roots and leaves, and these are used for many health purposes. The roots can be sliced like Jerusalem artichokes, and all parts of the plant are used in many herbal preparations. In the United Kingdom, these species are associated historically with a well-known refreshing cordial made from dandelion and burdock roots. The fact that it grows very easily and is not fussy about its growing conditions, has made it a widespread successful weed species on roadsides and waste ground. If cultivating this species, therefore, remove seed heads before their dispersal to reduce its invasive potential. Great burdock tends to be the main species grown for its roots and, as its name suggests, it is the larger of these group of species.

DESCRIPTION
Stout, fast-growing, biennial to short-lived perennials, classified within the daisy and thistle family, though their prickles are nowhere as fearsome as those of thistles. They grow to 0.5–1 m tall, with great burdock growing to >2 m tall. They form leaves and a storage root within the first year, and numerous flower stems in their second spring.

Leaves: Large, up to 40 cm long, from the base of the plant, producing quite dense shade beneath them. Oval to heart shaped, with a pointed or rounded tip, alternate, often with reddish leaf veins. Their undersides are grey-green with fine hairs, which reduce moisture loss. Are coarse and often have wavy margins.

Flowers/seeds: Not as showy or large as many thistles, they are egg-shaped, compact (~2.5 cm diameter), with many small mauve-purple florets clustered together in heads within a hemispherical receptacle that has long green bracts. Are borne singly or in doubles and triples from leaf axils and the apex of the flower stems. Once the flower has formed its seeds, the rounded capsules bear many hooked wiry hairs, like Velcro, and these species are believed to have been the inspiration for this useful product. The seed heads become easily detached from the plant and then tenaciously hold onto any animal hair or feather surfaces they encounter, so aiding their widespread dispersal. Flowers are borne from mid to late summer and seeds ripen in autumn. Pollination is by bees and insects.

Roots: Long, coarse taproots, similar to those of parsnip, but thinner. Has white dense central storage tissue. Can grow to 0.5–1 m long, but are only ~2–4 cm in diameter.

Harvest/storage: The roots are best harvested in autumn, and possibly through the winter months, but the roots may then be more woody. Should be harvested before the flower stems form. Can be tricky to dig up due to their depth and, consequently, are often damaged in the process. They can also be grown in long hollow pipes or tubes, deep compostible boxes or in trenches that have been pre-dug to depth. Harvested roots are usually washed and then stored in a fridge or a cool place.

Food

Young taproots just need washing but with winter-harvested taproots, remove the outer skin. The roots can be chopped and added to soups and stews; they have a crisp, pleasant, sweetish aromatic flavour, not unlike Jerusalem artichoke, to which it is related. Often used in the same way as cooked carrots, though are not usually eaten raw. May be soaked in warm water for ~10 minutes to remove any bitter flavours.

In Japanese cuisine, the roots may be thinly sliced and braised with carrot, soy sauce, sesame oil and a little sake. Alternately, they may be dipped in batter to make tempura, or added to sushi instead of fish. Cook until tender, but still crisp. The roots can be roasted. In Britain, a popular fizzy drink, called dandelion and burdock, was commonly sold, and became popular on hot summer days. The drink is occasionally still seen for sale, but unfortunately does not include either dandelions or burdock. However, the 'real' cordial is now undergoing a revival. Both the roots and seeds can be used to make this cordial.

The young leaves and stems can be gathered and cooked. Any stringy fibres should be removed (as with globe artichokes), with the centre of the stems and leaf bases being the most tender and tastiest. Their flavour is then good, and not unlike that of globe artichoke. The leaves can be dried and used to make a tea. The seeds have been used, or have been sprouted and used in salads, though care needs to be taken as the seeds are armed with hooks.

Nutrition/medicinal

It became a popular food in macrobiotic cooking. It is rich in fibre, with relatively good amounts of protein for a root. Has good quantities of the minerals potassium, manganese, magnesium, iron, zinc and calcium.

Like other members of this family, burdock contains the carbohydrate inulin. This compound increases the populations of 'good' gut bacteria, may improve the effectiveness of the immune system and increases the absorption of calcium. It prevents constipation and, consequently, is likely to reduce the incidence of bowel cancer. It binds with compounds that are involved with the production of cholesterol, and so may indirectly lower cholesterol levels. Because inulin is not digested in the gut but is instead fermented in the large intestines, it may have the side effect of causing flatulence. However, not harvesting the roots until after a frost (or placing them in a fridge), or leaving them in the sun for a few days initiates the conversion of inulin by the enzyme inulase, into fructose. This sweetens the roots and reduces their flatulence effects. The roots are very low in calories because inulin is not absorbed by the body, and burdock is thus an excellent alternative carbohydrate for diabetics and for those worried about weight gain.

The plant has been found to contain good amounts of antioxidants. The roots have long been used to purify the blood and to treat gout, psoriasis and skin ailments, and are believed to increase milk production in nursing mothers. It has been used to treat arthritis, rheumatism, sciatica and to reduce joint swelling and calcium deposits, as well as being used to treat kidney stones.

Has anti-fungal and antibacterial properties, which are said to be due to polyacetylenes found within the root. The plant has been shown to lower blood-sugar levels in some animals. *Warning:* A few people have an allergy to inulin. Like many other members of this family, the crushed leaves and stems can cause skin dermatitis due to the lactones they contain, and these effects may be compounded if exposed to sunlight.

Other uses

An oil extracted from the root has long been considered to be excellent for the hair and scalp, and has been used to treat dandruff and other scalp disorders, to slow hair loss, to improve hair strength and increase its shine. Modern research has shown that the oil is indeed rich in phytosterols and essential fatty acids both which improve scalp and hair health, as well as improving the function of sebaceous glands and hair follicles. It is claimed that regular use of burdock oil helps restore and maintain a healthy scalp and hair. Extracts from the seeds seem to have similar properties.

Wrapping the roots in polythene prevents them from drying out. Some people dry the roots for longer-term storage.

CULTIVATION
Easy.
Location: Can grow in full sun or light shade, and will grow in light woodland.
Temperature: Can grow in a wide range of temperatures, from cool- to warm-temperate. As the tops die back in autumn, the underground roots can survive winter in freezing temperatures.

Soil/water/nutrients: Can grow in a wide range of soils, from wet almost waterlogged soils, to dry, sandy soils. In general, prefers drier soils. Can grow in moderately heavy clay soils, though the taproots are then likely to be forked and more irregular. They are not very nutrient demanding and can be grown in poor-quality soils, but moderate additions of nutrients will give better growth.
Pot culture: Sometimes grown in containers to control their spread and make them easier to harvest, though need a deep container with loose compost to get the best taproot growth. Can be grown in tubes or decomposable pipes.

Food
The leaves have a sweetish, anise-like aroma and flavour. Russian tarragon has a coarser, some say more bitter, flavour, whereas French tarragon is spicier and more refined. It is a popular culinary herb and is added to many Italian and French recipes. It is one of the four herbs used in the traditional French *fines herbes*. Tarragon is much used across Europe and North America to flavour tomato dishes, fish recipes, and to flavour vinegar as a dressing. The young leaves can be added to salads. Tarragon goes well in egg dishes and is a common ingredient in white sauces. The young leaves and stems can be lightly steamed and eaten as an asparagus substitute. An essential oil is commercially extracted from the plant, and is used as a flavouring and an aromatic.

Nutrition/medicinal
The leaves contain some calcium, iron and manganese. The essential oil is extracted by steam, and mostly contains estragole (methylchavicol: ~70%), ocimene, phellandrene, camphene and pinene. Extracts (Tarralin) from the leaves, when given to diabetic and non-diabetic mice, significantly lower blood-glucose levels to a similar extent as known antidiabetic drugs, and so could have a role in managing diabetes. These extracts did not affect insulin or glucose levels of non-diabetic mice, and this compound has been found to be safe and non-toxic.

Tarragon contains phenylpropanoids, which have significant anti-platelet activity, and can prevent blood clots forming. In Iran, this plant has been historically used to treat epilepsy: recent studies have confirmed that the essential oil does have anticonvulsant and sedative properties. Compounds within the leaves have bacteriocidal properties. Tarragon has insecticidal and antifungal activity. Interestingly, tarragon, as well as potato and wheat, contain low quantities of natural benzodiazepines, which, in larger amounts, pharmaceutically, act as sedatives, anticonvulsants, muscle and anxiety relaxers and as hypnotics. It is said to have antispasmodic and anti-inflammatory effects, and has been taken for various digestive and menstrual problems. The leaves, chewed or macerated, have a mild, topical anaesthetic affect, and are used to ease toothache and gum problems.

Other uses
Its narrow, small leaves are attractive in the herb garden or a herbaceous border.

can be dried or frozen for later use. Freshly picked, they have a sweet, warm, aromatic fragrance. For drying, the leaves are best dried fairly quickly at ~50°C before storing in a dark, cool, airtight container. They reabsorb moisture easily, so dry storage is important.

Roots: Russian tarragon has long, spreading, fibrous, surface roots, so care needs to be taken with mechanical cultivation to avoid root damage. The roots of French tarragon are less spreading, but still benefit from the protection of an organic mulch.

CULTIVATION
Russian tarragon is easy; French tarragon is more particular.

Location: Grows best in full sun in cooler regions, but is best provided with light shade during the hottest part of the day in Mediterranean-type climates. Somewhat wind hardy and can be grown near to the coast.

Temperature: French tarragon grows best in warmer, sunny climates; Russian tarragon is a tougher, more cold-hardy plant. Because the tops die back in winter, the plants are fairly cold hardy once established, but their shallow roots are susceptible, so plants benefit from a protective mulch in cold weather. French tarragon is more likely to be killed by freezing temperatures, and so is best taken indoors.

Soil/water/nutrients: Russian tarragon can grow in a range of soil types, and seems to actually grow better if the soil is not too nutrient rich. Once established, it is quite drought tolerant. French tarragon grows best in moderately nutrient-rich loams and needs fairly regular moisture. Neither is tolerant of waterlogging. An organic mulch helps retain moisture, provides nutrients, suppresses weed growth and gives protection from winter cold. Grow in somewhat acidic to slightly alkaline soils: pH 5.0–7.5.

Pot culture: The smaller more delicate French tarragon could be ideal for growth in a container, and can be easily given protection in cold weather. Give plants good-quality, free-draining compost and regular moisture.

Planting/propagation: *Seed:* French tarragon rarely, if ever, sets seed. However, Russian tarragon can be grown from seed and is, in general, easier to propagate than French tarragon. Sow the fine seed and barely cover with fine soil. As a household usually needs only one or two plants, tarragon can be sown in trays and then seedlings pricked-out and grown-on before planting out once the soil has warmed. *Cuttings:* Plants can be divided and either root- or crown-divisions can be made. Are best divided in spring, and then established in pots before planting out at ~50 cm apart. Have spreading root growth, so need enough space between plants to allow this. Plants grow quite quickly, and can be re-divided every 3–4 years to give new stock, and rejuvenate growth.

Pests and diseases: Few problems, though slugs can sometimes be a problem.

Arthrospira platensis
Spirulina
PHORMIDIACEAE

Arthrospira platensis (syn. *Spirulina platensis*), *A. maxima* (syn *Spirulina platensis*), *A. fusiformis* (syn. *Spirulina platensis*)
Aphanizomenon flos-aquae

Confusingly, the Latin name of the main spirulina species has recently changed, with the literature often still using its older genera name, *Spirulina platensis*; however, it is more correctly known as *Arthrospira platensis*. The other spirulina species, *A. maxima* and *A. fusiformis*, may just be forms of *A. platensis*. *Aphanizomenon flos-aquae* is another cyanobacteria, used in similar ways to *Spirulina*. In the wild, the species *A. platensis* has a widespread occurrence in Africa, Asia and South America. These primitive organisms, classified as a cyanobacterium, are usually blue-green-coloured bacteria that are able to photosynthesise, and make a nutritious food.

Cyanobacterium may be single-celled, or the cells can aggregate to form tiny filaments or colonies. Very primitive life forms, they were one of the first living creatures to evolve on Earth, dating back 3.8 billion years. They are the precursors to all other plants, including seaweeds, and probably to animals. Spirulina, as a food supplement, is now often grown in controlled environments, which ensure non-contamination by other microbes.

It is tremendously nutritious compared with most foods, its cultivation takes up very little space, does not need soil, just needs light and a source of nutrients, and produces large crops of highly nutritious biomass. It can be grown in brackish water and produces 20 times more protein per acre, and needs 20 times less land than soybeans. It needs 200 times less land than that required for beef production. It is the ideal food for a highly populated world, but many people resist spirulina as a food source due to its colour and texture. It is, however, often added to food products to increase their nutrient and protein content, and is then found to be acceptable. It was not produced 'artificially' until the early 1960s, in Japan. In the 1970s, production began in Mexico, and then later in Australia and the United States. For more than 30 years, interest in this crop has increased phenomenally.

Much research has been conducted on spirulina for its minimal impact on the environment and its nutritional qualities. Most spirulina is now produced in the USA, India, China and East Asia. In a few countries, e.g. New Zealand, it has been embraced, and forms the base of a wonderful-tasting green, nutritious drink, often mixed with bananas, mango and other fruit juices. It is commonly sold dried in powder or tablet form. Spirulina is a food that can be produced under adverse conditions in places with little room and as such, it has been proposed as a potential food by NASA and the European Space Agency as a fresh food for long-term space missions.

DESCRIPTION

Primitive creatures, these prokaryotes have no central, membrane-bound nucleus (as do 'higher' eukaryote cells); they are more bacteria-like than most other cell forms, including algae. The cells contain a complex system of fine strands of material, which do contain some chlorophyll, but mostly contain another photosynthetic pigment called phycocyanin, and some carotene. Like plants, cyanobacteria can use water in the light-trapping reaction, but in anaerobic conditions can use hydrogen sulphide, and nitrogen. This unique ability to use atmospheric nitrogen (e.g. to reduce nitrogen gas to nitrates), which no other higher life form can, created an enormous opportunity for millions of other species and life forms to evolve, and to use this fixed nitrogen to produce enzymes and proteins for life. This group of organisms began what is possibly the most amazing biochemical set of reactions on Earth: the trapping of energy from the sun to make compounds to survive and multiply, and the conversion of nitrogen gas into oxygen. In the beginning, there was virtually no oxygen in the atmosphere. These tiny organisms are thought to be responsible for making the Earth's atmosphere oxygen rich, and largely changing it into the composition it is today. These creatures caused an explosion in biodiversity and evolution of multitudes of life forms to fill the niches developed in water, and on land.

Food

Spirulina is either used in drinks with cold fruit juices, or can be sprinkled onto foods such as soups, stir-fries or even salads. It is best not cooked, as this reduces its nutritive value. It does not have a strong flavour, and is mild and pleasant. In Mexico, it is added to candies. In Japan, India and Singapore it is added to nutritional appetisers. It is sometimes used as a colouring. In France, it is incorporated into a vegetable pâté.

Nutrition/medicinal

Spirulina is packed with nutrients; when dried, it contains an amazing ~65% protein, which includes a wide range of amino acids, including all the essential amino acids: it has a richer and more complete protein profile than any plant. It is very rich in iron, copper and manganese, with some potassium, magnesium and sodium. It is hypothesised that the photosynthetic pigment it contains, photocyanin, may have been the first to evolve, before chlorophyll, as it contains both haemoglobin and iron at its core. This gives spirulina its rich iron content. Chlorophyll (from plants), in contrast, just has magnesium at its core, whereas the animal oxygen-carrying pigment, haemoglobin, contains iron. It is possible that phycocyanin was the original precursor of these two essential molecules.

Spirulina is very rich in the B vitamins, i.e. riboflavin and thiamine, and probably B12, which is often lacking in vegetarian diets. It is very rich in vitamin A (~23,000 IU) as beta-carotene, having more than 10 times that of carrots.

It is very rich in vitamins D and K. However, because spirulina does not contain vitamin C, lemon juice (or similar) is often added to spirulina-based foods: the added vitamin C promotes synergistic reactions with nutrients within spirulina. Spirulina contains a little fibre.

A large number of research papers have been written on spirulina, including many on its medicinal benefits. The photosynthetic pigment, photocyanin, seems to stimulate the immune system. It increases production of infection-fighting cytokines, and the production of both red and white blood cells; it also increases T-cell counts. Substances within spirulina have shown marked anti-herpes and anti-HIV activity, and significantly inhibit HIV-1 replication. It is suggested that further development of these substances might yield novel candidates for broad-spectrum antiviral drugs.

In clinical trials, it has been shown to reduce anaemia and improve weight gain in both HIV-infected and HIV-negative malnourished children. It has been found to protect against hay fever, and may help reduce the severity of strokes as well as improving recovery. It may reduce the prevalence of neurodegenerative diseases.

Other uses

It is fed to poultry and is said to make hens' eggs yellow as well as improving the birds' health. It has been used as flamingo food to make them pink, and has been fed to cattle with claims of accelerating growth, speeding up sexual maturation and increasing their fertility.

Despite their tiny size, they are one of the major primary producers in the world's oceans.

Form: Spirulina often form slender, cylindrical filaments of cells that are corkscrew in form. They are usually coloured blue-green, though can be olive-green or reddish brown, depending on their environment. Unlike plants, including algae, these creatures are not surrounded by a cellulose wall, which makes them easier to digest as a human food. Cell division is by binary fission.

Harvest/storage: In the right conditions growth and multiplication are fast, and yields can be high in a short time. In the past, spirulina was only cultivated in open-channel, aerated raceway ponds, which were stirred continually to keep the liquid in motion. Although this method is still used, other cultivation methods use closed growth-containers to gain more sterile conditions. This reduces contamination by other organisms, i.e. some of these can produce toxic byproducts, but closed production systems are more costly to run. Initially, the organism is refined and placed in tanks of warm water (~30°C), with a very alkaline pH (pH 8–10), to which a wide range of minerals is added. This includes sodium bicarbonate, many minerals, plus a range of trace nutrients. The resulting brew is then supplied with 12 hours of light in every 24, and the mix is regularly

checked to maintain nutrient balance, correct pH, etc. Unusually for a crop, it can be harvested year round. At harvesting, the cells are removed by filtration; they are washed to remove excess salts, and then acid is added to neutralise pH. The cells are crushed to break up the filaments, and are then dried, though temperatures need to be exactly right to avoid reducing nutrient and compound quality. The resulting powder is stored in airtight packaging out of direct light.

Location: Spirulina occurs naturally in tropical and subtropical lakes that have alkaline waters with high concentrations of carbonate and bicarbonate.

Globe'), plus some varieties that have flesh that consists of alternate bands of rings of pink and white (e.g. 'Chiogga', from Italy, with temperature fluctuations apparently causing the distinctive banding). These non-red varieties do not stain like red types, but also do not contain the same amount of betalains (see Nutrition p. 112).

Harvest/storage: There are many varieties: some selected to produce an earlier spring crop; others for an autumn crop. Beetroots are best harvested when still young, ~5 cm in diameter. Older beets become hard and fibrous. Takes 50–100 days until harvesting, dependent on climate. The whole plant is pulled from the ground and the shoots are often removed to reduce moisture loss. Leaving some shoot with the beet increases their attractiveness, but does reduce their storage life. They can be stored in a cool place without their tops for several months and are best stored with quite high humidity, or they dry out. Some gardeners store them in the ground until late autumn, after removing their tops. A few of the younger leaves can be harvested during the growing season and used as a vegetable.

CULTIVATION
Easy.

Location: They prefer a sunny location, though can tolerate light shade. Can tolerate, and often grow better in, maritime locations.

Temperature: Prefer a cooler climate though will grow in the subtropics. Can be grown as a winter crop in warmer areas. Hot weather induces plants to flower in the second year. The swollen roots do not tolerate freezing temperatures, and should be harvested or protected for over-wintering.

Soil/water/nutrients: Grow best in a lighter soil due to their root development: stoney or clay soils impede storage-root expansion. Do best with a moderately nutrient-rich soil and regular moisture. Dry periods can cause hard, shrivelled roots and slow growth. Growth is best in slightly acid to neutral soils: pH 6–7. Can tolerate saline soils more than many vegetables.

Pot culture: Could be grown in pots of compost, though generally are not. Consider growing the ornamental-leaved beetroots if short of space.

Planting/propagation: Almost always by seed, which is large enough to sow individually. Germination is good. Briefly soaking the seeds before sowing can speed up and improve rate. Sow shallowly in rows, covering with ~1 cm of fine soil. Seedlings can be thinned as they grow. The young, tender shoots make an excellent addition to salads, or they can be transplanted to another area. Thin plants to ~20 cm for beetroot.

Reduce weed competition, particularly when young, and keep seedlings moist until established. Seed can be sown at intervals throughout the spring and summer to ensure a regular supply of young beetroots. In warmer regions, they can be sown in autumn for a late winter/early spring crop. Rotate this crop to reduce disease risk.

Pests and diseases: Have few problems, though the spinach flea beetle can damage leaves, but usually not too seriously. It can be spread from chickweed and pigweed, so eliminate these weeds from the vicinity. Also can have problems with leaf spot (various fungal diseases), leaf miner, a few viruses and rots, if the soil is cold and wet.

Beta vulgaris cicla
Chard (Swiss chard, silver-beet, spinach beet, perpetual spinach)
CHENOPODIACEAE (SYN. AMARANTHACEAE)
Relatives: beets, spinach, quinoa, amaranth, celosia

Chard is related to many nutritious, useful crop plants. Many varieties of *Beta vulgaris* have been selected, and virtually all parts of the plant (roots, shoots, leaves and seeds) of many species can be eaten. *Beta vulgaris* species originate from the Mediterranean region. There are many *B. vulgaris* varieties, which are mostly divided into two main groups: the beets, which include beetroot, mangels and sugar beet (see p. 111); and the leaf vegetables, which include chard, and is valued in many countries for its tasty, nutritious leaves. The Greeks were enjoying the leaves in at least 400 BC. Chard, similar to spinach, though its taste is milder and its oxalic acid content not as high, is extremely easy to grow, can be grown in cooler climates, supplying greens through the winter months, and suffers from few pests and diseases. Often grown in parts of Europe and the United Kingdom, as well as North America. Chard has become particularly popular in New Zealand, where it is known as silver-beet, and virtually every vegetable garden includes a few plants. These plants can be easily fitted into a small garden, and many varieties have ornamental leaves.

DESCRIPTION

They are biennials, producing leaves in the first year, and then flowering and setting seed in the second year, though they are usually harvested by the end of the first year. In colder areas, growth slows during the winter and then resumes in spring, but the stems and leaves remain alive. In warmer regions they are often grown as an autumn and winter crop.

Leaves: The standard varieties have large, deep green leaves, often with a deep red tinge, particularly the stems. They have a thick, succulent stem, which can be white or red, depending on variety. The leaves are long, often deeply folded between the veins, shiny, mostly growing from a central crown, with younger leaves towards the centre. 'Argentata' is a traditional variety, with dark green leaves, silvery white midribs and flavoursome leaves. However, there are several wonderfully colourful varieties such as 'Bright Lights', which has stems that can be coloured from yellow to orange to deep red; 'Bright Yellow' (self-explanatory), and 'Charlotte' with pinkish red stems.

Flowers: Insignificant, small, greenish yellow, sometimes reddish, in long, upright clusters. Pollination is by wind. They are not self-fertile, but its pollen will fertilise other members of this species in its vicinity.

Seeds: Some of the Chenopodiaceae produce highly nutritious, small, edible, dried fruits (often thought of as seeds), e.g. quinoa and amaranth. Formed in the second year, often numerous, distinctly knobbly in shape, 0.1–0.2 cm diameter.

Harvest/storage: Chard can be harvested over several months, from when they are young. Take care not to pick too may leaves from one plant at one time. Try to pick stems cleanly from the plant to avoid damage and entry of pathogens through ragged wounds. If the weather isn't too hot, the harvesting season can last several months. Leaves are best used fresh, though can be stored for a few days in a polythene bag in a fridge.

Roots: Has fairly shallow roots for water and mineral uptake, so needs care with mechanical cultivation. Unlike their close relatives the beets, chard does not form large storage taproots.

CULTIVATION

Very easy.

Location: Prefers a sunny location, though can tolerate light shade. Can tolerate, and often grows better in, maritime locations. Fairly wind hardy.

Temperature: Prefers a cooler climate, though will grow in the subtropics, where it is better grown as an autumn to winter to spring crop. High temperatures cause the plants to bolt, and growth is poor in hot weather.

Soil/water/nutrients: Can be grown in a wide range of soil types, from sandy to quite heavy clay soils. However, it does best with a moderately nutrient-rich soil and needs regular moisture. Will tolerate wet soils for a short time. Dry periods cause slow leaf growth and poor leaf expansion. Grows best in slightly acid to neutral soils: pH 6–7. Has a marked resistance to manganese toxicity. Can tolerate salt more than many vegetables.

Pot culture: Could be grown in pots if short of space. Choose ornamental varieties with brightly coloured stems, and position these potted plants among the flowering annuals.

Planting/propagation: *Seed:* Almost always by seed, which is large enough to be easy to sow. Germination is good. Briefly soaking the seeds before sowing can speed up and improve rate. Sow at a shallow depth in rows, covering with ~1 cm of fine soil. Seedlings can be thinned as they grow.

The young, tender shoots make an excellent addition to salads, etc., or they can be transplanted to another area. Thin plants to ~30 cm apart for chard. Reduce weed competition, particularly when young, and keep seedlings moist until established. Seed can sown at intervals

uses

Food
A few leaves can be removed from young plants as soon as they are established, though with moderation. Individual plants go on to provide fresh leafy greens for many months, through the winter, until they flower. The very young leaves are great in salads. Older leaves can be lightly steamed or stir-fried. Some cooks serve the green leaves and diced stems separately. The stems are crisp and juicy, with a celery like texture and a mild flavour. The leaves taste a little like spinach, but are not as acidic. When cooked, they do not reduce in volume as much as spinach.

Nutrition/medicinal
The leaves are very rich in carotenoids (vitamin A: one serving providing ~140% of RDA); they have good quantities of vitamin C and are very high in vitamin K (one serving providing almost 400% of RDA). They are particularly rich in the carotenoid lutein, which is known to help improve vision and significantly slow the progression of age-related macular degeneration (by as much as 40%). Lutein is protective against heart disease. They contain virtually no fat or calories. The compound, betaine is found within this family, particularly beetroot, and to a lesser extent in chard: trials have shown that betaine may reduce the multiplication of cancer cells. Recent research has indicated that betaine helps the body's hormonal system to deal with depression and may help reduce cardiovascular disease. **Warning:** The leaves sometimes contain relatively high levels of oxalic acid, so should be eaten in moderation, particularly by those with risk of arthritis, kidney stones and gout.

Ornamental
There are several ornamental varieties of chard, with colourful yellow and green leaves with red to orange to yellow midribs, e.g. 'Bright lights'.

throughout the spring and summer to ensure a regular supply of young leaves. In warmer regions, best to sow seed in late summer or autumn to supply a crop of leaves through winter and spring. Rotate this crop (and other Chenopodiaceae) to reduce disease risk.

Pests and diseases: Have few problems, though the spinach flea beetle can damage leaves, but this is usually not too serious. It can be spread from chickweed and pigweed, so eradicate these from the garden margins. Also can occasionally have problems with leaf spot (various fungal diseases), leaf miner, a few viruses and rots, if the soil is cold and wet.

SIMILAR VARIETIES

Perpetual spinach: Another variety of *Beta vulgaris cicla* though the leaves of this type are somewhat smaller, and are more spinach like. They are more like chard in texture, and as their name suggests, the more they are picked (within reason), the more they resprout and grow. A particularly valuable crop for the winter months, and tends to be more popularly grown than chard in the United Kingdom and some European countries. Grows well in good-quality soil, and seldom bolts before its second year. Its very young leaves are excellent in salads, and the older leaves can be used in the same ways as chard or spinach.

Bixa orellana
Annatto (achiote, atsuwete, achuete, urucum, lipstick plant, achiotl, aploppas)
BIXACEAE

One of only two genera within the Bixaceae family. Annatto is derived from the fleshy covering surrounding the seeds of achiote, a perennial shrub, indigenous to the Caribbean and Central America. Annatto is valued for its culinary uses, though is mostly used as a food colouring and to colour textiles, cosmetics and other products. It is a popular species in Central and northern South America, as well as the Caribbean, with most commercial production in Brazil. However, due to its introduction by the Spanish, it is also grown and utilised in the Philippines. Historically, it has long been used by the peoples of Central America; the Mayan people used it as a body dye in preparation for going to battle, and to colour craft items, as well as food. They and other native peoples have used the whole of the plant for a wide range of diverse medicinal purposes. Its species name, *orellana*, is after a Spanish explorer named Francisco de Orellana, who helped in the destruction of the Inca Empire. Although a tropical species, it could be grown in a container in a glasshouse in cooler climates, and makes an attractive plant with abundant pretty flowers and bright red clusters of fruits.

DESCRIPTION

A bushy perennial that forms a large shrub or small tree, growing to 2–8 m tall with a thin, smooth, brown trunk. Commercially it is usually kept to a small manageable size.

Leaves: Evergreen, heart-shaped, shiny, sometimes with reddish veins. Spirally arranged up the stems. Mid to dark green above, more greyish beneath.

Flowers: Has clusters of 10–50 attractive, simple, white to pale pink/mauve, 4–7 petalled flowers that are lightly fragrant and 4–6 cm in diameter. These have numerous stamens and a central ovary. Flowers are mostly borne in spring, though some can be formed throughout the year. Pollination is by bees and insects, all of which love the flowers.

Fruits/seeds: Forms many almost spherical pod-like fruits that become hard and capsule-like as they mature. They usually turn from green to bright red as they ripen and are covered in short, dense, red prickly spines. They are borne in tight clusters that take 5–6 months to form

after flower fertilisation. Most ripen in late summer to early autumn. When ripe, the pod splits into two to reveal numerous (~50) tiny seeds, which are each embedded in orange-red fleshy pulp. The seeds are triangular, deep red in colour and only ~0.4 cm long.

Harvest/storage: Trees can produce large crops; however, usual yields are 4–5 kg of dried seed per tree. Plants grown from seedlings take longer before they start to produce fruits, but plants grown from cuttings begin to produce good yields after 2–3 years, increasing in subsequent years. Seedling plants yield less than those grown from cuttings. The ripe fruits are collected when mature, but before they split open to release their seeds. The bunches of capsules are snipped from the tree. The capsules can be crushed and the seeds separated out. Seeds are best stored in a cool, dark, airtight container. More commonly, to extract the dye, the capsules are soaked and crushed with the seeds in water, and the fleshy outer layer of the seeds is allowed to settle out.

though cannot tolerate waterlogging. They prefer soils that hold more moisture and can grow in quite heavy soils rich in clay. In sandy soils, they benefit from added organic matter or a mulch to retain moisture. A liquid feed as they are growing is beneficial. They grow best at slightly acid to neutral pH: 5.5–6.5. They respond to moderate additions of limestone to the soil, but if the soil is too alkaline, then manganese deficiencies are likely.

Pot culture: The ornamental varieties of kale are ideal as a pot plant on a deck or balcony. They are smallish, compact and very colourful. Remember, though, that they need some cold/frosts to produce their most vivid leaf colouring, so won't be as attractive if grown inside or during the summer months. Use a good-quality compost, keep moist, and mulch around the plant.

Planting: Can be planted at intervals from early spring until autumn to ensure a regular crop. They are, however, usually planted as a winter crop. For this, the seeds should be sown at least 6 weeks before the first winter frosts occur, and the young plants should be gradually acclimatised to lower temperatures. Space at ~50 cm apart, with rows ~0.8–1 m apart. An organic mulch around the plants once they are established reduces weed growth and conserves moisture. At the end of the season, remove old stems or leaves, as these can be repositories for several diseases. It is recommended to rotate this crop in soils where brassicas have not been recently grown.

Propagation: Sow seeds at ~0.5–1 cm depth and barely cover with a fine soil. Some reports say the seeds need some light to germinate well. They are usually sown in rows *in situ*, or can be broadcast, but weed control is then trickier. Can be sown in trays or pots, then grown-on and planted out as seedlings. Germination is good, and a few plants can supply a lot of greens. Space or thin plants to ~40 cm apart. The seed keeps well and may still be viable after 4 years, though is best sown when fresher.

Pests and diseases: Flea beetles can be a major pest, attacking the young leaves and causing considerable damage, sometimes killing young plants. Planting tomatoes between these species is said to reduce attacks. Aphids attack young shoots, and can rapidly develop in numbers. Caterpillars (or cabbage worm), via the cabbage white butterfly, are less of a problem on kale, but do attack collards. Try to pick off any caterpillars, which are commonly seen on the undersides of leaves. Slugs sometimes eat the leaves. Check plants at regular intervals for signs of pest damage. The application of wood ash sprinkled around plants can deter slugs and some other pests. Clubroot can be a problem in some regions, particularly if the soil is acidic. Problems with the fungal disease *Fusarium* wilt, which blocks the vasculature of the plant, can kill plants, though this is less of a problem in these older-style brassicas. Kale and collards may be susceptible to root rots, with these often passed on through infected transplants. Crop rotation, the use of clean seed and uninfected seedlings can minimise many pest and disease problems.

SIMILAR SPECIES

Kai lan, *Brassica oleracea alboglabra*. A cool- to warm-temperate annual that probably originates from around the Mediterranean, but is now most popular in China and Southeast Asia, where it is grown for its young fleshy stems and leaves, as well as its edible flowers. Tends to grow in warmer climates than kale or collards, and so makes a good summer crop, otherwise similar to kale and collards. Although a biennial/short-lived perennial, it is usually grown as an annual, growing to ~0.5 m tall. Plants provide good yields. Cultivation requirements are as above.

Brassica oleracea botrytis
Cauliflower
BRASSICACEAE (FORMERLY CRUCIFEREA)
Relatives: broccoli, cabbage, Brussels sprouts, kohlrabi, mustard, cress

Forms of this vegetable were thought to have been cultivated more than 2000 years ago in regions around the eastern Mediterranean. Over the past few hundred years it has remained a popular vegetable, particularly in countries such as Italy (where varieties with larger heads are thought to have been originally selected), in France and, more recently, in the United Kingdom, as well as in China and India. It is a vegetable that needs considerable care with cultivation to produce a large head with quality creamy-white florets. Closely related to cabbage, broccoli and the other brassicas, this vegetable, although not having the depth of flavour of the other brassicas, readily mixes with other vegetables, is wonderful with a cheese sauce and is easily digested.

DESCRIPTION

An annual, that has been selected to form a very large, white, multi-flowered head. The plant grows to ~0.8 m tall and, similar to other brassicas, has a coarse, thick stem. Different varieties have been developed: either early spring-sown to give a summer harvest, or sown later in spring to give an autumn harvest, or late summer-sown to overwinter and produce an early spring crop. Only the over-wintering varieties are frost hardy, and actually need cold before flowering is initiated. Early varieties tend to form smaller plants.

Leaves: Large, grey-green with wavy edges: typically brassica-like. Have thick midribs and leaf veins.

Flowers: Many, tiny, yellow, although the cauliflower heads are usually picked before they open. If the heads form well, then many flowers are packed together in florets, and these florets are further packed together to form larger floret groupings. Flowerheads are usually creamy white, though varieties, such as 'Violetta di Sicilia' ('Violet Sicilian') with eye-catching reddish purple heads, can be found. A cross between cauliflower and broccoli, these varieties with purple flowerheads are believed to be more disease resistant, easier to grow and more tolerant of heat, though, unfortunately, they lose much of their colour when cooked. 'Green Macerata', as its name suggests, has lime green heads and a good flavour. Pollination is by bees and other insects. Both male and female structures occur within the same flower: plants are also self-fertile.

Harvest/storage: Takes ~13–15 weeks from sowing to harvest, depending on temperature, variety, etc. When the cauliflower head first expands, it is initially covered by small green protective leaves. As the head expands, these are pushed aside. For the cauliflower to remain white and compact it needs to be blanched: this is usually achieved by wrapping the larger lower leaves around the head and loosely tying them at the top, so enveloping the head. The head is then left for 1–3 weeks, depending on temperature, before harvesting.

Determining the right time to harvest can be tricky to get optimum head size – do not harvest too soon, but pick before the florets begin to separate. Having regular peaks within the tied leaves should determine this. Self-blanching varieties are available, though their reliability to do this seems to vary. Cauliflowers are cut below their head, leaving several leaves attached. Once cut, the head can be kept for several days in a fridge or, for longer storage, cauliflowers can be pickled or frozen.

Roots: Fairly shallow: needs care with mechanical cultivation.

CULTIVATION

Needs more attention and pandering than many veggies.

Location: Prefers a site in full sun in cooler temperate climates, but a little light shade in warmer areas. Can be grown in maritime locations, but is not very wind tolerant.

Temperature: Young plants are sensitive to cold, and are killed by temperatures near freezing. Mature plants are more tolerant of cold, but, apart from the winter varieties, are more sensitive to frosts than most other brassicas. This is a temperate species, though planting time can be adapted to climate, i.e. it can be planted in late winter in warmer climates. It needs warm, but not hot temperatures to form a good head. If it is too cold, then only small heads are formed; if too hot, then the head may fail to

Food

Not as strongly flavoured as other brassicas, though the coloured cauliflower–broccoli crosses (e.g. 'Violet Sicilian') have more flavour. The blanched flowerhead of the common cauliflower makes a good accompaniment to other vegetables, or is traditionally served with a cheese sauce. It can be lightly steamed (long cooking destroys all its flavour), it can be cut into small florets and eaten fresh in salads, or the small florets can be stir-fried with other vegetables. It is good in curries (see Nutrition below). The florets are often pickled. The young leaves at the base of the head can be eaten.

Nutrition/medicinal

Amazingly, 3-day-old sprouts of broccoli and cauliflower contain 10–100 times higher levels of glucoraphanin than do the corresponding mature plants. This antioxidant compound is now known to reduce the risk of cancer as well as reducing blood cholesterol. It induces enzymes, that are involved in cell DNA repair.

The mature plants contain good levels of fibre, and are very rich in vitamin C, so do not overcook this vegetable, or use it fresh. Also contain some vitamin K and the B vitamins, folate and B6. Have some potassium and manganese.

Research has shown that the juice from cauliflower is effective in reducing several types of pathogenic fungi, including *Candida*. The red-headed cauliflowers contain greater amounts of antioxidant anthocyanins. Eating cauliflower, along with turmeric (e.g. in curry) can lead to reduction in the occurrence, and even help reverse, prostate cancers. Turmeric is rich in curcumin; cauliflower (and other brassicas) are rich in isothiocyanates; together, in mice, they work synergistically to reduce tumour growth and stop its spread. *Warning:* Like the other brassicas, cauliflower contains compounds that can adversely affect the functioning of the thyroid gland in susceptible individuals. Those with thyroid conditions may only wish to consume brassica species in moderation.

Ornamental

The red-headed cauliflower varieties are eye-catching in a planting.

uses

develop at all. Because of this, in hotter climates, the early varieties might be more suitable, so that they have formed a head before the summer heat. Conversely, summer varieties may be better in cool temperate regions, where late spring frosts are a threat, but the summers are cool.

Soil/water/nutrients: To grow well, cauliflower needs a nutrient-rich, loamy soil. Can be grown in somewhat heavier soils, but not in heavy clay. Extra organic matter to hold moisture needs to be added to lighter soils. The plants need regular moisture and a good supply of nutrients, particularly of nitrogen. However, too much fertiliser can result in sappy growth, which encourages pests and pathogens. A lack of nutrients, however, causes poor head formation: tricky to get it just right! To get good heads of cauliflower, the plants must grow rapidly and they need warmth, nutrients and moisture. They grow best in neutral to slightly alkaline soils (pH 6.0–7.5); add lime to acidic soils. They are not tolerant of waterlogging. Because this vegetable seems to readily take up compounds and heavy metals from the soil, a home-grown cauliflower can avoid this risk.

Pot culture: Could be grown in a container if short of space. This species is ideal for raised beds where they can be more easily cosseted.

Propagation: Germinates in a few days if placed in warm, moist compost. Sow at ~0.5 cm depth and cover with fine soil. Seedlings are pricked out while still quite small and are generally grown-on in individual cells or pots until ~10 cm tall. Give them lots of natural light or they become leggy.

Planting: Dig the soil well before planting out young plants, and incorporate generous amounts of well-rotted compost or similar. Also, wet the soil before planting to help plants establish. Plant seedlings at ~40 cm apart for spring varieties and ~60 cm apart for larger autumn varieties. Commercially, they are planted in rows.

Early varieties are planted out once all risk of frost has passed and the soil has begun to warm up. Summer varieties are planted out in late spring; over-wintering varieties are planted in mid to late summer. For the latter, the plants need to be established before the cold weather arrives. Weed control is important, particularly when the plants are young.

Pests and diseases: There are various potential problems, many of which are common to all the brassicas. Among the pests are cabbage worms (or caterpillars), which can cause extensive damage to the heads and leaves; flea beetles, which love the leaves of young plants and can cause serious damage; and aphids, which go for the young shoots and can build up to large populations in a short time. Also stem and turnip gall weevils. Other problems are cabbage root fly and clubroot in acid soils, with the latter sometimes causing serious losses of plants (keep pH above 6.5). Fungal diseases, such as black rot, can be a problem if plants are crowded, experience long periods of high humidity or receive too much nitrogen. Rotation of crops reduces the incidence of many diseases.

Brassica oleracea capitata
Cabbage
BRASSICACEAE (CRUCIFERAE)
Relatives: Chinese greens, Brussels sprouts, broccoli, kale, mustard

A vegetable usually grown in colder temperate regions, which, in the past, has received bad press for being overcooked, smelly and boring. This is a shame, as either lightly cooked or stir-fried it is delicious. The wild parents of the modern cabbage were more leafy, lacking a compact head, and are thought to have been cultivated at least 2000 years ago in Asian regions. It is thought that the Celts introduced them into Europe, and the Romans probably cultivated them around the Mediterranean regions. However, it has only been over the past few hundred years that cabbages with a more compact form have been developed. Cabbage is a particularly important vegetable in Eastern and Northern Europe, and in Russia where it is frequently pickled and often forms a staple vegetable through the long, cold winters. The species name, *oleracea*, refers to cabbage's distinctive smell, and *capitata* refers to its head-like growth.

Food

Different varieties tend to be used in different ways, but, for all types, the secret is not to overcook them. This makes it smell and taste dreadful, and destroys most of its nutritional benefits. Red cabbage is often pickled. It has an interesting taste and, if finely cut, it can be added to salads ,where its colour shows off the greens. If it is to be cooked, add a splash of vinegar to the water to prevent red cabbage losing its redness and turning a washed-out blue colour (due to a pH change).

Green cabbages have thin almost white leaves in their interior and these are popular in coleslaws, kimchi and sauerkraut. The latter two are made by 'fermenting' the cabbage for a few days in salt. Too much salt impairs the flavour; too little allows undesirable microbe populations to develop. A ratio of ~35–1 (of cabbage to salt) is recommended. The sliced cabbage, salt and spices are sealed with water into storage jars that are then left for 2–4 weeks (see Bibliography). Some people find this fermented dish easier to digest than other cabbage preparations.

Finely shredded savoys are delicious stir-fried with other vegetables and perhaps with bacon or prawns. They can be finely cut and added to salads, though some find their taste too strong. The leaves are tasty if stuffed with rice and other ingredients. Traditionally, they were often prepared with corned beef. Savoys, when boiled, have a less strong sulphur smell than green cabbages do. Cabbage can be sliced, briefly blanched and frozen.

Nutrition/medicinal

Cabbage contains good quantities of fibre, which is associated with preventing colon cancer. The outer leaves are rich in vitamin A and K; savoy cabbages are rich in vitamin C. Has good levels of folate plus some potassium and manganese.

Eating brassicas, along with turmeric (e.g. in curry), can lead to reduction in the occurrence of, and even help reverse, prostate cancers. In China, research has shown that isothiocyanate-rich cabbage and similar species reduces the risk of breast cancer by 45%. They may reduce the risk of lung, colon and stomach cancers.

The isothiocyanate, sinigrin, has been shown to kill tumour cells and inhibit their division. These benefits seem to be effective only if the cabbage is not overcooked. The juice from cabbage is associated with healing peptic ulcers, possibly due to its high amino-acid glutamate content. ***Warning:*** Some people develop flatulence after eating cabbage because of some indigestible fibre. More seriously, like brussels sprouts, cabbages contain compounds that can interfere with thyroid function. People with thyroid problems may wish to avoid eating too much, though cooking is said to reduce or eliminate this effect.

Ornamental

Some ornamental varieties have been developed with pink, red or mauve rosettes of leaves surrounded by larger green leaves, and others have been selected to have deep red leaves.

Other uses

The juice from red cabbages can be used as a pH indicator, being red in acidic solutions and turning blue in alkaline.

DESCRIPTION

Familiar to all, are the large heads of compressed leaves. There are many hundreds of modern varieties, many with attractively coloured leaves that can be various shades of green, to red and purple. The shape of the cabbage head varies from rounded, to flattened, to open, to tight, to being almost pointed. The plant forms a single stem, growing to ~0.5–0.8 m tall. The stem is thick and coarse. Cabbages can be divided into three main groups: the green or Dutch cabbages, with green outer leaves and fine, almost white, densely packed, smooth leaves within; savoys (e.g. 'Vertus Savoy'), which have dark green crinkly, attractive heads; and red cabbages (e.g. 'Red Drumhead', forming dense heads weighing 1–2 kg, 'Regal F1 Red'). More unusual heirloom varieties can be found, such as 'Palm Tree di Toscana' (also known as black cabbage), a type of savoy cabbage that has dark green, kale-like leaves.

Leaves: Numerous, usually tightly packed around a white, thick stem. Distinctive midribs and leaf veining. Cabbage varieties range from those with smooth leaves, to crinkled leaves, to red leaves (see above), The red-leaved varieties (e.g. 'Ruby Perfection'), are popular as a contrast in salads. The attractive branching pattern of the leaves is evident when the cabbage is cut in half.

Flowers: If allowed to flower, these are four-petalled, in small clusters and bright yellow in colour. Drops in temperature to near freezing can initiate flowering (or bolting). Pollination is by bees and other insects. Male and female organs occur in the same flower. Most varieties will pollinate each other.

Fruits/seeds: Similar to mustard seeds in shape and size.

Harvest/storage: Takes 6–12 weeks before the cabbages are ready to harvest depending on variety and climate, etc. Early cabbages are often smaller, weighing 0.5–2 kg; later varieties can weigh up to 3 kg. However, they can grow much larger. Apparently, the world record for the largest, heaviest cabbage was set in 1989 by Dr Bernard Lavery, in Wales. He grew a cabbage that measured a staggering 3.5 x 4 m, and its official weight was 56.24 kg! Normally, cabbages are harvested by pulling the whole plant up and the stalk is cut off in the field. Alternately, some gardeners leave the stalk with the

need to be picked when they are fully formed, but before they fully ripen, as these dry and dehisce, shattering to scatter the seed. The seeds of Indian mustard are often more commonly used commercially as they do not shatter as readily as those of white or black mustard. For a small crop, seed pods can be gathered and dried, or the plants can be cut and allowed to dry in the field and the seed pods then gathered. The young leaves can be harvested over a period of time from ~6 weeks after seed sowing. Older leaves are tough and develop a strong, unpleasant flavour. The leaves are best eaten fresh as they can only be kept for ~3 days in a sealed bag in a fridge; they soon wilt and lose their flavour. They can, however, be quickly blanched and then frozen for later use.

Roots: Have both shallow and deeper roots.

CULTIVATION

Easy.

Location: Prefers a site in full sun, is tolerant of maritime conditions, and is quite wind tolerant.

Temperature: Can grow in a wide range of temperatures from cool temperate to regions where temperatures reach nearly 30°C.

Soil/water/nutrients: Grows best in a good loam, but will grow well in lighter sandy soils, though does not grow well in heavy clay soils. They are fairly drought hardy once established. Can grow in soils with a wide pH range, from acidic to alkaline: pH 4.5–8.0. Can be grown as a lay crop because they do not deplete the soils of nutrients.

Pot culture: These easy-to-grow plants could be grown in pots with other salad greens.

Propagation/planting: Mustard seed can remain viable for up to 5 years if stored in dry, dark, cool conditions. The seed germinates very well in a few days. It can be broadcast sown or sown in rows. Sow at ~1 cm depth and thin seedlings to ~10 cm between plants (the removed seedlings can be eaten). Commercially, mustard is often either sown in early spring for a mid summer harvest, or is sown in summer for an autumn harvest. For home production of mustard greens, the seed can be sown at intervals to obtain a continual supply. Weed control is important until the plants are fully established. Volunteer seedlings readily appear the following spring after a previous crop, so pod removal before they shatter is advised if no more are wanted.

Pests and diseases: Generally have fewer problems than many brassicas, though aphid attacks may occur, particularly in soils rich in nitrogen, which encourages sappy growth. Cabbage loopers and caterpillars (the young of cabbage white butterflies) can be a problem: check regularly for signs of infestation. Flea beetles can damage the leaves of young plants: severe attacks can kill seedlings. Various fungal diseases, such as mildews and rots, can be a problem in soils that have had previous infections or if there is high humidity.

Brassica rapa (syn. *B. campestris*)

Turnip (turnip greens, neeps)

BRASSICACEAE (CRUCIFERAE)

Field mustard (wild mustard, mustard spinach, bargeman's cabbage) (*Brassica campestris* (syn. *B. rapa campestris*, *B. rapa*, *B. ruvo*))

Relatives: pak choi, rape, mustard, cabbage, broccoli, swede, cress

In the botannical literature there is extensive crossover between *Brassica campestris, B. rapa* and *B. napus* (rape), with many overlaps and conflicting definitions, e.g. some include *B. campestris* within or as *B. rapa* (and variations of), and the usage of *B. rapa* and *B napus* often overlap. Here, they are dealt with as separate species, with *B. campestris,* usually known as field mustard, enjoyed for its highly nutritious leaves, and *B. rapa*, which includes many subspecies, used for its edible taproot and leaves. The latter may have been selected from *B. campestris*. Subspecies of *B. rapa* include the many varieties of Chinese greens, but also turnip. Rape (*B. napus* is described on p. 121), and the closely related mustards on p. 137.

Both *B. rapa* and *B. campestris* may be natives of Europe or of Asia. Field mustard (and to a lesser degree turnip) is often found growing on waste ground, on the margins of cultivated land and in the hedgerows of Europe and Britain. The leaves of mustard spinach are highly nutritious, though have a strong brassica flavour. The turnip has a long history of usage, and both *B. campestris* and *B. rapa* may have been harvested from the wild in Neolithic times. These species were used in India about 3000 years ago, and later by the Greeks and Romans. In modern times, the turnip is well known in northern Europe for its white, rounded, storage root, which is tasty if eaten when small and young. Its greens are also sometimes eaten. Turnips are widely grown to feed livestock.

DESCRIPTION

Field mustard is an annual, growing to 0.3–1 m tall. Turnips are annual or biennial, depending on when the seed is sown, and grow to 0.8–1.5 m tall, forming leaves and a rounded, storage taproot in the first year. Seeds sown in late summer produce flowers and seeds in the following year.

Leaves: Field mustard and turnip leaves are ~30 cm long, ~5 cm wide and deeply lobed, like those of dandelion. They are often greyish green. With more or less wavy margins, they clasp the stem with no leaf stalk, alternate. Those of the turnip tend to be rougher and tougher, though varieties of turnip, such as Chinese cabbage, have been selected for their tasty leaves, as have varieties of *B. campestris,* known as turnip broccoli or broccoli raab. The young leaves and flower shoots of the latter are produced in their second spring and are popular with Italians. They have an asparagus-like flavour.

Flowers: Small, bright mustard yellow. Simple, four-petalled, arranged in small racemes up the flower stem. They are initiated by long, warm, summer days, so seeds sown in early summer may bolt. Seeds sown in late summer are less likely to bolt, and instead flower the following spring. Pollination is by bees and insects. Both male and female parts occur within the same flower, and flowers are often self-fertile.

Pods/seeds: Rounded, small seed pods that contain small, brown-black seeds. The seeds are rounded and ~0.2 cm diameter.

Roots: Within the first year, turnips form a globe-shaped, white storage organ at the apex of a long thin taproot (~15 cm long), from which the leaves emerge. The turnip is actually the swollen base of the stem, adjoining the root, and not the root itself. The turnip has a white dense texture, though is moderately juicy and crisp when young. It has a white 'skin' that is often mauvish on its upper surface where it has been exposed to light. New varieties have been selected with skins of other colours, e.g. red, yellow, green, and a variety of shapes. Small lateral feeder and water-collecting roots sprout off the long, thin taproot, which is usually removed when harvesting.

Harvest/storage: The young leaves of field mustard or of Chinese cabbage can be harvested over several weeks from ~6 weeks after seed sowing. Picked leaves encourage the formation of new growth. Older leaves are tough and develop a strong, unpleasant flavour. The leaves are best eaten fresh and only keep for ~3 days in

uses

Food

All parts of the turnip have an almost radish-like flavour, though are not as hot and spicy. The younger leaves of field mustard can be harvested during the season and can be added to salads or lightly steamed as a vegetable, as can the leaves from the turnip variety, Chinese cabbage. Turnip leaves can be used for greens, though are tougher and stronger in flavour. Varieties, often known as turnip broccoli or broccoli raab, are popular with Italians as a winter green. They are left to overwinter and then produce tasty leaf sprouts, young stems and young flowerheads, much like broccoli early in their second year. They have a flavour that is said to be similar to asparagus.

Turnips' 'roots' are much better if eaten when still small and young, and fresh from the garden. Their taste is often underestimated, as they are frequently sold when too mature, or they are overcooked. Young turnips can be finely sliced and used in salads, are good in stir-fries, and can be lightly steamed with vegetables such as leeks, then sprinkled with grated cheese and accompanied with horseradish. They are good added to soups and stews, or can be cooked for longer and then mashed and combined with potato or kumara, along with cheese, salt and pepper. The seeds are often used in India to make a type of rapeseed oil, which is used in culinary dishes.

Nutrition/medicinal

The greens are wonderfully nutritious and are rich in fibre and protein (~10%), and contain virtually no fat. They are rich in vitamins A, K and C, a serving giving ~150% of the RDA of vitamin A, 175% of vitamin K and ~50% of vitamin C. They contain a little vitamin E, are rich in the B vitamins, and are high in folate with good levels of B6. The leaves are rich in minerals with good quantities of calcium, manganese and copper, and some iron, magnesium and potassium. However, prolonged cooking is likely to reduce concentrations of many of the above.

Turnip roots contain some protein, and good amounts of vitamin C, with some B vitamins and minerals, particularly manganese and potassium. Historically, all parts of the turnip plant — its seeds, roots, leaves and stems — have been used to treat various cancers. Like the other brassica, turnips and field mustard contain compounds that are converted to isothiocyanates when cut or chewed. These are known to have various health benefits, including reducing the risk of certain cancers as well as reducing blood cholesterol. It induces enzymes that are involved in cell DNA repair. *Warning:* Brassicas contain compounds that may interfere with thyroxin production in those who are susceptible; such individuals should avoid overconsumption.

Other uses

Turnip roots and their tops are widely used to feed livestock. They are highly nutritious compared with grass, and are comparatively rich in protein. Stock can therefore develop health problems if introduced to this feed after being on poor pasture. Initiate any feeding programme slowly to avoid this. Turnip roots may contain compounds that deter various insects, so they can be mashed with water to make a repellent for aphids, red spider mites and flies.

a plastic bag in the fridge. They can, however, be quickly blanched and then frozen for later use. Turnips can grow fast, needing only ~8–10 weeks before the first turnips are harvested. Spring-sown turnips can be harvested in early summer, or autumn-sown turnips can be harvested through winter. They are best dug up while still ~5–8 cm in diameter, though turnips can grow to ~15 cm in diameter if left. Young turnips are sometimes sold with their leaf tops, which makes them attractive, but reduces their storage time by exacerbating moisture loss. Without their tops, they can be stored in a bag in the fridge for a couple of weeks. They can be stored in a dry, dark box for extended periods or, in milder winters, the roots can be left in the ground to 'store' until needed. However, beware of slugs, birds and other creatures that may also enjoy them. Older turnips are often fed to livestock.

CULTIVATION

Easy.

Location: Can grow in full sun or semi-shade. Fairly tolerant of maritime conditions. Moderately wind tolerant.

Temperature: Turnip grows best in cooler temperatures; is fully frost hardy and is grown in places such as Canada and northern Europe. However, it can be grown in warmer climates, such as the southern states of the US, southern Europe and India. Timing of growth to avoid hotter weather produces better turnip growth. Field mustard grows in cool- to warm-temperate climates.

Soil/water/nutrients: Both species grow best in a good loam. They will grow in lighter sandy soils, but not as well in heavier clay soils, particularly if these are wet. A well-dug, loose soil is needed to form turnips; stoney soils inhibit their formation. The turnip was traditionally grown in poor-quality soils, which were then used to graze livestock, thereby improving the soil. However, turnips do respond to organic matter, particularly that with extra phosphates. Field mustard is fairly drought resistant once established, turnips less so. They grow best in soils with a pH of 5.5–7.5.

Propagation/planting: The seed can remain viable for several years if stored in dry, dark, cool conditions, though is better used fresh. It germinates very well, in about a week. Both species can be sown in rows outside, and then the seedlings thinned as they emerge. They grow best if well-rotted manure or compost is incorporated into the soil before seed sowing. Turnips can be sown in early spring to produce an early summer crop. If planted in later spring, they are likely to bolt in the summer heat and set seed before they form a 'good sized' turnip. Alternately, turnip seed can be sown in late summer for a winter crop. Field mustard is usually sown in spring. Sow at ~0.5 cm depth. The seed is small so that if sown too deeply, the germinating seedlings do not have adequate resources to reach the soil surface. Thin field mustard to ~10 cm between plants, and turnips to 20–30 cm. Weed control is important until the plants are fully established. Seeds that have been released in previous years readily produce volunteer seedlings the following year.

Pests and diseases: Generally has fewer problems than many brassicas. Aphids, cabbage loopers and caterpillars can be a problem. Flea beetles can damage the leaves of young plants; severe attacks can kill seedlings. Various fungal diseases, such as rots, can be a problem in wet soils or areas that have had previous infections. Clubroot is a problem in some areas: avoid replanting in the same soil for at least 5 years to minimise this risk.

Calendula officinalis
Calendula (pot marigold, garden marigold)
ASTERACEAE (COMPOSITAE)
Relatives: lettuce, Jerusalem artichoke, thistle, endive, sunflower

Calendula is one of about 25 species which belong to the large Compositae or daisy family. *Calendula* species originate from regions around eastern Europe through to Iran, though are now popularly grown in gardens around the world, and have become naturalised on waste ground in many countries. Of the *Calendula* species, some are annuals, some perennials. *Calendula officinalis* is the most popular ornamental species and is used for its flavour and its medicinal properties, particularly to reduce inflammation and as an antibacterial. It is also rich in antioxidants. Its species name, as with other 'officinalis' species, was because of its use as a standard pharmaceutical product. This species has long been used by the ancient Greeks, Romans and Arabs, as well as peoples across India. These bright, cheerful, easy-to-grow annuals look wonderful in the flower garden. Their petals can be used in salads and as a saffron substitute, plus they have wound-healing properties. Note that another common ornamental annual plant, called marigold, is from a different genus: *Tagetes*, and is not used as a replacement for *Calendula* spp.

DESCRIPTION

A half-hardy annual, usually grown as an ornamental for its bright yellow and orange flowers. It has a compact bushy shape, growing to 30–50 cm tall. Normally does not need supporting.

Leaves: The pale green, fuzzy, obovate- to lanceolate-shaped leaves are pungent when crushed. They are simple and spirally arranged up the stems.

Flowers: The bright, cheerful yellow and orange flowers will bloom for much of the year in warmer regions, and from late spring into autumn in cool-temperate regions. The flowerheads are composed of numerous tiny central flowers surrounded by a disc of petal-like rays. They can be 8–10 cm wide and have a pleasant, spicy aroma. They open in early morning, and close part-way through the afternoon, or sooner if the weather is cloudy and wet. Pinching out the tops of the main stems produces more flowering lateral branches, though the flowers may not be as large. Removing any dead flowers prolongs the flowering season. Pollination is by bees and insects.

Fruit/seeds: The seeds are actually achenes, with a single seed within the outer layer. 'Fruit' size and shape is variable, but are often sickle shaped, ~5 cm long, pale cream in colour.

Harvest/storage: The flowers are harvested as they open. From seed germination to flower formation can take as little as 7–9 weeks. The petals are either used fresh, or can be dried for later use. Spread the petals out thinly on some mesh to gently dry. They tend to stick together and to surfaces they are in contact with. Store the dried petals in a cool, dark, airtight container.

Roots: Has a fibrous root.

CULTIVATION

Very easy.

Location: Grows best in full sun, though will grow in light shade. Fairly wind tolerant and can be grown near to the coast.

uses

Food

The petals of the flowers look great as a garnish and are wonderful at brightening up a green salad. Can be used in soups, and are sometimes used as a substitute for expensive saffron: if cooked with rice or added to breads, they impart a golden-yellow colour. They have an interesting flavour, being sweet at first, but with a salty sometimes bitterish aftertaste.

Nutrition/medicinal

The flowers were historically, and still are, used to reduce bruising; to treat sprains, cuts and insect bites; to treat acne; and to reduce inflammation and bleeding. The herb can be taken internally or topically, depending on where the problem is. It has been used as a stimulant and to treat abdominal cramps and constipation. Recent studies have shown that marigolds have both spasmolytic and spasmogenic activities, which gives validity to its traditional usage for these ailments. The flowers have been shown to have anti-inflammatory, anti-viral and anti-genotoxic properties. In mice, they have been shown to kill cancer cells and to activate lymphocytes, which help fight disease. However, in another study, although extracts showed anti-cancer properties at low doses, higher amounts actually increased the number of damaged cells: this dual effect is known as hormesis.

Marigolds have significant antioxidant properties, hence the effectiveness of the flowers in treating various inflammatory and allergic diseases. The flowers are very rich in the carotenoid lutein which, research has shown, can improve eyesight and slow the progression of macular degeneration by up to 40%. Lutein is protective against heart disease. Marigold has been shown to be effective against several peridontal disease-causing bacteria: perhaps an extract could be mixed with toothpaste or a few leaves chewed.

Herbal extracts that included calendula have been given to children to resolve the pain and symptoms of non-serious otitis media (ear pain). Results have shown that due to *Calendula*'s antibacterial activity, its immuno-stimulation ability, antioxidant activity and anti-inflammatory effects, the extract resulted in significant improvements and had no side effects. It was cheaper than, and reduced the need for, prescribed antibiotics. The flowers have antiviral properties and studies have shown they possess anti-HIV properties. *Calendula* have hypoglycaemic effects, can inhibit the activity of gastric emptying, and gives a gastroprotective effect. Historically, *Calendula* has been used to treat stomach ulcers, liver complaints and conjunctivitis (pink eye). It has been used to treat fungal infections such as athlete's foot, ringworm and *Candida*.

Ornamental

One of the most popular and easy-to-grow annuals, this smallish plant can be grown in the tiny garden or in a flowerpot. Its bright orange and yellow blooms cannot help but lift the spirits. The flowers are excellent for cutting and using in fresh-flower bouquets. There are many ornamental varieties, many of which have multiple rows of ray petals and come in a wide range of shades from pale yellow to deep red. There are also several dwarf varieties.

Other uses: The plants attract a number of butterfly larvae. A yellow dye can be extracted from the flower, which is used to colour foods such as cheese and butter, as well as other products. The petals are added to skin creams, even baby creams, and have a soothing effect. The plant is believed to repel plant pests, such as aphids, and prevent them attacking nearby plants.

of chillies, as well as varying with variety, also varies with cultivation, e.g. heat, moisture, and environmental stress. Hot sun gives them a hotter flavour. They are not at all frost hardy, and grow better in warmer climates, though can be grown in a glasshouse, window sill or similar in cooler temperate regions. In particular, they need hot, dry weather while the fruits are forming.

Soil/water/nutrients: Grow best in good-quality loam or sandy soils. Do not grow well in heavy soils. Are very sensitive to over-wet soils, so good drainage is essential. Do not need particularly nutrient-rich soils, though benefit from an organic mulch to suppress weed growth and help retain moisture. Can grow at a wide range of pH, from a quite acidic pH 5 to an alkaline pH 8.

Pot culture: Perfect for pot culture, and can then be sited in a sheltered, sunny spot in cooler regions. Grow a selection of varieties to experiment with the different types. Ensure they have good-quality compost, are watered regularly, but have good drainage.

Planting/propagation: *Seed:* Usually grown from seed, which can be taken from last year's crop or supermarket fruits, as long as they haven't been treated. They need a long season of growth; therefore, in cool-temperate areas, start them indoors in early spring. Sow thinly in trays or cells and keep warm and moist, but ensure good drainage by mixing grit, vermiculite or sand with the compost. Cover seeds with 0.5–1 cm of fine soil. The hotter chillies need lots of heat (>20°C) to germinate and grow well, and they also take longer to germinate (6–8 weeks). Soaking the seeds before sowing can speed up and improve germination. Sparsely cover with soil. Once germinated, seedlings often succumb to fungal disease, so keep the soil moist, but not too wet, and provide good ventilation around plants. Growth rate varies, with species such as *C. chinense* growing slower than *C. annuum*. Plant out once all risk of frost has passed and the soil is beginning to become warm. Space plants at 30–60 cm apart,

depending on their final size. Pinch out tops to encourage a bushier plant. *Cuttings*: Being a short-lived perennial, shoot cuttings can be taken in spring, and these should root well.

Pruning: Pruning back sprawling branches in autumn can reinvigorate the plant and extend its life and cropping potential.

Pests and diseases: Have very few problems: little will attack these plants, though a mosaic virus can distort and damage the leaves. This cannot be treated, and it is better to destroy any infected plants to avoid its spread.

Carthamus tinctorius
Safflower (false saffron, American saffron)
ASTERACEAE
Relatives: sunflower, globe artichoke, Jerusalem artichoke, lettuce, endive

A member of the sunflower family, this plant is now mostly grown for the excellent-quality oil extracted from its seeds. Originally native to southern Asia, it was cultivated and utilised for thousands of years in China, India, the Middle East and Egypt. In Egypt it was used to colour cloth, and the human skin, including to anoint mummies before they were bound. It became more widely known and cultivated in southern Europe in the Middle Ages, and the Spanish introduced it into Mexico and into parts of South America. It was brought into the US in 1925, with cultivation now mostly in the west. Historically, in the US, it was more often grown for the extractable dyes from its flowers. Deep yellow to orange to red, these were used to colour foodstuffs and fabrics, often as a cheaper substitute for saffron.

Recently, safflower has become more valued for its seed oil, which is higher in polyunsaturates than virtually any other oil, and has excellent culinary properties. Not surprisingly, many new varieties have been selected for their oil properties, as well as their ease of cultivation. However, despite its culinary benefits, only a small amount is grown worldwide compared with most oil crops, with most grown in India, and some in the US, China, Mexico, parts of

South America and in Australia. The oil is most popular in Japan, with a little being used in North America, but it is less commonly encountered in Europe. In China it is mostly grown for its medicinal properties rather than for its oil or dyes. An interesting, quite ornamental though spiny plant to grow, its seeds can be used like those of sunflower, its young shoots are edible, and a dye can be extracted from its flowers.

DESCRIPTION

An erect annual plant, growing to 0.5–1.5 m tall when in flower. Thistle-like, with a main stem, branching towards the apex to form laterals and sublaterals with numerous flowerheads, and spiny leaves below. Many varieties have been developed, mostly for their oil, but also for reduced spines and disease resistance. The better known of these are 'Gila', adapted to arid conditions and gives high yields, and 'Frio', a more cold-hardy variety that gives good oil and protein yields.

Leaves: Its margins have many, long thin spines. Grey-green, oval to lanceolate, 10–15 cm long, ~3–6 cm wide, with thick waxy cuticles. Initially, the plant forms a basal rosette of leaves: these have few spines and can be harvested for eating. When a few weeks older, it forms flower stems which bear smaller leaves that have many spines. Upper leaves clasp the stems.

Flowers: Attractive, rounded heads of many tiny florets, thistle-like, but are deep yellow, orange or red in colour. Occasional white-flowered varieties also occur. Heads are 2.5–3.5 cm in diameter, with 1–5 flowerheads per plant.

The flowers are surrounded by spiny, leaf bracts and are borne in mid summer for ~4 weeks. Has both male and female parts within most flowers. Pollination is by bees and insects, but can be self-pollinating.

Seeds: Each flowerhead forms 15–35 white, shiny, oval

uses

Food

The first young leaves can be eaten fresh in salads or can be lightly steamed. The seeds, like those of sunflower, are tasty to eat and can be gently roasted, fried or used raw in salads. The oil is light in flavour and colour, and is similar to sunflower seed oil. Its very delicate flavour makes it good in many foods, including dressings, margarine, for general cooking and in liqueurs. It is more heat stable than many oils, not giving off smoke or smells at high heat; also, its consistency does not change at low temperatures. It can be added to many processed foods without affecting their flavour. The colouring extracted from its flowers is often used as a cheap substitute for saffron, and is used to colour a wide range of foods, including cheese, sausages, pickles, breads, rice dishes and soups.

Nutrition/medicinal

Safflower oil contains more essential unsaturated fatty acids and has less saturated fatty acids than virtually all other edible vegetable seed oils. The seeds contain a lot of oil for their weight (30–45%). Different types of safflower have been developed: some are rich in monosaturates (e.g. oleic acid: ~30%), others in polyunsaturates (e.g. linoleic acid: ~60%). It is rich in vitamin E.

Its high unsaturated fat content makes it good for lowering cholesterol levels and, thus, reducing heart disease. Monounsaturated oils have been shown to reduce LDLs, but not HDLs in the blood. The seeds are rich in protein, containing 15–25%. They contain good amounts of magnesium, copper, phosphates, zinc, iron and manganese, and of the B vitamins, particularly thiamine,

with some B6 and folate. The seeds are rich in flavonoids.

Recent research has shown that safflower seeds contain a lignan glycoside that has an anti-oestrogen activity equivalent to tamoxifen. Its serotonin-like compounds can reduce atherosclerotic lesions, probably because of their strong antioxidative activity. The seeds and their oil have been used as a sedative and a laxative to treat a range of maladies, including menstruation problems, and to treat diseases such as measles and scarlet fever. The oil has been used topically for rheumatism, sprains and sores. The red-orange colouring of its flowers is derived from the flavonoid carthamin. The leaves are rich in antioxidant flavonoids, particularly luteolin and quercetin. They have been used as a tea in the Middle East to prevent miscarriage and to treat infertility.

Ornamental

Its spiny nature means that although it has heads of colourful flowers, it needs to be sited away from thoroughfares: perhaps planted in a clump in the vegetable garden or towards the back of annual beds.

Other uses: Water-insoluble red and water-soluble yellow dyes can be extracted from the flowers. These are used in cosmetics, and to dye cotton and silk, including materials used to make carpets. The oil has been used in candles and is now used in varnishes, lubricants and as a drying oil in paints. It makes a good alternative to linseed oil for artists using oil paints, and has the advantage of not yellowing. The seed is often used in bird seed mixes with the benefit that it is apparently unpalatable to squirrels.

small, dry fruits (achenes), each ~0.7 cm long, and each containing a single seed. The outer hull around the seed makes up about half of its weight. The fruits are enclosed within leaf-like bracts, similar to those of the globe artichoke.

Harvest/storage: Young basal leaves can be picked early in the season; these have few if any spines. The flowers can be picked as they open, and then dried for later usage. They are used in several Chinese herbal remedies. The dried flowers are stored in a dark, dry, cool, airtight container. Seedheads take 4–5 weeks to form and mature after flowering. They can be collected as they mature, in late summer. Left to dry in an aerated place, the seeds can be easily shaken free. Alternately, because the fruits do not usually fall as they ripen, they can be harvested direct from the flowerheads, when the leaves and stems have become brown and the fruits are white and fully mature.

Roots: Have a deep taproot that penetrates to 1–2 m in depth.

CULTIVATION
Easy, though prickly.

Location: Grows best in full sun, and in regions that have longer summer days (>14 hours), which induce flowering; therefore, grows poorly nearer to the tropics. Despite its height and form, it is moderately tolerant of wind and hail. Can be grown near the coast.

Temperature: Grows best in warm-temperate climates, though some varieties (e.g. 'Gila') have been selected to grow in hot, desert-like regions. Conversely, its seedlings can withstand cooler climates than many crops, and can be grown in the same regions as wheat and barley. Most varieties however, are not very frost hardy, so seedlings should be planted in late spring in regions where there is a risk of late frosts. Young plants, still in the rosette stage, may be damaged by temperatures below freezing but they usually recover. Once plant-stem elongation commences, plants are much more susceptible to cold damage.

Soil/water/nutrients: Will grow in a range of soil types, from fairly heavy clays to light sandy soils. Grows best in soils that receive regular moisture, but have good drainage. Its deep taproot enables it to survive periods of drought, but growth is reduced. Plants are very susceptible to any waterlogging: a few hours of flooding can kill them. Grows best in soils of pH 5.8–7.5. Not fussy about soil-nutrient status, usually not needing extra fertiliser in most soils, though the addition of organic matter helps conserve moisture and gives better growth. Its deep roots can obtain nutrients from further down in the soil than most crops.

Pot culture: Could be grown in deep pots as a colourful annual if short of space, though its spininess makes it a poor choice for a deck or near thoroughfares.

Planting/propagation: The seed is sown in spring in cooler regions, either inside or *in situ* for larger crops. Sow outside only when the soil has begun to warm. In warmer regions, the seed can be sown in early winter. Cover seeds with ~1 cm of fine soil; germination only takes 7–14 days at ~15°C, though it will germinate at much lower temperatures (down to ~3°C). If grown in pots, use deep pots and handle the taproots carefully when transplanting. Space or thin seedlings to 10–15 cm between plants, though commercially they are often grown much closer together. Weed control is very important around young plants, as they are easily out-competed, but their spininess makes this problematic. Therefore, it is best to start off with weed-free soil. Also, rotate safflower (and other members of this family) to avoid build-up of soil diseases.

Pests and diseases: Its main disease problem is its susceptibility to many fungal diseases, e.g. *Phytophthora and Pythium* (root rot), *Alternaria* (leaf spot), *Verticillium* (wilt). Important to rotate this crop to different soils. Also avoid overcrowding and regions that have high, constant humidity. Has much fewer pest problems because of its waxy cuticles and spines, though has been known to be attacked by wireworms, aphids, caterpillars, leaf hoppers and thrips.

Carum carvi
Caraway (Persian cumin)
APIACEAE (UMBELIFERAE)
Relatives: coriander, parsley, carrot, dill, celery

Caraway is another member of the large Umbeliferae family, which includes many other aromatic spices and herbs, plus vegetables such as parsnip and carrot. Originally native to Europe or from regions towards Asia, it is now cultivated in many parts of the world, and has long been popular in India, the Middle East and in regions around the Mediterranean. It is a popular flavouring in several traditional Middle European dishes and breads. Evidence of its popularity and usage in Middle and Eastern Europe go back thousands of years. Today it is cultivated in a wide range of climates and locations from Finland, down through Middle and Eastern Europe, to North Africa, with the Netherlands being the main producer. It is a temperate species, and although usually only known for its seeds, its leaves and roots are also edible. Because it is not too fussy about soil type, and takes up little room, this species deserves to be fitted in the herb or flower garden. It has several useful medicinal properties.

DESCRIPTION

Often grown as an annual, but can be a biennial, this herb grows to 0.6–0.8 m at maturity, but is only ~0.3 m tall during the first part of its life. The plant has a carrot-like appearance.

Leaves: Ferny, finely cut, mid green, resembling those of fennel or carrot. Form a rosette initially and grow from a basal crown, finally producing taller flowering stems.

Flowers: Very small, white, numerous, arranged in umbels at the tops of stems. Borne in early to mid summer. Pollination is by small insects: flowers are too tiny for bees and most insects.

Fruit/seeds: Often called a seed, but actually a small dried fruit (called a schizocarp) consisting of two carpels, with each carpel containing a single seed. Are formed in autumn, and are small (~0.3 cm long), becoming brown when ripe. Are curved with longitudinal ridges.

Roots: Forms a long taproot for storage, which looks similar but is not as large as parsnip.

Harvest/storage: The younger leaves can be harvested throughout the season, leaving enough for the plant to keep growing. The fruits are gathered as they change colour from green to brown; if left too long, the fruits are scattered. Harvest the stems and umbels, and place in a dry, aerated place to finish ripening and to dry. Place them on racks above sacking or paper to catch fruits that drop. Once dry, the umbels can be easily threshed to release the fruits. These can then be stored in a cool, dark airtight container. The roots can be harvested during the autumn and winter months, if the seed has been planted in spring. If left until the second spring/summer, then roots lose their moisture and begin to become woody.

CULTIVATION

Fairly easy, though weeding is important.

Location: Prefers a site in full sun or with light shade.

Temperature: Is a cool-temperate species, but can be grown in the cooler months of subtropical climates. Is frost hardy once established and acclimatised. However, sudden drops of temperature below freezing can kill back the leaves. Are best mulched or given protection through colder winters.

Soil/water/nutrients: Although plants grow best in lighter soils or loams, they will survive in heavier soils, but then taproot growth is likely to be inhibited. Loosen heavier soils to depth and add gypsum to aid root penetration. Although they grow best with regular moisture, they need good drainage and are not tolerant of waterlogging. Not

uses

Food

The young leaves can be added to salads, or to soups and stews. The seeds are popularly added to breads, cakes and confectionery as a flavouring. They are added to traditional vegetable recipes, go well in potato soup and in cabbage dishes, such as sauerkraut. A few can be crushed and sprinkled onto meats especially lamb and pork. Add a few seeds to cream or cottage cheeses, to dips and potato salads. They have a distinctive licorice- or anise-like flavour that is sweetish and quite powerful. Its flavour does not mix well with many other herbs or spices, though it is often mixed successfully with garlic in sausages and prepared meats. The essential oil extracted from the seed is used medicinally, as well as in liqueurs such as Kummel, and in cordials. The roots can be cleaned and lightly steamed or roasted. Roast caraway root tastes similar to roast parsnip and some say it is superior in flavour. The Romans ate them mixed with milk and made into a bread.

Nutrition/medicinal

The leaves are rich in vitamins C and A. The seeds are fibre rich, with a little vitamin C and the B vitamins. Contains good amounts of iron, with some magnesium, phosphorus, calcium and manganese. Historically, this plant — particularly the seeds — have been used to treat rheumatism, colic, eye infections, flatulence and toothaches. Its action as an antispasmodic of smooth muscle means it has been used to treat non-ulcerative digestive problems, to prevent flatulence and to relieve menstrual cramps. It has been used by nursing mothers to increase milk production.

The seeds are rich in an essential oil, containing 6–8% by weight. The oil is rich in carvone, in particular, but also limonene, with some germacrene. Studies have shown these compounds to be potential anti-cancer agents, including against colon cancer. Carvone, in particular, has been shown to induce the detoxifying enzyme glutathione S-transferase, which is a powerful chemo-preventative agent. The fruits exhibit significant potential to lower lipid levels in normal and hyperglycaemic rats. Thus, caraway may help reduce heart disease and diabetes by reducing hyperglycaemia without affecting plasma insulin concentrations. Caraway is rich in antioxidants, particularly quercetin. It is an effective antibacterial and antifungal, controlling several pathogenic organisms. For this reason, it is added to mouthwashes and toothpaste, and is used to prevent the spoilage of various foodstuffs. Carvone is an effective insect repellent. The powdered seed has been used topically to reduce bruising.

Ornamental

Planted in groups, their feathery foliage and masses of small white flowers are attractive in a flower bed.

Other uses

The oil is used in soaps, lotions and as a perfume. It is used as an anti-fungal and root-sprouting suppressant on potatoes.

climate and does not tolerate too much fluctuation in temperature. However, can be grown in warm-temperate areas if planted in a sheltered, sunny spot, or could be grown in a glasshouse or similar in temperate regions. Plants are not at all frost hardy.

Soil/water/nutrients: Grows best in almost pure sand, needing only 1% organic matter and can grow in poor-nutrient soils. Prefers deep, well-drained, moist soil; is not drought tolerant. Grows best in slightly acidic to neutral soils.

Pot culture: In cooler regions, if fresh seed or cuttings can be obtained, these species could be grown in containers. Give plants a sand-based compost, but water regularly except during the cooler months. Avoid freezing temperatures. Plants respond well to pruning, so can be easily kept to a manageable size.

Food uses

Cinnamon is obtained from the dried inner bark of the shoots. It has a fragrant perfume, tastes aromatic and is sweet; when distilled it only gives a very small quantity of oil with a delicious flavour. Although cassia and cinnamon have similar uses, cassia is cheaper and more abundant; Ceylon cinnamon has a more delicate flavour thought by most to be superior. It is used in a wide range of foods: cakes and other baked goods, milk and rice puddings, chocolate recipes and fruit desserts, particularly with apples and pears, coffee, curries, French toast, eggnog, teas, pickles, puddings and rice dishes. It is common in many Middle Eastern and North African recipes, to flavour lamb stews or stuffed eggplant.

It is used in curries and rice pilau dishes and in garam masala spice mix. It may be used to spice mulled wines, creams and syrups. In Mexico, it is drunk with coffee and chocolate, and brewed as a tea. In India, cinnamon is used whole and the bark pieces are fried in hot oil until they unroll (which releases the fragrance). The temperature is then reduced by adding other ingredients such as tomatoes, onions or yoghurt. The cinnamon chunks can be removed before serving. When powdered cinnamon is used, it should only be added shortly before serving as cooking can make it become bitter. The unripe fruits are used in confectionery and in potpourri. In addition, the stem buds can be used instead of the bark, though are somewhat less aromatic.

Nutrition/medicinal

The main constituents of cinnamon are cinnamaldehyde, gum, tannin, mannitol and the flavonoid coumarin, and an essential oil that contains aldehydes, eugenol and pinene. The leaves yield 70–95% eugenol, which can be used as a clove substitute. It is thought to have been used at least 4500 years ago, and Chinese herbalists still recommend it for relieving nausea, fever, diarrhoea and menstrual problems. Historically, cinnamon has been used to ease all types of digestive problems. It may reduce spasms of the smooth muscle of the gut, and so eases complaints such as indigestion, irritable-bowel syndrome and flatulence.

Cinnamon oil contains a phenol that has antifungal and antibacterial properties, and has been added to foods, such as meat, to reduce pathogenic food-borne diseases. It is effective at killing the bacteria that cause tooth decay and gum disease, and so can be added to toothpaste.

Also, due to its bacterial activity, it has been shown to help clear up urinary-tract infections that are caused by *Escherichia coli* bacteria and vaginal yeast infections caused by *Candida albicans*. During the bubonic plague, sponges were soaked in cinnamon and cloves and placed in sick rooms. It may help prevent stomach ulcers, possibly by controlling the bacteria *Helicobacter pylori*. Recent studies have shown that cinnamon has antidiabetic properties, and may help people with adult-onset (type-2) diabetes to metabolise sugar better. Some reports claim that cinnamon reduces the amount of insulin necessary for glucose metabolism. In addition, the coumarin it contains has blood-thinning properties, increasing the blood flow in the veins and decreasing capillary permeability; therefore, it should probably be avoided by those taking anticoagulants. **Warning:** The amounts of cinnamon normally used in food are non-toxic, although a few people do experience allergic reactions after eating this spice. When cinnamon oil is applied to the skin, it can cause redness and burning. Cinnamon essential oil, taken internally, can cause nausea and vomiting.

Like all essential oils, any internal intake needs to be done with great caution as the compounds are highly concentrated. Taken internally, it can cause nausea and vomiting; there are reports that it may even cause kidney damage. The substance coumarin, although has a sweet, warm aroma (similar to that emitted from freshly cut grass), with a vanilla-like flavour, should only be ingested in small amounts as it is moderately toxic to humans, affecting the liver and kidneys. However, it is much more toxic to rodents, and is thus often included within rat and mouse killing preparations (e.g. as warfarin and brodifacoum).

Ornamental

If uncoppiced, they form attractive trees with red bark, attractive delicate flowers and leaves that often become flame-coloured in autumn.

Other uses

Cinnamon can be burned as an incense; it has a pleasant smell, stimulates the senses, yet calms the nerves. Its smell is said to attract customers to a place of business. The root bark smells like cinnamon and tastes like camphor, which it yields on distillation.

Propagation/planting: *Seed*: the most common method, but is difficult. Best to use fresh, washed seed. Germination takes 15–20 days. Keep seedlings moist (but not wet) and shaded for ~6 months. *Cuttings:* Are difficult and should be put under mist or kept continuously moist. Take semi-hardwood cuttings of ~10 cm length with at least two leaves. Dip the cutting in rooting hormone and plant in sandy, gritty, but moist compost. Place bags in a shaded area to root. Rooting should take 45–60 days. Rooted cuttings can then be carefully transplanted into pots with compost to encourage faster more vigorous growth before planting out in their final position. Avoid handling the roots, as they don't tolerate transplantation when they get larger. Keep young plants in a shaded place and water regularly. *Air layering*: Done using semi-hardwood shoots. A ring of bark is removed from a semi-hardwood area and then a rooting hormone is applied. Moist natural fibre is then secured to the area by wrapping in polythene to avoid moisture loss. Rooting takes place in 40–60 days. Well-rooted air layers can then be cut from the mother plant and planted in a potting mix in a shaded place, and kept moist. Trees should be spaced at ~3 m apart. Grow best with light shade while young; this results in healthier, rapid growth.

Pruning: Commercially, cultivated trees are usually kept coppiced, so that they form numerous thin stems and the tree remains within easy reach to be harvested. They are kept to 2–3 m tall. Some growers cut the trees back close to ground level. Only coppice trees every 3 years or so, or they are likely to become stressed and not grow as well.

SIMILAR SPECIES

Chinese cassia: *Cinnamomum cassia.* Native to south-eastern China, where it has long been used, with usage recorded in Chinese herbals dating back more than 4500 years. It also has a traditional use as a flavouring and was one of the spices traded along the ancient spice routes. It is still mostly grown in Vietnam and in Indonesia. A very similar species to cinnamon, the evergreen cassia tree grows to 7–10 m tall, and forms an angular crown. It has long oval leaves (~20 cm) with yellow flowers. The bark from the cassia tree is aromatic, like that of cinnamon, but is coarser, darker, and thicker, and the outer greyish corky bark is often not removed. Whole branches may be harvested, unlike the smaller strips taken from cinnamon. It is a cheaper spice than cinnamon and, consequently, cinnamon powder may be contaminated with cassia, or cassia might often be called cinnamon, particularly in the United States.

Unground, cassia is much thicker and naturally rolls inwards from both sides, like a scroll, compared with the finer, single roll of cinnamon. In addition, the small (1.2 cm long) unripe fruits can be harvested and dried, like cloves, and have a pungent aroma and flavour. The tree needs a tropical climate to grow well, and its cultivation needs are similar to those of cinnamon. The coarse bark is very hard and much more difficult to grind than cinnamon. The bark and buds are commonly used in soups, curries and spicy casseroles, though seldom in desserts, as cinnamon is. It has similar medicinal properties to cinnamon, including antidiabetic properties. It may lower blood pressure. However, it does contain coumarin, which should be only consumed in moderation. Similar species include the Indian cassia *(C. tamala)*, of which the bark and leaves are used; Indonesian cassia *(C. burmanni)*, often imported to North America, and commonly sold as cinnamon; Saigon cassia *(C. loureirii)*, which is often grown in Japan and Korea; Oliver's bark *(C. oliveri)*, an Australian cinnamon substitute; and camphor laurel *(C. camphora)*.

Coix lacryma-jobi
Job's tears (Chinese pearl barley, adlay, hatomugi)
POACEAE
Relatives: wheat, rye, oats, rice, bamboo, barley, corn

An attractive tall grass, native to Eastern Asia, it was widely grown there before the introduction of maize. In China, it has been a valuable food crop for thousands of years, and is now often grown as a food crop in India and Japan. Although valued as a cereal, it is also a medicinal plant, with monks from China having long used the healing properties of this species. Modern research largely confirms many of its historical uses. It is also often grown as an ornamental in gardens in warmer regions of the world, and has become naturalised in India, the southern United States, the Pacific and the Caribbean. Because of its versatility in growing in many soil types and conditions, this species has become a weed in many areas. However, the seeds of this ancient crop are packed with protein, containing more and a wider range of amino acids than rice, wheat, barley or rye. The plant is also attractive and easy to grow.

DESCRIPTION

An annual, though, with adequate care, it can be grown as a perennial in warmer regions. Is a member of the grass family. Often forms several shoots (tillers). Plant is 1–2.5 m tall.

Leaves: Dark green, long (~20–50 cm), lush, and relatively wide (~5 cm) for a grass. Leaf veins run longitudinally, stomata occur on both sides of the leaves, and the leaves sheath around each other to form the stem. Has C4 photosynthesis, enabling it to continue photosynthesising on hot days, when most plants have closed their stomata; and enables improved water-use efficiency.

Flowers: Numerous clusters of 2–3 small, insignificant, whitish or greenish white flowers arranged in spikelets, in spring. Male flowers occur above the female. The male flower produces copious pollen as they are wind pollinated. They are often self-fertile and flowers are borne in late summer.

Seeds: White (occasionally red or blue-black), shiny, produced in autumn. There are hard- and soft-shelled varieties; the hard-shelled types are notoriously hard, making the grain difficult to access. Seeds are oval with a pointed tip, looking like a rose hip, with the remains of the calyx at the tip.

Harvest/storage: Can be harvested at 16–20 weeks after seed sowing. If left too long, the stems can break, and the seed is scattered or is taken by birds, etc. The heads of seeds are cut and hung to dry. They can then be threshed to remove the husks, though this is difficult with varieties with hard seedcoats. If dried sufficiently, and then kept dark and dry, the seed can be stored for several months.

Roots: Spreading, and sometimes deep.

CULTIVATION

Easy.

Location: Prefers a site in full sun, but, in intense heat, prefers a semi-shaded site. Too much wind can knock the stems over.

Temperature: Grows best in warm to hot climates; it will grow in cooler regions, though more slowly. Not frost hardy, so seed needs to be sown in late spring/early summer in regions where late frosts are a risk.

Soil/water/nutrients: Not too fussy about soil type, and can grow in sandy soils through to quite heavy clays. As with most plants, this species will grow fastest with better yields in good-quality loams with regular moisture. It can grow in soils that are poor in nutrients, but yields are likely to be reduced. Adequate and regular moisture induces the formation of more stems (tillering) and, therefore, more seeds. They are fairly tolerant of wet and problematic soils: they often naturally grow on waste ground. Can tolerate acidic to alkaline soils. Do not seem to be very drought tolerant, producing poor yields.

Pot culture: Could be grown in pots as an annual or biennial. Attractive plants. Give good compost and water regularly.

Planting/propagation: *Seed:* Sow at ~2 cm depth. Germinates easily, but may take 2–4 weeks. Needs warm temperatures (~22°C) for germination. The seedlings then grow quite rapidly. Space seedlings at ~50 cm apart.

Food

The grain can be lightly cooked for ~10 minutes and is used as a carbohydrate source. Add flavourings (e.g. salt, pepper, spices, butter, etc.). Often added to soups and stews. Sometimes used as a rice substitute. It has a nutty taste, and can be made into a type of porridge and can also be prepared with sugar and dried fruits. It is often ground into a flour, particularly in India, where it is then made into various breads. It can also be simply removed from its husk and eaten as a snack. Various beverages are prepared from the grain: a non-alcoholic barley water and a tea, as well as alcoholic beers and spirits.

Nutrition/medicinal

The seeds are easy to digest, and have good quantities of protein (14–18%), which includes most amino acids. Is rich in the B vitamins niacin, thiamine, riboflavin, B6 and folate. Contains some calcium and phosphates, but is low in other minerals (compared with millets). Medicinally, it has long been used as a tonic, to ease digestive problems and to treat many types of cancer. There is recent evidence that the compounds can reduce tumour-cell division and may help reduce the formation of tumours. The seeds are rich in iron and contain oleic acid, which is thought to reduce vascular disease. It has been used to treat a wide range of other ailments, including beriberi, catarrh, dysentery, headache, rheumatism, pleurisy, fever. It is eaten in eastern Asia to promote health and vitality, and is often given as a convalescent food. It is even used to cleanse and vitalise the skin as well as to improve the flow of breast milk. Its high fibre levels are thought to reduce constipation and intestinal disease. It is thought to boost the immune system and may have analgesic properties. People who suffer from coeliac disease, a genetic disorder that disrupts digestion if gluten is consumed, can use gluten-free Job's tears as a substitute. However, the absence of gluten means that, on its own, it is not good for bread making.

Ornamental

This species is quite ornamental, and could be grown in a herbaceous border, perhaps with other grasses.

Other uses

The hard seed grains are used as beads to make necklaces, etc.

Cryptotaenia japonica
Mitsuba (trefoil, Japanese honewort, Japanese wild parsley, san ye qin)
APIACEAE (UMBELLIFERAE)
Relatives: carrot, parsley, celery, parsnip, dill

There seem to be only two members of the *Cryptotaenia* genus. Both have pleasant-tasting leaves enjoyed fresh in salads or as a garnish. *Cryptotaenia japonica* is probably a native of Japan, where it still harvested from the wild as well as being cultivated. The other species is *C. canadensis*, which as its name suggests, is thought to originate from northern America. Mitsuba (*C. japonica*) is grown throughout the year under glass in Japan, and is a popular vegetable during the colder months of the year. It is grown in Korea and China, other Asian countries and in California. It can be grown easily in cooler climates. Similar in appearance and taste to its relative celery, the smaller leaves and stems are often blanched and used in salads and clear soups. It has a distinctive flavour. The name 'mitsuba' is Japanese for three leaflets.

DESCRIPTION
A fast-growing, versatile, short-lived perennial, similar in appearance to celery or angelica, but more spreading and somewhat smaller, growing to ~0.5 m tall. Often grown as an annual.

Leaves: Usually trifoliate, oval, with pointed tips and slightly serrated margins. Leaves are flat, like those of Italian parsley. On long, fleshy leaf stalks, 10–15 cm, though with blanching these can grow to ~30 cm long.

Flowers: Small, insignificant, numerous, arranged in a flat disk. Pinky white in colour. Flowers have both male and female organs. Pollination is by insects.

Harvest/storage: The stems and leaves of plants as they come to maturity are often wrapped to blanch them for a week or so before harvesting. Usually the whole plant is pulled for use. Could leave a few plants to self-seed.

Roots: Forms a thickish storage taproot, off which grow many lateral roots.

CULTIVATION
Easy and versatile.

Location: Can be grown in full sun, though is likely to grow better with a little shade in hotter regions. Can be grown in quite deep shade.

Temperature: Can grow in a wide range of temperatures, from cool-temperate to subtropical. Once established, it is fairly frost hardy, tolerating temperatures down to ~–10°C. Can be grown as a winter crop in warm-temperate regions.

Soil/water/nutrients: Grows best in nutrient-rich loams, but can also grow in a range of other soil types, from sandy to fairly heavy soils. It will tolerate periods of wet, but not extended waterlogging. Is not very drought tolerant, and grows best with regular moisture.

Pot culture: Could be grown in a container and sited in a shady location near to the house. Consider growing the regular and purple-leaved forms together for contrast.

Propagation/planting: *Seed:* Grows well from seed, with germination not being as slow as with many other members of this family. Soaking the seeds for ~12 hours

uses

Food
Its young leaves and stems have a pleasant, spicy taste and smell, not unlike chervil or celery. The chopped blanched stems and leaves are often added to salads or are used as a garnish, or are briefly steamed or stir-fried. In Japan, they are often added to clear soups and stews, or can be coated in batter and deep fried to make tempura. Cook only briefly to avoid destroying their flavour. They go well with eggs and seafood. The roots can be eaten. The seeds can be used as a seasoning or can be sprouted and used in salads.

Nutrition/medicinal
Historically, this plant has been used in Asia as a tonic, and to treat colds and fevers, as well as to treat 'women's problems'. **Warning:** There is a report that if eaten in quantity the leaves may be toxic; however, this may actually apply to its fellow species, *C. canadensis*.

Ornamental
An ornamental variety, *C. japonica atropurpurea*, has attractive purplish red leaves that look good planted next to plants with fine-cut pale green foliage, e.g. fennel or ferns.

before sowing can further speed up germination. Cover thinly with ~1 cm of compost. Can be sown at intervals from spring into summer, or into autumn in warmer areas for a continual crop. *Cuttings:* The plants can be divided in spring or autumn. Space or thin plants to ~30 cm apart, though some gardeners plant them closer together to encourage the formation of longer edible leaf stalks.

Pests and diseases: Few problems, though is loved by slugs and snails. Sprinkling wood ash around plants may deter pests, as this encourages a local bird population.

Cucumis sativus (*C. vulgaris*, *C. longus*)
Cucumber
CUCURBITACEAE

West Indian burr gherkin (Jerusalem cucumber, prickly-fruited cucumber) (*Cucumis angurra*); Karela (bitter cucumber, balsam pear) (*Momordica charantia*)

Relatives: pumpkin, melon, squash, zucchini

A fast-growing, subtropical species originating from India where it has been cultivated for more than 3000 years. It belongs to the gourd family and is closely related to melons and pumpkins. Long ago, it was introduced into Asia and China, and, later, into Europe. It become popular in England from the 1600s, being traditionally associated with delicate sandwiches served with afternoon tea. The first cucumbers were small, prickly and bitter, and probably originate from *Cucumis harwickii*, a native of the Himalayas. Longer, sweeter cucumbers were selected at least 400 years ago. They are now a very popular vegetable worldwide, with China growing the most. Fairly easy to grow, giving good yields, but they need heat, particularly at first, and freely draining soil.

DESCRIPTION

A fast-growing annual that has tendrils enabling it to quickly climb up structures to ~2 m. The plant forms a leafy canopy, under which the fruit are formed.

Leaves: Large (8–14 cm long), three lobed, with irregularly toothed margins, thin, but with a roughish surface. Have long leaf stalks.

Flowers: Pale yellow, ~6–8 cm wide, bell shaped, with five almost fused petals, on petioles that grow from the leaf axils. Solitary, often accompanied by a coiling tendril. Pollination is by bees. There are several flower types: the most common is that male flowers are formed first (initiated by long days and higher temperatures), and these are followed by bisexual flowers (initiated by shorter autumn days and cooler temperatures). Poor pollination causes misshapen fruits, which often have shrivelled ends. Some cucumber varieties only produce female flowers and are able to set fruit without being fertilised. These form tiny, unformed seeds, which are popular in glasshouses, where pollinators are often excluded (e.g. 'Armour', 'Diva', 'Tasty Queen'). A variety's flowering habit should be marked on the seed packet.

Fruits/seeds: Usually long, usually green skinned, though sometimes brown, and sometimes with knobbles. The skin thickness depends on variety and cultivation methods. The longer, thinner-skinned cucumbers are usually known as Chinese or telegraph cucumbers and they are often lightly ribbed lengthways. A few varieties have been selected to have rounded fruits (called 'lemon' or 'apple') with a yellowish colour, and are sweeter (e.g. 'Lemon', 'Mini White'). Cucumbers are picked when they are still immature. If left for longer, the central seeds enlarge and the flesh and skin becomes bitter, though many varieties today have been selected to not become bitter as they age (e.g. 'Diva', 'Green Dragon', 'Mini White'). They vary in length from a few centimetres to over 30 cm long, and are ~5 cm in width. The variety 'Armenian Yard Long', as it name suggests, can grow to a metre long, and becomes curved. The skin of smaller varieties is often tougher, so is usually removed for salads. Cucumbers contain many small seeds that form along the centre of the length of the fruit. In non-pollinated types, these are hardly noticeable. In pollinated types, these can become quite large and not very edible as the fruit matures. They are oval, long, flat, pale tan. The seeds are surrounded by very juicy, pale green flesh.

Harvest/storage: Plants start producing quickly. After ~6–7 weeks the first cucumbers are formed, and then these expand rapidly within the following couple of weeks. They need to be harvested regularly as, if left to mature, the vine stops producing new fruits. If picked, plants can continue to produce fruits for many weeks. Yields can be very good. Pick when smaller for pickles, but leave until longer for use in salads. Are best stored at ~12°C, and can then be stored for several days; placing in a plastic bag will help retain their juiciness. Temperatures near freezing cause rapid cell collapse.

Roots: Fine, some are deeper, but also has shallow feeder roots, which can be easily damaged, so needs care with mechanical cultivation.

CULTIVATION

Fussy about the conditions it grows in.

Location: Needs to be grown in full sun and a site sheltered from strong wind.

Temperature: Is very susceptible to frost damage, so needs to be planted out only after all risk of frost has passed. Also, in cooler-temperate regions, growth will be much improved if it can be grown in a glasshouse, tunnel or conservatory, although some varieties have been selected that are more cold hardy (e.g. 'Diva', 'Tasty Queen'). In warm-temperate regions and the subtropics, it can be planted outside, and seedlings can be started earlier in the year. Needs regular daily temperatures of ~25°C.

Soil/water/nutrients: Older-style varieties are susceptible to periods of drought; more modern varieties, less so. Cucumbers grow much better with regular moisture, though are also sensitive to any standing water. In particular, they need moisture during fruit swelling. They grow best in medium-textured, nutrient-rich loams. Moisture retention is poor in sandy soils, and root penetration is poor in heavy soils plus these increase the risk of fungal root disease. Cucumbers need soils rich in well-rotted organic manure or compost, with additions of e.g. blood and bone. Need a reduced nitrogen to phosphate and potassium ratio: too much nitrogen results in excess leaf growth and less fruit formation. Grows best at a soil pH of 6–7, preferring more alkaline than acidic soils. Are best rotated around different garden sites to reduce pest-and-disease problems.

Pot culture: They could be grown in large containers, and then placed in a sunny location. They need good-quality compost, lots of nutrients, regular moisture, but free-draining soil. They need a trellis or wires to scramble up – this ensures the fruits do not touch the ground and improves yields.

Planting: Plants need quite a bit of room to grow as they have a scrambling, spreading growth. Commercially they are usually planted in widely spaced rows (2–3 m apart), though could plant smaller species in between. For smaller-scale production, small areas of soil are prepared by incorporating organic matter and nutrients, and slightly mounding this soil. Mounds are prepared at ~60 cm apart. It is important to cultivate well before planting, as the soil needs to be loose to allow root penetration. It is also important for the soil to be warm. Establish plants in small groups of 3–4, and site against pre-placed wire netting or a trellis for the plants to grow up. Plants grown without a support have smaller yields, and the fruits are more easily damaged. Weed control is important around young plants. Once the plants are ~50 cm tall, an organic mulch around them helps retain moisture and suppress weed growth. Gardeners often mulch with black plastic. Encourage plants, initially, to attach themselves to their support.

Food

The long cucumbers are a traditional familiar addition to salads, and in dainty sandwiches served with afternoon tea. Make a tasty salad with tomato, onion, balsamic vinegar and a little sugar. Varieties such as 'Lemon' have a particularly crisp, mild, pleasant flavour. Some add cucumber to stews and soups. Wonderful made into the cold Greek soup, tzatziki, where it is blended with dill, yoghurt, garlic and a little olive oil. Cucumber slices make a good garnish. Cucumbers are very popular pickled when small as gherkins. Varieties, such as 'Amour' which have dark green fruits, ~10 cm long, 'Homemade Pickles' with medium green, crisp fruits and good yields, have been selected specifically for pickling. Pickling varieties, are often more spiny, and are best picked when still small. A recent variety, 'Mexican Sour Gherkin', which is also similar to melon in shape, has been developed to have a pickled flavour, even when fresh. *C. anguria* is a species specifically grown as a gherkin (see below).

Nutrition/medicinal

Do not contain many nutrients, though have reasonable quantities of vitamin K, with some vitamin C and A, as well as a little potassium, magnesium and manganese, B vitamins and a little fibre. The fruits are cooling and soothing: the flesh is used to soothe scalds and skin inflammations, and slices are placed on the eyelids to cool and refresh the eyes. The cucumber flesh is said to 'clean' the digestive system. The seeds are more nutritious, and are rich in oil (~25%), containing ~50% oleic acid. They are said to have diuretic and cooling properties. They have been used to eradicate internal parasites.

Warning: Some find that the skin (and sometimes the flesh) causes indigestion. Many find cucumbers cause wind or burping, though many new varieties have been developed that do not have this effect, e.g. 'Armenian Yard Long', 'Long White Wonder', 'Soo Yoh'. The leaves have been used to induce vomiting. The germinating seeds may contain toxic compounds.

Ornamental

There are some quite ornamental varieties, such as 'Chinese Sweet Cucumber' (also known as 'Painted Serpent Cucumber'), which has long, thin fruits that are often curled and have green-and-white-striped ridges running lengthways.

Pickling cucumbers tend to be tougher, and may be grown outside; some salad cucumbers can be also grown outside, though are more often grown in glasshouses.

Propagation: Seeds taken from fruits often do not

Food

The pleasantly aromatic fruits are used in a wide range of dishes as a flavouring, although the seeds of caraway are often used in preference, as some find the flavour of cumin too strong. They have a fairly hot, rich, slightly bitter flavour, which, when added to dishes, tends to draw out the flavours and sweetness of foods. They are often roasted or fried before being added to a dish to release their full flavour. They are very popular in Indian cuisine, where they are added to curry sauce mixes, dahl, popadoms and chapatis, as well as to cooling yoghurt. The seeds are popular in Middle Eastern cuisine, and are used to flavour dips, breads and meat recipes. They are used in Europe to add a distinctive flavour to sausages and cheeses. They are sometimes used in cakes and sweet foods. An essential oil is extracted from the seeds, which is used as a flavouring and medicinally.

Nutrition/medicinal

The seeds contain some vitamin A and C, plus some of the B vitamins. They are particularly rich in iron, with some calcium, magnesium and manganese. Have been historically and widely used to treat digestive problems and for liver complaints. The seeds contain compounds that relax spasms of smooth muscle, and so relieve intestinal problems and prevent flatulence. Was believed to stimulate the sexual organs. In the West, coriander is more popularly used medicinally; cumin has similar properties to coriander, though the latter is more often preferred as a flavouring. The seeds have significant antioxidant properties and reduce free-radical-mediated oxidative stress. They can reduce blood glucose levels and may aid in the treatment of diabetes mellitus. The seeds also have strong chemopreventive potential to reduce the formation of carcinogens. The seeds can decrease increases in lipid levels caused by alcohol intake, and thus reduce hepatotoxicity. Cumin extracts are particularly effective at controlling *Helicobacter pylori* bacteria, which can cause stomach ulcers, and does so without risking antibiotic resistance, as can occur with conventional treatments. The seeds have antibiotic properties against several other Gram-positive and Gram-negative bacteria. The seeds produce a good-quality essential oil (~2.5%). The main aromatic compound is cuminaldehyde; it also contains many minor compounds. Extracts, if chewed, have been used to relieve the pain of toothache. It can be used to control the larval growth of some insect pests.

Other uses

The essential oil is used in perfumery.

---

for their medicinal values. The seeds are rich (~50%) in the essential oil thymol, which has powerful antibacterial and antifungal properties, as well as reducing digestive complaints, including diarrhoea and flatulence, and is used to treat chest infections. The oil includes pinene, cymene, limonene and terpinene. Historically, in India, the seeds were thought to have aphrodisiac properties. Still most commonly cultivated and used in India, they are also used to a lesser extent in Arabic cuisine.

Cuphea spp.
Cuphea (bat face, tiny mice, Mexican heather)
LYTHRACEAE

Cigar flower (*Cuphea ignea*); also *C. lanceolata*, *C. viscosissima*, *C. paucpetala*, *C. leptopoda*, *C. wrightii*, *C. tolucana*, *C. procumbens*, *C. micropetala*

A genus of about 250 species, often grown for their ornamental value, but have recently been researched and cultivated in Oregon (USA), Italy and France, and also to lesser extent in Greece, Portugal and Spain, for the abundant oil extracted from their seeds, which is very rich in lauric acid and other fatty acids. Originally from Mexico down to Peru, most species need a subtropical or tropical climate to grow well, but a few species can be grown outside during the summer in temperate climates. The ornamental value of its colourful flowers means that it is often grown either outside, or as a glasshouse or conservatory plant in cooler regions. Interest in these species for their oil production centres around countries with warm-temperate climates, where they can be cultivated *en masse*. The usual main source of lauric acid and other similar fatty acids, is tropical coconut and palm oil. Developers hope that this species might partially replace the need for these tropical species, and thus reduce transport costs as well as dependency on outside sources. Several *Cuphea* species can produce these seed oils, and a few of the more cold-tolerant or commercial species are described below.

DESCRIPTION

Species can be annuals or evergreen perennials. Most species are fast growing but only form small plants. All parts of the above-ground plant are covered with short sticky hairs, which make handling them tricky. *C. ignea*, a perennial shrub, only growing to ~30 cm tall with about the same spread; *C. viscosissima* is an annual, growing to ~50 cm tall. For oil production, crosses between *C. viscosissima* and *C. lanceolata* show the most commercial and agronomic interest.

Leaves: *C. ignea* has small (2–5 cm long), mid-green, evergreen leaves. Leaves are lanceolate with smooth margins. The common names of several *Cuphea* species are after heathers, which the leaves resemble.

Flowers: Tubular, 2–3 cm long, varying in colour from yellow to red to violet. Singly or in clusters. Have a long flowering period from spring through summer, and sometimes later. In more tropical climates, plants can flower for most of the year. Flowers have both male and female parts. Flowers of *C. ignea* are borne singly from leaf axils and are bright scarlet, with purple, black and white markings at the tubes entrance. Are particularly attractive to nectar-eating birds, such as hummingbirds and honeyeaters, but also to some butterflies. Flowers can be self- or cross-pollinating.

Fruits/seeds: Has small (~0.5 cm long), oval, hard fruits that form in autumn and can remain on the plant over winter. These contain small, oily seeds.

Harvest/storage: The small seeds are tricky to harvest commercially due to the stickiness of the plant and because the seeds tend to drop as they mature. However, plants flower and produce seeds only 6–10 weeks after the seedling stage.

CULTIVATION

Location: Prefer a site in full sun, though in hotter weather plants benefit from light shade. Flower colour is said to be improved if grown in light shade.

Temperature: Most species need a subtropical or tropical climate to grow well, but a few are more hardy and can be grown outside during the summer in cooler temperate climates. More cold-hardy species include *Cuphea ignea*, *C. viscosissima*, *C. cyanea*, *C. miniata*. For perennials, do not allow temperatures to fall much below ~7°C in winter.

Soil/water/nutrients: Grow best in soils rich in organic matter that receive regular moisture, though only need minimal watering during the colder months. Can grow in a range of soil types from moderately heavy to sandy-textured soil, and in moderately acidic to somewhat alkaline soils: pH 5.5–7.5.

Pot culture: Ideal for growth in pots, and perennials can then be moved inside in colder weather. Make a great floral display on decks and ledges. Give good-quality compost and water regularly. Site in a sunny, but sheltered spot.

Planting/propagation: *Seed:* Sow seed in early spring, inside, and thinly cover the small seeds with fine soil. Give warmth (~13°C) and moisture. Germination is fairly slow,

uses

Food

The oil, a medium-chain triglyceride, has various uses, particularly within candy and chewing gum, to reduce the use of saturated fats, improve flavour and to act as a flow carrier and solvent.

Nutrition/medicinal

The oil from the seed is rich in various fatty acids, lauric acid (the same as in coconut and palm oil: dodecanoic acid), caprylic and capric acids (single fatty acids), and myristic fatty acid (a saturated fat). Specific species are rich in different types of oil, i.e. are very rich in either caprylic, capric, lauric or myristic acid. Of these fatty acids, caproic, caprylic and capric acids do not raise levels of LDLs ('bad' cholesterol); however, lauric, myristic and palmitic acids do increase the production rate of LDLs. *C. carthagenensis* induces a significant reduction in plasma cholesterol in rats; other *Cuphea* species may have similar qualities. The oil may have antimicrobial properties. This is converted to monolaurin (lauricidin) in the body, which has antiviral, antibacterial and antiprotozoal properties by removing the lipid coat around viruses (e.g. HIV, herpes, cytomegalovirus, influenza), plus some bacteria (e.g. *Listeria*, *Helicobacter pylori*), yeasts (*Candida*) and some protozoa (e.g. *Giardia*). There is some evidence that these species reduce protozoan infections, possibly due to their flavonoid content, of epicatechin in particular, but also kaempferol and tiliroside. Also, strangely, the oil is claimed to promote weight loss. The medium-chain fatty acids do not circulate in the bloodstream, but are sent directly to the liver and are immediately converted into energy. Thus, the fat is used to produce energy rather than being stored as body fat. The seeds are fairly rich in protein.

Ornamental

The more cold-hardy species can be grown as bedding plants in cooler-temperate regions; otherwise, species need to be grown under glass. In warmer, frost-free regions the perennial species can be grown outside. They are mostly grown for their attractive flowers.

Other uses

The oil is used in soaps, detergents and cosmetics, and is being researched for usage in pest-and-disease control. Lauric acids are widely used in cosmetic and shampoo products as sodium-dodecyl-sulphate. The molecular structure of this compound means that, unlike most fats, it reacts with water as well as other fats, and so allows water to 'dissolve' other fats such as grease on skin or oils on hair. It has a long shelf-life and said to be safe to handle.

taking 14–21 days. The seeds have an unusual seedcoat that is covered with fine microscopic hairs. Prick-out seedlings and grow-on until large enough to plant out, but only once the soil has begun to warm up and all risk of frost has passed. *Cuttings*: Cuttings from young, lateral shoots of perennials can be taken in spring. Remove the lower leaves and insert into a gritty sand-compost mix. Give light shade and regular (but not too much) moisture while they root. Keep temperatures at 15–20°C. Grow-on and plant out when established. Space plants ~15 cm apart. Commercially, they are being trialled as a crop rotated with soy and maize, with the added benefit that the sticky hairs of cuphea reduce the occurrence of some pests (e.g. rootworm) that attack maize and soy.

Pruning: Perennials can be trimmed in autumn to remove straggly, older growth. Plants can be almost cut to the ground to rejuvenate them, and will resprout from the base. However, perennials are seldom kept for longer than 2 years as older plants become woody and produce fewer flowers.

Pests and diseases: Few pest problems reported. Their sticky hairs trap most potential pests, such as aphids and other small insects, and there are few disease problems.

Curcuma longa
Turmeric (haldi, haridra, manjal)
ZINGIBERACEAE
Relatives: ginger, galangal

A monocotyledonous member of the ginger family, the rhizomes of turmeric are valued for the deep yellow spice they produce, which is included in almost all Indian cuisine. It is used in many Asian recipes, and in Chinese and Japanese cuisine. Its history of usage in India is thought to stretch back at least 2500 years. It is still used in ceremonies, particularly weddings, and is associated with bringing good luck, fertility and prosperity. Although southern India supplies most of the world's turmeric needs, some is also grown in Pakistan and Bangladesh, as well as in other tropical regions of the world (e.g. the Caribbean). Originally thought to be from South and Southeast Asia, this species is not found in the wild, but was probably selected or discovered long ago and has been widely cultivated ever since. It is thought that one of its parents is wild turmeric (*Curcuma aromatica*). Turmeric has recently become the focus of hundreds of scientific research papers for its many potential, diverse medicinal properties. Although a plant of the tropics, this attractive species can be grown in cooler climates as a pot plant, inside, as long as it is provided with warm temperatures year round. If you can get hold of a section of rhizome, it is well worth having a go.

DESCRIPTION

An attractive, monocotyledonous, perennial plant, growing to 0.6–1 m tall. Forms storage rhizomes that produce the following year's leaves from small buds along their length. Stems grow up from the rhizomes each year, produce flowers, and then die back until the next season.

Leaves: Long and oval with pointed tips, arching as they become taller. Elegant and lush in appearance. Are typical of a monocot, with younger leaves growing out from the centre and top of the sheathed leaves. Are bright green and can grow to be ~1 m long.

Flowers: Exotic and attractive, mostly white, but also some pale yellow. Many small flowers are arranged in a dense apical spike on tall flower stems. The flowers are fragrant.

Seeds: Does not produce viable seed; only propagated vegetatively.

Roots: Has yellowish brown knobbly rhizomes and thick feeder roots that grow off these. Unsurprisingly, the rhizome looks similar to that of ginger, but its centre is a dull orange colour. Rhizomes are ~3 cm in diameter and ~8 cm long.

Harvest/storage: Takes 7–10 months after planting until the rhizomes can be harvested. Are dug up as the leaves begin to die back and become yellow at the end of the season. The leaves and flower stems are removed. The rhizome is washed and then boiled for about one hour in slightly alkaline water. They are then dried artificially, or in the sun for several days, before their outer skin is polished to remove roughness. The dense orange storage tissue is then ground to produce a deep yellow, aromatic powder. It is reported that in some local Indian markets, the ground powder is adulterated with other substances as well as with ground rhizomes from similar species; the ground spice sold abroad is less likely to be contaminated. Store ground turmeric in a dark, cool, airtight container to retain its flavour and colour.

Food

The spice is widely used in all types of Indian curries, from mild to hot. Its flavour is subtle compared with most curry spices, with its main taste due to curcumin. It has a warm, aromatic flavour that is not hot, but is slightly bitter and somewhat drying. It imparts a strong yellow colour to the foods it is added to, and is used in rice dishes, curry sauces and dahl. It is used commercially to colour various foodstuffs, e.g. mustards, relishes and pickles, as it has a strong colour but not an overpowering taste, and is much cheaper than saffron. It is used to colour cakes, biscuits, custards, butter and cheese. In Japan, it is made into a popular tea. The younger leaves can be used as a flavouring in dishes.

Nutrition/medicinal

The spice contains some vitamins C and A, as well as the B vitamins (particularly B6). Is rich in iron and manganese. Turmeric is undergoing a huge surge of scientific interest because of its main compound, curcumin. Curcumin seems to have many important medicinal properties. Hundreds of papers have been published on this species, most of which address these medicinal properties. Several trials are ongoing to study its use to treat various diseases. In particular, turmeric has recently been found to have exciting potential in slowing down the progression of the neurodegenerative disease, Alzheimer's. This is suggested as a reason why this disease is so uncommon in India. Alzheimer's is linked to the formation of protein knots in the brain called amyloid plaques and to protein neurofibrillary tangles (tau); turmeric has been shown to reduce the number of the former by ~50%.

The curcumin it contains has been shown to have very powerful antioxidant and anti-inflammatory properties. Recent research has found that people who regularly eat curcumin-based spices have a much lower incidence of colon cancer. It suppresses the proliferation of several types of tumour cell, and there is evidence of it even inhibiting cancer metastasis. It has shown some effectiveness against cancer of the pancreas, breast, ovary, prostate, rectum, as well as multiple myeloma.

In India, turmeric has historically been used to treat many ailments, including pulmonary complaints, liver disorders and rheumatism, with its efficacy for the latter being partially confirmed by recent studies. It has been found to aid digestion, by reducing spasms of the smooth muscle of the gut and to boost the immune system.

Curcumin has shown some protection against the formation of cataracts, against liver injury and to repair damage after heart attacks and strokes. It has been found to help treat some sexually transmitted diseases such as gonorrhoea and chlamydia. There is some evidence for it treating cystic fibrosis. It has antibacterial activity and is reported to have activity against *Helicobacter pylori* (which can cause stomach ulcers) and *Staphylococcus aureus*. If all the above (and other research not reported here) isn't enough, it has also been found that eating brassicas with turmeric has a synergistic effect, increasing the medicinal value of both foods. Externally, preparations are used for their antiseptic properties on cuts and burns, including difficult-to-heal wounds. **Warning:** Although the vast majority of studies have found positive benefits from curcumin, turmeric in very high amounts should perhaps be avoided by those receiving anticoagulant medications, and by women receiving chemotherapy for breast cancer.

Ornamental

An attractive species, it has a tropical, lush appearance, with ornamental, fragrant flowers. Can be grown in the flower border in a warm climate, or in a pot in colder regions. There are ornamental varieties that have showier, larger, brightly coloured flowers.

Other uses

Sometimes used as a dye for clothing, but its colour is not very light fast. Has been used in sun-tanning creams, and in India it is often used to colour the skin in ceremonies. As a dye, if it is mixed with alkaline fluids (e.g. baking powder) it turns bright red, but when mixed with acid (e.g. vinegar) it produces yellow. The colours it produces are considered sacred in Hinduism and Buddhism.

CULTIVATION

Location: Prefers light shade, and needs a sheltered site away from wind.

Temperature: Needs a semitropical, but preferably a tropical climate to grow well. Is damaged by temperatures much below ~10°C. However, it can be grown in glasshouses or as a house plant in cold-temperate regions, and be placed outside during the warmer days of summer. If growing inside provide adequate light and keep the leaves clean of dust. Makes an interesting pot plant, though may not produce many rhizomes grown by this method.

Soil/water/nutrients: Needs good-quality, organic-matter-rich loam to grow well. Prefers lighter soils: rhizome formation is poor in heavy soil. Needs regular moisture, and is not drought hardy, or tolerant of waterlogging. Grows best in slightly acidic to neutral soils: pH 5.7–7.0.

Pot culture: A good method to grow this species in cooler climates. Give plants a wide pot to spread out in, good-quality compost with lots of organic matter and regular moisture when actively growing. In winter, keep plants warm, but with less moisture. Site plants in a warm, semi-shaded, protected place.

Planting/propagation: The rhizomes can be dug up at the end of the growing season and cut into sections, each with at least 2–3 healthy eye buds. Plant sections horizontally in ~4 cm of good-quality compost and give light shade, regular moisture and heat (>20°C). Once established, the rooted sections can be transplanted to their final position. Plants are spaced at ~50 cm apart. Rhizomes can be sometimes obtained from Asian or Indian speciality food shops, and may grow if they haven't been chilled or treated with fungicides.

Pruning: If not harvesting each year, the old leaves can be removed at the end of the season to tidy them up.

Pests and diseases: Not too many problems, though if grown as houseplants, can be attacked by the usual problems such as red spider mite and scale insects.

Curcuma zedoaria
Zeodary (Indian arrowroot)
ZINGIBERACEAE
Relatives: galangal, turmeric, ginger

Related to ginger and galangal, and closely related to turmeric, the rhizomes of zeodary are used as a flavouring and medicinally, with several recently discovered medicinal properties being explored. A very attractive, ornamental perennial, it is mostly grown in China, Northern India and Korea, where it is used as a food flavouring and medicinally. There are two types of zeodary: one has long rhizomes; the other has rounded.

DESCRIPTION
The shoots and flowers die back at the end of the season, and the plant over-winters as storage rhizomes.

Leaves: Has attractive, long, leaves that have a deep purple line running along their centre. These grow to ~1 m tall and grow out in groups from buds on the rhizomes.

Flowers: Has showy, beautiful, deep pink individual flowers that emerge before the leaves. They often also have colourful bracts. Flowers grow on ~30 cm stems that have evolved for the flowers to emerge early before the leaves and other competing vegetation, allowing better fertilisation and exposure to sunlight. The flowers can last for about a month, making a wonderful garden display.

Roots: The plant has chunky, fleshy roots, which grow off the rhizomes. These are knobbly and have yellowish inner flesh. They are the underground true stems of the plant, off which grow the lateral leaves and flowers. These extend in length annually, with younger rhizomes producing the most vigorous stem and flower growth. They grow near to the soil surface.

CULTIVATION
Similar to that of turmeric and ginger.

Location: Can be grown in open sun or with light shade,

Food
The flesh of the rhizomes has a warm, aromatic, fairly hot flavour, somewhat resembling ginger. It has a camphor-like aroma. It is used to flavour various foods, such as noodle recipes. It has a stronger flavour than ginger, and should be used with care so that its flavour does not overpower that of other ingredients. It is often added to fish and meat dishes. The young shoots and rhizomes are used as a vegetable in chutneys. When chewed it is said to turn the saliva yellow.

Nutrients/medicinal
The rhizomes are rich in starch, but also contain curcumin, camphor, pinene, arturmerone and curcumeme. They are likely to have similar health benefits to turmeric. Historically, it has been particularly important in Chinese and Korean medicine. It has been used for digestive problems, as a stimulant, to treat atherosclerosis, as an anti-inflammatory and is believed to have growth-regulating properties.

Recent research has found it has significant anti-inflammatory effects. It has antimicrobial activity and can kill the larvae of some mosquito species. Several research projects have found that it may play important roles in the inhibition of cancer metastasis: in one trial it was found to decrease tumour size in mice and prevent chromosomal mutation. It is being investigated for its possible ability to treat cervical cancer. It exhibits potent antiproliferative and antifibrogenic effects in chronic liver disease, and has been shown to have potent analgesic properties.

Other uses
Extracts of this species have been used in perfumery. Makes a wonderful garden ornamental plant, with long-lasting beautifully coloured flowers.

uses

though prefers a sheltered site away from cold winds.

Temperature: Is not frost hardy. Prefers a warm-temperate to subtropical climate. In cooler climates, can be grown as a container plant, and then given protection during colder weather. However, plant leaves die back in winter, and a thick mulch over the rhizomes can give adequate protection in marginal temperature zones.

Soil/water/nutrients: Prefers well-drained soil, though is not too fussy about nutrient status. Grows best in lighter soils that allow spread of the rhizomes, but does not need deep soil. Prefers soil of pH 5.6–7.0. Does not tolerate waterlogging, but regular moisture during the growing season gives the best growth.

Planting/propagation: Can be easily propagated in autumn, from sections of rhizome that contain at least 2–3 healthy eye buds. Allow the cut surface to heal and become dry before laying them horizontally within moist, warm compost to root and form shoots. Space established plants at ~0.3 m apart.

Cymbopogon spp.
Lemongrass (citronella grass, fever grass)
POACEAE

Lemongrass, West Indian lemongrass (*Cymbopogon citratus*); lemongrass, Malabar grass, East Indian lemongrass (*C. flexuosus*); citronella (*C. nardus*); citronella (*C. winterianus*); palmarosa, rosha grass, Indian geranium (*C. martinii*)

Relatives: grasses, bamboo, wheat, rye, corn

There are about 50 species of *Cymbopogon*, and the lemongrasses, as the common name suggests, are monocotyledonous species. They originate from Asia, Australia and India, and prefer warm-temperate to tropical climates, though some species are more cold hardy. Lemongrass is particularly popular in Thailand, Vietnam and neighbouring countries. Lemongrass is a popular herb in India and in the Caribbean. Over the past few years it has become much more widely used and recognised by cooks in Europe, Australasia and North America. Apart from its usage as a flavouring in foods, it also has medicinal uses. Other *Cymbopogon* species, very closely related to lemongrass, produce citronella, an oil often used to repel insects, including mosquitoes, and it is used widely in aromatherapy. These species are relatively easy to grow, though are grown as annuals or need protection if grown in colder climates. They are attractive, wind-hardy species, plus they have a fabulous aroma.

DESCRIPTION

Tall, grassy, perennial plants. Forming clumps, its coarse leaves arch outwards as they mature, making an attractive display. Several species are used as flavourings, but the main ones are *Cymbopogon flexuosus* (cochin, Malabar grass) from India and *Cymbopogon citratus* from Sri Lanka, with the latter being the main species commonly grown and encountered. These species grow to ~1 m tall, with the same or more spread. Commercially, they are only grown for ~4 years before being replaced. Citronella oil, used as an insect repellent and aromatherapy oil, is derived from members of this genus. The essential oil is derived from *C. nardus* and *C. winterianus*, with both thought to originate from Sri Lanka. These species grow taller than lemongrass, to ~2 m, and their leaf bases are often tinged red. *C. winterianus* is considered to be of superior quality. A further species is *C. martinii* (palmarosa, rosha grass or Indian geranium); the main compound within its essential oil is geraniol, which is used widely in perfumes and in aromatherapy. This species grows to ~1.5 m tall and has finer leaves. There are several Australian species, though these are not usually used as flavourings or for their oils.

Leaves: Long, up to 1 m for lemongrass species and 1.5–2 m for citronella species. Grass like, thin, narrow, upright and arching at maturity. Have a coarse texture and are pale blue-green in colour, though young shoot are yellowish green. Fragrant when crushed.

Flowers/seed: Rarely produce flowers in colder regions. Male and female flowers are borne separately on the same flowerhead. Male flowers produce lots of pollen. Flowers are insignificant individually, and are yellow-green in colour. Pollination is by wind.

Harvest/storage: Young plants should be left for about 3 months to establish before starting to harvest the leaves. The bases of the young leaves can then be harvested through the rest of the growing season. If not used straight away, harvested shoots can be stored in a plastic

Food

The young shoots are chopped and used as a seasoning in many Asian recipes. It adds a fine lemon flavour to sauces, curries, soups, as well as seafood and fish dishes. It makes a popular lemon-flavoured tea: simply shred a leaf lengthways to expose the inner oil glands and steep in hot water for a few minutes. Citronella oil is sometimes used to flavour teas.

Lemongrass is often used with ingredients such as galangal, chilli and coriander. Although best used fresh, it also dries well, and is sometimes ground into a powder. The outer, older leaves become too tough to be eaten; however, sections can be crushed to release their lemony oil and then added to dishes, with the crushed stem then removed after cooking or marinating.

Nutrition/medicinal/other uses

The main flavour of lemongrass is from citral. This compound has been shown to have potential anticancer properties. Citronella oil contains good amounts of geraniol and citronellol, with both these compounds having antiseptic properties, and they are used in soaps and cleaning materials. The essential oils from these species have calming properties when used topically, and have antifungal and antimicrobial properties. Compounds within them are effective against the yeast pathogen *Candida*.

Lemongrass is used to induce relaxation and reduce depression, and the oil is used to soothe aches and pains. A tea is drunk to treat headaches and reduce respiratory ailments. Citronella oil has many uses; in particular, it is burnt to repel mosquitoes as well as providing a light source. Compounds, such as piperetone within these species, are particularly effective at repelling and even inhibiting the larvae of a number of insects, and more effectively repel mosquitoes than almost all other essential oils tested. Extracts have effective antibacterial activity against several pathogenic food-borne bacteria (e.g. *Escherichia coli*, *Listeria* spp., *Salmonella* spp., *Campylobacter* spp., *Clostridium* spp.) and could be added to food products to prevent contamination. The efficacy of these compounds is increased when they work together, rather than being separated into their individual components.

These species work synergistically with pharmaceutical antimicrobial drugs against *Staphylococcus aureus*. The essential oil from lemongrass has been shown to be effective against *Helicobacter pylori*, a bacterial pathogen that causes stomach ulcers; also, because they are not a traditional antibiotic, they work without the development of acquired resistance.

The fragrance of citronella, derived from citrol and geraniol, is used in cosmetics, soaps, and in aromatherapy. Palmarosa oil, derived from *C. martinii*, is widely used in aromatherapy, and to reduce tension and stress. Citrol is becoming widely used in many environmental cleaners and degreasers; it has a wonderful fragrance and cleans without the use of lots of chemicals. Its refreshing, degreasing properties make it an effective addition to skin cleansers. The compounds within these species and their oils have been tested, and are safe internally and topically, though, as with all essential oils, the oil should be only ingested in small amounts.

Ornamental

Are attractive as specimen plants if allowed to mature. Look good with large-leaved dicot species.

bag in a fridge for a couple of weeks. They freeze well without any loss of flavour, or can be dried. The essential oil from these species can be obtained by either steam or alcohol distillation.

CULTIVATION

Fairly easy.

Location: Prefers a site in full sun. Is wind hardy, and its long leaves look attractive moving in the breeze. Can be grown near the coast.

Temperature: Although native to subtropical and tropical climates, they can be grown in warm-temperate climates, or even in cold-temperate regions if given winter protection. They are semi-cold hardy, and may tolerate temperatures down to ~–2°C. Plants become dormant during the winter months. Mulch or cover the roots of plants in colder regions; in regions with regular frosts, plants are best grown in a container that can be moved inside.

Soil/water/nutrients: Although not too fussy about nutrient status of the soil, plants grow better with incorporation of organic matter and enjoy a feed or two of liquid nutrients during the growing season. Plants do need good drainage, and grow well in sandy soils, but also need regular moisture, though much less moisture during the winter months when not actively growing. In particular, add organic matter to sandy soils to help retain moisture. Do best in climates with higher humidity. Prefers slightly acidic to neutral soils: pH 5.0–6.5.

Pot culture: Although they are large plants when mature, can be grown in a container in colder regions, and then brought inside during the winter. Give free-draining gritty compost, regular moisture, and regular nutrients while actively growing.

Planting: As specimens, space plants at least 1 m apart. As annuals or short-lived perennials, can be spaced much closer.

Propagation: *Seed:* Only seems to set seed in warmer climates; however, seed is available through specialist seed merchants. The fine seed should be thinly sown and only just covered (~0.5 cm) with soil. Germination usually takes 7–14 days, though can take up to 6 weeks. Seed needs warmth (20–25°C), as well as moisture. Prick-out seedlings and grow-on until large enough to plant out in spring. *Cuttings*: Often propagated by division. In warmer regions, plants can be lifted in spring or autumn and the roots separated into plantlets; in cooler climates, best to only divide plants in later spring to avoid cold temperatures until plants are fully established. Insert plantlets into moist, warm compost to establish, before planting out in their final positions. When lemongrass is bought for cooking,

stand it in a glass of water and it will often form roots (if it has not previously been allowed to dry out). Look for signs of rooting when purchasing. As soon as these start to emerge, insert the stalks into moist, warm compost.

Pruning: Last year's growth can be trimmed back to ~15 cm in spring to encourage the formation of new harvestable shoots. If trimmed in autumn, winter cold is liable to injure the plant.

Pests and diseases: Few problems.

Cynara cardunculus
Cardoon (cardoni)
ASTERACEAE (COMPOSITAE)
Relatives: globe artichoke, lettuce, Jerusalem artichoke, thistle, sunflower

Very similar in appearance to the globe artichoke, though tends to form a taller plant. Like its close relative, the flower buds can be eaten, but are smaller and more fiddly to handle; it is more usually valued for its edible leaves. Less grown and less appreciated than the globe artichoke, it may have been eaten by the Greeks, but was popular with the Romans. It is sometimes grown around Mediterranean regions, and is most popular in France and Italy, but is gaining popularity as a more unusual vegetable within the United Kingdom. It is cultivated in some areas of the United States and Australia. However, in warmer climates, in pastoral locations, this plant's seeds can be readily dispersed, posing a potential weed problem (e.g. in southern Australia and California).

DESCRIPTION

This is a hardier and tougher species than the globe artichoke. If left to grow normally, the plant can reach about 2 m in height with several stems, and mature plants can spread as wide as they are tall. It is a short-lived perennial. In warmer climates it retains its leaves year round; in colder regions it tends to regrow from its roots each year. There are spiny and spineless varieties, with the spineless being much preferred.

Leaves: Its attractive grey, green, long leaves (0.8–1.8 m) are thinner than those of the globe artichoke. They are deeply lobed and have prominent midribs. For culinary use, a few young leaves can be removed during spring and early summer. Or the older leaves can be blanched when ~1 m tall, normally by mid summer. They are wrapped together and covered with sacking, paper, or cardboard to blanch them. This makes them whiter, much more succulent and without bitterness. The leaves should be wrapped while they are dry. Blanching takes ~4 weeks; if left for too long, fungal disease can set in and the centre crown can deteriorate.

Harvest/storage: If blanched, the whole can be harvested in late summer, and then used as a vegetable. Takes ~14 weeks until blanched leaves can be harvested; young leaves can be picked sooner. Removal of the all blanched leaves can weaken the plant though, and gardeners tend to resow cardoons annually or biannually

if grown for blanching. The leaves are cut at their base, leaving the basal crown intact. The leaves can be stored for a few days within a fridge (but not frozen), but are quite large and take up considerable space. Or they can be stored for a few days in the cool inside a polythene bag to maintain humidity. The flowerheads can be harvested before they begin to open and the hearts can be eaten (see below).

Flowers: If left to mature, the flowers form from spring onwards, depending on climate and age. Established plants flower sooner than first-year seedlings. The heads are rounded, globe like, smaller than those of the globe artichoke and composed of many bracts. When mature they open to form a dense head of purple, thistle-like flowers, which the bees and butterflies love. The flowerheads contain both male and female flowers. The globes are harder and denser than those of globe artichoke, and only the very centre is soft enough or large enough to be edible.

Fruit/seeds: The seeds are actually small, dry, simple fruits called achenes, each containing a single seed. They form with 'wings' that make them very mobile. In some regions this makes them a potential weed problem. Remove the head before they seed to eliminate this risk, or cover the head with a polythene bag if growing for its seed.

Roots: Forms clumps of tuberous roots, off which spread deeper roots. Needs a loose soil to root well.

Food
The unopened flowerheads can be boiled for ~30 minutes, and the outer scales removed, with the flower structures, to leave the central heart. This, although small, can be tender and tasty. The young leaves can be eaten fresh in salads and treated in the same way as celery. They can be lightly cooked. For blanched leaves, the older, outer leaves are removed to leave the younger leaves, the stems and the tender central crown. This is often sliced into sections horizontally and then simmered for a short time. They have juicy, tender midribs. They can be eaten as an accompanying vegetable, or added to soups and stews, though are best when their individual, pleasant, but mild, flavour can be appreciated. Dribble with garlic butter, or crumble a white cheese over them. They can be added to a range of Mediterranean recipes with e.g. olives, eggplant, courgettes and tomatoes. Their taste is difficult to describe, but is less strong than brassicas, and some say is slightly reminiscent of celery.

Nutrition/medicinal
Has good quantities of folate, and some magnesium and potassium, but also sodium. All parts contain a bitter compound, which is reduced in young or blanched leaves. Good levels of fibre, which includes inulin. This is not actually digested, but encourages the multiplication of 'good' gut flora, so improving digestion and reducing the risk of colonic cancers. Because it is not digested, it has no calorific value, but gives the sensation of having eaten. Its inulin content may be as good or better than that of Jerusalem artichoke (see p. 239), *also see* Warning below). Recent research has found that this species helps improve vascular endothelial function, which may be of particular importance in the elderly, as this reduces the risk of cardiovascular problems. In trials, when it was fed to older rats, it was found to restore their vascular 'suppleness' to that of young rats. The leaves contain the antioxidants chlorogenic acid and cynarin, which may help prevent cancers and may have a protective effect on the gall bladder and liver, as well as improving digestion. In the past, this plant was used to treat hepatitis and other liver complaints. The leaves contain compounds that act as antimicrobials, particularly fungal. **Warning:** A few people have an allergic reaction to inulin, so treat cautiously until this is known.

Ornamental
Makes a great ornamental within a herbaceous border if left to mature. Looks good with plants with purple or reddish foliage.

Other uses
A yellow dye can be obtained from the leaves and stalks. The flowerheads, if cut, last a long time and are good in dried flower arrangements.

CULTIVATION
Easy to grow.
Location: It grows best in full sun. Because of its height, it is not very tolerant of exposed locations, though if growing for blanching this is not as relevant. It grows well in maritime salt air.
Temperature: Can be grown in Mediterranean-type climates, but is then best grown during the cooler months, i.e. start off the seeds in late winter, or late summer for a late autumn crop. Cardoons grow best in regions with warm, but not too hot, summers, such as northern France, southern United Kingdom, and northern California. If the weather is too hot, the leaves become bitter. It is not very frost hardy, and severe frost can kill the roots. Less severe frosts tend to cause the tops to die back, though the roots are usually fine. Mulch (e.g. straw) during cold weather for added protection.
Soil/water/nutrients: Prefers a fairly nutrient-rich, deep, loamy soil. Can grow in sandy soils, but cardoons do need regular moisture to grow well. Extended dry periods result in tougher leaves and stunted growth. Growth is poor in clays due to restricted root penetration. Grows well in regions with higher humidity, though is not tolerant of waterlogging. It grows best with a soil pH that is mildly acidic, pH 5.5–6.5.

Pot culture: Could be grown in large pots to make an interesting annual plant.
Planting: Plants can be spaced at ~0.7 m apart, but are better if given more space to spread. If grown for ornamental purposes, they need to be planted at least 1.5 m apart. They readily fit into a herbaceous border, and if some are not harvested, they form a tall, attractive plant. Generally do not need staking or attention once established. If harvested for their leaves, the plants seldom last much longer than a couple of years before their vigour is reduced. Otherwise they live for 4–5 years, but do benefit from their tubers being divided to form new plants.
Propagation: Seed: Often grown from seed. Germination is good, within a few days. The seeds can be sown individually in trays. Seedlings can be pricked-out and grown-on in cells or pots before planting outside once all risk of frost has passed. *Cuttings:* Sections of young shoots with some root, if possible, can be gently removed from the crown in spring and summer, and established in pots. The tuberous roots can be divided in late autumn, and placed in beds or pots to over-winter and should establish new leaves and roots in spring. Plants are rejuvenated by division, which is best done every 2–3 years.
Pests and diseases: Few problems.

Food

The seeds are often removed from the pods just before use and the pod discarded, as some find the pod texture too woody; it has little flavour. The seeds can be used whole or are ground to a powder, which is best done just before usage. Cardamom is richly, sweetly and deeply aromatic, and has a distinctive, warm flavour, which is a little like ginger, nutmeg and cinnamon. This spice is used in both sweet and savoury dishes. It is combined with other spices in curry sauces, in pilau recipes and in dahl, as well as various vegetable and meat dishes. It is added to betel pan. It is coated with sugar and used as a confectionery in India. In Scandinavia, it is used as an ingredient in and on scones, cakes, waffles and other bakery products. Can be added to whipped cream and used as a dessert topping, and added to rice puddings. One recipe recommends mixing it with mango, yoghurt and ice to make a smoothie. The seeds, either whole or ground, are used to flavour tea, often with other spices. One of its main uses is mixed with ground coffee beans to make a very popular Arabian beverage called gahwa. Its essential oil is used to flavour various foods and drinks, including liquors and mulled wine.

Nutrition/medicinal

The seeds contain good quantities of fibre, a little vitamin C and the B vitamins. They are very rich in manganese, with a little iron, copper, magnesium and calcium. The oil within the seeds is very rich in palmitic, oleic and linoleic fatty acids, and contains cineol and alpha terpinyl acetate. The seeds are rich in oleoresin, a mix of oil and resin (also found in *Capsicums*), which gives cardamom much of its aroma, flavour and medicinal properties. It contains cineol and limonene, which add to its aromatic properties. An essential oil can be extracted from the seeds. The oil has antibacterial properties, and is used to preserve foods, particularly meats such as sausages, with only a small amount needed to be effective.

Historically, cardamom has been used for digestive problems, including food poisoning, and it is still valued for its stomach-calming properties. Extracts have proven analgesic properties, antispasmodic and anti-inflammatory properties, and have been shown to help relieve gastro-intestinal disorders. The seeds are chewed to cure bad breath, and have been used to treat sore throats. Research shows it can reduce the formation of clots in human blood and lipid peroxidation, so helps those at risk of heart disease. In China, cardamom is given to children suffering from coeliac disease (intolerance to the gluten found in certain cereals) to help relieve the symptoms. They have been used to treat various skin conditions, and modern natural skin creams and soaps sometimes include it. The Arabs consider it to have aphrodisiac properties.

Ornamental

If the climate is suitable, it makes a terrific, exotic large-specimen plant or can be grown in a larger border, with its tall shoots of large leaves and metre-high flower shoots. Could be grown in cooler climates within a heated greenhouse or similar. Because it loves shade, it could be grown as a large house plant.

Other uses

The ground seeds have been added to tobacco. The large leaves have been used as plates and to wrap food in.

Roots: Forms a system of robust rhizomes for storage of nutrients to develop the following season's shoots.

CULTIVATION

Location: Needs a site in light shade, because it doesn't grow well in full sun. Also needs to be sheltered from wind.

Temperature: Needs a tropical climate with temperatures >20°C; will be killed by temperatures anywhere near freezing. Possibly the least cold-hardy species described in this book, but it is included because it could be grown in a pot inside if given a hot, steamy environment, e.g. a heated bathroom.

Soil/water/nutrients: Grows best in soil rich in organic matter, with additions of well-rotted manure or fertiliser, with more nitrogen and less potassium. Needs regular moisture, but not waterlogging; too much moisture can result in leaf tips becoming brown.

Pot culture: Could be grown in a large pot inside in cooler climates. Give good-quality compost, good drainage, but plenty of moisture and humidity, shade, and lots of warmth. In winter, give plants less water.

Planting/propagation: *Seed:* Can be grown from seed, but it must be fresh: viability is said to decrease very rapidly, in as soon as 7–10 days, so unfortunately, store-bought seed will not germinate. The seeds are best carefully removed from the pods as this speeds up germination: should then germinate in 7–14 days, though older seed takes longer. Sprinkle the fine seed on a compost-sand mix and only just cover with fine soil. Keep moist, warm and shaded. Seedlings are grown-on in pots for about 2 years before planting out in their final, shaded location. *Cuttings:* Easily propagated by dividing the rhizomes into sections. Each section should be healthy and have young growth. Lay the rhizomes horizontally in moist, warm compost and cover with ~8 cm of soil. Commercially, they may be planted singly or in groups of 3–4, with groups ~3 m apart.

Pruning: Remove any leaves or stems that are damaged or diseased, or any brown leaves.

Pests and diseases: Few problems, though is reported to be eaten by monkeys, rats, lizards and porcupines in India and Sri Lanka.

Amomum spp.: black or brown cardamom (Kravan, Java cardamom, Bengal cardamom, Siamese cardamom, white or red cardamom): Native to Asia and Australia, the pods of this species are sometimes used as a flavouring, but are mostly used medicinally in India, and to a lesser extent in China and other East Asian countries. Of this genus, the species *A. subulatum* is commonly cultivated and used in Indian spice mixes, e.g. in garam masala. The other main species, *A. tsao-ko*, is used in Chinese cuisine, e.g. in some meat dishes and pickles. Their pods are considerably larger and have a coarser aroma and flavour than green cardamoms. They are more camphor-like. They are dried over a flame, which gives them a rougher texture, a dark reddish brown colour and a smokey aroma and taste. Medicinally, these species are used to treat gum and teeth infections, to relieve respiratory congestion, to treat sore throats and inflamed eyelids, and for digestive ailments. They have been used as an antidote to both snake and scorpion bites.

Eleusine coracana (Finger millet): see *Pennisetum glaucum* p. 326

Elsholtzia ciliata
Vietnamese balm (crested late summer mint, Vietnamese mint, ray kinh gioi)
LAMIACEAE (LABIATAE)
Relatives: mint, lemon balm, thyme, rosemary, lavender

Vietnamese balm is in the same family as many other wonderfully aromatic, culinary herbs, and is one of about 25 species within the *Elsholtzia* genus. The leaves from this Asian plant are highly regarded for their spicy, aromatic, lemony flavour. Native to Korea, Japan and China, this species has now become naturalised in many parts of the temperate northern hemisphere. It can be found in northern Europe, is common in Siberia, and is found in parts of north-eastern United States and eastern Canada. It is considered invasive in some areas of the United States. It is often found growing on hillsides, sometimes at considerable altitude, and beside roads. Despite its common name, it is more a plant of temperate regions, but has become valued in the cuisine of Southeast Asia, and is frequently sold in markets. In Europe, it is often grown as an ornamental plant. It is easy to grow, takes up little space, and has attractive flowers so this plant deserves a spot in a flower bed or the herb garden.

DESCRIPTION

An erect annual, growing to 0.4–0.8 m tall, it has four-sided slightly downy stems.

Leaves: On long leaf stalks, are simple, opposite and alternate at 90° angles up the stem. Are oval to lanceolate, 4–10 cm long, slightly downy, with distinctive toothed margins. The underside of the leaf is covered with tiny oil glands, which give the leaves their strong citrus aroma.

Flowers: Typical flower shape of this family with bilateral symmetry and upper and lower lips. The pale dusky pink to mauve flowers have both male and female parts, and can be self-fertile. Borne from mid summer until early autumn in erect spikes, 4–10 cm long, from leaf axils, though with the largest flowers at the apex of the plant. Pollination is by bees and insects.

Harvest/storage: The young leaves can be harvested throughout the season, but are considered to have their finest flavour just as the plant begins to flower. The leaves are best used fresh, but they can be dried for later use. Store in a cool, dark airtight container. The seeds can be gathered just as they ripen within their capsules.

Eryngium foetidum

Mexican coriander (culantro, spiny coriander, bhandhanya, fitweed, recao, wild coriander, spirit weed, ngo gai, sawtooth, long coriander, recao)

APIACEAE (UMBELIFERAE)

Relatives: parsley, coriander, dill, fennel, carrot, celery

Most of the 200 species within the genus *Eryngium* are from warm-temperate to tropical climates, and include the well-known species of sea holly. Most have grey-green leaves that are often spiny, and are adapted to dry, coastal locations. Although a native of Central America and the Caribbean, Mexican coriander has become a particularly popular culinary herb in Vietnam, Singapore, Malaysia, Thailand and India. It is cultivated, and grows naturally, in regions around the Caribbean and is sold in Central American and Caribbean markets. Its species name indicates the strength of flavour and aroma of its leaves, which are used to flavour hot, spicy recipes. It is often known as culantro and, when dried can be mistaken in flavour for cilantro (coriander), though is stronger in taste. Due to increasing numbers of Asian and Central American people now living in North America, Australasia and parts of Europe, the popularity of this herb has spread, with significant amounts of dried and fresh product being imported. Local cultivation is also being trialled.

DESCRIPTION

A slow-growing biennial species that produces leaves and a storage taproot in the first year, and flowers and sets seed in the second. However, it is often grown as an annual in cooler regions, as it is mainly grown for its edible leaves. Grows to 25–40 cm tall in the first year, though the flower stem can become taller.

Leaves: Leaves grow spirally from a shortened stem, and form a basal rosette. Are thick, waxy, tough and have clearly toothed margins, with the teeth being more spine like and sharper on older leaves and on the smaller leaves growing on flower stems. Elsewhere, the leaves are fully edible. They are lance shaped (~30 cm long, ~5 cm width), with a rich green to blue-green colour.

Flowers: Small, in umbel-like clusters at the apex of tall flower stems, which form in the second year. The outer calyx is green and the flower corolla is creamy white. Pollination is by bees and insects.

Fruits/seeds: Has small, rounded, knobbly fruits. The numerous small seeds can be collected once the fruits have ripened and turned brown.

Harvest/storage: A few leaves can be picked and used fresh when needed throughout the season. Harvesting can commence when plants are about 10 weeks old. They are of better quality in the first year, and become tougher and less flavoursome once the flower stems begin to form. Remove any forming flower stems to prolong the harvesting season. Excess leaves can be successfully dried or frozen. Unlike many herbs, the dried leaves of this species retain much of their colour and flavour. However, the fresh leaves are best used immediately after picking. They can be kept for a few days in the fridge.

Roots: Has a storage taproot, which grows 10–16 cm long, off which grow thick, spreading, regularly branched feeder roots.

CULTIVATION

Location: Although it can grow in full sun, it grows much better in light to heavy shade. If grown with too much light and heat, leaf size and yield are reduced, and plants bolt early producing more flowers. The flavour and aroma of plants are said to be better if they are grown in the shade. The longer days at higher latitudes can also induce plants to bolt, producing more flowers but low leaf yields. Growers are trying to select varieties that do not have this property so that plants can be more easily grown in regions outside the subtropics and tropics.

Temperature: Although native to hotter climates, plants do not like intense heat. They are not frost hardy, and need to be moved inside or covered if colder weather threatens. Less cold hardy than coriander.

Soil/water/nutrients: Can be grown in a range of soil types from sandy to moderately heavy, but likes regular moisture and the addition of organic matter. Soils with moderate nutrient content, particularly of nitrogen, are said to give better leaf growth. Grows best at pH 6.3–7.5.

Pot culture: Ideal for growth in pots or a wooden box in cool-climate regions, and can then be protected during colder weather. As it can be grown in shade, it is sometimes grown as a houseplant in cooler regions. Give plants good drainage, with good-quality, fairly nutrient-rich compost.

Planting/propagation: *Seed:* Is better to use fresh seed as older seed loses its viability. Usually started off

Food

The spicy leaves of this herb are often used in marinades. It is sometimes used instead of the leaves of coriander, but has a stronger flavour. In Asian cuisine, it is added as a fresh flavouring to spicy hot soups, stir-fries and noodle dishes. In South and Central American cuisine, the chopped leaves are added to salsa and to other sauces, which are served with a wide range of savoury dishes. It is used in soups, stews and bean dishes. It can be added to chutneys for its flavour but also acts as an appetite enhancer.

Nutrition/medicinal

The plant has very good amounts of vitamin A (10,460 I.U.), and some of the B vitamins, particularly riboflavin, as well as vitamin C. Also contains some calcium and iron. Historically, the leaves and roots have been used to stimulate appetite, to treat digestive problems. They work by soothing smooth muscle spasms of the gut, and so ease flatulence, stomach pains, treat colic, etc. They have been used as an aphrodisiac, to reduce fevers and to treat pulmonary infections, such as colds and flu. They have been used to treat diabetes, as a fungicide, an antiseptic, a germicide and a viricide. Research has shown that it can act as an anticonvulsant. Extracts have been shown to have topical activity against various inflammations. The essential oil contains carotol, farnesene, anethole and pinene.

Ornamental

This plant has attractive leaves, so makes an interesting addition to the herb garden or can be grown as a pot plant.

from seed, which takes considerable time to germinate: 14–28 days. Sow thinly on peaty soil and just cover (some advise germinating without covering seeds). Keep warm (>22°C), moist and shaded. Grow seedlings on in shade in free-draining compost until large enough to be planted out. Give plants regular moisture, but they need good aeration and good spacings as seedlings often suffer from fungal damping off. In cooler regions, can be grown on in pots or in a glasshouse. Space plants at least 15 cm apart. Handle gently, as the taproots dislike disturbance. *Cuttings*: May be propagated by root cuttings but percentage take can be poor because of their poor tolerance of root disturbance.

Pruning: Any forming flower stems should be removed to encourage more leaf growth and prolong the harvesting season.

Pests and diseases: Has few problems, though root-knot nematodes have been reported, as well as occasional fungal leaf-spot diseases. Some gardeners say that the flowers encourage populations of beneficial insects, e.g. ladybirds and lacewings, and plants may help repel aphids.

Erythronium spp.
Dog's tooth violets
LILACEAE

Dog's tooth violet (*Erythronium dens-canis*); American trout lily (syn. dog's tooth violet, adder's tongue) (*E. californicum* (syn. *E. revolutum*)); white dog's tooth violet (white trout lily) (*E. albidum*); katakuri (*E. japonicum*)
Relatives: tiger lily, star of Bethlehem

A small genus containing about 25 species, with origins from Asia, to Europe and North America, they are related to the lilies, and not to violets as their common name suggests. These monocotyledonous plants, which naturally grow in springtime in woodlands, have delicate flowers and mottled attractive leaves. Its pretty flowers open before the surrounding herbage has had time to grow up and while most deciduous trees are still in bud, enabling pollination and exposure to light. Although they are more usually regarded and grown as ornamentals, most species have edible bulbs (though see Warning below), which have a pleasant, sweet flavour. The main edible species are the dog's tooth violet, the American trout lily, white dog's tooth violet and katakuri. A popular spring ornamental in Europe and Britain, the dog's tooth violet originates from central Europe through to Asia; the American trout lily is from the west coast of North America, spreading from Canada down to southern California; the white dog's tooth is from central North America, from north to south; and katakuri is from east Asia, particularly Japan: there are numerous ornamental varieties of these. Although the corms have a good flavour, many gardeners are reluctant to harvest these beautiful plants, and young corms take several years before they start producing flowers. The answer would be to plant lots of them each year, so there are enough to enjoy for their flowers, and a few to harvest and eat.

DESCRIPTION

Small perennial monocotyledonous plants, the dog's tooth and white dog's tooth violets only grow to ~15 cm tall, with the American trout lily being larger, at ~30 cm tall. They form storage bulbs to get them through the winter. In spring, the bulb sends up flower stems, closely followed by leaves. These leaves, which have died back by mid summer, photosynthesise to produce starch and sugars to be stored within the bulb for next year's early growth.

Leaves: Narrow to broad lanceolate, mid-green, attractive leaves; they are often flecked with maroon, brown or silver, depending on the species.

Flowers: A welcome and beautiful flower in spring. The drooping flowerhead has six recurved delicate petals (like a turk's-cap lily) which are mauve-pink in many species, and has three stamens and a central style that hang downwards. The flowers are held individually on arching deep-red fleshy stems. The flowers of American trout lily are mottled, often white and mauve, and those of white dog's tooth are usually white, though occasionally yellow. Those of *E. americanum* and *E. gigantum* are a lovely deep yellow colour. Flowers are 4–7 cm in diameter. The seed ripens by early summer. The varieties of *E. californicum*, 'White Beauty' and 'Pagoda' are more vigorous species, growing more quickly and flowering sooner. Pollination is by bees (including bumble bees) and insects.

Roots: The bulbs of dog's tooth violet are white and oblong and, with a bit of imagination, could resemble a dog's tooth. They form successive younger bulbs around them as the plants get older. Bulbs can be ~6 cm long and ~2.5 cm wide in the American trout lily, but are smaller in the dog's tooth and white dog's tooth. All have feeder roots growing from their base. Although small, the bulbs are tender and tasty. Some species have stoloniferous growth, with underground stems spreading to new areas of soil to form new plants; these species are said to produce fewer flowers than non-stoloniferous species.

Harvest/storage: The bulbs are harvested once they have reached a good size, which can take 3–4 years, or longer. They are best harvested in autumn or early winter, when rich with sugars and starch. Perhaps harvest some for eating and replant the rest for future crops. The leaves can be harvested in spring, but great care is needed to not harvest too many, otherwise the bulb does not form sufficiently and the plant will die. Please do not harvest plants from the wild.

CULTIVATION

Location: Prefers a site in light shade, and can be grown on slopes.

Temperature: Most are cold-hardy species, over-wintering as bulbs, and their early flowers and leaves are able to withstand late spring frosts. There are reports that the American species need more heat before they will flower and are not as cold hardy.

Soil/water/nutrients: They grow best in organic-matter-rich loamy soils, which are moist, but are not waterlogged. Prefer a slightly acidic to neutral soil, and grow better in lighter textured soils, with clay soils inhibiting bulb expansion. Can grow in somewhat alkaline soils as long as organic matter has been incorporated.

Pot culture: Ideal for growth in tubs or pots, around the edges, with a larger specimen plant in the centre. Near to the house they are a welcome sight in spring. Perhaps grow in pots and take them indoors for a spring floral display.

Planting/propagation: *Seed:* Can be grown from seed, though the progeny can be variable. Also, they can take 3–5 years before they mature or are large enough to flower. Sow the fine, fresh seed in pots in autumn, and allow it to over-winter in a cold frame. Only give occasional moisture. The seedlings may need more than 2 years of growth before they are large enough to prick-out and grow-on separately. Weed control is important around

Food

The corms have a pleasant, sweet taste, though some describe them as acrid. They can be lightly roasted or fried, and enjoyed with other vegetables. Can be added to stir-fries, or can be eaten raw, finely sliced and added to salads. The bulbs can be dried and ground to make flour, which is used in cakes, etc. The bulbs of katakuri are used in Japanese cuisine, mostly for their starch properties. The flour is used to thicken soups and sauces, and does not gel when cooled. It is included in dumplings and confectionery. The leaves of these species can be lightly cooked.

Nutrition/medicinal

Historically, these species have been used as a diuretic, as a stimulant, as a contraceptive, to reduce fevers, but also to induce vomiting. These species contain sesquiterpene lactones as alpha-methylene-butyrolactone. This inhibits the secretion of granular contents from platelets and neutrophils, and research indicates its efficacy in treating migraines and other similar conditions (however, this compound is also responsible for its dermatitis-like reactions: see below). The plant is said to relieve coughs, and has been used to eliminate intestinal worms. The leaves and bulbs have been topically applied to reduce swellings and to treat various skin problems.

Warning: A few people have adverse skin reactions after handling the cut bulbs or leaves. There are reports that some of these species act as an emetic; this seems to primarily refer to *E. americanum* and *E. grandiflorum*, so treat these with caution.

Ornamental

Mostly grown as ornamentals for their welcome colour and the delicacy of their flowers after a long grey winter. They are often planted in light woodland, under specimen trees in rockeries, or sometimes in lawns.

Pot culture: Can be grown in containers near to the house or on a deck. Excellent summer flower show.

Planting/propagation: *Seed:* Can be grown from seed, but most modern plants are derived from hybrids, and so any progeny derived from seed will be variable. Sow seed in spring and cover with ~1 cm of soil. With warmth and moisture, germination takes ~3 weeks. Prick-out seedlings and grow-on until ~15 cm tall, or until the following year in colder regions, before planting out. *Cuttings:* Because of variability from seed production, vegetative propagation is the usual method, and is easy and successful. Clumps can be divided in spring or autumn, and the tubers either established in pots before siting in their final position, or simply planted where wanted. In colder areas, gardeners often recommend leaving division until early spring so that the new plants are not damaged by the winter cold. Divide clumps every 3–4 years by digging up and gently pulling apart the plantlets. Space new plants at ~45 cm apart. Ensure that the crown of the plant is buried less than 2 cm deep, to pevent rot. Because the flowers only last a day, gardeners who grow them for ornamental purposes, often plant them at periods during the summer season to prolong their season.

Pruning: The old leaves and stems are often cut back to ground level in winter.

Pests and diseases: Very few problems, though there is a gall midge that can damage the flower buds, so destroy any infected buds. Slugs and snails may sometimes be attracted to young plants.

SOME SPECIES

Hemerocallis citrina: Often grown in China for its good-quality, edible young flowers. This species has flowers that open in the evening, and smell a little of lemon, hence its species name.

Hemerocallis dumortieri: A vigorous daylily that produces numerous flowers from early summer.

Hemerocallis fulva: A good species for its tawny-coloured edible flowers, its edible young leaves and has vigorous rhizomes, which even spread widely around and through paving if allowed to. Most varieties are hybrids. The flowers are usually harvested just after they have opened, and are good added to salads.

Hemerocallis lilioasphodelus: Another species grown for its edible flowers and rhizomes. The taste of the flowers, though, is reported to be variable.

Hemerocallis minor: Has edible flowers that open in the evening, and reasonable-sized rhizomes.

Hordeum vulgare (syn. *H. distichum* (two row), *H. tetrastichum* (four-row))
Barley
POACEAE
Relatives: wheat, rye, rice, oats, millet, bamboo, corn

A widely cultivated, important member of the grass family, it is the fourth most commonly grown cereal, after wheat, rice and maize, and is a staple food to many. Probably the first of the cereals to be harvested and eaten from the wild: it is thought that it was being gathered and eaten by pre-Neolithic man ~10,000 years ago. It then became one of the first cereals to be cultivated. The Egyptians are known to have used barley extensively in breads and to make beer. Its cultivation and usage then spread to many parts of the world, and it is particularly valued for its cold tolerance, as well as its ability to grow in poorer-quality soils than many crops, including rye and wheat. It is now widely grown in Russia, Canada, the Ukraine and other northern countries, as well as in many hot countries, such as India and Africa. It was thought to have originally evolved from the species *Hordeum spontaneum*, a species that grew wild in the Middle East (as did many of the original cereals). Unlike several of the cereals, it does have an ordinary diploid chromosome number. Many varieties and types of barley have been selected for different uses. Much is now grown to feed livestock, but its other main use is to make malt for beer.

It comes in three main types: two-, four- and six-row, with the latter having a larger, plumper spike. The six-row types can be divided into three further types: malting barley, for beer; tall, bearded and spring barley, which is often planted in autumn for a spring harvest; and winter barley, usually grown in warmer regions and is often grown to feed livestock. The two-row is the oldest type, and is the most similar to *H. spontaneum*. It is usually planted in spring, for an autumn harvest, and is used to make malt and to feed livestock. Although malt can be extracted from other cereals, barley is the preferred choice due to its high enzyme levels. The ears, depending on variety, can be bearded or non-bearded. Bearded forms tend to be the older type of the two and have awns (hairs), ~7–8 cm long; these are attached to each seed, and originally evolved to aid in seed dispersal. Commercially, bearded types are more tricky to plant and process, and livestock do not like eating the hairs, but they are the best for malting for beer. Barley is a very undervalued grain for eating; it has wonderful quantities of fibre, antioxidants and many other health benefits and deserves to be re-discovered and used much more widely.

DESCRIPTION

A faster-growing crop than wheat. It grows to ~60–120 cm in height, depending on variety, and forms one main stem, i.e. it does not tend to tiller.

Leaves: These sheath and wrap around the stem, alternately, becoming smaller near the apex. Lanceolate, ~25 cm long, ~1.5 cm wide, smooth.

Flowers: Insignificant, yellow-green in colour. Pollination is by wind. They form in threes, in spikelets at the top of stems.

Seeds: With the hulls removed, which may have a

Food

The grain is often used to make malt for beer and whisky, to make malt vinegar, and the sweet malt, rich in the sugar maltose, is often used by bakers. To malt barley, the grain, still with its hull, is washed, then soaked at ~16°C for less than 8 hours. The grains are then drained of water and spread thinly on trays that are kept warm, humid and dark, but are well ventilated, for ~2–5 days, until the sprouting shoot has attained ~75% the length of the grain. Soaking the seed for a longer period than 8 hours leads to anaerobic conditions which kills it. Once the seed has sprouted, it is then rapidly dried (roasted) at 40–50°C for ~24 hours. This quickly halts the germination process, and traps the nutrients within the seeds at a stage when they are just becoming activated by the many enzymes. The variations in roasting method affect the malt's characteristics, and the consequent brew. The malted barley should then have a crunchy, sweetish taste.

Barley grains can be cooked whole (with the hulls removed), though this does take a considerable time. Placing them in a blender is said to separate most hulls from the grains. Processed barley can be bought as pearl barley, though this has had its fibre-rich bran layer removed, and consequently some of its health benefits. Barley grains can be purchased as pot/scotch barley, which has been less processed. For home processing, roasting is said to make the outer hull easier to remove. Barley grains can be boiled and eaten like rice, or can be added, with other vegetables or meat, to soups and stews. They can be made into a pilaf or added to salads. The grains have a pleasant, sweetish, nutty flavour.

The roasted grains can be ground to make a soothing hot beverage, often mixed with milk, or can be mixed with lemon, honey and water, then chilled to make a refreshing summer drink. Ground, the flour can be added to biscuits or breads. Barley is sold as barley flakes and can be used in the same way as oat flakes, or the grains can be toasted and cracked to make barley grits, which are similar to bulgar, and can be used in the same way (see wheat). The seeds can be sprouted and then allowed to grow into 'grass', either in soil or a soilless medium. (Must be sprouted before placing on the growth medium.) The grass can then be harvested and used like wheatgrass added to juices. Or the seeds can be simply sprouted and eaten in salads.

Nutrition/medicinal

The grains of barley (particularly two-grain types) are very high in enzymes, more so than most other cereals, making them excellent for malting. Has a high protein content and excellent quantities of fibre (50%). Has good levels of the B vitamins, thiamine, niacin and B6, and of the minerals manganese (in particular), very high in selenium (a powerful antioxidant), plus good amounts of magnesium, phosphorus and copper. The latter may help relieve rheumatoid arthritis.

Being a whole grain, it is high in antioxidant phenolics, as yet are largely unexplored scientifically. If these are eaten as a group (rather than as individual components in supplements), they are thought to have many important health benefits. Barley's high fibre content is excellent for digestion, for reducing the risk of colon cancer (as well as haemorrhoids) and, indirectly, for lowering cholesterol levels. Barley contains plant lignans, which are converted within the body to compounds that are thought to protect against hormone-related cancers, e.g. breast cancer.

The digestion of fibre encourages the populations of beneficial bacteria within the intestines. These bacteria produce by-products which help maintain the health of the cells of the colon and are involved in lowering cholesterol. This is in addition to constituents within the fibre that bind to cholesterol-producing compounds (particularly LDLs), which are then eliminated from the body. Barley has been shown in trials to be better than other grains at reducing glucose and insulin responses in type-2 diabetics. An alkaloid within the grain called gramine, can be converted to isogramine. This was discovered in the 1930's to have significant local anaesthetic properties: it was used to make lignocaine (xylocaine). This safe compound has been widely used in dentistry for many decades. **Warning:** Barley contains glutens, which some are allergic to, though their amount and reactivity are not as high as those within wheat (see p. 425).

Ornamental

The bearded forms of barley are particularly ornamental. Consider planting a few patches of them amongst annuals or as a contrast species amongst low-lying, broad-leaved plants. Or perhaps, best of all, amongst field poppies.

Other uses

Often used to feed livestock, particularly the beardless varieties. Chickens like the grains sprouted. The stalks make good straw bedding for stock. The stalks have been used to make hats.

beard, the seeds are more rounded than those of wheat, but are about the same size. Only two of the spikelets of the two-row forms are fertile; all three of the four- and six-row forms are fertile.

Harvest/storage: Takes only 60–70 days from planting in spring until seed harvesting, even at low temperatures. Autumn-planted varieties need ~60 days once they have started growing in spring. Once the seed is ripe, the plants are cut, bundled and stood to dry (if you do not have a mechanical harvester!).

CULTIVATION

Could be grown in a small area. Is hardy and adaptable to a wide range of soil types and temperatures.

Location: Prefers full sun; does not grow well in shade. Also grows better with some protection from wind as the stems can break/bend (lodging), which makes harvesting difficult.

Temperature: Depending on variety they can grow from semi-tropical to almost arctic conditions. Grow in soils that are too cold to grow rye or wheat. Will grow from the Ukraine down to latitudes 10° north or south of the equator. Is grown from Norway, to Africa, to India. However, does not do well in the humid tropics. Often grown as a winter crop in hotter regions.

Soil/water/nutrients: Grows best in lighter soil with a neutral to slightly acidic pH, though can tolerate a pH range from 4.5 to 8.3; however, may suffer from aluminium toxicity in very acidic soils. Does not tolerate waterlogging well, but likes some moisture. Will grow on nutrient-poor soils, so is often the chosen crop in regions that have difficulties growing wheat. Indeed, growing barley on nutrient-rich soils can lead to more disease problems, particularly in soils rich in nitrogen.

Pot culture: Could be grown in a pot, perhaps with other grain types. Interesting for children to see the different cereal types and to watch their rapid growth.

Propagation: Fresh seed should give excellent rates of germination: ~90%. Germination occurs in 2–5 days in warm, moist soil, perhaps longer in cooler weather.

Planting: Some varieties have been selected to be planted in autumn, to grow through the winter to produce a spring crop; others to be planted in spring for the more traditional autumn crop. Because they can be planted at different times of year, and have a short growing cycle, they are often fitted in between other agricultural crops. The seed is usually sown *in situ*, scattered thinly in drills at ~2 cm depth, in rows ~20 cm apart.

Pests and diseases: Like most of the cereals, they are vulnerable to a number of diseases when planted as large monocultures. On a small scale, these problems are far less likely, or if they do occur, are less likely to be serious. However, potential problems include a virus (transmitted by aphids) that can damage the seeds. Many fungal diseases, including rusts, are the main problem, particularly in warm, humid regions; however, resistant varieties have been developed. Plant bugs and aphids can attack plants, but usually do not seriously damage plants.

Hyssopus officinalis
Hyssop
LAMIACEAE (LABIATAE)
Relatives: mint, rosemary, lemon balm, sage, thyme

The *Hyssopus* genus consists of about ten shrubby species, and is a member of the Labiatae family, which also contains many well-known popular culinary herbs. Hyssop, which originates from regions around the eastern Mediterranean into Central Asia, has a long history of usage as a culinary herb, for its medicinal properties, but also for its pleasing aromatic qualities. It was popular with the Greeks, with its Greek name 'esob' meaning 'holy herb', and was used for various purposes in temples. The Egyptians valued this species medicinally, associating it with cleansing of disease. In the Bible, it is likely to be the herb referred to 'Purge me with Hyssop, and I shall be clean'. Its species name, as with other '*officinalis*' species, was because it was a standard pharmaceutical product. It was often used as a strewing herb, scattered on floors to release its fragrance when walked upon. The plant was taken to other parts of Europe and Asia, and from there, much later, to North America, where it has become naturalised in places. It used to be included in most cottage gardens in England, though is now much less widely grown. It fits well into a herb garden, and can be grown as a low aromatic hedge, it is fully cold hardy, and its leaves, young stems and flowers can be used both as a flavouring and medicinally. Several unrelated species are sometimes incorrectly called hyssop: hedge hyssop (*Gratiola officinalis*), a possibly poisonous plant and a member of the Scrophulariaceae family; and giant hyssop, Mexican hyssop and anise hyssop, all from the unrelated *Agastache* genus.

DESCRIPTION

A fragrant, erect, bushy, short-lived perennial shrub, growing from 0.4–0.8 m tall, with about the same spread. Has the distinctive square stems of many members of this family. Tends to be grown as a short-lived perennial.

Leaves: Long (2–5 cm), narrow, mid green. Are strongly aromatic when lightly touched. Are borne opposite, and in alternate pairs up the square stem. Are virtually evergreen, though can lose their leaves in very cold winters or in adverse climatic conditions.

Flowers: Pretty, numerous, are usually a blue-purple colour, but there are also pink- and white-flowered varieties. Those with blue flowers are more commonly used medicinally due to their greater essential-oil content. Flowers are two-lipped and tubular, 1–2 cm in diameter, and have both male and female parts. Are borne on the apices of erect flower spikes, in whorls, from mid summer to autumn. Can be self-fertile. Bees love the flowers, and they are visited by butterflies and hoverflies.

Harvest/storage: The leaves and young stems of hyssop are usually commercially, harvested just as the flowers open, but they can be harvested before. However, if left till after flowering, the texture and flavour of the leaves deteriorate. For drying, harvest leaves on a dry day. They dry easily, and can be kept for several months, but do lose much of their fragrance and flavour. Store in a dark, cool, airtight container.

CULTIVATION

Location: Prefers a site in full sun, and in a fairly sheltered spot. Can be grown near the coast.

Temperature: Can grow in a range of climates from cool-temperate to subtropical. Is frost hardy once established, and can tolerate temperatures down to ~–20°C.

Soil/water/nutrients: Needs a free-draining soil and does better in lighter sandy soils or loams. Can grow in a range of soil pH conditions, from slightly acid to limestone or chalk soils: pH 6.0–7.5. Will grow in thin soils and is fairly drought hardy once established. Not too nutrient hungry, though will grow better if organic matter is incorporated into the soil.

Pot culture: Could be grown in containers near the house where their aromatic foliage can be appreciated. Perhaps plant with contrasting foliage herbs such as fennel or dill.

Planting/propagation: *Seed:* Can be grown from seed. Although germination is quick, seedling growth is slow, so the seed is best sown inside in trays, and given some heat and regular moisture. They can then be easily kept weed free until seedlings are large enough to plant out by autumn, or by the following spring in colder areas. Sow seed in early spring in warm, freely draining compost or soil. *Cuttings:* Cuttings from new basal growth, 6–9 cm long, can be taken in late spring, preferably with a heel. The lower leaves are removed, and the cutting is inserted into gritty compost to root. Give cuttings light shade until established. Cuttings usually root well. The roots of mature plants can be divided in spring, with plantlets established in pots before planting in their final positions. Space plants at ~20–30 cm apart for a hedge, or wider apart in the herb

Food

The leaves and young stems are used to flavour savoury recipes, such as soups, pies, bean dishes and stews, but also, sparingly, in fruit salads. Can be added to green salads. It has a refreshing mint-like, but sharp to slightly bitter taste, and is excellent as a garnish with greasy meats and other foods. Can be added to stuffing and sauces. The leaves have a marked flavour; they should be used with restraint so that they do not dominate. The flowers are edible, and make an attractive garnish. Dried leaves are said to be significantly inferior in flavour, but are used to make a tea. The essential oil is used in liqueurs.

Nutrition/medicinal

Historically, leaves from hyssop were used to treat coughs, sore throats and other chest complaints, acting to expel phlegm, but also to treat jaundice. It is believed to relax peripheral blood vessels and can, thus, promote sweating. The leaves have been used as a poultice on cuts, bruises and wounds. Plants have antiseptic and antibacterial properties. Hyssop extracts have antiviral properties, and to exhibit strong anti-HIV activity. Studies have shown that hyssop inhibits the digestion of complex carbohydrates, but not of simple sugars, and so could be a useful supplemental food in hyperglycaemia.

The plant contains antioxidant flavonoids and tannins, a bitter substance called marrubin, and several phenols, particularly carnosol. The essential oil contains cineol, pinene, plus several monoterpene derivatives. The essential oil is extracted by steam distillation, and is used to relieve anxiety, mental exhaustion and depression, and to increase alertness. Varieties with blue flowers produce more oil (0.5–1%) than pink- or white-flowered varieties. Many of the compounds hyssop contains are similar to those found in rosemary and sage. **Warning:** Like all essential oils, internal consumption should be undertaken with great caution: in larger quantities, this oil can cause convulsions. The leaves or flowers should not be consumed during pregnancy: it is said they can induce contractions.

Ornamental

Often grown as an ornamental, and as a low, aromatic hedge. Would make a fabulous herbal hedge mixed with lavender and rosemary. Its attractive flowers attract the bees. A popular plant in the herb garden.

Other uses

Its essential oil is used in several perfumes. The dried leaves are used in potpourri.

Lablab purpureus (syn. *Dolichos lablab*)
Hyacinth bean (lablab bean, Egyptian bean, Tonga bean)
FABACEAE (FORMERLY LEGUMINOSAE)
Relatives: peas, lentils, Phaseolus bean species, lupins

Its origins are unknown, but hyacinth bean probably originated in the tropical parts of Africa. It needs a warm summer to grow well; it is now cultivated pan-tropically, as well as in subtropical and warm-temperate regions. A relative of peas, beans and lentils, this bean is from a different genus, and it looks somewhat like an ornamental runner bean. It has a long history of cultivation and usage in many parts of North Africa, and many varieties exist. In North Africa and in parts of Asia, this species is cultivated and utilised for its edible flowers, leaves, young seeds and pods. In other regions, such as the United States, it is usually grown as a fast-growing ornamental climbing species, often as an annual, for its fragrant mauve flowers and attractive foliage. In Australia, in particular, it is being trialled and assessed as a potential green manure and forage crop. It is quite drought tolerant and produces abundant foliage that contains good amounts of nitrogen, making it a good animal feed. The hyacinth bean is easy to grow in the right location, and provides fragrance, colour, shade and food.

DESCRIPTION

Although it can be grown as a perennial in warmer climates, it is often grown as an annual elsewhere. A fast-growing, vigorous climbing plant with tendrils, it reaches heights of 0.8 m (but more often 2–3.5 m) depending on variety, location, etc. Stems are a purplish colour.

Leaves: Deep greeny-purple with attractive veination. Leaves are compound, in threes, each 7–15 cm in length, and each with an oval to cordate shape. They are smooth above, but lightly downy below.

Flowers: Many, small clusters of attractive, rose to mauve to purple, pea-like flowers, from leaf axils. Have a rich and pleasant aroma; are borne from mid to late summer, or longer if the weather remains warm. Flowers have both male and female parts. Flowers are recommended for attracting bees, butterflies, other insects and hummingbirds.

Pods/seeds: The flat, shiny purple pods ripen in autumn, so adequate time is needed for these to mature before any early-autumn cold weather arrives. Are ~10–15 cm long, with pointed tips, and contain 2–8 oval seeds, which can be white, cream, red, brown or black, depending on variety, and are sometimes mottled. They all have a conspicuous white hilum.

Harvest/storage: Needs only 70–120 days before the pods and seeds are ready to harvest. Young pods and beans can be picked before this time. Flowers and young leaves can be gathered as needed.

Roots: Forms a symbiotic relationship with nitrogen-fixing bacteria, which form nodules on the roots. This enables plants to grow in poor-nutrient soils, as nitrogen is commonly the rate-limiting nutrient; in return, the bacteria receives protection and sugars from its host. Has deep roots that are said to extract moisture from ~2 m depth.

CULTIVATION

Location: Grows best in full sun or in very light shade, in a sheltered spot. The older, more traditional varieties only flower and fruit in response to shorter day lengths; however, many modern varieties have been selected to flower in longer days, making them suitable for growth in more temperate latitudes. Choose varieties that either respond to longer day length or are day-length neutral. 'Highworth' is a short-day variety; 'Rongai' and 'Endurance' are longer day types.

Temperature: Prefers warm-temperate to tropical climates, though can be grown in more temperate climates if grown as an annual and sited in a warm, sheltered site, or grown under glass. Prefers daily temperatures of 18–30°C, but will tolerate temperatures down to ~4°C. Established plants may even be able to tolerate light frosts, as they are more cold hardy than some other tropical legumes (e.g. cowpea).

Soil/water/nutrients: Can grow in a range of soils, including those that are relatively deficient in nutrients; however, growth is improved if soils contain good amounts of organic matter, plus a little extra sulphur and phosphorus. Will grow in lighter sandy soils, but also in quite heavy clays, as long as they do not become waterlogged for extended periods.

Grows best with regular moisture, though, once established, is quite drought tolerant. It may, however, lose its leaves in longer periods of drought. Grows best at slightly acidic to neutral soils, pH 5.2–6.8. Plants are not tolerant of saline soils, which rapidly kill the foliage.

Pot culture: Could grow this species in boxes or containers if short of garden space, and if living in a temperate region that only has a short, warm summer. The pot plant can then be given extra warmth to extend the season. Give good-quality soil or compost, but not too much fertiliser. Water now and then, but not too often. Makes a tremendous ornamental show on a deck or by the house; use a trellis or stake plants to support them.

Planting/propagation: *Seed:* Soaking the seeds for ~4 hours before sowing speeds up and increases the germination rate. Sow the largish seeds in 3–8 cm of moist, warm compost in trays, or *in situ*, and give light shade. Takes 2–4 weeks to germinate, and needs temperatures over 20°C, so are best sown inside in colder regions to extend the growing season. Prick-out and grow-on seedlings before planting out at ~30 cm apart when all danger of frost has passed and the soil has begun to warm. The plants should be sited near to a fence or a sturdy structure they can climb up. Can be planted in groups, like runner beans, and grown up long sticks arranged as a wigwam or in rows. In warmer climates, and if the seeds are not harvested at the end of the season, volunteer plants readily form the following year. Commercially, it may be interplanted with maize.

Pests and diseases: Very few problems; occasionally get a few aphids and Japanese beetles may nibble the leaves.

uses

Food

Young, fresh pods and beans can be lightly cooked and eaten like runner beans, or other fresh beans, and make a sweet, tender vegetable. Use in the same range of dishes as fresh peas and beans. The young fresh beans are said to be excellent lightly stir-fried, and eaten simply with a little black pepper and a knob of butter.

The dried beans should be cooked before eating because the raw beans contain toxic compounds (see Warning below). Cooked, they are used in the same way as other beans, in curries, stews, soups, but also make good-quality tofu or can be fermented into tempeh, in the same way as soybeans. The beans can be sprouted, and the shoots eaten in salads and sandwiches. The leaves are said to be edible, but need to be cooked. The flowers can be added to dishes or used as a garnish.

Nutrition/medicinal

The leaves have good amounts of proteins, and unlike many legumes, do not contain high tannin levels. The seeds contain lots of protein, ~20%, with good amounts of the amino acids aspartic and glutamic acids, leucine and lysine. Have good quantities of fibre (~8%), and of the vitamins A, B and C, though the latter are reduced after cooking. Good amounts of manganese, calcium, copper, phosphorus, potassium, selenium and iron. The pod contains good amounts of vitamin A.

Historically, the plant has been used to counteract various poisons, to treat digestive ailments and to reduce blood sugar levels. It is said to prolong blood coagulation time, and so lessens the formation of clots.

The juice from the pods has been used to treat ear and throat inflammations. The dried, mature seeds have been used to expel internal parasites as an aphrodisiac, as an astringent, to reduce vomiting and diarrhoea, and to lessen alcohol intoxication. The bean contains kievitone, a breast-cancer-fighting compound. **Warning:** Some report that the mature beans are poisonous, containing dangerous levels of cyanogenic glucosides, which need repeated washings, plus cooking, to remove. Others claim they are not at all toxic.

Recent studies report that it is only toxic if large amounts of uncooked or unrinsed mature beans are eaten. They seem to be fine eaten when young, but it is probably prudent to thoroughly cook mature beans, discarding water they have been soaked and cooked in before adding them to other ingredients (e.g. stew). Initially boil the beans for 10 minutes at a high temperature, and then rinse them several times to remove any toxins.

Ornamental

Makes a terrific, ornamental, quick-growing vine; can be used to form a living, summer shade plant over an arbour, trellis or deck. Has abundant pretty, fragrant blossoms, attractive green to purple foliage, plus eye-catching purple pods. Can be grown as an effective, short-term groundcover.

Other uses

These relatively fast-growing plants, with their ability to fix nitrogen, make them a good green manure species. The leaves and stems are often used as food for livestock.

Lactuca sativa
Lettuce
ASTERACEAE (COMPOSITAE)

Lactuca sativa asparagina (syn. *L. s. augustana*, *L. s. angustata*): celtuce
Relatives: chicory, endives, dandelions, sunflower, globe artichoke

The original wild lettuce is *Lactuca serriola*, a plant still found growing wild in Europe and Asia; it has prickles and a bitter, acrid taste. It has been used more as a narcotic than as a vegetable for thousands of years and there is evidence that the Egyptians were eating wild lettuce ~4500 years ago. Both the Egyptians and Romans ate *L. serriola* and *L. virosa* to induce sleep and relaxation. It was eaten to stimulate the appetite as well as being associated with male fertility. From the wild species, the Romans may have been the first to select less bitter varieties, from which a multitude of lettuce varieties has developed. Everyone is familiar with lettuce; the ubiquitous salad ingredient, which, unfortunately, is often served limp and unimaginatively. However, crisp, fresh lettuce, straight from the garden, is something else, and does not have to be restricted to salads. It is very quick and easy to grow, taking up very little space, and grows best in cooler weather. With home-grown lettuce, you can be sure that it does not contain unwanted chemicals or residues, which, unfortunately, some commercially produced lettuces do.

DESCRIPTION

An annual (or sometimes a biennial), with many leaves growing from a basal crown. Its central short stem is white and contains a white latex-like fluid. The shape of the lettuce head varies with variety.

Leaves: Oval to rounded, usually with more or less wavy margins. Thin, varying in colour from almost white, to yellow, to dark green, with many varieties having red- to bronze-coloured leaves. Texture varies from soft and floppy, to crisp and upright, depending on variety. Leaf frilliness or waviness varies hugely, with many of the loose-leaved lettuces having particularly attractive leaves. There are literally hundreds of varieties, but these can be divided into three main types: head lettuces, leaf lettuces and stem lettuces.

The head lettuces are subdivided into the crisp, tight-headed cabbage heads (e.g. icebergs, most popular in the United States); and the softer, somewhat looser tight-headed butterheads (e.g. 'Bibbs', 'Buttercrunch') popular in Europe. These, as their name suggests, form a tighter head that is more cabbage-like. 'Grenoble' is a large, red-tinged iceberg type. Types such as 'Buttercrunch' have no bitterness and have dark green outer leaves with yellow-green centres. 'Perella Rougette Montpellier', an Italian looser headed type, is tinged attractively deep red. 'Tom Thumb' is a miniature English variety, handy for growing in pots or if very short of space.

The leaf lettuces that have leaves that are open and spreading, are subdivided into the taller, more oval-leaved crisp Cos or romaine lettuces (e.g. 'Paris Island Cos'); and the loose-leaved, softer non-headed varieties (e.g. 'Lollo Roso', 'Red Sails', 'Black-seeded Simpson'). 'Freckles' is an Australian Cos type, with its leaves speckled maroon. An attractive but also flavoursome lettuce is 'Rouge d'Hiver', which originates from Europe and has leaves that range in colour from green, to deep red, to bronze. 'Drunken Woman Fringed Head', an old Italian variety, has ornamental, curly, red-tinged leaves. 'Canasta' is another ornamental lettuce, originally from Bavaria, that has bright green leaves tinged red. 'Lolita' is a frilly leafed type with deep-red-coloured leaves.

The stem or celtuce (Chinese lettuce, asparagus lettuce) has large, white, crisp stems and is used more for these than for its leaves. It is pale in colour, and forms a long, thin, compact head (see below).

Flowers: Lettuces can bolt in too much heat, and then they form a flower stalk with a small, bright yellow flowerhead that is similar in appearance to a dandelion. Flowerheads contain both male and female flowers, and can be self-fertile. Pollination is by bees and insects, but they can also set seed without a pollinator.

Seeds: Botanically, they are small fruits or achenes. Fine, flat, can be pale and white (and need light to germinate) or dark brown/black. Because they are small, they are tricky to sow thinly. Cos has somewhat larger seeds. Purchased seed is often pelleted for easier sowing and handling.

Harvest/storage: Lettuces take ~6–12 weeks from seed sowing to harvest, depending on growing conditions and variety: the loose-leaved types tend to be the quickest. Harvest before fully mature, and certainly before the formation of a flower stalk. If the latter occurs, then the leaves become bitter and tough. The plants are best cut in the morning, while still crisp from taking up moisture during the night. If the roots are left in the soil, they often resprout to form a second smaller crop

Food

Fresh, crisp lettuce, with a drizzle of olive oil and balsamic vinegar is delicious. A salad with a mix of lettuce varieties can work well. If adding other salad leaves, ensure these do not overwhelm the delicate flavour of lettuce. Older lettuce leaves can be stir-fried, and are very tasty cooked in this way with seafood and other vegetables, but should only be briefly cooked. Chinese stem-lettuce is often lightly steamed or stir-fried, and is popular in Asian cuisine. It is delicious with a little soy sauce and sesame oil. An edible oil has been extracted from the larger Cos lettuce seeds.

Nutrition/medicinal

Nutritional value varies with lettuce type. As with most vegetables and fruits, those lettuces with a bitter flavour and with more colour also contain more nutrients and antioxidants. For these (e.g. butterhead and red-leaved types), the leaves are rich in vitamins A and K, plus many other phytonutrients; they also contain good levels of folate and some manganese, potassium and iron. Unfortunately, the paler lettuces (e.g. icebergs) are very poor in nutrients. Lettuces contain a modest amount of fibre, and most of this is within the stems; therefore, the Chinese lettuce has the greatest quantities of this. **Warning:** Wild lettuce contains a compound that is similar to opium (lactucarium) and has opiate properties, but is not addictive like opium. However, in excess, it has caused death. Historically, the white latex-like substance from the stem was dried and smoked, though other experiments have definitely not had pleasant outcomes (see the Bibliography).

Ornamental

Not immediately thought of as an ornamental; however, they are often grown as such, with a row or group of them sited between colourful annuals. The different varieties, with leaf colours ranging from bronze, to red, to yellow, to green, make a satisfying display. They take up little room, and can be fitted into the smallest garden.

Other uses

The white juice has been used to treat warts.

(particularly Cos-type lettuces). Wash harvested lettuce briefly and store in a polythene bag in the fridge where it will store well for several days. It keeps longer if the leaves are not separated or cut in any way. Avoid placing lettuces with fruits as these often produce ethylene, which induces the lettuce to age more rapidly.

Roots: Fairly fine and shallow, so take care with mechanical cultivation. Mulch around plants to help retain moisture and add nutrients, but this can also harbour pests such as slugs.

CULTIVATION

Easy.

Location: In full sun in cool-temperate regions if grown in spring or autumn, but needs some shade during the summer in colder climates and needs year-round shade in hot climates. A site that gets some morning or evening sun, but is shaded the rest of the day, is ideal. Bright sun scorches the leaves of some varieties, leading to areas of brown tissue. Some gardeners blanch their lettuces to make them whiter and to reduce any bitterness of the leaves, but most modern varieties have been selected to not be bitter.

Temperature: Almost without exception, most varieties prefer cooler summers. Too much heat makes the leaves bitter and induces the plant to bolt. However, 'Australian Yellow-leaf' is an exception and is more heat tolerant than most other varieties. As its name suggests, it has eye-catching yellow leaves, it grows larger than many varieties and is more bolt resistant. For most varieties, if the weather is likely to be hot, grow lettuce as a spring or autumn crop as usual, but plant summer crops in a shaded area. The tight-headed crisp, iceberg varieties, in particular, need cooler conditions; if the temperature becomes too hot they do not form properly. For this reason, bolt-prone varieties are sown/planted as early in the year as possible, or late in the year (after the summer heat). If heat becomes an issue, cover the plants with cloth or brush to shade them. The loose-leaved, non-headed varieties are less fussy about temperature. Lettuce could be grown as a winter crop outside in warmer climates. If acclimatised, they should survive a light frost.

Soil/water/nutrients: Not too fussy about soil type or pH, and will grow in most soils as long as they are not too acidic: pH 6–7. Will grow in sandy soils, but also fairly heavy soils, though the ideal is a good loam with plenty of organic matter. Lettuces do need regular moisture, but do not tolerate waterlogging. Generally they need more moisture than the average rainfall can supply. Time watering for the evening or early morning, and try not to leave too much water on the leaves in bright sunshine, as these easily scorch.

Pot culture: Ideal and decorative for pot culture if short of space. Because they come is so many varieties and shapes, they make an interesting display among/with other pot plants, or even on their own, particularly many of the colourful, frilly leafed varieties.

Planting/propagation: The seed is best sown fresh: stored seed rapidly loses its viability. The seed is fine and is best mixed with a little fine sand to make sowing easier. Sow thinly as germination is usually good, in ~6–10 days. Sow more thinly than one would think as overcrowding of seedlings is a common error. Indeed, the other problem is too many lettuces ready to eat at the same time. The ideal is a few seedlings at about 3-week intervals. Sow at ~0.5 cm depth and cover with very fine soil; note that some varieties (e.g. many of those with white seeds) need light to germinate, and

Food

The outer flesh of the root is softer and sweeter; its harder inner core is more starch-rich. The root is said to have a tangy taste that has overtones of butterscotch. The fresh roots are sometimes eaten fresh, but are more usually baked or roasted and eaten with other vegetables or meat. They are often dried, and then develop a sweeter, spicy, musky flavour; are often traditionally added to puddings and jams, or may be boiled in milk to make a sweet porridge. They are added to a sweet liqueur, or made into a beer, or the ground, dried root can be used to make a hot or cold beverage. A flour can be made from the dried root, and is used in baking. The leaves are sometimes eaten either fresh in salads or are lightly steamed. They have a strong aroma and taste (similar to cress) due to their glucosinolate content.

Nutrition/medicinal

For a root, they are unusually rich in proteins, which includes the essential amino acids lysine and arginine. The tubers contain good quantities of fibre, but are also rich in sugars, mostly as sucrose. They are very rich in iron (~16 mg/100 g) and iodine, and contain some calcium, zinc and selenium, with some vitamin C (~25 mg/100 g) and the B vitamins niacin and B6. The roots contain some linoleic, palmitic and oleic acids.

Historically, this plant has always been thought to increase fertility of both people and livestock, and has been used as an aphrodisiac, to influence hormonal levels and to stimulate the immune system. Recent research has shown that the roots and leaves do contain aromatic isothiocyanates that seem to act as prostaglandins and sterols. These compounds have been shown to reduce the incidence of cancers, such as breast and liver. Root extracts have been taken by menopausal women to relieve unpleasant symptoms. This species is often included in aphrodisiacs, and has been shown to increase spermatogenesis; however, it does not increase testosterone levels, as some reports claim.

The roots contain macamides: these compounds are similar to anandamides, which are known as 'bliss' compounds. Anandamides are neurotransmitters found naturally within the brain, and are sensitive to compounds found within cannabis. They are also important in the management of short-term memory and pain relief, as well as in the initial implantation of the embryo in the uterus.

Root extracts can relieve stress: in rats, these compounds can reduce or even eliminate the occurrence of stress-induced ulcers, reduce elevated corticosterone levels by reducing the weight of the adrenal glands (which occurs with stress), and even out plasma levels of free fatty acids produced by stress, which may help ease indigestion. Traditionally, the roots have been eaten to increase energy, endurance and stamina, and to promote mental clarity. They contain small amounts of alkaloids, saponins and tannins, but these do not seem to pose any health concerns.

Other uses

Its roots may secrete allelopathic compounds that deter the growth of other plants, including weeds, around it.

Lepidium sativum

Garden cress (pepper cress, pepperwort)

BRASSICACEAE

Relatives: watercress, landcress, mustard, Brussels sprouts, cabbage

Garden cress was gathered and eaten by the Egyptians and Persians and was enjoyed by the Greeks and Romans, who ate it in spicy salads and with bread. It is found growing wild from North Africa to the Himalayas, and is thought to be originally from western Asia, but then rapidly spread to Europe and other parts of Asia. It is now naturalised in numerous parts of Europe, the United Kingdom, as well as North America. It was popular in the Middle Ages, and was enjoyed by the nobility. Garden cress is a member of the *Lepidium* genus, of which there are ~150 members, though *L. sativum* is the usual species grown for its salad greens. Unlike watercress, it can be grown in ordinary soil. It can be grown until mature, and its leaves harvested; however, in Europe and the UK, it is usually consumed as young sprouts harvested from small tubs and is often then known then as 'mustard and cress'. There are several varieties of *L. sativum*, and these are produced year-round as a popular addition to salads. The three main subspecies of *L. sativum* are *latifolium*, *vulgare* and *crispum*. These have been listed according to their increasing drought tolerance, with *L. sativum crispum* being the most tolerant. *L. virginicum* (pepperweed) is a similar species, native to the US, which is not cultivated, but its leaves are sometimes gathered from the wild.

DESCRIPTION
Can grow to ~50 cm tall, and is a short-lived perennial, though is usually grown as an annual, and often as a short-lived, quick-crop-sprouting seed.

Leaves: Long, oval, with a grey-green colour. Often divided into three leaflets, with long leaf stalks. The variety 'Crinkled', as its name suggests, has crinkled, wavy-margined leaves, which have a sweet to spicy flavour.

Flowers: White or pinkish, small (~0.3 cm), in dense groups, with the largest group being apical on the flower stem. Below, they grow from the leaf axils. Four-petalled and simple, they are borne from spring until summer. Heat can initiate early flowering, though varieties such as 'Crinkled' are more resistant to bolting; once plants begin flowering, leaf growth virtually ceases and their flavour becomes impaired. They are popular with bees and other insects. Both male and female parts occur within the same flower, and flowers can be self-fertile.

Seeds: About ~0.3 cm long, similar to mustard seed. Tan or black in colour.

Harvest/storage: The young shoots of garden cress can be cut with their stalks. Or, plants can be left to mature, and then leaves harvested over several weeks, though older leaves are not as flavoursome. Fast growing: harvesting of leaves can start after only 3 weeks, with good yields.

Roots: Forms fairly deep, fibrous, spreading roots.

CULTIVATION
Very easy.

Location: It prefers a site in semi-shade, though can be grown in sun in cooler regions. Shade promotes the formation of larger leaves. It can even grow in quite dense shade and can be grown near the coast.

Temperature: It may continue growing outside through milder winters, if given some protection, e.g. a cloche. Also, consider pots of cress on a sunny window sill through the winter months.

Soil/water/nutrients: Does not need running water, but does grow better with regular moisture, which promotes larger leaves. Dry periods can initiate bolting. Can be grown in most soil types, as long as they are fairly rich in nutrients and consistently moist. Can be grown in somewhat acidic to somewhat alkaline conditions: pH 5.5–7.5.

Pot culture: Can be very easily grown in pots for winter or out-of-season use.

Planting/propagation: Garden cress grows well and easily from seed. For a crop that is grown to maturity, the seed can be broadcast or is more usually sown in rows, and then seedlings thinned to ~10 cm apart as they mature. Sow the small seeds at a shallow depth of ~0.5 cm. Germination takes 4–8 days, and germination rates are good, so sow seed thinly. Keep young plants moist. Garden cress grows quickly, and the younger leaves are

uses

Food
In Europe and the UK, the sprouted seedlings are the usual part eaten, often added to salads or used as a garnish with egg or potatoes, and sometimes in sandwiches. They have a pleasant, mild, peppery flavour. Leaves from older plants can be mixed with cottage cheese and fruit to make a delightful, tasty, light salad, or, can be added to soups, stews, etc. Some eat the leaves with bread and butter, lemon, vinegar or sugar. The root can be eaten and has a radish-like flavour, but is a bit tough.

Nutrition/medicinal
Garden cress is packed full of minerals, and is rich in iodine, iron, calcium, sulphur, potassium and manganese. Also contains very good quantities of beta carotene (vitamin A), as well as vitamin C. It is very rich in vitamin K. Contains some fibre, protein and folate. As with other brassicas, much of its distinctive flavour is derived from isothiocyanates. These compounds are produced from other precursor compounds, glucosinolates, when the plant is injured. Research has shown that isothiocyanates may prevent cancers and heart disease. Indeed, compounds from cress have been shown to strongly inhibit the formation of liver, breast, lung and colon cancers, more so than most other brassicas. Historically, garden cress leaves were used as a source of nutrients (e.g. for vitamin C), to purify the blood, to stimulate the appetite and to eliminate internal parasites. It was burnt and used on insect bites to reduce swelling. The seeds were regarded as an aphrodisiac. Garden cress seedlings are very nutritious, with high levels of protein, and are rich in vitamins A, B and C, as well as several minerals. **Warning:** Some reports say that the seeds, eaten in quantity, can induce abortions.

Other uses
Historically, the water obtained from the mashed leaves was used as a hair conditioner and tonic, and was believed to prevent hair loss.

the best; therefore, sowing at regular intervals (about every 2–3 weeks) ensures a continual crop throughout most of the year. Can be sown outside from spring, after all risk of frost has passed, onwards into autumn, or later in warm-temperate or subtropical climates. Covering the plants with a cloche during winter keeps some growth going during colder weather. Minimise weed competition around plants, particularly when young. For sprouted seedlings, the seeds are best soaked in warm (not hot) water for a few hours before being scattered on blotting paper or a thin layer of sand to germinate with warmth and moisture. They are

best kept in a fairly dark place for the first couple of days or so after they have germinated to become etiolated, with long stems, before placing on a window sill for a further couple of days, to green-up before harvesting. If sown with mustard seeds, it should be noted that cress seeds can take 2–3 days longer to germinate, so are best started off first. The variety 'Moss Curled' is a popular sprouting variety. The young cotyledonous leaves (sprouts) can be eaten 4–6 days later. Seeds are best sown when fresh, but can be stored for 2–3 years if kept cool and dry.

Pests and diseases: Has few problems.

Levisticum officinale
Lovage
APIACEAE (UMBELIFERAE)

Levisticum scoticum: Scottish lovage (sea parsley)

Relatives: fennel, angelica, dill, parsley, carrot, celery

Lovage is a tall, perennial, aromatic herb. It belongs to the same family as many other aromatic herbs, plus vegetables such as carrot and celery. Its genus name is derived from the Latin 'ligusticus', which is the name of an Italian shoreline opposite Genoa where it was commonly found growing wild. Its growth, aroma and flavour are similar to those of celery, but are stronger. Originally native to southern Europe, it is now grown in many temperate areas of Europe. It is particularly popular in Germany, where it is known as the Maggi herb because of its similarity to this commercial flavouring. It is popular in France and in countries bordering the Mediterranean. It was a popular garden herb in English cottage gardens. It has a long history of usage, with both the Greeks and Romans, with the Romans particularly valuing it as a food flavouring. Later it was a popular medicinal plant in the Middle Ages. Later, still, it was used as a substitute for angelica in Britain and has been used in a wide range of foods and medicines, as well as to make a wine, flavour fish, and was used as a diuretic. It is quite easy to grow and, once established, will self-seed or can be easily divided. Quite a large species, only a few plants are generally needed, perhaps sited towards the back of the herb or veggie garden. An under-utilised species, virtually all parts of this plant can be used as a seasoning or vegetable.

DESCRIPTION
A hardy, tall perennial herb, which forms a long storage taproot. The whole plant, including the roots, has a strong celery-like aroma. The plant looks similar in appearance to angelica. The stems and leaves die back in winter, and sprout afresh in spring. It initially forms a rosette of basal leaves, and then forms flower stems at least 0.8–1.6 m tall. The stems have a few leaves, and are thick but hollow, becoming branched towards their apex, with these topped by umbels of tiny flowers.

Leaves: Mid to dark green, very similar in form to those of celery, and have a celery-like aroma when crushed. Are shiny and are deeply divided into more-

or-less three wedge-shaped leaflets, which have deeply toothed margins.

Flowers: Has numerous, small yellow-green flowers arranged in umbels that are borne in mid summer. However, removal of flower stems induces further leaf growth, if that is what is required. Flowers have both male and female parts, and can be self-fertile. Pollination is by small flying insects.

Seeds: Its tiny aromatic fruits (schizocarps), often incorrectly called seeds, consist of two carpels, each containing a single, small seed. The fruits are yellow-brown in colour, have an elliptical, crescent shape and three winged ribs.

pods are unlikely to mature before the cold weather sets in. Yields from plants are variable. The pods are picked when fully mature. Older varieties of this species may have pods that dehisce, with the pods drying and then springing open to release their seeds. These therefore need to be picked just before full maturity. Harvested pods are dried and then crushed to release their seeds, with pod fragments winnowed. Seeds are dried and stored in a dry, cool container.

Roots: The roots form a symbiotic relationship with nitrogen-fixing bacteria (*Rhizobium* spp.), with the plant able to receive extra nitrogen, and the bacteria gaining protection and sugars from the plant. Lupins form very dense clusters of root hairs, known as proteoid roots, particularly in humus-rich soil and when the plant is actively growing. These enormously increase the surface area for absorption of nutrients, and particularly benefit the absorption of slow-moving nutrients such as phosphate (but also calcium, magnesium, various micronutrients). Proteoid roots enable plants to grow much better than they would with normal root-hair development. The plant forms a short but penetrating taproot.

CULTIVATION

Location: Grows best in full sun. Plants do not seem to be affected by daylength, so can be grown and will flower and set seed in most latitudes. Can be grown at altitude or near the coast, and is fairly wind tolerant.

Temperature: Can grow in a wide range of temperatures, from cool temperate to the tropics, though needs a drier climate. Mature plants are said to be somewhat frost hardy, and will grow in temperate climates, but early, more severe autumn frosts can kill plants that are still forming and maturing pods.

Soil/water/nutrients: Not too fussy about soil type, and will grow in poorer nutrient soils. Prefers a lighter-textured soil. If adding fertiliser, plants may grow better with more phosphorus and potassium, but extra nitrogen

is wasted as this prevents or reduces the plants' symbiotic relationship with bacteria. The addition of sulphate (as gypsum) may increase the seed's sulphurous amino-acid methionine content (see Nutrition). Plants grow best with regular moisture, particularly while flowering and forming pods, though are, generally, quite drought hardy once established. Plants grow best in freely draining soil, and do not tolerate waterlogging or high humidity. They grow best at slightly acidic to neutral soils of pH 5.6–6.8.

Pot culture: Could be grown in pots if short of space, to make a long-lasting ornamental flower display and also an edible crop. Add leaf mould and organic matter to the compost to encourage beneficial bacterial and fungal associations. Water moderately.

Planting/propagation: *Seed:* The seeds can be soaked for ~24 hours to soften the seedcoats, before sowing either outside *in situ* or inside. Usually sown *in situ*, but can be started off in trays or pots, particularly in cooler regions to extend the long growing season they need. Cover with ~1–2 cm of fine soil, and keep warm, shaded and moist. The seed can be treated with fungicide, as loss of seed and young seedlings through fungal disease is high. The seed should be fully ripe for sowing. Germination takes 7–21 days, and weed competition should be curtailed around young plants. Growth is slow at first; plants are particularly susceptible to disease and pest attacks at this time. Space or thin plants to ~0.3 m apart.

Pests and diseases: Unfortunately, in its native area, this species is susceptible to various pests and diseases, so efforts are being made to select more resistant varieties. The fungus *Colletotrichum* is particularly damaging, causing anthracnose, which can attack stems and leaves of younger plants, as well as pods and flowers, also causing die-back and stem lesions. Efforts are made in indigenous regions to plant this species in disease-free soils. In addition, high humidity and wet soils increase the likelihood of infection. Various weevils can attack the roots and stems.

Lycopersicon lycopersicum (syn. *Solanum lycopersicum*)
Tomato
SOLANACEAE

Solanum uporo: cannibal's tomato

Relatives: aubergine, potato, tamarillo, aubergine, peppers, deadly nightshade

Originally from South to Central America, possibly the Andes region, Chile, Ecuador, Bolivia through to Mexico, this vegetable, though botanically a fruit, is known by all. It is not certain if the tomato was cultivated by the indigenous populations, but the Spanish took it back to Europe, the Caribbean and to Asia (via the Philippines). Its popularity rapidly spread across the Mediterranean regions, where it suited the climate, and was soon widely adopted particularly in Italy. The name tomato is thought to be derived from the Spanish 'tomate', which was derived from the Aztec, 'xitomatl', meaning 'plump fruit'.

Although a frost-sensitive plant, as all gardeners know, the tomato can be grown in a sunny spot, even in cold-temperate regions (some varieties have been grown in Siberia), and can produce a fresh, nutritious, juicy, sweet crop for several weeks. Can be grown in the smallest garden, or in pots on a window sill or deck. There are thousands of varieties of tomatoes, from small bushy plants producing small, sweet cherry tomatoes, to larger commercial types that have thicker skins and often less flavour, to the oval Italian plum tomatoes that so popular canned and puréed, and the large beefsteak tomatoes, ideal for grilling and barbecues. Tomatoes are said to be top of the world's most favourite-vegetable list: even children love them. Consider planting a few different types to enjoy their multitude of uses, colours, shapes and flavours.

DESCRIPTION

A bushy, fast-growing, short-lived perennial, though usually grown as an annual. Can grow from ~0.5 m to more than 2 m tall, depending on variety. If untrained, it forms a bushy plant with many laterals and sublaterals. Its weak stem means that it is often sprawling, lying on the ground if not supported. The many tomato varieties can be divided into two types: those that are smaller, more bushy, need little to no staking, and produce most of their fruits within a shorter harvesting period; and taller, climbing tomatoes, which do need staking, but produce greater yields of fruits over a longer period.

Leaves: Dark green, deeply lobed, 10–25 cm long, with leaves larger at the base of the plant and on the main stem. Are composed of 5–9 long, oval leaflets that have irregularly toothed margins. Are covered with hairs

uses

Food
Fresh in salads; as a garnish; or added to a myriad of Mediterranean-style recipes; sun-dried; puréed; made into sauces for pastas, pizzas, etc.; gorgeous soups, both hot and cold; sandwiches, served with cheese and pickles; made into a tasty healthy juice; added to pies and stews; ketchup; combined with vodka and spices to make a bloody Mary; delicious dribbled with olive oil, black pepper and garlic and then grilled: great for breakfast on wholemeal toast with avocado. Green and red tomatoes make wonderful chutneys.

Nutrition/medicinal
Tomato fruits are wonderfully rich in carotenoids (vitamin A: ~900--1300 I.U.), as beta-carotene, lycopene, lutein and zeaxanthin: these confer cardioprotective and chemopreventive activities. They are particularly rich in lycopene (3 mg/100 g of fresh tomato), though yellow tomatoes contain less. Also contain good quantities of vitamin C (15--40 mg/100 g), and some vitamin K. Tomatoes have good amounts of potassium and little or no sodium. They have a low GI, contain virtually no fat and have a little protein.

Lycopene gives tomatoes their wonderful red colour, and is a very powerful antioxidant: there is strong evidence of it treating and preventing several forms of cancer. Several studies report that lycopene reduces the occurrence and impact of existing prostate cancers, possibly by 30--40%. There is also evidence that it may reduce the incidence of ovarian cancers. Its antioxidant properties reduce damage caused by UV light to the skin, i.e. sunburn, particularly those with delicate skins. It has been recommended that those who work regularly in the sun include more lycopene-rich foods in their diet: studies have found reductions in UV damage of between 20--40%. Unlike many other vitamins and antioxidants, its efficacy actually increases with cooking and processing, i.e. pureed, as a sauce or as sundried tomatoes, where their flavours are intensified; plus the addition of olive oil further promotes its absorption.

In these concentrated forms, tomatoes have greater amounts of B vitamins, particularly niacin, thiamine and riboflavin, and become richer in vitamin K. Levels of minerals too are wonderfully enriched, with greater levels of manganese, potassium, copper, phosphorus, iron and magnesium.

Tomatoes can also reduce the development of several age-related diseases, reduce cardiovascular disease and have anti-inflammatory properties. **Warning:** All other parts of the tomato plant (i.e. leaves, roots) are poisonous. Although grafting is relatively easy amongst the Solanaceae family, care is needed as members of this family contain powerful alkaloids, which could be passed into the grafted fruit, e.g. potatoes have poisonous fruits, as does deadly nightshade.

Ornamental
Tomatoes are good planted in the flower bed amongst other species: this reduces the pest-and-disease risk, adds interest and saves space.

Other uses
The natural insecticide they contain is sometimes utilised by gardeners as an organic spray, by mashing up and liquidising the older leaves.

(trichomes) that, when broken, release their distinctive tomato-plant pungency and a liquid that repels predators.

Flowers: Are 1–2 cm wide, with five, yellow, pointed petals, bright yellow stamens and a yellow calyx. They form in clusters of 3–12 on short spurs (trusses) immediately off the main stem initially, and then off lateral stems, and not from the leaf axils. The trusses form from the base of the plant upwards. Borne from mid summer through to late autumn, unless grown under glass with artificial lighting to produce crops almost year round. *Pollination:* Flowers are usually bisexual and can be self-fertile or fertilise other flowers on the same plant, but the pollen does need to be transferred. For this reason, they need wind, insects or manual transfer of pollen from the male stamens to the female stigma. Therefore, pollination can be a problem in glasshouses, where there is little wind and no insects. Unlike most flowers, the pollen is produced within the stamens, rather than at the tips, and needs to be vibrated by a bee's proboscis or by wind to release it. Wilder or older varieties are more likely to need cross pollination between plants.

Fruit/seeds: A rounded berry, usually in small clusters along longish stalks, known as a truss. They vary in size enormously depending on variety, from small, tasty, sweet cherry tomatoes (~2 cm diameter) to large beefsteak tomatoes (~12 cm diameter), with many shapes and sizes in between. Are usually red, but can get yellow-, orange- or purple-skinned varieties, and even some that are streaked in several colours. Some purplish Roma Italian plum varieties look more like tamarillos or eggplants. Are formed of two halves, and have a smooth, waxy, shiny skin. Beneath the skin is a layer of edible, juicy, succulent flesh; inside which is a central, pulpy region containing many small, edible seeds, though these are not digested and pass straight through the gut. Indeed, this has evolved as a very successful means of vegetative spread.

Seed companies now sell a wide range of tomato varieties, including many of the heirloom types, which although they may not produce as large yields or such regular-shaped fruits, are often much tastier. A few to look out for are the black tomatoes, from regions around the Black Sea. These have dark red to almost black flesh around the seeds, and have a rich, complex flavour (e.g. 'Black Krim', 'Black from Tula'). A very sweet, tasty popular Amish heirloom tomato is 'Brandywine Pink'. Non-red tomatoes include the 'Delicious', which although it remains green when ripe, does become fairly sweet; 'Gold Nugget', which yields cherry-sized sweet bright golden-coloured fruits; 'Yellow Pear', which produces pear-shaped mild-flavoured yellow fruits; and 'White Cherry' has pale yellow cherry fruits when ripe.

Harvest/storage: Takes 75–85 days from seed sowing to harvest of most tomato varieties. Climbing varieties of tomatoes can be picked over a period of weeks, often up to the first frosts, which then kill the plant. Can be picked when not quite ripe (turning from green to red), and placed in a sunny spot to ripen or with other ripening fruits (as the ethylene gas these emit helps ripen the tomatoes). Most commercial tomatoes are picked unripe to extend storage times. However, fully vine-ripened fruits are considered to have a better, sweeter flavour. For the best taste, do

not store them in a fridge, and eat them slightly warm. Even better, eat them when they are just freshly picked. Tomatoes do not store for very long, though they can be dried, bottled, puréed, juiced or canned.

Roots: They have relatively shallow roots and are susceptible to drought and to damage by strong winds. Adventitious roots readily form where the stem touches the soil.

CULTIVATION

Need cosseting to get the best fruits, though gardeners all over the world consider the labour well worth the rewards.

Location: Tomato plants need to be grown in a sheltered, warm, sunny location.

Temperature: The tomato is a subtropical plant and needs warm/hot, sunny days to grow and fruit well. Young plants should only be planted out once all risk of cold has passed. Plants are not at all frost hardy. However, they need a relatively long growing season, so gardeners in cooler regions start seedlings off inside early in the year to 'extend' the growing period. Some gardeners then continue growing the tomatoes inside under glass or in a conservatory during the summer to ensure they receive adequate heat.

Soil/water/nutrients: Grow best in a organic-matter-rich loam, or a sandy loam. If the soil has a significant clay component, mix in gypsum and organic matter, and

Food

The younger leaves can be added to drinks to give a lemony flavour. A few can be finely chopped and added to fruit or green salads, though their flavour is fairly strong, so needs discretion. Can be added with other herbs, such as rosemary, thyme and the mints to a wide range of dishes; lightly cooked, its flavour blends in with the other herbs.

Can also be added to ice-creams, and is used with lemons and limes to increase their citrus flavour in foods. Can be used as a substitute for lemongrass. The dried leaves retain their scent, and it makes a good lemon-flavoured tea, which can be drunk hot or iced.

Nutrition/medicinal

The leaves contain ~0.1% essential oil, of which most is citronella, with some caryophyllene, neral, geranial, citronellol and geraniol. Historically, the leaves have been used to treat stomach and digestive problems as well as stress and anxiety. Balm has been shown experimentally to induce relaxation, relieve stress and to induce regeneration in humans. The essential oil, applied as aromatherapy, has been found to be effective in relieving agitation in people with severe dementia, including those with Alzheimer's disease, and to be clinically safe and improve their quality of life. Out of many plants tested, balm has shown a significant ability to enhance or restore mental functions, including memory.

It has been also shown to have antibacterial properties against several species, some antifungal properties and has powerful antioxidant properties. Compounds within it, particularly citrol, have anti-tumour properties. Extracts from the leaves have been shown to be effective in topically controlling the *Herpes simplex* virus, and it has been used to treat both genital and oral infections. Some studies claim this is due to its rosmarinic acid content.

In animal studies, the leaves affect the immune system, in both humoral and cellular responses. Compounds within the leaves have potent anti-HIV-1 activity. On a lighter note, Mrs Grieves (*A Modern Herbal*) reports that 'John Hussey, of Sydenham, who lived to the age of 116, breakfasted for fifty years on Balm tea sweetened with honey, and herb teas were the usual breakfasts of Llewelyn Prince of Glamorgan, who died in his 108th year'.

Ornamental

Their wonderfully bright coloured leaves makes them excellent as a contrasting foliage plant. They make an great groundcover (though may need controlling), and can be planted along the sides of paths or thoroughfares; when crushed, they release their delightful lemony aroma. There are attractive variegated varieties: these need regular trimming to encourage new fresh variegated leaf growth, as older leaves tend to lose their colour.

Other uses

The dried leaves retain their lemon scent and are used in potpourri. An essential oil can be extracted from the leaves, and this is often used in perfumes and air freshener products. The leaves when crushed and rubbed onto skin have been said to help deter mosquitoes. Recent research has also demonstrated the powerful ability of balm-leaf extract to kill the larvae of some mosquito species.

Location: Grows best in full sun or in light shade. Prefers a little shade in hotter, drier climates. Fairly wind hardy. Can be grown near the coast.

Temperature: Can grow in cool-temperate to sub-tropical climates. Plants are frost hardy, but in regions with heavy frosts, they benefit from a mulch applied around the runners and roots. Dies back in cold winters, but usually resprouts from its perennial roots and runners in spring.

Soil/water/nutrients: Is not fussy about soil type and can grow in sandy soils to heavy clays. Is not nutrient hungry, so can be grown in tricky areas of the garden, though its spread needs controlling. Is fairly drought hardy once established, but regular moisture gives better growth. Can grow in fairly acidic to somewhat alkaline soils, pH 5.3–7.5.

Pot culture: Ideal for growth in a container, where its spread can be controlled. Not fussy about soil type, or a little neglect. Plant species with contrasting foliage near it for the best display. Place pots close to where people sit so they enjoy its fragrance.

Planting/propagation: *Seed:* Seed can be sown in spring, and germinates in 7–14 days. Grow seedlings on until large enough to be placed in their final location. However, is much easier to propagate this species vegetatively.

Cuttings: Very easy to propagate vegetatively. The runners can be cut into sections, to include some roots, and buried at a shallow depth in compost. Plants can be divided in spring or autumn. Take cuttings while plants are actively growing in spring and early summer. Very easy and successful. Take cuttings from young shoots and remove their lower leaves before inserting the cutting into gritty, moist compost to root. Have a good success rate.

Space plants at ~30 cm apart for groundcover, or plant individually among other herbs, but as with mint, will need to be planted within a barrier (e.g. buried bucket without a base) to prevent its spread.

Pruning: Older plants can become leggy and untidy. Remove older stems to induce new fresh growth. Can be pruned with shears.

Pests and diseases: Has very few problems.

Mentha spp.
Mints
LAMIACEAE (LABIATAE)

Spearmint (common mint; *Mentha spicata*), peppermint (*M.* x *piperita*), apple mint, pineapple mint (round-leaved mint) *M. suaveolens* [syn. *M.* x *rotundifolia*]); long-leaved mint (*M. longifolia*), watermint (*M. aquatica*); pennyroyal (*M. pulegium*); lemon mint (*M.* x *piperita citrata*); Corsican mint (*M. requienii*); curly mint (*M. spicata crispii*); Japanese peppermint (corn mint, field mint; *M. arvensis*)

Relatives: sage, rosemary, thyme, balm

There are 25–30 species within the *Mentha* genus. These mostly originate from Europe, though some are from Asia, a few from Australia and one from North America. Known to virtually everyone as the scent and taste of fresh spearmint, excellent in sauces, drinks and in a wide range of cosmetics and food products. The aroma of freshly crushed mint is hard to beat. Apart from spearmint, many other *Mentha* species are cultivated, and are known for their culinary, ornamental or herbal properties. The *Mentha* species readily hybridise, their origins are sometimes difficult to ascertain, and their names can vary accordingly. The Japanese are believed to have used *M. arvensis* medicinally at least 2000 years ago. Mint was popular with the Romans for its clean, cooling aroma and properties. Within the mints, the species spearmint, peppermint, apple/pineapple mint, Japanese peppermint and long-leaved mint are particularly well known. Spearmint, peppermint and Japanese mint are particularly rich in menthol, which has been and still is used in many medicinal products, and has cooling, antiseptic and analgesic properties. As all gardeners know, they are extremely easy to grow, and spearmint, in particular, will thrive in the poorest soil, though does spread tenaciously through the herb bed and beyond, or even creeps out of the container it was put in to control its spread. However, even the smallest garden should have at least a couple of types of mint.

DESCRIPTION

They are spreading perennials, producing stems or runners that grow outwards either just on or just below the soil surface, rooting as they go. These then produce lateral upright branches that grow leaves and flowers. Flowering shoots grow to ~20–70 cm tall, depending on species. Some of the many types of mint are briefly described below. **Spearmint** (*Mentha spicata*) has rich green almost hairless leaves and a wonderful fresh aroma and flavour; it is the most widely utilised culinary herb and is used in a range of toothpastes, cosmetics, aromatic products, etc. It is native to Europe and the UK. **Peppermint** (*M.* x *piperita*) is a hybrid between spearmint and watermint; it has the strong penetrating flavour and aroma of watermint. Its leaves, unlike most other mints, are on stalks. **Apple mint** and **pineapple mint** (*M. suaveolens*), as their names suggest, have a fruitier aroma and flavour and they are often considered to be the best culinary mints. They have pale green, rounded leaves, which are covered with fine hairs, with this texture not liked by all. **Long-leaved mint** (*M. longifolia*) has a good mint flavour; it has thinner, longer, but woolly leaves. **Watermint** (*M. aquatica*) grows wild in Europe and the UK on the margins of fresh or somewhat brackish water. Its narrow, almost hairless dark green leaves have a pronounced aroma and taste, which is too strong for many. **Pennyroyal** (*M. pulegium*) is another pungent mint, more commonly used as a medicinal herb; it has a more upright and branched form. **Lemon mint** (*M.* x *piperita citrata*), closely related to peppermint and a hybrid, has smooth leaves and a lemon flavour. **Corsican mint** (*M. requienii*) is a smaller, pretty plant with much smaller leaves and is often grown in pots. It is more cold sensitive though, and has a strong peppermint-like aroma and a flavour not liked by all. **Curly mint** (*M. spicata crispii*), as its common name suggests, has dark-green curly leaves, which are popular as a garnish, though are not rated for their aroma or flavour. **Japanese peppermint** (corn mint, *M. arvensis*) has smoother, softer leaves and a very good flavour and aroma. It is often grown commercially instead of spearmint.

Leaves: All have distinctive square stems. The leaves are opposite, and are oval with pointed tips and serrated

Food

The young pods are possibly the most popular part of this plant to be eaten, and are known as drumsticks. They can be eaten raw in salads, or can be lightly steamed or added to stir-fries, and then taste like fresh beans or like asparagus. They are a common ingredient in curry, korma and dahl. The sweet seeds can be removed from older pods and lightly fried and then eaten like peanuts, or they can be gently cooked like peas. The younger leaves can be eaten fresh in salads or can be lightly steamed and served as greens; they are often added to curry dishes and to pickles. Pieces of root can be scraped and the finely cut outer flesh is similar in flavour to horseradish, and has been used as a substitute. Research, however, now questions its safety (see Warning below). Even the sweet flowers are edible, though should be cooked, and are added to cooked dishes or are fried in batter. The oil from the seeds is edible, and has been used in salad dressings and for cooking.

Nutrition/medicinal

The seeds contain very good amounts of protein (~30%) and oils (~40%), and a little fibre. The oil is composed mostly of oleic (~65%), with some palmitic and stearic fatty acids, with composition not dissimilar to that of olive oil. The oil is clear, has little aroma and resists rancidity. The seed contains bactericidal and fungicidal compounds. The pod (without seed) contains a little protein and fibre, though has good amounts of calcium, phosphate and iron. It is very rich in vitamin C (~120 mg/100 g), with a little vitamin A. Together, the seeds and pods contain all the essential amino acids.

The leaves are particularly rich in calcium, phosphate and iron. They are wonderfully rich in vitamin A (~11300 I.U., including carotenoids) and in vitamin C (~220 mg/100 g), with some of the B complex. In addition, leaves contain oestrogenic substances and the anti-tumour compound, -sitosterol. The flowers are rich in potassium and calcium. Compounds within the outer root are able to reduce spasms of smooth muscle by reducing the activity of motor fibres, which accounts for several of its medicinal uses.

Historically, several parts of the horseradish tree have been used to treat tumours. The leaves and pods have significant antibiotic and anti-tumour activity, which are thought to be mainly due to their isothiocyanate content, similar to that found within brassicas. It has been found to significantly increase quantities of antioxidants. Plant extracts are effective against Staphylococcus aureus. Juice extracted from the root has been used topically to stimulate blood flow and reduce skin irritations. The crushed leaves have been used externally to help heal sores and for headaches. The tannin properties within many parts of this plant have been used for digestive problems and to treat diarrhoea. A leaf extract has been shown to be effective at lowering blood sugar levels somewhat within 3 hours of ingestion, and so may have uses for those with type-2 diabetes. The roots have been taken as a tonic, to ease problems with menstruation, to expel phlegm. The oil from the seed has been used topically to treat skin diseases.

Historically, women in the Sudan have long used the crushed seed to purify drinking water. This usage has been extensively trialled: one experiment found that the crushed seeds reduced the number of coliform bacteria by ~90% within 20 minutes. It is thought that water-soluble cationic proteins from the seeds bind to particles within the water and flocculate them; these particles then settle out and can be decanted before the water is used. Work is currently under way on this process so that it can be more widely utilised in regions of the world that have unclean water. Trials in Malawi showed that the crushed seeds could be used in continuous water-flow systems and produced water of similar quality to that treated with aluminium sulphate. Used in this way, the seeds have been shown to pose no serious threat to human health.

Warning: The root bark contains ~0.1% alkaloids, mostly as moringinine and spirochin. In large doses, the former can act as a cardiac stimulant and raise blood pressure, and the latter is a nerve-paralysing agent. In large doses, both of these compounds can be fatal.

Ornamental

Makes an excellent ornamental specimen tree in warmer regions. Has attractive feathery foliage, fragrant flowers for most of the year, and interesting and edible pods.

Other uses

The seeds are high in a clear, non-drying oil (~40%) called Ben oil. This is valued for its lubricating properties for the fine parts of machinery (e.g. clocks), and is used in cosmetics, soaps and hair products. The wood yields a blue dye. The bark yields tannin, used in treating leather, and produces a coarse fibre that can be used as filling or to make mats, etc. The wood exudes a gum, which is white at first, drying to yellow, and finally reddish brown. This is used as a tragacanth substitute. The leaves are fed to livestock, and the trees are sometimes planted to form a barrier hedge. This species is being researched for biomass production. The wood is used to make cellophane.

of waterlogged soils, but can grow in regions with high rainfall. Grows better in lighter sandy soils or loams, though will tolerate heavier clay soils. Will grow in low-nutrient soils, but the addition of organic matter and some well- rotted manure or fertiliser can result in better growth and yields. Can grow in a range of soil pH values, from acidic to alkaline, pH 5.0–8.0, with some reporting an even wider range.

Planting/propagation: *Seed:* Can be grown from seed. This needs no pre-soaking or other pre-treatments. Viability of fresh seed is ~80%, but this decreases to 50% in ~12 months. Cover seed with ~2 cm of soil. Seed germinates fairly quickly and seedlings can then be grown-on in pots under light shade. They grow rapidly, and young plants can be planted in their final positions within a few months. They are best grown in deep biodegradable pots; when planting out handle the roots carefully as they are easily damaged. Seedlings and young plants need regular moisture until established. *Cuttings*: Often grown from long stem cuttings (>1 m) taken from new growth. Insert deeply into moist warm compost, in light shade, to form roots. Space rooted cuttings or seedlings at ~3 m apart, or more for specimens. Space closer together if planting as a screen.

Pruning: Remove any damaged or diseased wood, and attend to any ragged breaks as branches break easily. Commercially, growers prune or pollard trees to <1 m height following harvesting to promote branching, increase pod production and make future harvesting easier.

Pests and diseases: Has few problems, however, root-rot can kill plants if the soil is too wet. The leaves and pods can be attacked by caterpillar species, aphids, scale insects, borers and fruit flies, though these attacks are unusual.

Murraya koenigii (syn. *Bergera koenigii, Chalcos koenigii*)

Curry-leaf tree

RUTACEAE

Relatives: rue, orange, lemon, grapefruit, Sichuan pepper

The curry-leaf tree is a shrub/small tree found growing indigenously in regions of India and towards Burma. It is often found growing in woodlands. A member of the same family as many other strongly aromatic plants, such as rue, the curry-leaf tree is also related to the citrus species. It is a very popular spice in southern India and Sri Lanka. From India, this plant was taken through Africa to South Africa, and has spread to many Southeast Asian countries. As well as a flavouring, it has been long used in India, and the Far East, including China, to treat a wide range of medical complaints. Its usage in Europe and Britain has led to its unhelpful common name because, although it can be added to many curry-type recipes, it is not an ingredient in the curry mixes served in the West. Instead, it has a much finer flavour and, in India, is mixed with a variety of different spices and ingredients in different types of dishes. Although a subtropical/tropical species, this plant can be successfully grown in a container and then given protection in colder climates. It can be trimmed to size, has fragrant flowers, eye-catching and edible fruits, and its leaves can be harvested as a flavouring. Another species, also often called 'curry plant', after its spicy-flavoured leaves, is the European *Helichrysum italicum* (see p. 83); however, this is quite a different species from a different plant family. Its flavour is more sage-like and it is considered inferior by most chefs, compared with the finer quality of *Murraya koenigii*.

DESCRIPTION

A large shrub to small tree, 3–5 m tall, with the same spread. All parts having a spicy curry aroma when crushed. Can be fast growing in good soil with a suitable climate; slower growing elsewhere. Its many stems are marked with lenticels, and its thin bark peels off in strips to expose white wood beneath. There are reported to be three types of this species: a dwarf, spreading form; the usual, medium-sized type, which grows fast and tall; and a slow-growing, but more fragrant, type known as 'Gamthi'.

Leaves: Deciduous, ~30 cm long, compound, consisting of ~12 pairs of leaflets, often with a terminal leaflet . Leaflets are long and thin, ~5 cm long, ~2 cm wide, with short leaf stalks. Have smooth margins and are mid-green in colour.

Flowers: White, small (~1 cm diameter), with five fused petals forming a funnel. Are borne in large, loose clusters at the apices of branches. Are sweetly fragrant. Have both male and female parts within each flower. Are borne from mid to late spring. Pollination is by bees and insects.

Fruit/seeds: Round to oval, ~1.5 cm long, shiny. Turn from green to dark purple, almost black, when ripe. The flesh is a wonderful blue colour. There is a large (~1 cm), central green seed, but this is poisonous. Fruits are borne in large bunches and ripen from late summer into autumn.

Harvest/storage: The younger leaves can be picked as a flavouring ingredient all season. They are much better used fresh, ideally from your own tree. When dried or kept even for a day or two, they lose much of their flavour. To store, they can be kept in a fridge for a few days or can be quick frozen. The ripe fruits are picked from late summer onwards, but discard the seeds. Several harvesting sessions are needed during the fruiting season. Healthy plants give good yields of fruits, with ~4.5 kg considered as an average yield from one bush during a season.

Roots: Deep and fibrous.

CULTIVATION

Location: Can grow in full sun or in a light shade.

Temperature: Prefers warm-temperate to subtropical climates, but could be grown in cool-temperate regions in a container and given protection during the colder weather. However, some reports say that acclimatised plants can survive light frosts. Best to grow them in a sunny, sheltered spot in cool-temperate locations, and mulch roots and cover plants if necessary.

Soil/water/nutrients: Grows best in moderately nutrient-rich soil, and benefits from the addition of organic

Food

The leaves are used to flavour various spicy dishes, and add a depth and pleasant taste to foods. They are often toasted or briefly fried just before use. They are added to vegetable, lentil and fish recipes and, because they are soft, do not need to be removed before the food is served. They go well in sauces with coconut milk and other spices. The leaves, after being lightly fried, may be added to pickles and chutneys. They can also be finely chopped before use, and then added to egg or cheese dishes, or can be mixed with potatoes in samosas, etc. The ripe, sweet fruits are edible, and are popular in the areas where these plants are mostly grown. However, they do have an aroma that some find unpleasant. More importantly, the seeds are reported to be poisonous, so should be discarded.

Nutrition/medicinal

The fruits contain ~65% moisture and ~10% sugars, with some fibre, and they are fairly rich in vitamins and A. Fruits contain reasonable amounts of phosphorus, calcium and magnesium, with a little iron. They are high in antioxidant anthocyanins, and are used for a range of medicinal purposes. The leaves are very rich in carotenoids (carotenes, lutein) and vitamin E, plus have useful amounts of the B vitamins, folic acid and riboflavin. They contain iron, calcium, phosphorus and zinc.

The leaves, bark and roots have been used as a tonic and to ease digestive problems. The fresh leaves have been eaten to stop diarrhoea, vomiting and to cure dysentery. They have been used to treat various skin problems. Their uses in China and other Asian countries include as an analgesic, an antioxidant, to improve vision and to regulate fertility. Research has shown that leaves can reduce total serum cholesterol, and LDL and VLDL, while increasing HDL ('good' cholesterol), and they can lower the release of lipoproteins into the blood. Also, interestingly, the leaves are a traditional Indian remedy for diabetes. Many recent research projects have found that they do decrease blood glucose levels, and so they have been suggested to be of clinical importance in improving the management of high cholesterol levels and type-2 diabetes. The plant contains compounds that inhibit the action of the enzyme pancreatic alpha-amylase, which would normally help break down simple sugars. Therefore, curry leaves slow the digestive breakdown of sugars and prevent rapid rises in blood sugar level.

The essential oil contains many compounds, though mostly caryophyllene, aromadendrene, selinene, phellandrene, pinene. It has been found to have strong antibacterial and antifungal activities. In India, the twigs of this species, like neem, are used as a toothbrush, and reduce gum disease and strengthen teeth. Research has shown that chewing the leaves reduces halitosis and improves mouth hygiene.

Ornamental

The curry-leaf plant is quite ornamental, and makes an interesting shrub for the herbaceous bed, or can be grown as a hedge. It has bunches of wonderfully fragrant flowers, colourful, edible fruits and aromatic leaves.

spread of plants can be easily controlled. Keep the leaves growing and watered until they die back; some of the bulbs can then be harvested.

Planting/propagation: *Seed:* Sow thinly in autumn or early spring and cover with ~0.5–1 cm of soil. Seeds should germinate in 7–14 days, and germination rates should be good. Thin seedlings and grow-on for a couple of years until they have formed bulbs. Lift at the end of the second season, separate out the bulbils and plant out in their final positions. It takes longer to get harvestable bulbs and flowers from seed. *Cuttings:* Established clumps can

be divided and bulbs gently teased apart before replanting. Bulbs are spaced at 10–16 cm apart, either in an informal design or in rows. Place bulbs at ~5–8 cm depth. It takes a year or two before the plants start to form further bulbs. If growing among grass, avoid mowing the leaves after the plant has flowered, as these are needed to build up storage reserves within the bulb. If wanting to control their spread, mowing will sap their reserves.

Pests and diseases: Few problems, though a fungus occasionally causes blackening of the leaves.

Oryza sativa
Rice
POACEAE (GRAMINEAE)
Oryza glaberrima: African rice
Relatives: wheat, rye, oats, grasses, maize, bamboo

Rice is the world's second most important food crop (after wheat), and has been cultivated for thousands of years in Asia; records show that relatives of modern-day rice were being grown in China ~5000 years ago. Although there are more than 8000 varieties, there are only two main species of rice, with *O. sativa* being by far the most common. Its ancestor is believed to be the wild-rice species *O. rufipogon*, with modern-day rice not occurring naturally in the wild, but originating from selections. Most of the world's 300 million acres of rice is grown in Asia, India and China. Rice is also an important food in South America. Wild rice (*Zizania aquatica*) is a different species.

DESCRIPTION
A member of the grass family, this monocotyledonous ancient crop does need specific conditions to grow well. It grows to 0.7–2 m tall, depending on variety, with taller varieties tending to lodge (stem breakage). Varieties with short, stiff stems are preferable. Usually produces some tillers as it grows, with more being produced by some varieties or if plants are grown with more space around them. Only early-season tillers produce seed heads. It is usually grown as an annual, though can produce tillers and live for longer in warmer regions, to form a more spreading plant. For all the thousands of varieties, there are only two main environments in which they grow: either upland types (i.e. often at altitude) that need less or no flooding (though do need regular moisture); and lowland swamp rice, which is usually grown in flooded soils in river-basin regions. The majority of rice grown is the latter type. Rice fields are flooded mostly to reduce weed competition; the rice can tolerate flooded conditions, but the majority of weed species cannot. Rice can be grown in ordinary soil, but does then need regular weeding or herbicide applications. The type of rice grain can be divided into three main groups. **Japonica:** Generally short grained. Plants are hairy and have stiff, short, upright stems, and freely form tillers with numerous flower stalks (panicles).

They have no awns. Mostly grown in cooler regions of Asia, in Europe and the US. **Indica:** Generally long-grained. More suited to tropical/subtropical regions. Plants have less stiff, spreading stems with numerous panicles. They have no awns. **Bulu:** Of lesser importance. Tends to be intermediate between Japonica and Indica. Mostly grown on islands around Southeast Asia. Fewer panicles, but kernels are larger. Have awns.

Leaves: Grass-like, long (~1 m), narrow (~2.5 cm), pointed, veins running lengthways, stomata on both sides of leaf, they sheath the stem.

Flowers: Long, terminal panicles, 10–25 cm long, with many flattened spikelets of flowers at the apex. They are pollinated by wind, and are often self-pollinating.

Seeds: Vary in size and shape depending on variety, from short and plump to long and thin, with many intermediate shapes. Short- or round-grain rice is plump, has a high starch content and is sticky when cooked. It is used for risotto, desserts and sushi. Long-grain rice is a thinner grain, less starchy and remains separate when cooked. It is used to accompany savoury dishes. Types include Basmati and Jasmine.

Harvest/storage: Takes 4–6 months from germination to harvest, depending on location and variety. Rice plants are usually harvested with a scythe and hung to dry for

uses

Food

Like all grains and nuts, poorly stored damp, cooked or uncooked grains can become contaminated with toxic *Aspergillus* fungi; if in doubt, throw it out and do not keep cooked rice for long in the fridge. There are many types of rice, including short grained for desserts, cakes, soups; medium grained; long grained for use with curries, etc.; glutinous rice, which has more sugar and less starch, and is used to make sticky desserts; risotto (Arborio) rice; Basmati rice, an aromatic rice grown mostly in India; and Jasmine rice, another aromatic rice. Many of these types can be purchased either as brown or white rice. Rice is the major component of billions of people's diet and is often the main ingredient accompanied by pieces of vegetable, meat or fish, plus various flavourings such as soy, chilli and garlic. Rice can be added to soups, stews, and is the main carbohydrate in most Chinese, Indian and Asian recipes. Commercially, it is included in many breakfast cereals, confectionery products and desserts. It is used to make certain beers and is distilled to make Saki. Rice is usually simply boiled until soft and eaten before it becomes mushy and sticky (except for sticky rice). In Indian cuisine, the rice is often pre-fried in oil with spices to add flavour, before boiling.

Nutrition/medicinal

To gain more nutritional benefits, soak brown rice for ~20 hours in warm water (38°C) prior to cooking. This activates various germination enzymes, which extend the range of nutritional compounds within the grain, particularly gamma-aminobutyric acid (GABA). This compound acts as an important neurotransmitter in the brain, improving neuronal communication and reducing anxiety, improving sleep and reducing blood pressure. Brown rice (i.e. with its bran) unpolished, is much more nutritious than white rice. Brown rice contains some fibre, ~10% RDA of protein. It has a low GI of 23. It is rich in the B vitamins, particularly B6, niacin and thiamine, plus some pantothenic acid. It has good quantities of some minerals, particularly the antioxidant selenium, and also of manganese, magnesium and phosphorus.

Rice bran, consisting of the seed coat of the grain, has a very low GI of 7, is rich in fibre and contains ~32% RDA of protein. Bran contains some vitamin E and wondrous quantities of the B vitamins: >200% RDA of thiamine, >200% RDA of niacin, ~240% RDA of B6, plus folate and riboflavin and lots of pantothenic acid. Similarly, bran is incredibly rich in manganese, phosphates, magnesium, zinc, iron, copper, potassium and selenium.

White rice has a higher glycaemic index of 30, has less fibre and protein, and fewer minerals than cooked brown rice, though does still contain some selenium and manganese. It also has much lower levels of B vitamins (hence the occurrence of beriberi in some Asian communities that eat predominantly white rice). Due to its much lower nutritional content, white rice is often sold fortified with added minerals, etc.

The outer bran layer, found in brown rice can lower blood pressure, help control glucose levels and lower cholesterol. Rice bran seems to reduce bladder cancer in mice, particularly if fermented with *Aspergillus oryzae*, and research is being conducted on compounds from fermented bran to be used in cancer treatments. The lower GI of brown rice, bran and brown rice flour result in reduced risk of cardiovascular disease, compared with diets high in white rice, which have been shown to increase this risk. Rice, traditionally, has been used to treat many types of digestive ailments and to stop diarrhoea and vomiting. Rice is generally considered safe for those on a gluten-free diet. Externally, rice has been used to treat various skin problems, including psoriasis, sores and swellings.

Other uses

Rice husks are rich in potassium and make good compost. The harvested stems are used for thatching, as a fuel and to feed livestock. Rice is processed to make rice paper. Most bran is used to feed livestock. Paddy fields are often a haven for many animal species, such as water birds and amphibians, which help to keep insect pest numbers down.

~2 weeks, before being threshed and winnowed to separate out the rice grains. Removal of the husk around the grain is tricky, although the Japanese sell small hand mills that can dehusk rice. Commercially, rice goes through a number of preparation stages once harvested. Unpolished rice still retains its hull, seedcoat (the bran) and its germ (embryo); it is hard and abrasive and is usually fed to livestock in this form. Brown rice has had its hull removed, but still retains its bran and germ, and thus most of its nutrients. White rice has its husk, bran, germ and some of the endosperm removed; it, therefore, has had most of its nutrients removed. It consists primarily of white storage, starchy endosperm. White rice is often parboiled before distribution to strengthen the grains and this increases thiamine content. It is often polished and some white rice has various nutrients added to fortify it. The bran that is removed from white rice is rich in protein, oils and B vitamins, as well as various minerals; most of this is fed to livestock.

CULTIVATION

Location: Needs to grow in full sun, and is not tolerant of strong winds. Most rice varieties need short days to grow well, though some long-day varieties have been developed.

Temperature: Requires temperatures of >22°C for at

least 40 days of its growth; cool temperatures during the day or night reduce its growth and increase susceptibility to disease. Prefers a tropical or subtropical climate. Growth ceases below 10°C and temperatures of ~5°C can kill plants. Upland rice is more tolerant of cooler temperatures.

Soil/water/nutrients: Rice needs a good supply of fresh, preferably running, water, and growth is better if this is warm. Needs moderately nutrient-rich soils and a pH of 5–7.5. A fine soil that allows easy planting and harvesting above a clay impermeable layer is ideal, thus preventing water from draining downwards. The addition of organic matter is advantageous, and crop rotation is recommended.

Pot culture: As an experiment, rice can be grown in trays where water levels can be easily controlled. It makes an interesting school project.

Planting/propagation: Seed can be tested for viability by soaking in salty water: those that sink are viable and the rest should be discarded. The saved seed is then washed free of salt. Rice seeds need an extended period of soaking to germinate; this is unusual as the seeds of most species are killed by much more than a couple of days of soaking. For small-scale cultivation, seed can be germinated by tying the rice in a muslin bag and immersing this in a warm water bath to soak for 25–30 days. The germinating seed is then removed and left to dry for a few hours. Traditionally, the germinated seed is laid in seed beds and lightly covered with fine sand with netting placed over this. It is kept warm and well watered, and the seedlings are transplantable in about a month. The soil in the seedbed is then thoroughly soaked to enable the seedlings to be pulled up without root damage. They are sown in the paddy field in rows, ~20 cm apart, with 2–3 seedlings inserted into wet soil. The paddy fields have been previously levelled, to ensure an even water depth, and the soil tilled to ~30 cm depth. A channel is dug around the field's perimeter, ~50 cm deep, and the removed soil placed externally to form a dyke. The channels are lined, these days with plastic, to prevent the water from escaping outwards. The water, apart from being needed by the plant, also suppresses weed growth.

For the first 3 weeks, the water level is kept to ~5 cm depth while the seedlings root and become established. After this time, competing weed growth is less important, though plants do need to be watered each morning, but then warmth and sunshine during the remaining day are encouraged. Plants are grown on for ~6 weeks, (weeded if necessary) until the flowerheads start to form. The paddy is then re-flooded to ~5 cm depth during seed pollination. As the ripening seed turns yellow and begins to hang downwards due to its weight, the paddy is drained for about two weeks to allow the plants to dry out before harvesting.

Pests and diseases: Rice is susceptible to a very wide range of fungal diseases (particularly rice blast (*Magnaporthe grisea*)) and to nematode attacks, due to the wet, humid conditions it is grown in. Insect attacks are less problematic.

OTHER SPECIES

African rice, *Oryza glaberrima*. Has been grown in some areas of West Africa for thousands of years. It was grown 2000–3000 years ago along the Niger River, and is now a staple food to ~15 million people along the Ivory Coast. Many varieties have been selected by the women in these regions (the main tenders of this crop). Despite its flavour being preferred by many, it is now being largely replaced by *O. sativa*, which was originally introduced by the Portuguese in the 16th century. Its demise is unfortunate, as the African species is more suited to the environment, and there are attempts now to halt this decline (see Bibliography). There are a few crosses between African rice and *O. sativa*. The two species are similar, but the African rice grain is redder, smaller and darker in colour. Its panicles are straight and simply branched. Unfortunately, African rice seeds tend to scatter, the grain is difficult to mill and the yields are lower, but it is more resistant to various diseases and to weed competition. It can be grown in poorer soils, tolerates fluctuating water levels better, and its flavour is said to be better.

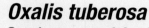

Oxalis tuberosa
Oca (yam, sorrel, kao)
OXALIDACEAE
Oxalis tetraphylla: iron-cross plant
Relatives: wood sorrel

The oca (or yam as it is also known) is grown for its small, colourful, red, waxy, knobbly tubers. Originally native to South America, it was a staple food of the Andean Indians, second only to the potato, and is thought to have been cultivated there for at least 4000 years. Oca is still a very popular crop in some high-altitude regions of South America, particularly in areas of Bolivia, and in Central America (particularly Mexico), but this crop is now grown little outside these regions. It is however, grown in New Zealand, where it is thought to have been introduced by immigrants from Chile in the late 1800s. However, there are collections of more than 400 accessions found in Peru and Ecuador, and research is ongoing to improve this potentially versatile crop. In New Zealand and in Australia it is grown at a small scale and, when in season, is a popular vegetable that is widely available, being most popularly roasted with other vegetables to accompany meat roasts. Its genus name, *Oxalis*, is derived from a word meaning sharp or tangy, and refers to the tangy-tasting leaves of this genus. Oca is a versatile carbohydrate crop that has potential for much wider cultivation in temperate regions.

DESCRIPTION
A small (20–30 cm tall), attractive, perennial, bushy but sprawling plant. Usually grown as an annual, with its tubers harvested in late autumn. Many varieties are known in South America, though few are found outside this region, except for in New Zealand.

Leaves: Alternate, delicate, divided into three leaflets, resembling those of clover. *En masse*, they often have a luxuriant, attractive appearance. The leaves fold together at night or when the plant is stressed to conserve moisture. Leaves have long, sappy stems that mostly grow from a basal crown; these can be coloured yellow, to green, to reddish. The leaves and stems usually die back in winter, particularly in colder regions.

Flowers: May have loose clusters of pretty, bright orange-yellow or purplish, five-petalled flowers that form on the top of a flower stalk. Flowers are borne during summer. However, many varieties of oca never form flowers. If they do, then both male and female parts occur in the same flower. Pollination is by bees and insects.

Seeds: Rarely sets seeds: mostly spreads vegetatively.

Roots: The tubers are not true roots, but are swollen, underground storage stems, which form in groups within the soil. The skin of the tubers is smooth and almost shiny, and usually an attractive pinkish rose colour, though some are yellowish or purplish. They are small (4–12 cm long), and are often finger sized, cylindrical, with irregular, cylindrical grooves along their length. The flesh is waxy, dense and usually white, though can be yellowish or purplish. Many South American varieties only produce tubers if the day length is short (less than 12 hours). During longer days, these varieties form above-ground stems instead, and only start to produce underground storage organs in response to shorter, autumn days. However, if frosts occur at this time, then tuber formation can be poor. Varieties do exist that are less day-length sensitive.

Harvest/storage: The tubers are ready to harvest once the top shoot dies back in autumn. Takes 6–8 months to form tubers after first planting. Dig up carefully to avoid damaging the thin skin. Once harvested they become sweeter if left to dry in the sun for a few days. Can give good yields of 2–4 kg per plant, and plants take up little space. Can be stored for several weeks in a cool, dry place.

CULTIVATION
Easy.

Location: They prefer a site in full sun. Some varieties are short-day plants (see above), other varieties, e.g. those found in New Zealand, seem to not be as day-length sensitive. Often grown at altitude in South America, but can be grown near the coast in a sheltered location.

Temperature: They can grow in a range of temperatures from cool-temperate to subtropical. They are fairly cold hardy once established, and although frost can kill back the stems and leaves, the underground tubers should resprout in spring. The plants do not grow well in hot climates where temperatures exceed ~28°C: plants wilt and tuber production is poor.

Soil/water/nutrients: Grow best in good-quality loam that includes organic matter. Do well in lighter sandy soils that have regular moisture. In heavy, clay soils, the

Food

When freshly harvested, some tubers have an acidic flavour, which mellows after being dried in the sun for a few days. Freezing is also said to reduce acidity. Many tubers are not acidic and have a sweet flavour, even when raw. The tubers have a waxy texture and a pleasant nutty flavour when cooked. They are not usually eaten raw. They are often roasted and eaten with roast meats and other vegetables. They can be briefly boiled, and are then similar to Jerusalem artichokes in flavour, or can be baked, or sliced and fried. They can be added to soups and stews. They have a more interesting texture and flavour than modern potatoes. In Peru, they are frozen overnight then mashed to form a powder that is added to desserts, porridge, etc. In Mexico they are sometimes eaten raw, sprinkled with lemon, pepper and salt. They are sometimes pickled. The stems, flowers and leaves can be eaten and used like spinach. Indeed, the flowers and leaves of all *Oxalic* species are edible.

Nutrition/medicinal

The tubers contain variable amounts of protein, but usually ~5%. They consist mostly of easy-to-digest carbohydrate, with virtually no fat. They have good quantities of calcium and iron, though much of this may not be available due to oxalic acid content. The skins and outer pith contain good amounts of antioxidant anthocyanins. ***Warning:*** The tubers and leaves do contain oxalic acid, so need to be consumed in moderation; bitter/acidic tubers contain more, whereas sweet tubers have very little. Some reports say that levels can be as high as those found in spinach, so those at risk of rheumatism, kidney stones or gout, should only eat this plant in moderation. Oxalic acid also binds calcium, making it unavailable to the body, and affects iron uptake. Cooking can leach away some oxalic acid, as does curing for a few days in the sun.

Ornamental

Quite an attractive plant in leaf, though it may not flower. Perhaps grow it with other members of this genus that do flower and have edible leaves (see below). Would fit in well to a flower border as well as the veggie garden.

roots and tubers fail to grow properly; cold, wet soils or waterlogging can kill plants. Can grow in slightly acidic to somewhat alkaline soils: pH 5.5–7.5.

Pot culture: Can possibly be grown in a container.

Planting/propagation: *Seed:* Not usually cultivated from seed. *Cuttings:* The tubers can be planted whole, or cut into sections that include 1–2 eyes and planted at ~6 cm depth in warm, moist compost in spring. Plant ~25 cm apart. Soil can be periodically mounded up around the plant, in the same way as potatoes, to encourage the formation of further tubers. May be propagated from stem cuttings.

Pests and diseases: They are susceptible to a number of viral diseases in South America, but these do not seem to be a problem elsewhere. Heat and high moisture can make them susceptible to bacterial diseases of the sappy stems. Can be attacked by a potato beetle in South America. Otherwise, they seem to have few problems. The tubers are rich in a soluble protein called ocatin, mostly found within the pith and skin. This compound inhibits the growth of several plant-pathogenic bacteria and fungi, thus conferring natural resistance to many pathogens.

OTHER SPECIES

Iron-cross plant, *Oxalis tetraphylla* (syn. *O. deppei*). Originally from Central or South America, this plant is now found growing wild in many temperate countries. A small (20 cm tall), easy-to-grow, hardy plant that produces edible leaves throughout the summer, into autumn. Grows to ~20 cm tall with a spreading habit to ~35 cm. The leaves and stems die back in winter, but the roots are fairly frost hardy (down to ~–7°C). As its name suggests, it often has four leaflets, rather than three, like other members of this genus. Has pretty, small, five-petalled pinkish and white flowers. It grows best in freely draining soil in full sun, and can out-compete the growth of many weeds. Can be propagated from seed or by root divisions. The leaves and flowers have a tangy, lemony flavour, and are good added to salads. However, like other members of the *Oxalis* genus, they do contain oxalic acid (see the Warning above). Makes a good summer ground-cover plant.

Location: Prefers a site in full sun: does not grow well in shade. Too much wind can break the stems (lodging).

Temperature: Grows best in warm to hot climates; although it can grow in cooler regions, growth is slower. Is not frost hardy, so needs to be sown in late spring/ early summer in regions where late frosts are a risk. Mature plants are reported to survive an autumn frost.

Soil/water/nutrients: Not too fussy about soil type, and will grow in sandy to quite heavy clays. Will grow in soils that are poor in nutrients, though adequate nitrogen will give a better crop. However, too much nitrogen results in sappy growth, increased risk of disease, and increased lodging. Too much nitrogen content can also be toxic to livestock. As with most plants, these species grow fastest in good-quality loams with regular moisture. Given adequate moisture, they also tend to form more stalks, and therefore more seed (tillering). However, they can be more drought tolerant than many crops once established, and are often grown in soils that are problematic where, for various reasons, other crops cannot be grown. Most millet species, though, cannot survive waterlogging. Millet grows best in soils from pH 5.5–7, though will grow outside this range.

Pot culture: Could be grown in pots, possibly with other grass species.

Planting/propagation: *Seed:* The seed is either sown in rows or is broadcast. Because the seed is small, only cover the seeds with ~0.5 cm of fine soil. Need temperatures of ~24°C for germination, which is usually rapid, taking 3–6 days. Millets grow quite rapidly, and as long as the soil was weed-free before seed sowing, they can generally out-compete most weeds that emerge later. *Cuttings:* Root sections can be taken, and these should root. Over-winter in a glasshouse or similar in cool-temperate climates. Millets can be grown with legumes, with the latter providing nitrogen, and the former providing biomass and tolerating poorer soils.

Pests and diseases: Has few pest or disease problems. Occasional problems with the fungal diseases that attack other cereals, such as smuts and rusts. Chinch bugs and grasshoppers have been reported to attack millet. Birds and rodents are the main problem and are attracted to the ripe seeds.

SPECIES

Fonia, *Digitaria exilis.* Is one of the main *Digitaria* species that is gathered and cultivated from the savannahs of western Africa. It forms a delicate grass, growing to 30–60 cm in height. It is an important staple food for many people in Ethiopia, Sudan, Mali, Burkina Faso, Guinea and Nigeria. It has smaller grains than other millets, but is fast growing and can be grown in very poor, dry, or acidic soils. It can be harvested within 6–8 weeks after seed sowing, which makes it extremely important as a quick food crop. The grain is rich in methionine and cystine and is used to make a porridge, couscous, bread, spaghetti, and for beer. Other *Digitaria* species used for food crops are *D. iburua* (black fonio), which is grown in Africa, and *D. compacta* (raishan), a minor cereal grown in northern India. The leaves and other byproducts from these species are valuable livestock fodder.

Barnyard millet (Japanese millet, billion-dollar grass) (*Echinochloa crus-galli*); bourgou (*E. stagnina*); antelope grass (*E. pyramidalis*); shama millet (*E. colona*); Japanese millet (*E. frumentacea*); *E. esculenta*; *E stagnina*. A group of species that are found in many regions of the world. Their seeds are used for food, and their leaves are used to feed livestock. They are sometimes grown for food for people in Africa,

Food
The grain can be lightly cooked for ~10 minutes and used as a carbohydrate source, with the addition of flavourings (e.g. salt, pepper, spices, butter, etc.), or is sometimes prepared with sugar and dried fruits. It is often prepared as a type of porridge. It is better eaten when freshly cooked, as it goes hard and unappetising if left. Millet is often ground to make a flour, particularly in India where it is made into various breads. Various beverages are prepared from the grain, both non-alcoholic and alcoholic (beers and spirits).

Nutrition/medicinal
The seeds of these species are easy to digest. Cooked, millet has good quantities of protein (12–14%), and contains most amino acids, particularly glutamic acid. It even contains some lysine, which is often deficient in cereals, e.g. maize. The seeds are rich in fibre, but much is converted during cooking. Millet is rich in the B vitamins, especially niacin, thiamine, riboflavin, B6, pantothenic acid and folate, and also the minerals manganese, copper, iron, phosphorus, potassium, magnesium and zinc, and some selenium, although the levels of all these are considerably reduced with cooking. People who suffer from coeliac disease, a genetic disorder that disrupts digestion if gluten is consumed, can use gluten-free millet as a substitute. However, the absence of gluten means that, on its own, it is not good for bread making.

Ornamental
Some of the species are quite ornamental, and could be grown within herbaceous borders, or within a themed ornamental grass-species bed.

Other uses
The leaves are a valuable source of hay, and good yields can be obtained. The stalks are used for weaving, house construction, etc.

uses

India, Japan and Asia, but in the United States and Australia they are usually grown as bird and livestock food. Like the other millets, these species can grow in dry, poor-nutrient soils. Recent research has shown that their seeds contain antioxidants. **Bourgou** is an important crop in regions of Africa, and its sugary stems are undergoing a revival. Similarly, **antelope grass** and **shama** millet are also grown in Africa for food and to feed livestock. **Barnyard grass** is common in the warmer regions of Europe, where it often grows wild. It can grow in cooler regions than many millets. It is grown in Asia and India as a food and for livestock, but also in the United States, primarily as livestock fodder. A tall grass (up to 1–1.5 m), it is one of the few millets that is tolerant of waterlogging and is often found growing in standing water and prefers more nutrient-rich soils.

E. frumentacea is grown in poorer soils in northern India and Pakistan and its seed is often used as a food crop.

E. esculenta is sometimes grown in China, Korea and Japan as a food crop but also to feed livestock.

E. stagnina is sometimes cultivated in Nigeria to provide flour, but also to make beverages.

Finger millet (African millet, ragi), *Eleusine coracana.* Originally a native of Africa, it is still grown there in dry, poor soils, but also in Northern India. It is an important crop to millions who have little other food. The plants are markedly disease resistant and the seed can be stored for long periods. As its name suggests, its seed heads are finger shaped and packed with small seeds. The seeds are rich in protein, particularly methionine. They are either prepared as a porridge or are ground to make a flour.

Proso millet (syn. broom corn millet, common millet, hog millet, white millet), *Panicum miliaceum.* Was utilised in China more than 7000 years ago, and has long been used in India and Russia. Today, it is mostly grown in China, the United States, India, the Middle East, Eastern Europe and Russia, where it is mostly used for bird food. It can grow in cooler temperatures and at higher latitudes than many other millets. It grows to 0.5–1 m tall and has an appearance that is not dissimilar to corn, with wide leaf blades. It has a small, compact seed head. Harvesting can be done in 10–12 weeks. Its small seeds come in a variety of colours. The leaves of proso are hairy and are less popular as forage for livestock. It is fast growing and, like the other millets, it can tolerate dry, nutrient-poor soils. Indeed, it seems to respond poorly to regular moisture and nutrients.

Little millet, *P. anicum sumatrense.* Mostly grown in India, and can grow at high elevations. A grass, 30–90 cm tall, with heads of very small seeds. It can grow in poor, dry soils. This species has been little studied.

Pearl millet, *Pennisetum glaucum.* Probably originates from Eastern Africa, this species has been gathered and cultivated for at least 4000 years. It is now widely grown in other areas of Africa and India as a food crop, but also in the United States mostly as bird food. It grows 1–2 m tall, though modern varieties are being selected to grow smaller to reduce the risk of lodging. It takes ~9–10 weeks from seed sowing until harvest. It has deep roots and is very tolerant of dry soils, high temperatures and low soil-nutrient status. Today, it is the main commercially grown millet, and is often grown for human consumption. It is a staple for many people in India and Africa.

Foxtail millet, *Setaria italica.* The second most common commercially grown millet. Its history of usage stretches back to ~4000 BC in China, and it is still often grown in China, India, Russia and the United States. In China it used to be an important staple crop. A slender, fast-growing plant to 1–1.5 m tall, it has narrow, hairless leaves, compact, dense seed heads, with easily removed small seeds that come in a variety of colours. Foxtails give good yields of grain compared with many millets, though the grain is small. These can be harvested after 8–9 weeks. The flowers are often self-pollinating. Can grow in dry, poor-nutrient soils. In China, it is a staple food for many poorer people living in arid regions; in the United States and Europe it is grown mostly for bird and livestock food.

Perilla frutescens (syn. *P. crispa, P. nankinensis*)

Perilla (green perilla, red perilla, beefsteak plant, shiso, Japanese basil, rattlesnake weed, summer coleus, jisoo, shisho, purple mint)

LAMIACEAE (LABIATAE)

Relatives: mint, spearmint, balm, basil, thyme

A native of Southeast Asia, this plant is widely used for its edible leaves and flowers, as well as its oily seeds. It is popular throughout Asia, but particularly in Korea, Japan and China, where the leaves and flowers are used in many dishes, plus it is a favourite ingredient in many spice mixes and pickles.

Historically, this plant has been revered in Asia, with people believing that it brought health and well-being; however, standing on it inadvertently brought dire bad luck. Recent research has confirmed, and even exceeded many of its historical medicinal properties, and it is likely that this plant will become more widely known, grown and used in the West. Perilla is grown and used in India. In the United States it has escaped to become a roadside weed, though it does not seem to pose a serious invasive threat.

Food

There are two main types: red and green perilla. Red perilla is mostly used as a colouring in pickled vegetables, is added to rice and is used to flavour beverages. Green perilla is the most common type used for its leaves. The leaves are usually eaten fresh, added to salads or used as a garnish. A mix of the different coloured leaves brightens up a dish. However, the green perilla is considered to have the better flavour, so ideally grow a mix of varieties. The leaves have a tangy flavour (can be slightly acid to salty), but they are also somewhat basil- or mint-like. They are sometimes lightly steamed as a vegetable. Green perilla is popular in Japan. The Japanese dip the leaves in batter and deep fry them for tempura, they use them for wrapping rice cakes, or they use the leaves as garnish with raw fish. The leaves are often added to various Japanese and Korean pickled sauces, e.g. umeboshi and shichimi (seven-spice mixture), and to rice dishes with other vegetables and fish. The seeds are rich in oil (30–50%), and this can be extracted and is used in Korean, Japanese and Chinese cuisine. However, the oil does not keep long due to its high content of linolenic acid, so do not store for long periods. The flowers are edible, they make an attractive garnish and the seeds can be added to breads and confectionery. The essential oil from the leaves is very sweet: more than 2000 times sweeter than sugar, and research is being conducted into its usage as a sweetening additive, as well as in perfumery. It used to be used in sarsaparilla.

Nutrition/medicinal

The leaves have good quantities of both vitamins A and C, and are rich in antioxidants such as quercetin. Red perilla, in particular, contains betalains: red betacyanins within the stems, and yellow betaxanthins within the flowers and leaves. Both are powerful antioxidants and may help prevent the formation of some cancers. Perilla has a long history in Asia, being used as an antimicrobial, to relieve asthma and other lung disorders, for stomach/digestive and cardiac problems, and as a tonic.

Research suggests that this plant can reduce the incidence of and treat existing cancers and has broad antimicrobial properties. Several compounds (particularly rosmarinic acid) are thought to be responsible for some of these actions. The leaves can effectively increase the rate of phagocytosis by white blood cells in immune reactions, thus aiding the immune system. Rosmarinic acid has been found to reduce the symptoms of hay fever allergies and to protect the liver against damage. In Japan, the leaves are often eaten as an antidote to fish and crab-meat allergies, and leaf extracts have been shown to have anti-depressive properties. The plant is effective at stopping constipation. The seed oil has medicinal properties, and is high in unsaturated fatty acids, particularly linolenic (omega-3 acid), linoleic, and oleic acids. In trials with rats, when compared with safflower oil, it gave the rats improved abilities. The seeds contain ~20% protein. **Warning:** A few people develop dermatitis after continually handling the plants. Cattle (and possibly other livestock) may develop pulmonary oedema after eating this species, though they usually choose not to eat it.

Ornamental

The coloured-leaved varieties make a great, useful addition to the flower border, and several ornamental varieties are available.

Other uses

The leaves can be distilled to produce an essential oil that has a sweet taste and smell, and is sought after in the perfumery industry and as a sweetener. A red food colouring is obtained from the leaves. The seed oil is used as a drying oil and as fuel, with its high linolenic oil content being valued as a lubricant and is added to varnish, printing inks, lacquers. Birds love the seeds and butterflies love the flowers. The leaves, rubbed on the skin are said to repel ticks and other insects.

DESCRIPTION

A smallish, bushy annual, resembling basil or a coleus plant. Is low-lying for most of the season (~20 cm), but then forms flowers, stems and smaller leaves to reach ~1 m tall at the end of its season. As all members of this family, it has distinctive square stems.

Leaves: Large, up to 15 cm wide and long, covered with fine hairs, roughly serrated and sometimes with wavy leaf margins. Oval with pointed tips: similar in shape to mint leaves. As one of its common names 'coleus' suggests,

DESCRIPTION
Vary from small bushy plants to fast-growing climbers. Usually annuals.

Leaves: Usually in three heart-shaped leaflets with pointed tips, arranged alternately up the stems.

Flowers: Typically legume (or 'pea')-like with five petals. The lower petal protrudes out beyond the upper folded petals. Often white or pinkish in colour. Pollination is by bees and other insects. Flowers are usually self-fertile, and have both male and female structures within the same flower, and are borne in spring.

Seeds: Beans come in variety of sizes and colours: there are many different species and varieties. They are often commonly named after the bean's colour, e.g. red, black, yellow, white, pinto. Usually bean-shaped, though can be flattened or more rounded. They are larger than peas. Most beans can be toxic if eaten raw, and should be cooked before use (see Warning below).

Harvest/storage: For fresh eating, the beans (bush, snap, runner, etc.) with their pods are picked at regular intervals from mid summer to autumn, depending on species. They are harvested while still tender. It takes ~50–70 days from sowing until harvest. The pods vary in colour depending on variety, but are usually green or yellow. For drying, the pods are left to fully mature and can be then simply left on the plant to dry naturally: this works if the humidity is not too high. Otherwise, they can be picked when the pod is beginning to change colour to yellowish/brown, and then left to dry in a warm, aerated place. Once dry, the outer pod is removed, and the seeds stored in a dry, cool, dark container. Can be kept for several months or longer. In the past, younger fresh beans were commonly stored with salt in sealed jars. It takes ~90 days from sowing until harvest. Pods should be harvested before severe frosts occur.

Roots: Fix nitrogen (see above). Not extensive, and are often near to the soil surface making them susceptible to extended dry periods and to mechanical cultivation.

CULTIVATION
Once established, plants need little care.

Location: Prefer a sunny site, though with a little shade in hot climates. Only moderately tolerant of wind; are best planted with other species around them. Generally, not tolerant of maritime locations.

Temperature: Most are not frost hardy, but often can be grown in cool-temperate climates as an annual. Start seedlings off inside to extend the growing season. They prefer growing temperatures of 20–30°C, and only grow

Food
Fresh, young beans, lightly cooked, are delicious. A popular vegetable to accompany traditional Western recipes. Most dried beans need soaking for ~6 hours before cooking (see Warning below), and then may need cooking for an hour or two. The use of a pressure cooker speeds this up. It is recommended that other ingredients are not added until the dried beans are cooked or they may prevent the beans from softening. Cooked, dried beans can be used in many ways: stews, pies, soups, curries, many Mediterranean dishes, salads. They can be added cooked and cold to salad ingredients.

Nutrition/medicinal
Beans have good amounts of proteins, often ~12–20%, and often have good quantities of the amino acids aspartic and glutamic acids, leucine and lysine. They are rich in the B vitamins, with folate in particular, but also riboflavin, niacin and thiamine. The beans, particularly with their pods, have good amounts of fibre, and contain some vitamin A. Vitamin C levels can be high in raw fresh beans, though this is reduced when the beans are cooked. They are often rich in manganese, copper, phosphorus, potassium, selenium and iron. **Warning:** The soaking and cooking water from dried beans should be discarded before the beans are added to the other ingredients (e.g. stew), as beans (particularly red kidney beans), often contain high quantities of phytohaemagglutnin, a glycoprotein lectin. This affects the cell's ability to transport protein and can cause agglutination of red blood cells.

Raw beans contain the highest levels of this compound, though much is lost during cooking. However, cooking temperatures must exceed 80°C or the toxicity can be worse; therefore, be wary of using slow cookers for beans. Initially boiling the beans for 10 minutes at high temperatures, and then discarding the water is said to remove most toxins. Toxic levels of phytohaemagglutnin can cause intestinal discomfort or pain, and in some cases, sickness and diarrhoea. Only a few beans may need to be ingested to get these symptoms, though symptoms usually pass within 3–4 hours without needing treatment. On the 'good' side, phytohaemagglutnin is used medicinally to trigger the synthesis of lymphocytes. In addition to phytohaemagglutnin, many beans infamously produce flatulence, but the addition of epazote (see p. 161) or asafoetida (p. 230) may reduce this.

Ornamental
There are some selected ornamental beans, particularly runner beans, which have colourful pods (e.g. 'Roquefort' with bright yellow pods; 'Purple Pole Bean' with purple pods; the dwarf French bean 'Tee Pee' with purple pods) or bright eye-catching flowers (e.g. 'Scarlet Runner' with lots of bright red flowers).

Other uses
Not removing the roots from the soil at the end of the season leaves much of the fixed nitrogen in the soil to act as a natural fertiliser. The leaves and stems of old plants can be used in compost.

slowly if it is cooler. Compare with peas, which prefer cooler weather.

Soil/water/nutrients: Prefer a good loamy soil with mid pH (5.5–6.5). In alkaline soils, beans often suffer from zinc deficiency. Can grow in sandy soils, but do not grow well in heavy clay soils. Grow best with regular moisture, but do not tolerate waterlogging. Not enough moisture often leads to poor bean formation and shrivelled pods. Compost dug into the soil before planting improves plant growth.

Pot culture: Good for growing in pots if short of space. Perhaps try ornamental runner beans, which will grow up canes and produce brightly coloured bean pods as well. Give the plants good compost to start with and lots of regular moisture.

Planting: Depends on species: smaller bush-type beans can be planted at ~15–20 cm apart in blocks or rows. Seeds can be sown at ~10 cm apart and then thinned if needed. Sowing seeds at intervals through the spring and summer gives a longer harvesting period. Regular moisture until the plants are fully established is important. Runner (or stick) beans are usually either planted in groups at the base of canes/sticks that are tied together wigwam style, or can be sown in two rows, ~40 cm apart, with the strings or sticks from the beans meeting along an upper horizontal ridge (inverted 'V' shape). Alternatively, they can be allowed to grow up fences or other plants (e.g. small trees, maize). Beans do not grow well with weed competition. Legumes benefit from being rotated around the garden to reduce disease risk and to improve soil in different areas.

Propagation: Easy from seed. Sow ~2–5 cm below the soil surface, depending on their size. Some reports recommend soaking for ~12 hours before sowing to soften the seedcoat; others say this practice can do more harm than good. Seeds are often started off inside in colder areas, the seedlings pricked-out and grown-on, and then the plantlets established outside once all risk of frost has passed. Seed can be sown *in situ*, but keep the soil moist (not too wet), until germination and during seedling stages. Mice seek them out, as they do peas. Can use seed from the previous year's crops, though make sure that it is disease free. Often, store-bought beans will germinate and produce plants. It can be fun trying out a few different types.

Pests and diseases: The seeds can be attacked by seed maggots, which are attracted to the germinating compounds: they can do extensive damage. Rapid germination in a warm soil reduces this risk. Can suffer from a number of diseases including aphid infestations, which can severely stunt plants. Beetles can do damage in some areas, biting holes into pods and seeds. Fungal diseases often occur, particularly if the climate is humid. Beans are also susceptible to several bacterial and viral diseases, particularly in hot, humid weather. Treatment of disease is often tricky and impractical. Try to reduce risks by supplying good ventilation around plants, by rotating legumes to different locations each year and by growing non-leguminous species in their immediate vicinity.

SPECIES

There are many bean types available to the home gardener,

with quite a few varieties of *P. vulgaris*. This species, along with some other *Phaseolus* species are described below.

Black beans (frijoles negro, Mexican beans, Spanish black beans), *P. vulgaris*. Beans are small, shiny and angular. The bean below the black seedcoat is white. Native to South America, they are most popular in Mexican and Central American cuisine. Pre-soak beans and cook well, discarding the water.

Brown beans (Swedish beans), *P. vulgaris*. Closely related to black beans, they were introduced from Sweden into the United States in the 19th century. Largish beans with a mild sweet flavour, they are often used in soups. Good amounts of magnesium and calcium.

Butter beans (sieva bean), *P. lunatus*. Closely related to lima beans and can be genetically crossed. Are smaller than lima beans, but are more tolerant of heat. Pods are more difficult to shell. See 'Lima' below.

Dragon-tongue bush bean, *P. vulgaris*. A variety originating from the Netherlands in the 19th century, it has strange, irregularly shaped pods, mottled purple over a yellow background. The pods grow to ~10 cm long, and young beans with their pods can be eaten, and have a good flavour. Alternatively, the beans can be left to mature and are then dried.

Dwarf/French beans, *P. vulgaris*. Small (~20–50 cm tall), bushy, easily managed plants. Are usually eaten while still tender with their pods. Need little care except for regular moisture. Flowers are usually white/pale mauve. Seed can be sown in rows or groupings. Easily fit in between other plants. Yellow wax beans are a popular variety of this bean, which, as its name suggests, has yellow pods that are tender and delicious.

Flageolet beans (haricot beans, cannellini beans, navy beans), *P. vulgaris*. If picked when still young and tender, they have a delicate flavour and are highly valued by the French. If matured and dried they are then known as haricot beans and should be pre-soaked before cooking. The beans are smallish, and white to light green in colour. Haricot beans are more usually known as 'baked beans': it is usually this bean that is combined with tomato sauce to make the famous product. Canned beans are very high in fibre, and have high quantities of protein, higher than most other beans. Fairly good vitamin B levels and the minerals phosphorus, potassium, magnesium, zinc, copper and calcium.

Kidney beans (red, pinto, pink, cranberry, New Orleans and others), *P. vulgaris*. Red, kidney-shaped beans, popular in 'Chilli con Carne'. Extra care needs to be taken that the water they are initially soaked or cooked in is discarded as these beans have the highest levels of phytohaemagglutnins (see Warning above). The plant is bushy, not a climber. The beans are good in casseroles and salads. Their roots may be dangerously narcotic.

Lima beans, *P. limensis*. Originally from tropical regions, these plants are perennial climbers, though are usually grown as an annual in temperate climates. Have yellow/white flowers. The pods are flat and ~12 cm long, each pod containing 3–6 beans. They need a sunny site, sheltered from wind, and grow best in fertile soils, with regular moisture, but not waterlogged. They benefit from the addition of a little limestone and an organic mulch

Pimenta dioica (syn. *P. officinalis*)
Allspice (Jamaica pepper, pimento, myrtle pepper)
MYRTACEAE
Relatives: myrtle, feijoa, guava, bay rum tree (*Pimenta racemosa*)

Allspice is derived from the small fruits of a small to medium-sized tree that is native to the Caribbean, Mexico and Central America. The Spanish 'discovered' the spice back in the 16th century, and called it 'pimienta', possibly confusing it with black pepper, but its flavour is not as hot and biting as that of peppercorns. Instead it has a warm and pleasant aroma and taste. Its common name, allspice, is derived from its aroma and flavour resembling many spices: i.e. cinnamon, cloves, nutmeg, juniper berries, as well as peppercorns. Until World War II, allspice was a more commonly used spice; however, many trees were felled during the war, and re-cultivation never really occurred. Nowadays, allspice is grown commercially in the Caribbean, in countries such as Trinidad, Jamaica and Cuba, as well as in Mexico, with little commercial cultivation occurring outside these regions. Although a plant of subtropical and tropical regions, this beautiful, small, aromatic tree could be grown in a container on a patio or in a glasshouse. However, it needs more than one plant to produce fruits and, even then, plants do not always produce flowers.

DESCRIPTION

Slow-growing, small to medium-sized tree, to ~10 m, though much smaller when grown in a container. Has attractive, whitish grey bark that peels off in thin strips. Leaves, fruits and bark all have a warm, pleasant aroma.

Leaves: Evergreen, attractive, large (10–20 cm long, ~5 cm wide), oval with pointed tips, shiny on their upper surface, rich mid-green, leathery. Leaves occur in opposite pairs. They are pleasantly aromatic, and contain numerous small, oil-storage pores on their lower surface. May shed their leaves in adverse conditions.

Flowers: Small, white, ~0.5 cm diameter, typical of this family, with reduced petals and many fluffy stamens or stigmas. Borne in clusters on flower stems that grow from leaf axils, with the flowerheads forming a domed, pyramidal shape. Plants usually either produce male or female flowers, so need more than one tree to set fruits. However, male plants are said to sometimes produce a few mixed-sex flowers and so occasionally set fruits. Male and female flowers are similar in appearance. Flowers are borne in mid summer and are pollinated by bees and insects.

Fruit: Rounded, small, ~0.75 cm diameter, green, turning purple-brown as they ripen. They have the remains of the calyx at their apical end, as do other members of this family, indicating the inferior ovary of this fruit. Fruits are borne in clusters near the ends of branches and have a pleasant warm, spicy aroma. The fruits contain a single (or sometimes two) largish seeds. Fruits do not take long to form after the flowers, and are harvested in early autumn. However, trees do not always flower and fruit when grown away from their natural environment.

Harvest/storage: Trees start to fruit when about 4 years old, and then go on yielding crops for many years. The bunches of fruits are picked when still green, just before they start to change colour and when they have their strongest flavour. Ripe fruits become sweet and are less aromatic. Both the fruit flesh and seeds are used to make allspice powder. The fruits are dried, often in the sun, and turn a reddish brown colour. They are then either stored whole or are ground. However, like most spices, the flavour of allspice is much better when freshly ground. The whole fruits and ground spice should be stored in a dark, cool, airtight container to retain quality.

CULTIVATION

Location: Can grow in full sun or in light shade.

Temperature: Plants grow best in subtropical and tropical regions. Mature trees are said to tolerate light frosts, however, the leaves can be damaged at temperatures below freezing, and smaller branches can be killed at –3°C.

Soil/water/nutrients: Trees grow best in moderately nutrient-rich soils, particularly when enriched with organic matter. They do not grow well in heavy soils. They need regular moisture when young, though mature trees can be fairly drought tolerant. Grow best in slightly acidic to neutral soils, pH 6.2–7, and are not tolerant of waterlogging.

Food

The fruit flesh and seeds are dried and powdered, and these are used as a flavouring in both savoury and sweet dishes. Particularly in middle and northern Europe, allspice is used when cooking meats, and is added to sausages, meat pies, stews, soups and pickled fish, as well as to some vegetables, particularly pumpkin, and to pickled vegetables. It can be added to pickles, barbecue sauces and ketchup, as well as marinades. It is added to desserts, cakes and candies. It has a warm, rich flavour that is slightly peppery, but not too hot, and is somewhat like cinnamon, cloves and nutmeg. It is used in various liqueurs, e.g. Benedictine and Chartreuse, and can be added to mulled wine. In the Caribbean, meat may be stuffed with the leaves and then the whole thing barbecued using allspice wood. It is an ingredient in Jamaican sauces, and is often combined with several other spices, including chillies. The aromatic oil, extracted from the seeds, leaves and bark adds aroma to various foods. A few of the fresh leaves can be added to various savoury dishes, and are used in the same way as bay leaves, being removed before the food is served. The leaves lose much of their flavour and aroma if dried, so are best used freshly plucked from the tree. They are often used to smoke meats.

Nutrition/medicinal

The spice contains some vitamins A and C, plus a little of the B vitamins. Also contains good amounts of manganese and calcium, with a little iron, magnesium, potassium and copper. The main aromatic compound from all parts of this plant is eugenol, which also gives cloves their characteristic aroma. The fruits contain 2–5% essential oil, most of which is eugenol, but also contain some cineol, phellandrene and caryophyllene.

Eugenol has long been used medicinally for its anaesthetic and analgesic properties, particularly to ease the pain of toothache. Allspice is used to calm spasms of the smooth muscle of the gut, and helps ease digestive complaints, flatulence, feelings of nausea, etc. In rats, it has been found to reduce the incidence of stomach ulcers. Compounds within allspice have a strong antioxidant and anti-inflammatory action. Medicinally, the diluted oil has been used topically to stimulate blood flow, and to treat rheumatism, cramps and to treat fatigue. It has been taken internally as a tonic, to relieve tension and exhaustion, and to treat depression. **Warning**: The essential oil, like all essential oils, should always be used with caution, internally or externally, and should be diluted for usage. Its eugenol component may irritate mucus membranes and the skin.

Ornamental

An attractive evergreen tree, valued for its flowers, but mostly for its aromatic properties. Can be grown as a specimen tree in warmer climates, or as a container plant in cooler regions.

Other uses

Allspice and its essential oil are used for their aromatic properties in cosmetics, perfumes, soaps, etc.

Pot culture: Although frost sensitive, this species makes a good container plant. It is slow growing and grows to fit the pot or size available. It makes an attractive, wonderfully aromatic pot plant for indoors, the patio or greenhouse. Give plants good-quality compost and regular, but modest amounts of moisture, and reduce watering during colder weather.

Planting/propagation: Usually propagated by seed, though these lose their viability quickly, so are best sown fresh. Sow in moist, warm compost at ~1–2 cm depth. Grow seedlings on in pots, in freely draining, good-quality compost, in light shade. Plant out once they have become a reasonable size, which may take 2–3 years. Space trees at least 3 m apart, unless controlling their size.

Pest and diseases: Few problems, though plants grown inside can suffer from the usual glasshouse or pot plant pests and diseases.

DESCRIPTION

A perennial species that does best in subtropical and tropical climates, growing to 20–30 cm tall. It is often more sprawling and spreading, with stems becoming more like runners. Typical of the wild members of this family, it has distinctive jointed stems.

Leaves: Smooth, rich-green to lime-green leaves that have distinctive reddish brown mottling towards their bases. The basal area of the leaf and their leaf stems are a deep red to purple colour. Leaves are oval in shape with acute pointed tips, are smooth and have untoothed margins.

Flowers: Not known if it flowers or sets seed.

Harvest/storage: The leaves are best used when fresh, though can be stored for a few days in a polythene bag within the vegetable section of a fridge.

CULTIVATION

Easy.

Location: Grows best in full sun in cooler sites, but can be given light shade when temperatures become higher than 28ºC, as plants tend to wilt in intense sun. Could be grown as an annual in cooler regions, and sited in a sheltered, sunny spot, or grown in a pot on a sunny window sill. Can grow near to the coast.

Temperature: Grows best in warmer climates; cold weather reduces growth. If fully acclimatised and established, plants may survive light frosts, but in warmer regions temperatures near freezing can kill plants. Best to err on the safe side and protect plants if freezing temperatures threaten.

Soil/water/nutrients: Grows best in regions that receive regular rainfall: is not drought tolerant. However, is not tolerant of waterlogging either, so needs freely draining soil. Can grow in somewhat acidic to neutral soils, pH 5.5–7. Grows best in moderately nutrient-rich soils. Add extra compost or organic matter annually, along with some bone meal or similar.

Pot culture: Ideal for cultivation in a pot in cooler regions, and can be sited on a sunny window sill or in a glasshouse, but needs regular moisture and good-quality soil.

Planting/propagation: *Seed:* Seems to seldom produce or be propagated from seed.

Cuttings: This is the usual propagation method. Pieces of young stem can be taken in late spring and early summer, and inserted either into moist compost to root, or placed in a glass of water until roots sprout. Percentage take is good, as this species readily produces roots from its jointed stems.

Pruning: Stems can become long and straggly. Cutting these back initiates bushier, more leafy growth, and extends the life of the plant.

Pests and diseases: Few problems, though if grown indoors, can suffer from the usual glasshouse pests such as whitefly and spider mite.

Food

The tangy, spicy, young leaves are popular in salads, spring rolls, in spicy soups and as a garnish on various noodle dishes. It is popularly eaten in a dish that includes fertilised duck eggs. They have an almost citrus flavour, and its relation to sorrel can be detected. It has a warm, coriander-like aroma and flavour.

Almost always used fresh, as drying results in loss of virtually all flavour. Vietnamese noodle dishes often include small pieces of chicken, pork or fish, plus steamed or raw vegetables, fresh onion leaves, fried garlic, citrus lime, mustard, chilli, fish sauce, plus other herbs. Because the flavours of Vietnamese cuisine are not as hot as those of neighbouring countries (e.g. Thailand), a wide range of herbs is used, including Vietnamese coriander, to give this region's food its distinctive taste. The leaves go well with seafood dishes, and mix well with ginger, garlic and sesame oil flavours.

Nutrition/medicinal

The leaves have good quantities of vitamin C, plus calcium, magnesium and manganese. An essential oil, called kesom, can be extracted from the plant, and is being researched as a crop in Australia.

The oil has a delightful citrus flavour and aroma. It contains the aldehydes decanal (~30%) and dodecanal (~45%), which occur at higher quantity in this species than in any other plant known. These are important commercially for flavouring and fragrance purposes. The oil contains an alcohol and humulene and caryophyllene.

The leaves have been historically used to treat digestive complaints, and topically to reduce swellings and eradicate spots. Sparse recent research has been conducted on the medicinal properties of this species. **Warning:** Studies have found that this species can reduce sperm counts in mice: it may have the same effect in humans, and has been historically used in Asia to reduce sexual urges. Apparently, it is often grown and eaten by Buddhist monks.

Ornamental

A not unattractive plant, with its coloured leaves and stems. It is easy to control, and could be grown alongside flowering species as a foliage plant.

Porphyra spp., *Laminaria* spp, *Undaria* spp.
Seaweed (edible)
PHAEOPHYTA (brown seaweeds); CHLOROPHYTA (green seaweeds); RHODOPHYTA (red seaweeds)

A few of the more common edible seaweed species are described below for those interested in harvesting them or discovering a little more about them. Structurally very different from land plants, they are algae, composed of many individual cells that form a simple macro structure, without veins or connective tissue or true absorbing roots. Instead, they absorb nutrients and moisture through their entire surface area; hence their thin fronds, and instead of roots, they have holdfasts, which do as their name suggests. Similar to more primitive life forms, their lifecycle is divided into two or more distinct stages, with the sexual stage consisting of individual free-living and swimming 'spores'. So different are these stages that sometimes biologists classified them as different species (e.g. nori seaweed) before it was realised that one 'changed' into the other. They are divided into three main groups depending on their colour: green, brown or red. Their colour is an indication of the light-catching pigments they contain, which, in turn, determine the depth that they inhabit below the sea surface. Green seaweeds generally grow closest to the shore, in shallower water, and contain just chlorophyll: they are also thought to be precursors of all the land plants. Brown seaweeds can grow at depth, though many of their fronds are not too far below the sea surface when the tide recedes. These contain fucoxanthin as well as chlorophyll. Red seaweeds can grow deeper than the other types (over 80 m depth) and contain a wide range of light-catching pigments (chlorophyll, phycoerythrin and phycocyanin), which are able to trap more blue light as well as other colours.

Seaweed needs the right location and conditions, and much of it is simply gathered from the shoreline. However, the aquaculture production of seaweed has become an important way to obtain this food in parts of the world. Edible seaweeds are very popular in Asian, and particularly Japanese, cuisine. They have been used as a food source for at least 2500 years in Japan, though initially were more usually eaten by the aristocracy. About 21 species of seaweeds are still widely utilised in Chinese, Korean and South East Asian cuisine. In these regions, much seaweed is produced by aquaculture. In Japan, the estimated total annual production of nori alone is more than US$1 billion, one of the most valuable aquacrops worldwide. Seaweeds account for ~10% of the Japanese diet. The main three species cultivated and eaten are nori (*Porphyra* spp., red seaweeds), kombu (*Laminaria* spp., brown seaweeds) and wakame (*Undaria pinnatifida*, brown seaweeds). However, edible seaweed also has a long and traditional usage in other parts of the world: the Welsh have historically eaten seaweed and it is still commonly seen and purchased as laverbread. The Scots and Irish have extensively used seaweeds. Similarly, in countries in the far-north latitudes with long, dark winters, where fresh land-grown vegetables are scarce, seaweeds have formed an important part of the diet.

DESCRIPTION

One of the main genus of edible seaweed is *Porphyra*. These are red seaweeds and are used to make Japanese nori as well as Welsh laverbread (the main British species are *P. dioica* and *P. purpurea*). Another popular edible seaweed in Britain is *Chondrus crispus* (a red seaweed, Irish moss, carrageen moss).

In China, Korea and Japan, the seaweed most commonly produced by aquaculture is nori (e.g. *P. yezoensis*, *P. tenera*). Nori is usually made into sheets that can be toasted to give them the characteristic dark green colour. Kombu (or kunbu) (e.g. *Saccharina japonica*, formerly *Laminaria japonica*, a kelp and broad-fronded, brown seaweed) is extensively grown around Japan and China. Wakame (*Undaria pinnatifida*, a kelp and a brown seaweed) is also popular in Japan and China, and is sometimes produced by aquaculture.

Other popular edible seaweeds are arame (*Eisenia bicyclis*, a brown nutritious seaweed), hiziki (*Hizikia fusiformis*, a brown almost black, tough seaweed), sea lettuce (*Ulva lactuca*, a very thin-fronded green seaweed, popular in Britain), sea palm (*Palmaria palmata*, a red seaweed), dulse (*Palmaria palmata*, a red seaweed popular in Britain, Iceland and northern Europe), and sea spaghetti (haricot vert de mer, *Himanthalia elongata*, a brown seaweed) rich in minerals and vitamins that is mostly used around France, hondawara (young *Sargassum* spp.) and miru (*Codium* spp., green seaweeds) used in soups. Agar is mostly obtained from *Gelidium amansii*, a red seaweed, with alginates often obtained from *Laminaria* spp.

Food

No seaweeds are known to be toxic, though some may be very tough and rubbery to eat! Seaweeds can be used in a multitude of recipes, in clear soups with miso, with noodles, such as soba, with various types of mushroom, sushi, stir-fries, and served as a 'vegetable' with seafoods. Kombu, popular in Japan, China and Korea, is used in various fish and meat dishes, in soups, as a vegetable with rice, and is added to bean dishes to make them more flavourful and easier to digest. Seaweeds, particularly the denser kelps, e.g. wakame, are pre-soaked before being added to soups, etc. Wakame soup is served with miso and at virtually every Japanese meal. Wakame is toasted, added to rice dishes, is used in sunomono salads, or can be coated in sugar and then tinned. Nori sheets are typically flaked and added to sauces and soups, or are used to wrap sushi. Nori may be just soaked and eaten as a snack, and is often added to crackers and biscuits.

Laverbread is made from well-cooked *Porphyra* species, which become mushy, dark green and pâté-like. Despite its appearance, it is very tasty and is traditionally served with toast and local seafoods, such as cockles. It is now becoming popular again and may even be served in pastas or in a spicy batter.

Apart from their usual edible uses, seaweeds are very important because of their agar, alginate and carrageen contents. These colloidal, gelatinous substances are used as thickeners, emulsifiers, food additives and to retain moisture in foods. Agar is used in a range of foods such as meats, desserts, beverages, as a moulding agent or binder, Carrageen is used in a similar way, to thicken salad dressings and sauces, and is used as a preservative in meat and fish products, dairy items and baked goods. Alginates are used in a similar way to carrageen, but are also included in various industrial processes.

Nutrition/medicinal

The seaweeds are nutrient rich, often more than most other plants. They are a very important source of iodine, and contain lots of iron, potassium, magnesium, calcium, phosphates, zinc and some selenium, and also sodium, though not as much as their flavour indicates. A disadvantage is that seaweeds will absorb toxic heavy metals if these are widespread in the water in which they are grown. Seaweeds are rich in the vitamins A, C, D (rarely found in other plants), E, K and the B vitamins, particularly thiamine and niacin. Laver seaweed is particularly rich in vitamin A.

Seaweeds contain some fibre, plus small amounts of protein, though nori is very rich in good-quality protein (25-35% dry weight) (also see *Chlorella* below). Nori is also rich in vitamin C, containing more than oranges. Seaweed contains good amounts of taurine, known to reduce the occurrence of gallstones and help control blood cholesterol levels. Taurine may reduce the liver damage caused by excess alcohol by reducing the build-up of fat around this organ. It may also help against obesity for similar reasons. Hiziki is rich in minerals, particularly calcium. It contains ~14 times more calcium than cow's milk, though hiziki does need >4 hours cooking in a pressure cooker. Once cooked, it is said to have an astringent, but nutty, flavour. Dried agar is wonderfully rich in folate, with some vitamin K, and is very rich in iron, magnesium, zinc, potassium, calcium and manganese. Seaweeds are low in calories and are, therefore, a good food for those concerned about weight gain.

Historically, seaweeds have been used to treat various medical conditions, such as arthritis, chest infections and even to expel intestinal worms. Edible brown kelps (e.g. *Fucus vesiculosus*, bladderwrack), have been shown to lower plasma cholesterol levels. Bladderwrack has been found to prolong the length of the menstrual cycle and exert anti-oestrogenic effects in pre-menopausal women. Studies suggest that seaweed may be an important dietary component (apart from soy), that is responsible for the reduced risk of oestrogen-related cancers observed in Japanese populations. It may reduce the pain caused by endometriosis. In particular, kelp may be beneficial to women with, or at high risk of, oestrogen-dependent diseases. They have been shown to have tumour-inhibiting properties.

Other uses

Seaweed extracts are often added to cosmetics and are thought to rejuvenate and moisturise the skin. From Edwardian and during Victorian times, seaweed baths were a popular therapy, found often in the coastal spa-towns of Britain. Seaweed is heated with hot water in a bath, often using brown bladderwrack (*Fucus serratus*), a very common species around Britain and Ireland. The heat releases the gel-like alginates from the seaweed, as well as minerals, and these are thought to be very therapeutic, particularly for relieving arthritis, rheumatism and similar complaints. Seaweed spa baths can still be found, particularly along the west coast of Ireland.

Seaweeds are often used as fertiliser and are great for increasing the organic-matter content of the soil while also adding lots of nutrients. Bear in mind that, unwashed, they are covered with sodium, and some plants may find this environment more difficult to grow in. However, most vegetables thrive in soil that seaweed has been added to. Agar, extracted from seaweed and sterilised, is the main media used to incubate bacterial, fungal and plant-meristem cultures. Various chemicals can be added to the agar to 'make' the cultures do different things, e.g. to form many roots or leaves, etc. Kombu, along with other *Laminaria* spp. are rich in glutamic acid, which is widely used to make MSG. Medicinally, alginates are used in wound dressings and in other products.

Harvest/storage: Collect freshly exposed seaweed from the beach, but choose a clean beach, free of industrial or sewerage outflows. They can be collected using a snorkel after the tide has just turned. Try to collect just fronds and avoid removing the holdfast as well, so the seaweed can regrow.

Once collected it needs to be used as quickly as possible: as is well known, seaweed begins to deteriorate rapidly and becomes very smelly in a short time! Place seaweed in a bag in the vegetable section of a fridge for a few hours for storage. For longer storage, the fronds are thoroughly washed with fresh water and then hung and dried fairly rapidly.

In Japan, many seaweed species are dried, and are then made into sheets, are sliced into strips, or are powdered for storage. Aquaculture-produced seaweed is mainly harvested during the winter months until spring.

CULTIVATION

In Asia, and particularly Japan, the popularity of edible seaweed has led to its production by aquaculture, as well as collection from the wild. It is grown by either seeding ropes with sporophylls (specialised leaflets that bear the sex cells: zoosporangia) or with a suspension of the sex cells (zoospores). The ropes are then suspended in seawater to form fronds; alternatively, bare rocky shorelines are seeded with sporophylls. Nori, a more delicate seaweed, is often cultivated on bamboo structures near to the shore. Cooler seawater gives the best growth.

OTHER SPECIES

***Chlorella* spp.** These belong to a genus of single-celled simple algae that have been recently termed a 'super food'. They are tiny (~5 μm diameter) and passively move about in water currents. Like spirulina (see p. 100), they are protein rich and full of nutrients, though some say the claims of their nutritional benefits may be exaggerated. Unlike spirulina, *Chlorella* contains just chlorophyll, and not the other photosynthetic pigments; however, it is one of the world's most photosynthetically efficient plants. It is very protein rich, containing ~45% dry weight, and includes all the essential amino acids. It contains ~20% unsaturated fats, carbohydrate and some fibre. It also has good amounts of vitamins C and E, as well as all the B vitamins. It has been claimed to strengthen the immune response, and so reduce the incidence of several serious diseases, with some saying that it is a powerful anti-carcinogen.

It is said that *Chlorella* can raise blood albumin levels. Albumin is a very important component of blood plasma, maintaining water balance between the blood and tissues, and thus helps maintain blood pressure. Because each *Chlorella* cell is coated in cellulose, the cells are crushed before usage to make them more digestible: cellulose is poorly digested by humans. *Chlorella* is easy to grow, too easy in some conditions when fresh water has become over-saturated with fertiliser run-off (i.e. rich in phosphates, nitrogen, etc.). *Chlorella* can be one of the algae that then begin to multiply exponentially, producing a thick soup of cells.

All oxygen is used up in their respiration and light cannot penetrate to the lower water regions. In extreme cases, the lake or pod can 'die'. However, if controlled, and grown in tanks, it is a very good way to make a nutritious food in little space using only water, sunlight and a few minerals.

Portulaca oleracea (syn. *Portulaca sativa*)
Purslane (little hogweed, fatweed, pusley, verdolago, portulaca, pourpier)
PORTULACACEAE
Miner's lettuce (blinks, Indian lettuce, winter purslane) (*Claytonia perfoliata* (syn. *Montia perfoliata*))

Purslane is believed to have been a widely cultivated and important crop, both for food and medicinally. It is thought that purslane was cultivated at least 4000 years ago, and was used across the Middle East to Eastern Asia, including by the Greeks and Romans. It was particularly popular with Arabs, who no doubt took it to Spain where it became naturalised and used as a food (though is less cultivated now). From there it was taken to South America. It used to be more popular in the United Kingdom and Europe in times past, and was often used in salads and stews.

Unfortunately, it is usually now thought of as a weed of arable- and waste-ground in the United Kingdom, Europe and North America, though is popular in Japanese cuisine where it has a variety of uses. It is a very successful wild plant as it is not fussy about soil type nor moisture level, and very readily grows from seed, or stem and root sections. It can even find its way through cracks in concrete. Purslane has tasty succulent leaves that are nutrient rich, and its seeds are particularly rich in omega-3 oils. It is very easy to grow in a wide range of conditions. It richly deserves to be more widely recognised and grown as a leafy vegetable and for its edible seeds: as long as its spread is controlled. There is also a sub-variety with golden leaves (*P. oleracea* var. *aurea*), though it tastes the same.

DESCRIPTION

A prostrate, trailing, succulent perennial in warmer climates, but an annual in cooler regions. It has many succulent, juicy, trailing, reddish, jointed stems. Grows fast to ~0.4 m tall, with a spread of 0.6–1 m.

Leaves: Thick, succulent and mucilaginous, usually oval in shape, though variable and can be longer and thinner, or more square. Virtually no leaf stem. Leaves are usually green but there are also golden coloured varieties. They are fairly small, ~2 cm long, ~1.5 cm wide, and are clustered at stem nodes and apices.

Flowers: Small, five-petalled, yellow, pretty, bell-shaped, usually borne singly, though sometimes in doubles or triples, from leaf axils. Only open for a few hours each

uses

Food

The leaves are crisp, yet juicy. The young leaves and stems are often added to salads, and can be used instead of cucumber. Charles II is believed to have enjoyed a salad prepared with purslane, lettuce, chervil, borage flowers and marigold petals, then dressed with oil and lemon juice. The leaves, when cooked for longer, tend to become mucilaginous, and are added to stews and soups. Younger leaves can be added to flans, omelettes, pies, sauces, etc., or can be lightly stir-fried with garlic and butter. In France, they are combined with sorrel to make a soup. The thick stems can be pickled in salt and vinegar for winter salads. The seeds are usually ground to make a flour, perhaps used in pancakes, cakes, etc.

Nutrition/medicinal

This hugely undervalued plant has tremendous nutritional properties. The leaves have a high moisture content, but are also rich in vitamin A (~2200 I.U.) and have good amounts of vitamin C (~15 mg/100 g), with a little of the B vitamins. Leaves have good amounts of manganese, magnesium, potassium, iron, copper and calcium.

The seeds of this species are very rich in omega-3 fatty acids (alpha-linolenic acid), with possibly greater amounts than any other plant. Omega-3 oils are very important in reducing levels of 'bad' cholesterol and reducing the risk of various cardiac diseases. Alpha-linolenic acid is also linked with a positive effect on the brain and may reduce various disorders such as depression, Alzheimer's disease, autism, schizophrenia, etc. It has even been associated with reducing some types of cancer.

The leaves are rich in powerful antioxidants, which work alongside vitamin C in the body to prevent free-radical damage of cells. The leaves contain plant sterols (beta-sitosterol) and allantoin. Beta-sitosterol, which only occurs in plants, significantly reduces blood cholesterol levels, and may reduce the incidence of several diseases. Allantoin is known to heal wounds, stimulate the growth of healthy tissue and reduce skin irritations: it is used in anti-acne creams, toothpaste, mouthwash, shampoo. Historically, the plant has been used as a tonic to prevent scurvy, as a diuretic, and for its soothing, mucilaginous properties. Its high mucilage content gives an emollient and soothing effect on the digestive system, regulating the bowels by reducing constipation, but also by reducing irritable-bowel syndrome-type disorders. It has recently been shown to heal and inhibit gastric ulcers. It also contains compounds (probably potassium related) that relax muscle fibres, such as those in the gut.

Purslane was believed to reduce bladder and urinary tract problems, it was used as an anti-inflammatory, including as an eye wash and to treat headaches. Recent research confirms its topical efficacy as an anti-inflammatory and analgesic when compared with certain synthetic drugs. It was used in Iran to relieve respiratory distress and recent research has confirmed that compounds within this plant do indeed reduce the severity of asthma attacks. *Warning:* Purslane may contain some oxalates, so perhaps should not be consumed in quantity by those with gout, kidney stones or rheumatism, etc.

Ornamental

Often grown as a quick ornamental groundcover plant for its flowers and attractive leaves. However, prevent it from scattering its seeds unless you want a garden full of purslane.

Other uses

Has been used to feed livestock, and is believed to be to animals. The Romans used the juice from leaves to deter ants, which seems odd as ants also visit the flowers.

Rosmarinus officinalis
Rosemary
LAMIACEAE (LABIATAE)
Relatives: mints, basil, thyme, sage, balm

Rosemary is another wonderful herb from the Labiatae family. Its name is derived from 'ros', meaning dew, and 'marinus', meaning from the sea, in reference to it often growing wild along the Mediterranean coast, where it is thought to have originated. Rosemary has been a popular herb across southern Europe for thousands of years. The Romans introduced it into middle Europe and the United Kingdom, where it has remained a well-known herb and ornamental plant. The Christian church has long used this plant as a symbol of fidelity at weddings and of remembrance at funerals, with sprigs being included in bouquets. It has long been valued as a flavouring herb, but also for its many medicinal properties. It is still a popular herb in Italy, France and the United Kingdom, with most gardens containing a plant or two. It is very easy to grow, needing little care (except for an occasional trim), but it does need well-drained soil and lots of sun. Recent research has confirmed its many powerful medicinal properties, and plants are now grown commercially for extraction of their essential oil. However, a few fresh leaves from a plant from garden, added to food regularly, will achieve the same benefits. Its species name, as with other '*officinalis*' species, was because of it being a standard pharmaceutical product. The flowers make an unusual garnish.

DESCRIPTION
A perennial, evergreen shrub, growing 0.6–2.0 m in height, depending on variety, but there are also some prostrate forms that only grow to ~30 cm. Rosemary is multi-branched, usually with upright, woody stems. Plants sometimes become straggly and woody after 3–4 years, and gardeners sometimes choose to replace them at that stage, though some specimens can live for more than 30 years.

Leaves: Needle-like, but flat, 2–3 cm long, numerous, clustered along and directly off the woody stems. Usually dark green, though there are varieties with a silvery stripe. They are resinous and wonderfully aromatic when crushed. The leaves are 'designed' to reduce moisture loss in hot sun, with a small size, thick leaf cuticle, resinous oils and a grey thick under-surface that reduces vapour loss from the stomata.

Flowers: Pretty, small, powdery blue, speckled flowers borne from spring into summer in temperate climates, but may flower in winter in subtropical climates. They are borne singly or in small groups up the stems from leaf nodes. Flowers contain both male and female parts. Great for attracting bees in particular, but plants are also visited by butterflies.

Harvest/storage: The younger, supple shoots are the best. Snip these off rather than pulling or breaking them, to lessen the likelihood of entry of fungal disease. Remove the shoot tips to encourage the plant to become more bushy. Strip the leaves off the stem, discarding any woody tissue. The herb is best used fresh, while still resinous and pungent. The leaves can be dried, slowly, for storage in dark, airtight containers, but its flavour is never as satisfying.

Roots: Fibrous and spreading, though not invasive. Are fairly shallow.

CULTIVATION
Easy.

Location: Loves the sun, with heat making the leaves more resinous and aromatic. Fairly wind hardy, but does not like cold winds. Can be grown near the coast, though excess salt spray can damage the leaves. Consider growing a prostrate form in these locations.

Temperature: Can grow in cool-temperate climates, but loves heat and sun, and does best in a Mediterranean-type heat. In cooler regions, plant in a sunny spot. Temperatures much below ~–10°C may kill back the shoots and buds. In areas with cold winters, rosemary is better grown in a container that can be covered or brought inside.

Soil/water/nutrients: Needs a well-drained soil to grow well: excellent on slopes or in freely draining gritty soils. Can be drought tolerant once established, though grows better with fairly regular moisture. Plants are not very nutrient hungry, and can grow in poorer soils. Growth in soils that are nutrient rich may result in faster growth, but herb flavour is often then reduced. Rosemary can grow in soils from neutral to alkaline, pH 6.5–7.5 or higher, so is very happy growing on chalk and limestone soils.

Pot culture: Could be grown in a pot and trimmed to size. The evergreen aromatic leaves and small pretty

Food

The leaves are either used whole, or are more usually chopped finely and added to a wide range of dishes to impart a spicy, warming flavour. It has a peppery, eucalyptus, or camphor-like aroma and taste. Goes wonderfully with other herbs such as sage and thyme, and is often used in stuffing, in sauces, sprinkled on potatoes with cheese and milk, and then baked, or added to vegetable stews or ratatouille. Also goes well with chicken and fish, and in pasta recipes. Unlike many herbs, cooking does not destroy its flavour. Often used to flavour meats, particularly lamb, where sprigs may be inserted in cuts made into the lamb joint before it is roasted. Often added to vinegar dressings or olive oil to flavour them. Finely chopped, a little can be added to jams, biscuits or jellies to add a touch of sophistication; however, rosemary has a strong flavour when fresh or dried, and too much can be overpowering.

Nutrition/medicinal

The leaves contain ~30% oil, all of which is unsaturated, and rich in omega 3 and omega 6 fatty acids. The leaves are very rich in carnosol, a powerful antioxidant and anti-inflammatory. This compound is being researched for many medicinal therapies, including to possibly treat Parkinson's disease. Rosmarinic acid, epirosmanol and ursolic acid are found in good amounts and are powerful antioxidants. It also contains carnosol, and some rosmanol and rosmarinic acid.

Research has shown that leaf extracts significantly reduced the incidence and number of cancerous skin tumours in mice by 45–60%, to reduce cancer within human bronchial cells, and reduce the incidence of colon and breast cancers in mice, with carnosol and ursolic acid being particularly effective. Compounds within rosemary may reduce free-radical skin damage caused by UV light and other factors. Rosmarinic acid, within rosemary, has potential in the treatment or prevention of bronchial asthma, spasmogenic disorders, peptic ulcers, inflammatory diseases, hepatotoxicity, atherosclerosis, ischaemic heart disease, cataracts and poor sperm motility.

Rosemary has been shown to be a significantly effective antithrombotic when included in the diet, thus reducing the incidence of heart disease. Historically this plant has long been used as a tonic and made into a tea to calm the nerves, cure insomnia and to cure headaches. The leaves have been widely used as an antiseptic: as a mouth wash and to clean wounds. Research shows that topical application of rosemary essential oil is effective at reducing the *Herpes simplex* virus. It is also an effective antibacterial agent. The leaves, made into a tea, are said to help relieve menstrual cramps and relieve digestive upsets. The crushed leaves or essential oil, have long been believed to help repel insects; research has proven it to repel at least four mosquito species. The oil has been used externally to relax muscle pain and stiffness, and is used in oil preparations to inhale for colds and chest congestion. ***Warning:*** As with all essential oils, any internal usage should be done cautiously. Excess consumption of these oils can cause serious toxicity. However, leaves from the plant are perfectly safe to use.

Ornamental

Makes a great evergreen screening plant in a herbaceous border, and a wonderful aromatic hedge, with blue flowers from spring into summer; the variety 'Miss Jessopp's Upright', as its name suggests, is good for hedging. Rosemary can be trimmed and pruned to fit the space available, and some use it for topiary. There are many ornamental varieties, with some tall and upright and others prostrate and sprawling (e.g. 'Prostratus').

Other uses

Rosemary's antiseptic properties, and its oils, have long made this a popular ingredient within shampoos. It has a wonderful fragrance, helps give the hair shine, treats dandruff, strengthens the hair, and is believed to slow the process of hair loss and greying. The leaves are often added to potpourri and other air-freshening products. The essential oil can be heated to release a wonderful fragrance. Its scent is said to stimulate memory, and to also induce good dreams if a sprig is placed under the pillow. The oil is used to add fragrance to soaps, perfumes, etc. The proven antiseptic properties of this plant have made it useful as a food preservative.

flowers are welcome near the house, and can be easily accessed for kitchen use.

Planting: Can be planted as an individual within a border, but also make a wonderful, fragrant, evergreen hedge. If planting for the former, allow ~80 cm between plants at least; for a hedge, space plants at ~30 cm apart.

Propagation: *Seed:* Can be grown from seed, but the seed is tiny, and it takes longer to get a first harvest. Germination can be slow. However, seedling plants are sometimes said to be of better quality. *Cuttings:* Mostly grown from cuttings. Take green cuttings in early to mid summer, with a heel if possible. Strip off lower leaves, and insert about two-thirds of the cutting into a gritty compost mix. Ensure this is free draining, but keep moist until roots have formed. However, note that wet, cold compost is the main cause of cutting failure, with young shoots succumbing to fungal rots. Grow cuttings on until large enough to plant out in their final location. Lower branches can be pegged down to the soil for layering in summer. Lightly score the woody stem partway along, and bury this portion, or bury the stem tips. It can take several months for roots to form. Wait until the new plants are fairly well rooted before removing them from the parent plant. Insert plantlets into a gritty compost mix, and keep partially shaded and moist until new shoots are formed. Plant out new plants in spring.

Pruning: Rosemary can become straggly, and removal of longer stems encourages a bushier neater form, with more fresh leaf growth. Older plants often become woody, with some branches dying back, so fairly severe pruning of dead wood will then rejuvenate the plant. Rosemary can be pruned to fit the space available, and grows better with a trim at least once a year.

Pests and diseases: Very few pest or disease problems.

Rumex spp.
Sorrels
POLYGONACEAE
Garden (syn. common sorrel, spinach dock) (*Rumex acetosa*); French sorrel (syn. Buckler sorrel, round sorrel) (*R. scutatus*); spinach rhubarb (*R. abyssinicus*)
Relatives: spinach, buckwheat, rhubarb, quinoa

The sorrels are members of a large and diverse family. Some members of this family are nutritious and are valued as a food and medicinally, e.g. buckwheat, spinach; whereas others are considered weedy and very difficult to eradicate, e.g. Japanese knot weed, dock. The sorrels consist of several similar species, among which *Rumex acetosa* (garden or common sorrel) and *R. scutatus* (French sorrel) are the most popular edible species. Their leaves are tangy and make a delicious sauce or soup, and the young leaves can be used in salads. They are easy to grow, are perennials and take up little room. Spinach rhubarb (*R. abyssinicus*) is a taller, coarser species, and its leaves are used like those of spinach. Other edible species include *R. acetolsella* (sheep sorrel) and *R. crispus* (dock), but both these, as many gardeners know, are difficult to eradicate and control in the garden, and might be best not encouraged. In addition, their flavour is much more acidic (see Warning below). These vegetables/herbs originate from Europe, and records of their usage in England and France go back hundreds of years. Apparently, it was popular in the kitchens of Henry VIII as a meat tenderiser. It has always been, and still is, a popular herb in France, and is used in many traditional recipes.

DESCRIPTION
A perennial herb that can live ~10 years with minimum of maintenance. The leaves of garden sorrel grow to 30–60 cm tall, those of French sorrel to ~30–50 cm tall, while Spinach rhubarb can grow to 2.5 m tall. The flower stalks of all sorrel species can be considerably taller.

Leaves: Garden sorrel leaves are distinctively, spear-head shaped, while those of French sorrel are more rounded and broader. Evergreen in warmer regions, more deciduous in colder climates, growing from the basal crown of the plant, on long leaf stalks. Younger leaves are often tinged reddish. Leaves of French sorrel are more delicate, and the variety 'Silver shield', the most commonly encountered, are variegated and silvery. The leaves of all species are hairless and smooth.

Flowers: Tiny, green or white, arranged terminally along tall, more or less branched, flower stalks. Some varieties of sorrel (e.g. 'Blonde de Lyon') may not flower for several years, if at all, though most species do flower annually in summer. Pollination is by wind. Male and female flowers are usually on separate plants, so more than one plant is needed to ensure seed production.

Fruits/seeds: Although called seeds the flower produces small, simple dry fruits, called achenes. The fruits are numerous, three-sided, angular, and easy to collect in autumn. May turn lovely shades of rich red as they ripen.

Harvest/storage: The younger leaves are more tender and have a better flavour, though most leaves from French and garden sorrels are good to eat. Harvesting of leaves can start ~4 months after seed sowing. Can then be harvested year-round in warmer regions, and as long as they are growing in colder areas. Simply snap or cut to harvest when needed, and use fresh. Even if flowers form in summer, plants continue producing edible leaves into autumn. Once picked, the leaves quickly wilt. Stored or dried leaves lose their flavour.

Roots: Many Polygonaceae species have robust, deep taproots. The roots of French and garden sorrel are more shallow and less invasive, making these species more susceptible to drought.

wanting a few plants. Plant out once the soil has warmed. Avoid handling or damaging the roots as they dislike being transplanted. There is evidence that yields are not as good from transplanted plants compared with direct-sown seeds; therefore, if growing from transplants, consider planting in biodegradable pots to avoid root disturbance. In warmer regions, summer-savory seed can be sown in autumn to produce a winter crop of leaves. Plant or thin seedlings to 10–20 cm apart for a dense planting or hedge, or to 30–40 cm apart for individuals. *Cuttings*: Winter savory plants can be divided in spring, with sections grown-on in pots in light shade until established. Cuttings of new growth can be made in late spring, and inserted in gritty, free-draining compost to root.

Pruning: Gardeners often remove the old flower stems of winter savory and tidy up any straggly untidy growth to encourage new stem growth in spring. It becomes woody and produces little new growth after 2–3 years, and is then usually replaced. Summer savory is replaced annually.

Pests and diseases: Few problems reported.

OTHER SPECIES

Lemon savory, *Satureja biflora*. A small, short-lived perennial only growing to ~20 cm tall, though is often only an annual in colder regions. Has small, light green leaves, which have, as its name suggests, a lemony citrus aroma and flavour.

Yerba Buena, *Satureja douglasii*. This is a low-growing, creeping perennial that is found growing wild in North America along the Pacific coast. It prefers rich, moist soil, and a shady site out of direct sun. It does best in cooler climates. It has long been used as a treatment for a wide range of ailments, hence its name meaning the 'good herb'.

Pink savory, *Satureja thymbra*. Native to the Mediterranean and most commonly encountered in Spain where it is sometimes used for culinary purposes. Only growing to ~30 cm tall, this perennial, evergreen species has fine foliage and produces numerous, small pinkish flowers in summer. Can be trimmed to keep it tidy and productive. Once established, this species is quite drought hardy. In cuisine, it is often mixed with other herbs and spices to make the mix 'zatar', and is used to make a herbal tea.

Jamaican mint bush, *Satureja viminea*. A small perennial, with little, oval, shiny, light-green leaves, this savory has a much more mint-like fragrance and flavour. It is easy to manage and grow, and is not invasive like spearmint can be. Can be grown in full sun or with a little light shade. Needs a warmer climate if grown outside, as it is not frost tolerant; however, could make a good container plant and be taken inside during the colder months.

Scolymus spp.
Spanish thistles
ASTERACEAE (COMPOSITAE)

Common golden thistle (*Scolymus hispanicus*); spotted golden thistle(*S. maculatus*); large-flowered golden thistle (*S. grandiflorus*)

Relatives: salsify, globe artichoke, Jerusalem artichoke, chicory, dandelion

These little known *Scolymus* species are sometimes grown in gardens around the Mediterranean for their roots and bases of their fleshy young leaves. They are known to have been valued by the Greeks. Their generic name 'Scolymus' is derived from 'skolos', which is Greek for spines, and refers to the very spiny leaves of this genera. As well as a food, these species have been used medicinally as diuretics and to reduce perspiration. Of the three species, *Scolymus hispanicus* is the most commonly cultivated for its edible leaves and root, with *S. maculatus* being a close second. Both are sometimes collected from the wild; *S. grandiflorus* is less commonly found or utilised. Unfortunately all species are very spiny, which makes them unpopular to grow and handle, however, their young leaves and roots have a very pleasant flavour, and deserve to be explored as an interesting new vegetable. In some countries where they have been introduced, they have become a local weed in arable land, e.g. in California and Australia. To reduce the risk of this, remove flowerheads before they set seed.

DESCRIPTION

Common golden thistle (Spanish oyster thistle, Spanish salsify), *Scolymus hispanicus*, is a similar species to salsify, with a long, white taproot, which some say has a richer oyster flavour than salsify. Its young leaves and stems are edible and are highly rated by many. A native of southern and western Europe, particularly Spain, but is found growing as far north as northern France.

The plant grows to 0.4–1 m tall, and all parts have a white, milky sap, as is typical of this family. It is a biennial, or sometimes a short-lived perennial in warmer regions, though is normally grown as an annual for its young leaves and tender root, both which become much tougher in subsequent years. Towards maturity, it forms a reddish flower stem with many apical flower stalks. Older stems are lined with wing-like, spiny bracts.

Leaves: In the first year, it forms a basal rosette of leaves, which are long (~30 cm), numerous, grey-green, thistle-like, somewhat spiny and lobed. They lie almost flat on the ground, radiating outwards and have attractive pale green veins. Young leaves have short fleshy stalks. Older leaves develop spines and have long leaf bases (bracts) that extend down the stem to form 'wings'; these are continuous along the stems. Leaves are deeply toothed and are often covered with fine hairs.

Flowers/seeds: In the second year, the plant forms an 'untidy' main spiny stem with several, spreading flower stalks. These bear numerous, dandelion-like (though their centres are not as dense), yellow to orange flowers, 2–3 cm wide, with larger ray-like petals around the circumference. The flowerheads are surrounded by spiny bracts. They only open during the day, closing each night, and live just for a few days. Flowers are borne from late spring to early summer, have both male and female parts and are self-fertile. Pollination is by bees and insects.

Fruits/seeds: Form rounded seedheads. The seeds, botanically, are small, simple dried fruits (achenes). These also bear rigid hairs, enabling them to cling to passing animals, humans, etc. Or the seedhead can break off to tumble away and disperse its seeds over a wide area.

Roots: Has a long, thin taproot that is similar to scorzonera in appearance. Has yellowish central flesh.

Harvest/storage: Young leaves and stems can be harvested in spring by pulling off the young whitish shoots and leaves with gloves. Gardeners can try blanching the young leaves, by covering with fabric or cardboard for a week or so before harvesting. This makes the leaves more tender. Unfortunately, heat induces the plant to form flowers, and the fleshy leaf bracts then become tough and acrid, so they can only be harvested for a short period in spring. Leaves harvested in the second year are tough and inedible. The storage taproots can be harvested in autumn or during the winter of the first year.

CULTIVATION

Easy: needs minimum maintenance.

Location: Can grow in full sun or a little shade. Can be grown near the coast, though does not seem to grow well at altitude. Fairly tolerant of windy sites.

Temperature: Grows well in hot Mediterranean-type climates. Can tolerate heat much better than salsify, but can also be grown in cooler temperate regions. May be fairly frost tolerant.

Soil/water/nutrients: Like salsify, it grows best in lighter soils where the roots can penetrate to depth. Is drought hardy once established, though regular moisture gives better growth. Prefers a moderately rich soil, but can grow in poor stoney soils. Benefits from the addition of organic matter to the soil before planting.

Pot culture: Could be grown as an annual in a pot, though its spiny nature makes it unsuitable near a deck or path; however, could be used as a security 'feature' barrier.

Planting/propagation: The seed has good germination rates, and can be stored for several years whilst retaining its viability. Does not contain seasonal inhibitors, and can germinate at any time of year with warmth and moisture. Germinates within a few days. Sow in moist, warm compost, just barely covering the seed with fine soil. Often sown *in situ*, in rows, thinning seedlings to ~30 cm apart.

Pests and diseases: Has very few (if any) pest or disease problems.

OTHER SPECIES

Spotted golden thistle (tagarnina, diente de porro, escólimo-malhado), *Scolymus maculatus*. This species is mostly valued for its young edible leaves. It is occasionally cultivated in a few regions around the Mediterranean. It is gathered from the wild in southern Europe (including Spain, Italy and Greece), North Africa and the Canary Islands, but is also found in parts of Southeast Asia. It grows wild on arable margins, ditches, waste ground and along tracks.

An annual plant with a grey-green, shiny appearance, to reflect the glare of the hot Mediterranean sun. All parts contain a white, milky, latex. Similar in appearance to *S. hispanicus*. The leaves are reduced to bracts, and are hard, sharp and tough. They are 'designed' to avoid being eaten, with reduced size and a tough covering to avoid desiccation. Leaves have long stems 0.3–1.3 m long, which are flattened and covered with irregular, spiny, toothed, hard, bract-shaped leaves. Basal leaves are longer and more oval, smooth, and have fewer spines. The wing-like bracts have gaps along the stems (unlike *S. hispanicus*), and these have hard, thick, white margins. Has yellow flowerheads that are borne singly or in groups of 2–4. They consist of many florets arranged in a flattened disc, surrounded by ray flowers that superficially look like petals. Has a row of black hairs around the perimeter. Flowers are borne from late spring to early summer. Seeds do not have stiff hairs to aid their dispersal. Pollination is by bees and insects.

Young leaves and stems can be harvested in spring. Unfortunately, heat induces the plant to bolt, and the fleshy leaf bracts then become tough and acrid, so only harvest for a short period in spring.

Easy to cultivate, the spotted golden thistle can grow in full sun or a little shade. It grows well in warm to cool-temperate climates, and may tolerate light frosts once established. Also tolerates hot, sunny days, with heat encouraging rapid growth of the basal leaves, but also

Food

The root is peeled. It can be sliced or diced, and fried, roasted or boiled and has a sweet, oyster-like flavour that is rated by some to be finer than salsify or scorzonera. Can be dipped in batter and fried. Many rate the flavour of these species highly. The base of the young leaves and stems, as well as the young flower or leaf buds, can be added to salads, soups, stews, pasta, or eaten with bread, cheese, sundried tomatoes. The plants are sometimes blanched to soften the leaves. The central, fleshy midrib of the young leaves and stems are the tastiest parts, being not dissimilar in flavour to globe-artichoke hearts. In some regions, this plant is valued more for its leaves than the edible root.

The fleshy part of the young leaves of the spotted golden thistle is said to be similar to that of the Spanish oyster plant, and are said to be delicious. The leaves are picked (with care to avoid the spines), and then cooked. Discard the tougher parts, just leaving the fleshy base, in the same way as eating globe artichoke bracts. These are added to soups and stews, served as a vegetable with meat, or can be baked with cheese, or roasted.

Nutrition/medicinal

Historically, the plant was used as a diuretic and extracts were used to reduce sweating. It probably contains inulin, like other members of this family. Inulin increases the populations of 'good' gut bacteria, may improve the effectiveness of the immune system, increases the absorption of calcium and prevents constipation. It may indirectly help to lower cholesterol levels. Because inulin is not digested in the gut, it is instead, fermented in the large intestines, which may cause flatulence.

Drying the roots for a few days in the sun, or giving them a short period of cold, sweetens their flavour and converts most inulin to fructose sugars. The roots are likely to be very low in calories, as inulin is not absorbed by the body, thereby making them an excellent alternative carbohydrate for diabetics or for those worried about weight gain.

Warning: A few people have an allergy to inulin, so use with caution until this is ascertained.

Ornamental

Could be grown as a prickly barrier to deter cats, dogs, etc. Produces many bright flowers, though is not the prettiest of plants.

Other uses

The flowers produce a yellow colouring, which has been used to adulterate saffron.

initiating flowering. It is tolerant of a wide range of soil types, from sandy soils, to quite heavy clays, to stoney soils: can grow in heavier soils than common golden thistle as it does not form the same deep taproot. Is tolerant of periods of drought once established, but grows better with regular moisture. However, is not tolerant of too much moisture, particularly not waterlogging. Benefits from the addition of organic matter to the soil before planting. Can grow in somewhat acidic to quite alkaline soils, pH 5.5–7.5.

The seed remains viable for at least 2–3 years. It is sown at ~1 cm depth in moist, warm compost in spring. Can be sown *in situ* or in trays/individual pots, and then transplanted out once the soil has become warm at ~40 cm apart. Grows better with weed control initially, otherwise needs minimal maintenance.

Has very few to no pest and disease problems.

Large-flowered golden thistle, *Scolymus grandiflorus* is a lesser known, but closely related species is *S. grandiflorus*. It is found growing in the wild, locally, in the eastern Mediterranean. It is very similar in appearance and growth characteristics to *S. hispanicus*, and is a biennial or short-lived perennial. Has continual winged bracts along its stems. Seeds have stiff hairs that cling to passing animals, etc. Its young leaves and roots are edible and can be used in the same way as *S. hispanicus*. Cultivation, soil type, nutrition, uses, etc. as described above.

Scorzonera hispanica
Scorzonera (black oyster plant, Spanish salsify, viper's grass, black salsify)
ASTERACEAE (COMPOSITAE)

Relatives: salsify, dandelion, lettuce, Jerusalem artichoke, endive, golden thistle

Closely related to salsify and to golden thistle, this member of the daisy family is mainly cultivated for its long, edible taproots. It is native to Spain, and is now found growing wild across southern Europe. It does not appear to have a long history of cultivation. Unusually, it does not seem to have been used by the Romans, and records of its usage from the wild begin only in the 16th century. It then became popular and was cultivated in France, Italy and Spain, but particularly in Belgium. It is now seldom commercially grown on a large scale, though is still cultivated to a limited extent, in Belgium, the Netherlands, France and Poland. Scorzonera is often grown by European gardeners, and its popularity has increased over the last few years as a more unusual, tasty, healthy root crop. Similar species, which can be grown and used in the same way but are not usually cultivated, are *S. mollis* and *S. undulata*.

DESCRIPTION

A short-lived perennial. Variable height, growing 0.3–1.2 m tall, though it is often grown as an annual or biennial. Faster growing and earlier maturing than salsify. It often forms only a single or a couple of main flower stems, off which grow several apical flowering branches. Typical of this family, all parts of the plant produce a white, milky sap. A few varieties are: 'Great Russian', which has a long root with black skin, and is popular in Europe; 'Lange Jan', which has a good-quality root; 'Duplex' roots have a good flavour, and give high yields; 'Elite Stamm' is productive and high-yielding; which is 'Schwarze Pfahl', similar to Elite Stamm.

Leaves: Variable, sometimes broad at the apex and narrower towards the base, or can be broader at their base, with pointed leaf tips. They are long, often fleshy. The young leaves can be blanched, by tying paper or cloth around them for a week or two before harvesting, to give them a delicate flavour. Leaves grow from a basal crown for the first year, or until it flowers (whichever occurs first).

Flowers: Yellowish, dandelion-like, 2–4 cm diameter, composed of many individual flowers grouped together in a flat disk, with larger ray flowers around the perimeter. The typical Compositae flowerhead has two sets of bracts around its base. The inner layer is upright initially, protecting the flowerhead, and only droops at the time of seed release. Several flower stalks grow off the main stem. Each flower lasts for a few days, opening in early morning, and closing again later in the day or in cloudy, wet conditions. After several days, they close and shed their outer petals, to form a feathery seedhead. Plants can flower in the first year, which does not affect root quality, but does reduce yield. More usually they are borne in the second year, from spring into summer. Pollination is by bees and insects, though some flowers are self-fertilised. Male and female structures occur within the same flower.

Fruits/seeds: The seeds are actually tiny, simple dry fruits, called achenes. The plant forms a head of these, like the dandelion, with these many fruits having pappus hairs at their apices enabling them to float easily in the lightest breeze. Fruits are long, white and pointed.

Roots: Has a long (~30–60 cm), thin (~2–4 cm), fragile, dark-brown-skinned taproot. The outer thin skin surrounds a white, fleshy storage tissue that releases a white sap when injured. The width of the taproot increases after it has reached full length towards the end of summer, and then annually.

Harvest/storage: Yields are moderate, and are somewhat better than those of salsify. The roots can be harvested at the end of the first season, or at the end of the second or third season. Unusually, older roots still retain their quality and flavour. Plants need 18–24 weeks after seed sowing before the roots are large enough to harvest, which is usually by autumn/early winter. Dig deeply around the long, fragile roots and carefully lift them from the soil. Cut off the older leaves rather than the top of the root: damaging the root causes the sap to flow and reduces its storage time. The roots can be left to 'store' in soil over winter until they are needed. In colder regions place straw over them for protection, or they can be harvested and stored in cool, damp sand or in a plastic bag in a fridge. Frosts are said to sweeten their flavour. Young leaves can be harvested during the summer for the first year, and used in salads, etc. Leaves

Food

The roots have a delicate, pleasant, globe-artichoke- or asparagus-like flavour; some say they taste like oysters. The thin, blackish skin can be easily removed once the root is cooked. This is often easier and less messy than peeling when they are raw, as their white sap then tends to bleed.

The white inner flesh can be eaten in a variety of ways. It is often sliced and added to stir-fries and then sprinkled with lime or lemon juice. Can be roasted, added to soups and stews, baked with tomato and meats or fish, steamed and served with a creamy sauce, sautéed in butter with herbs, be steamed as an accompaniment for fish or meat, grated with cheese, added to egg dishes, or even preserved in sugar.

The young roots can be thinly sliced and added to salads. Rubbing the flesh with lemon, prevents oxidation and discolouration. The roots can be dried and ground to make a coffee substitute, like chicory. The very young leaves and shoots can be eaten raw in salads, or somewhat older leaves can be lightly steamed — they have an asparagus/globe-artichoke flavour. Blanched leaves are even more delicate in flavour. The flowers can be used as a garnish in salads, and also have an unusual chocolate-like aroma. There is even a recipe for scorzonera-flower omelette.

Nutrition/medicinal

Uncooked and boiled, the root has good quantities of protein (8–10%). This consists of high levels of asparagine (which is also plentiful in asparagus), and may contribute to its asparagus-like flavour; and of arginine, a semi-essential amino acid needed for cell division, removing toxins in the urine, boosting the immune system, hormone release, fighting cancer and for wound healing; and histidine, an essential amino acid, particularly needed by children for growth, but also needed for tissue repair, especially of nerve cells.

Scorzonera has a very low GI and contains virtually no fat. Contains some vitamin C, and has good amounts of the B vitamins, particularly riboflavin and B6. Good amounts of the minerals manganese, phosphorus and potassium. Like other members of this family, scorzonera contains inulin as its main carbohydrate type. Inulin increases the population of 'good' gut bacteria, may improve the effectiveness of the immune system and increases the absorption of calcium. It prevents constipation and, consequently, is likely to reduce the incidence of bowel cancer. It binds with chemicals that are involved with the production of cholesterol, and so may indirectly help to lower cholesterol levels. Inulin is not digested, instead it is fermented in the large intestines, but does have the side effect of causing flatulence (though this is not as noticeable as with Jerusalem artichokes). As the inulin is not absorbed, scorzonera is an excellent alternative carbohydrate for diabetics and for those worried about weight gain.

It contains good levels of choline, an essential compound needed for cardiovascular and brain function, as well as for cell membrane composition and repair. Historically, scorzonera has been used for a wide range of ailments: as a diuretic, to purify the blood, to relieve stress and calm nervousness, as a cold relief, to relieve stomach ailments and even to treat snake bites (indeed its common name is viper's grass).

Ornamental

The flowers are quite pretty, brightening up the vegetable plot.

produced by the flower stem are tougher and have less flavour.

CULTIVATION

Fairly easy.

Location: Prefers a site in full sun. Is fairly wind hardy.

Temperature: Can grow in a range of climates from cool-temperate to warm/hot Mediterranean. When the leaves die back in winter, the plant becomes fully frost hardy.

Soil/water/nutrients: Plants grow best in deep, loose, sandy but organic-matter-rich soils: heavy or stoney soils inhibit or distort root penetration. They grow best with regular moisture, but can grow in drier soils once established (though root quality may be compromised). They can grow at a range of pH, from 5.5–8.0: can grow in chalk and limestone soils.

Pot culture: Not very suitable for growing in containers because of their long, fragile taproots.

Planting/propagation: Seed: The seed loses its viability after 2–3 years; better germination is obtained with fresh seed. Sow seeds in situ in early spring if wanting to harvest them in the first year, as they need a long season. However, early-sown seed is also more likely to bolt. Cover the seedlings with clear plastic in colder regions if temperatures near freezing are likely. Germination, with warmth and moisture, takes ~14 days and is usually good. Sow the seeds in rows at ~1 cm depth, and thin seedlings to 10–20 cm apart. Keep young plants moist and control weed competition, at least until fully established. It is tricky to grow and transplant seedlings because the long taproots break easily: plants then form malformed roots. If wishing to start them off inside as seedlings, consider growing them in long, biodegradable pots to avoid handling the roots.

Pests and diseases: Generally trouble free, though occasional fungal diseases, such as damping off of seedlings or white rust, can occur.

Secale cereale
Rye
POACEAE

Relatives: wheat, oats, barley, bamboo, rice, maize

The parents of rye may have been *S. montanum*, a wild species originally from southern and eastern Europe, or *S. anatolicum*, also from eastern Europe. Remains of rye grains have been found in Neolithic sites in Turkey, and it was cultivated for at least 2000 years in eastern Europe, often in colder, poorer soils where wheat struggles to survive. It was a main part of the diet for those who lived in central and northern Europe during the Middle Ages, often later to be replaced by potatoes. Rye is sometimes used as a whole grain or rolled, but mostly is used for making bread and adding to other flour types. It is also grown as a green manure and the grain is fed to livestock. It is not related to ryegrass, a very commonly planted pasture grass.

uses

Food
The seed can be sprouted and used in salads. It can also be cooked, like rice, but does need at least 40 minutes of cooking. Even then, it is quite chewy. Pre-soaking can reduce cooking time. The cooked grain has a pleasant nutty taste. It can be mixed with other grains, or added to salads, soups and stews. The grain is often rolled, like oats, and added to muesli cereals, cereal bars, cakes, muffins, bread, etc. The grain is often ground to make flour, which is very popular in middle and northern European (particularly German) breads. It gives a rich, fruity, distinctive taste, though the bread is usually heavier than wheat bread due to its lower gluten content and is, therefore, often added to wheat flour at a ratio of 1:3 mix. The flour comes in three colours: dark, medium or light, depending on how much bran has been removed. Pumpernickel rye flour is the darkest, coarsest and the strongest tasting, but also the most nutritious. The flour is often made into crisp biscuits for cheese, etc. Rye is used to make alcohol: e.g. rye whisky, beer and vodka. For beer, the seed is sprouted, like barley, and a sweet extract is separated out from the roasted grain.

Nutrition/medicinal
Rye grains are richer in fibre than many cereals, and are wonderfully high in protein (~25%), with good quantities of most of the amino acids, particularly glutamic acid, proline and leucine, but also lysine, phenylalanine, arginine, valine, glycine and alanine. It is low in fat, and is very rich in all the B vitamins, including folate and pantothenic acid. Being high in fibre, it has a relatively low GI. It has some vitamin E and K. It contains abundant minerals, particularly manganese, but also selenium (an antioxidant) and zinc, as well as phosphates, magnesium, copper and iron. All flour types retain most of their fibre, protein and minerals, with bran-rich dark flour retaining the most of both these and the B vitamins. Lighter rye bread, unfortunately, has much less protein, fibre, minerals and vitamins. The lignans in rye grain have been shown to be more effectively converted to entrolactones by bacteria in the gut than those from wheat, rice and most other cereals. There is evidence that entrolactones (which are phyto-oestrogens) can reduce the risk of heart disease and strokes, and have been shown to reduce blood cholesterol. Rye may possibly reduce the risk of some hormone-related cancers, such as breast cancer. Whole grains, including that of rye, have been shown to reduce the risk of colon cancer. Rye bread has been found to enhance early insulin secretion in people susceptible to deteriorating glucose tolerance and development of type 2 diabetes, thus, slowing the onset of these diseases. Historically, the seed has been taken as a laxative, and the mashed seeds have been used as a poultice for tumours. ***Warning:*** Rye does contain some gluten, though not as much as wheat, and can, therefore, cause an allergic reaction in those who have coeliac disease. Ergot poisoning: see above.

Other uses
The plants take up excess nitrogen from the soil, thus preventing it being leached, and this can then be re-circulated as a green manure. The stalks and leaves are therefore often ploughed in, after the grain is harvested. As well as adding organic matter, it is good for stopping erosion and increasing the water-holding capacity of poor soils. Residues of rye (particularly the roots) have allelopathic properties, and can reduce the growth of some weeds. It loosens the top soil and suppresses nematode populations. Rye's quick growth also out-competes many weeds. The grain is sometimes fed to livestock, though they may not find it as palatable as other cereals. The straw stalks can be plaited decoratively, and used to make mats, hats, etc.

DESCRIPTION

Rye is a monocotyledonous annual if grown during the summer months, but is biennial if planted in summer/ autumn to grow through winter. Grows to a height of 0.8–1.4 m. Typical cereal appearance.

Leaves: Long, narrow, pointed tips. Leaves sheath the stem, have longitudinal veins with stomata on both upper and lower surfaces.

Flowers: Forms compact seed heads (panicles) at the end of tall stems. Both male and female flowers are within the same panicle. Pollination is by wind.

Seeds: Longer and thinner than those of wheat. The grains with husks have long awns.

Harvest/storage: Although a hardier plant than wheat, it does have lower yields. Harvested either in autumn or spring (depending on when it is planted), when seeds begin to turn light brown, but are still 'juicy'. Harvested grain is rolled to remove the husks, and the grain dried for storage.

Roots: Spreading, soil stabilising.

CULTIVATION

Easy.

Location: Prefers a site in full sun, though can grow in some shade. Fairly wind hardy.

Temperature: Grows best in cool-temperate climates, and can tolerate frosts and temperatures well below freezing once established (more so than most cereals). Although rye can be grown in warm-temperate regions, it seldom is as wheat is grown preferentially.

Soil/water/nutrients: Can grow on poorer soils, particularly sandy soils. Does less well in heavy clays. Does not need high-nutrient soils, and can grow in soils that are fairly acid (pH 5.5) to neutral. Does less well in alkaline soils. Not able to grow well in wet, waterlogged or saline soils. Is fairly drought tolerant once established.

Planting/propagation: The seed readily germinates in less than 14 days if sown shallowly in fine, moist soil. Seed loses its viability more rapidly than most other cereals, so use fresh seed. Rye is often grown in spring for an autumn crop, but is also sown in late summer to autumn for a spring crop. For spring harvests, the seed needs to get a good start before cold weather sets in. Seed can be broadcast or sown in rows. Rotate plantings to reduce the risk of disease, particularly fungal infections. Rye competes well with weed growth. It has allelopathic properties that suppress the growth of many weeds, though this can also suppress the growth of other crops. Therefore, do not re-sow another crop until at least 3 weeks after harvesting rye.

Pests and diseases: Has fewer disease problems than wheat, though the most serious and likely one is ergot fungus, which infects the grain, leaving black fruiting bodies in the seed heads. This is poisonous to people and livestock, causing convulsions, miscarriage and necrosis of digits. It also causes hallucinations, being similar to LSD. Historically, unfortunately, this was a common occurrence when the grain was stored in damp barns during the winter months. Infected grain should be destroyed or can be soaked in a 20% salt solution for the ergot fragments to float separately to the surface; the grain should then be washed in fresh water before drying or usage. Rye can also be infected with other fungal stem rots, smuts, anthracnose and rusts, though crop rotation and selection of resistant varieties reduces these problems.

Sechium edule
Chayote (choko, sechium, cho-cho, Buddha's hands)
CUCURBITACEAE
Relatives: marrow, cucumber, courgette, pumpkin

A native of Mexico and Central America, chayote is thought to have been cultivated and used by the native peoples for thousands of years; however, because its seed does not store, its remains have not been found in archaeological sites. Chayote is still a popular vegetable in Central America, but also popular now in other parts of the world, including the Caribbean, China, Australia and New Zealand. It is a member of the gourd family, and forms a large, perennial vine. It produces very good yields of greenish oval fruits, which can be prepared in many ways. Its young leaves, shoots and its tubers are also edible. It is a useful plant that can be allowed to climb a fence or tree, and has ornamental properties.

DESCRIPTION

A short-lived (4–8 years), fast-growing, climbing perennial, which, if planted near a tree will climb up into its branches, though should not damage the tree. This vine can grow ~15 m in height/spread and has robust, grooved, hairy stems. The shoots die back each autumn, but regrow from the basal crown each spring for several years.

Leaves: Attractive, large, 7–14 cm long, variable in shape and can be oval, to heart-shaped, to palmate. They have a coarse texture, often with 1–3 tightly coiled tendrils

DESCRIPTION

This is a vigorous perennial vine with prickly stems and paired tendrils that help it scramble over the growth of other shrubs and trees. Some species can grow up to 50 m in length in the right environment. *S. rotundifolia* grows to ~12 m, *S. china* grows to ~4.5 m and *S. aspera* to only ~3 m.

Leaves: Large, up to ~30 cm, oval or heart-shaped, with pointed tips and longitudinal veining. Are shiny, dark green. Most species are evergreen. Are borne alternately along the stems. Have pairs of twining tendrils from the leaf nodes.

Flowers: If the plant produces flowers, then these are borne in white to green clusters in late spring to early summer. Some species, such as *S. aspera*, are wonderfully fragrant. Female and male flowers are on separate plants, so need more than one plant to produce fruits; in the wild, plants often form single-sex stands due to the dominance of vegetative spread. Pollination is by insects.

Fruits/seeds: Plants produce deep red to dark purple rounded drupes, ~1 cm in diameter, which ripen in autumn. These are grouped in dense rounded clusters along the stems from leaf nodes. The flesh has a dense texture and contains a central large seed. Although birds love them, humans do not.

Roots: The red-brown rhizomatous roots that can be >2 m long. They are tenacious and are the main means of spread, as fruits may not be formed. The rhizomes are

Food

The juice from the roots is used to make a root beer, which can be either alcoholic or alcohol free. Sweeteners and flavourings, such as vanilla, birch bark, nutmeg, anise, ginger and licorice root, and many others, may be added to the bitter juice. Sarsaparilla adds a foaming quality to the beer, which is best served cold, and is then at its most refreshing. Today, much of the root beer produced does not contain sarsaparilla, and most is carbonated. The roots can be diced and added to soups or stews. They can be dried and ground to make a flour, often used in cakes, puddings, sweet drinks, etc. Its young shoots can be eaten fresh or cooked, and are said to taste like asparagus. The flesh of the fruits is not usually eaten but the fruit of *S. china* is reported to be edible.

Nutrition/medicinal

Sarsaparilla has a long history of medicinal usage, which is still going strong today. The properties below apply to several *Smilax* species. In Central and South America, *Smilax* species have been historically used to treat a wide range of complaints, including sexual impotence, rheumatism and joint pains, headaches, skin ailments, and as a general tonic. Internally and topically, root extracts have been used to treat various skin problems, such as psoriasis and dermatitis, and also leprosy. Early usage of sarsaparilla in Europe was as a blood purifier, a tonic, a diuretic, to treat rheumatism, to promote sweating and to treat syphilis. It has had a long history of usage for syphilis and other sexually transmitted diseases throughout the world and was registered as an official herb in the US Pharmacopoeia as a syphilis treatment from 1820–1910. In China, sarsaparilla has been shown to be effective in treating syphilis in ~90% of acute and 50% of chronic cases.

Sarsaparilla roots contain plant steroids (sarsasapogenin, smilagenin, sitosterol, stigmasterol) and saponins. The saponins give the natural froth of root beer. Most of sarsaparilla's pharmacological properties have been attributed to these steroids and saponins. They are thought to facilitate the body's absorption of other drugs and phytochemicals. Sarsaparilla contains antioxidant flavonoids, which are said to be effective in treating autoimmune diseases and inflammatory reactions, as well as having liver-protective properties. Sarsasapogenin and smilagenin were included within a 2001 United States patent in preparations to treat senile dementia, cognitive dysfunction and Alzheimer's disease. The patent submitters claim that smilagenin reversed the decline of brain receptors in aged mice and restored their receptor levels to those observed in young animals, reversed the decline in cognitive function, and enhanced memory and learning. Another 2001 patent was filed for a *Smilax* species to treat psoriasis and respiratory diseases. Sarsaponin is thought to bind with toxins within the gut and inactivates them so this may be the reason for sarsaparilla's historic usage as a blood purifier. Sarsaparilla root also contains many compounds, including quercetin, ferulic acid, kaempferol and resveratrol. Sarsaparilla is now widely sold in health food stores. **Note:** The bark of sassafras species, which was used to flavour root beer, contains safrole, a compound that has been categorised as a mild carcinogen: for this reason, this compound is banned from usage. However, *Smilax* species do not contain this compound. No known toxicity or side effects have been documented for sarsaparilla, though ingestion of large-quantity dosages may cause gastrointestinal irritation.

Ornamental

Attractive vines, some with fragrant flowers, though vigorous and sometimes invasive. More controllable, smaller, cold-hardy species, such as *S. aspera* or *S. china* could be grown in cooler climates.

Other uses

The fruits are eagerly sought after by birds, which later disperse the undigested seed. The vine affords a good, protective area for small birds to make their nests. This and other *Smilax* species are often grown to make an unruly, prickly barrier hedge.

sticky when cut, have no aroma and a somewhat bitter flavour.

Harvest/storage: The rhizomatous roots are harvested at the end of the summer season. They are crushed and boiled to extract their juice, which is used in drinks.

CULTIVATION

Location: Prefers to grow in shade: its roots, in particular, benefit from being shaded and kept cool. Not tolerant of strong wind.

Temperature: Most are subtropical to tropical species, and are killed by temperatures near to freezing. A few species, such as *S. rotundifolia*, *S. china* and *S. aspera* are more cold hardy, and can tolerate light frosts.

Soil/water/nutrients: Grows best in an organic-matter-rich soil with regular moisture, and a pH of mildly acid to neutral: 5–6.5.

Pot culture: The more tropical species could be grown in a glasshouse or similar, in a container, in cooler countries; the more cold hardy can be planted in a sheltered, warm site outside.

Propagation: *Seed:* The more cold hardy species are said to germinate best after a period of freezing temperatures; even then, seed can take months or longer to germinate. Prick-out seedlings and grow-on for a year or two until large enough to plant in their final positions. *Cuttings*: Sections of healthy, young rhizome can be taken in autumn or spring and covered with ~10–15 cm of moist, warm compost. These should be left in light shade to form roots and shoots before planting out. Cuttings taken from young stem growth in summer, are said to succeed.

Pruning: The plants can be severely pruned back and will regrow from their underground rhizomes. They will usually even recover after fire.

Pests and diseases: Few problems.

Smyrnium olusatrum
Alexanders (black lovage, horse parsley)
APIACEAE (UMBELLIFERAE)
Smyrnium perfoliatum: perfoliate alexanders
Relatives: celery, parsley, angelica, dill, carrot, parsnip

Native to the Mediterranean region, alexanders is similar to many of the other aromatic culinary herbs from this family, such as parsley, angelica, dill and fennel, and to vegetables such as celery and parsnip. It grows wild in many parts of Europe, including the United Kingdom, and is often found growing along lanes and tracks, on banks, near the coast and beside watercourses. It is can be seen growing near the walls of historic buildings, possibly close to where it was once cultivated in gardens hundreds of years before. It is likely that it was gathered from the wild and eaten and used by Neolithic people and during the Iron Age. It has long been used as a flavouring, a vegetable and medicinally, and was popular with the Greeks who used the leaves, seeds and roots. The Romans also used this species and introduced it to many middle European countries, including Britain. Later, in the Middle Ages, it was often grown in the vegetable gardens of Britain, Italy, Spain and Belgium and was used medicinally, particularly in France. However, it is thought to have been superseded by the development of improved varieties of celery, which were much less bitter than wild celery or alexanders. It may now be undergoing a partial revival in interest, and deserves a place in the vegetable garden. However, in some situations, it can become somewhat invasive if allowed to freely self-seed. The distinctive aroma from its seeds was thought to be similar to myrrh, hence the derivation of its genus name.

DESCRIPTION

A biennial herbaceous plant that produces leaves and a storage taproot in the first year, and flowers and seeds in the second. Its flower stems can grow 0.8–1.2 m tall, becoming hollow with age, though the main leaf growth is much shorter. It often retains some leaves through the winter, when little else is green.

Leaves: Leaves are mostly divided into three, shiny, bright green leaflets, and are similar in appearance to those of parsnip. They are broad with toothed margins, and they have attractive flattened, sheath-like, concave leaf stems.

Flowers: Typically small and numerous, forming decorative umbels from mid spring to early summer. Flowers are an attractive yellow colour and have a slight, but sweet fragrance. Flowers can be either just male or have both male and female parts; the latter can be self-fertile. Attracts many species of small insects for pollination, particularly flies.

Seeds: Although often called seeds, the flower produces small dry fruits, called schizocarps, which consist of two

Food
The leaves, seeds and roots are edible. The plant as a whole, but particularly the leaves, have a strong, spicy aroma that is celery-like, and the seeds are said to smell like myrrh.

The leaves can be used in the same way as parsley, and make a garnish, or can be added to salads or sauces. Although they have a celery-like flavour, they are more bitter, and have a stronger taste, so add with care. Include them in soups and stews. The younger leaf stems can be eaten fresh: they are similar to celery, but have a sharper, tangier flavour. Both leaves and stems can be lightly steamed. Peel the roots, then dice and use them like parsnip. Traditionally, they were diced and soaked in vinegar or salt to make a pickle. Old recipes added mint, onion, raisins, toasted wheat and a little honey. This was mixed with two-parts syrup and one-part vinegar to make a pleasant sweet-and-sour relish, which was served with a little oil.

The flower buds can be added to salads. The seeds can be used as a flavouring like other members of this family (cumin, dill, etc.). Parts of this plant (possibly the seeds), were added as a flavouring to wine and mead.

Nutrition/medicinal
The leaves are high in vitamin C. They are rich in furocoumarins and acetylenic compounds, and contain several antioxidant polyphenols, including quercetin and kaempferol. Historically, parts of the plant (particularly its roots) were used as a diuretic and laxative, and as a blood cleanser. The seeds were used to relieve digestive problems, including flatulence, and they were taken on ships to counteract scurvy. Little recent research seems to have been done on the medicinal and nutritional properties of this species.

Ornamental
This is an attractive member of this family, with its bright green leaves and yellow umbels of flowers, though it can become invasive if allowed to self-seed. Plant in the herbaceous border or herb garden. Attracts a wide range of insect species.

carpels, each of which contains a single seed. The fruits are shiny, rounded, almost black in colour and are ridged. Each plant produces an estimated 3000–6000 seeds so gives excellent yields, but can also vigorously self-seed in the right locations.

Roots: Has a thick, elongated taproot that is often forked and has a gnarled appearance. Can penetrate to ~50 cm depth, though most of the thicker root is near the surface. Has whitish, dense flesh.

Harvest/storage: The younger leaves can be harvested throughout the season, but are best picked during the first year and before the flowers form. The younger stems can also be picked. Harvesting leaves and some stems keeps the plant growing vigorously. The leaves and stems can be blanched for 2–3 weeks before harvesting, by covering them, e.g. with cloth, to exclude light. Blanching makes their flavour less strong and reduces any bitterness. The roots are usually harvested in autumn into winter. In times past, they provided much-needed variation to the winter cuisine.

CULTIVATION
Easy.

Location: Can be grown in full sun, but can also grow with some shade. Is particularly happy growing near the coast and is tolerant of salt spray. Is moderately wind hardy.

Temperature: Can grow from cool-temperate to Mediterranean climates. Stems mostly die back in winter, and plants are then fairly cold hardy, but cannot survive very cold winters. Temperatures much below 5°C can kill plants unless the roots are well mulched.

Soil/water/nutrients: Grows best in loose, moderately nutrient-rich loamy soils, but also grows well in lighter sandy soils. Heavy soils can impede taproot growth. Prefers soil that is neutral to fairly alkaline (pH 6–8). In the wild, plants are often found growing on chalk or limestone. Although it prefers reasonable quality soil, it is less fussy than many of its close relatives, such as celery and carrots. Grows best with regular moisture, but is more drought tolerant than many other Umbeliferae species. It is not tolerant of waterlogging.

Pot culture: Although not ideal for pot culture, could be grown in a deep container, and given free-draining lighter soil to which compost has been added.

Planting/propagation: Grows well and easily from seed. Has larger 'seeds' than many of its relatives, so cover with 1–2 cm of fine soil. Germination can be fairly slow: 10–24 days, but is faster and better if seeds are given a period of vernalisation: i.e. a few weeks kept moist in the fridge (not the freezer). If sown in trays, prick-out seedlings and grow-on in pots before planting out. Transplant carefully as their taproots are easily damaged. If sowing in situ outside for a larger crop, weed control is important around the slow-germinating and delicate seedlings. Once established, any seed naturally left to set will readily form volunteers. Just reduce weed competition and add a little organic matter to provide nutrients.

Pests and diseases: Few problems. Plants attract many insect species, but these seldom do serious damage. However, plants can become infected with a rust that damages leaves and reduces growth: remove any infected leaves.

OTHER SPECIES

Perfoliate alexanders, Smyrnium perfoliatum. This is a very similar species and its young leaves and stems

of long, dry periods once established, but is also tolerant of wet soils and brief waterlogging. Prefers a slightly acid to neutral pH of 5.5–7, though some reports say it can tolerate alkaline soils up to pH 8.5. Can grow in sandy or heavy soils. Of the nutrients, the addition of extra phosphate is the most beneficial, though sorghum is often grown without any fertiliser additions. Too much nitrogen in the soil makes the plants fleshy and more susceptible to lodging (breaking), as well as to pests and diseases. Sorghum is tolerant of saline soils.

Planting/propagation: The seed is usually sown in rows, in spring, once the soil has become warm, and it is covered with ~2 cm of soil. Red sorghum plants are thinned to ~15 cm apart; sweet and broomcorn to ~25 cm apart. Plants can be spaced closer, but are then more susceptible to lodging as they get taller. If planting

as perennials, plant them further apart to allow for spread. For just a few plants, start them off in compost in trays and then plant out established seedlings. This method is useful in cold-temperate regions to 'prolong' the summer period.

Pests and diseases: May get the same problems as corn, though they are not usually as serious. A few insects may attack the ripening grains. The main problems are fungal diseases, such as downy mildew or stem rots, which can cause extensive damage, with leaves forming lesions and dropping off. Bacterial diseases can cause leaf spots or root rots, and particularly infect plants in humid climates; however, there are bacterial-resistant varieties. Maize dwarf mosaic, carried by aphids, can cause stunted growth and mottled leaves. Birds are particularly attracted to sweet-grain varieties.

Spinacia oleracea
Spinach
CHENOPODIACEAE
Relatives: chard, samphire, good King Henry, quinoa

A member of the ubiquitous Chenopodiaceae family, along with a range of other edible plants, spinach is, however, the only member of the *Spinacia* genus. Spinach leaves are full of vitamins and nutrients. Made famous by Popeye (though perhaps misleadingly), this green vegetable is regaining popularity after going through a period of being commonly served as an over-cooked mush. Now, it is often prepared in imaginative ways, and its young leaves are delicious fresh in salads. The history of its usage goes back at least 2000 years when it was gathered in Iran. It was also cultivated by the Greeks and Romans. Its usage then spread eastwards to China, southwards to northern Africa and westwards to Europe, later to be taken to North America and Australasia. A very adaptable, easy and quick-growing plant that can produce crops of leaves for extended periods, if planted to avoid the hottest part of the summer.

DESCRIPTION
A cool-season annual with somewhat fleshy leaves, though it can grow through winter into the following summer in warmer regions. The leaves grow to ~50 cm tall, the flower spike to >1 m. Newer varieties have been selected that grow faster, and less readily run to seed

Leaves: Vary with variety. Long (~15–30 cm), oval, with pointed tips, and often with a lobed base. Depending on variety they can be smooth or crinkled (savoy type), and can be oval or more rounded. Usually a deep, rich-green colour, though younger leaves are paler. They alternate up the short basal stem, and tend to be quite succulent and shiny. Leaf veins are quite prominent at the back of the leaf, and leaves have long, fleshy stalks. Initially, all leaves grow from a basal rosette, which can be more or less compact. As the flower stalk forms, the leaves begin to age, lose their flavour and turn yellow.

Flowers: A tall, branching, hollow flower spike grows

upwards from the centre of the basal leaves. Longer, hot, sunny days initiate flowering. Has many small, insignificant greenish white flowers in clusters. Usually has either male or female flowers on a plant, so needs more than one plant to set seed, but occasional plants have both flower sexes. Male flowers are said to bolt more readily than female plants. Many modern varieties of spinach have been selected to be more resistant to bolting (e.g. 'Approach F1', 'Hector'). Pollination is by wind.

Seeds: The seeds are small, simple, dried fruits (achenes). These can be smooth or prickly: varieties with smooth fruits tend to come from newer varieties, those that are prickly from older types. Fairly small, tan coloured.

Harvest/storage: Leaf harvesting can commence in as little as 6–8 weeks after seed sowing, once the plant is established. Leaves can be picked when required, though leave adequate young leaves to maintain growth. Some gardeners harvest the whole plant. Leaves can be harvested

Food

The leaves are tastier, crisper and more nutritious if harvested just before use. Older varieties of spinach (often with narrower leaves) tend to be more acidic in flavour; newer types with less oxalic acid (e.g. 'Hector'; see below) have a milder taste. Young leaves can be combined with other salad greens, or simply enjoyed on their own. They are wonderful with diced white cheese, a drizzle of olive oil, black pepper and croutons. Spinach only needs a brief cooking time, not much more than simply letting them stand in boiled water for a few minutes. Over-cooking makes spinach less tasty and greatly reduces the vitamin and nutrient levels, particularly vitamin C and folate. Use the water they have been cooked in for stocks or gravies: this contains much of the lost minerals. Spinach goes wonderfully with eggs.

Nutrition/medicinal

The leaves are very rich in beta carotene (vitamin A: ~20,000 I.U., one serving giving >350% of the RDA), very rich in vitamin K (~900 µg/100 g, equivalent to >1000 times the RDA), rich in vitamin C (~18 mg/100 g) plus some vitamin E. In particular, they are high in the carotenoid lutein, which can significantly slow the progression of age-related macular degeneration and cataracts, and is protective against heart disease. Spinach also contains some protein and has a very low GI. It contains good levels of folate, plus good amounts of riboflavin and B6. The leaves contain good levels of minerals, particularly manganese and magnesium, with some potassium, calcium (though see Warning below), zinc and a little selenium. They contain some iron, though not as much as was believed in the past, and despite the Popeye myths, most is not actually absorbed by the body. Some is bound with oxalic acid and thus becomes unavailable (see below), and the rest occurs as non-haeme iron (as it does in all vegetables, see Introduction).

However, vitamin C increases the absorption of iron by ~50%.

The leaves are rich in antioxidants (i.e. flavonoids, particularly quercetin), which may retard neuronal age-related disorders and cognitive behavioural problems, thus may help prevent neuro-degenerative diseases. Spinach may also reduce the incidence of certain types of cancer, such as lung, stomach, colon and skin. The leaves contain rubiscolins, which are classified as opioid peptides. These may affect the mind in some way, though quite how is not yet known. Historically, the leaves have been eaten to cure constipation, and for heart and lung disorders.

The seeds have been eaten to ease breathing disorders and for liver diseases such as jaundice. ***Warning:*** Members of this family contain oxalic acids, and spinach has greater concentrations than most. Smaller amounts are not a health risk, however, in larger regular quantities, these acids may lead to kidney disorders, increased risk of gout as well as interfering with calcium absorption. Conversely, data proving a direct relationship between oxalic acid intake and kidney stones are not conclusive. Other factors (e.g. genetic, high meat diet, etc.) are now thought to be of greater importance. Regarding calcium absorption, it is known that >90% of that found within spinach is not absorbed due to oxalic acids. Oxalic acid also binds to some of the iron, making it unavailable to the body. Cooking does not seem to reduce oxalic acid content. Many newer varieties of spinach have a lower oxalic acid content.

Ornamental

Although not particularly pretty, it can be planted in the flower bed among fine-leaved species to give contrasting form, or perhaps with silver- or red-leaved species.

Other uses

Its chlorophyll-rich leaves are used as a food colourant.

for 7 weeks or more if grown in the summer months, before they start to bolt, but can be harvested for much longer if grown as a winter crop in warmer regions. Spinach is best eaten fresh from the garden. It can be kept for a few days in a plastic bag in the fridge, but loses nutrients and flavour. Spinach can be frozen for longer storage and, of course, as Popeye knows, it can be canned.

Roots: Has lots of spreading fibrous roots, many of which lie close to the soil surface, therefore, take care that they are not damaged by mechanical cultivation.

CULTIVATION

Easy: minimum maintenance.

Location: Can be grown in full sun, or a little shade in warmer regions. Some shade encourages the formation of larger more succulent leaves. Fairly wind hardy and can be grown near the coast.

Temperature: Can grow in cold- and warm-temperate climates. In the latter, it is best grown as an autumn to winter to spring crop: it will keep growing throughout the winter, supplying leaves when little else is available. In cooler climates, it is generally planted in early spring for a summer crop or, if given a mulch and planted in a sunny spot, it may be planted in autumn and grown through the winter. It can tolerate temperatures down to at least −10°C once established. Older varieties, with spiny 'seeds', are said to be more cold hardy.

Soil/water/nutrients: Grows well in many soil types, from sandy to quite heavy clays. The presence of organic matter and nutrients (adequate nitrogen, phosphate and potassium) gives the best growth. Incorporate these before sowing or planting, though do not allow fertiliser to come into direct contact with seeds. Grows best at pH 6–7.5. Plants do not grow well in acid soils, and have stunted growth and yellow leaves. Add some lime if the soil is acidic. Most importantly, spinach needs regular moisture to produce well.

Pot culture: Could be grown in pots if short of space.

Planting/propagation: Sowing seeds at intervals of a few weeks maintains a continual supply of fresh, young leaves. The seeds germinate well and within 7–10 days. Sow seeds at 1–2-cm depth. Give moisture and some warmth (~20°C), though too much heat inhibits germination. Can be sown thinly in rows, and then thinned as they grow, to obtain a final spacing of ~20 cm or closer. Or, can be sown in trays, and then seedlings planted out in their final positions; this is a better method if short of space or if only a few plants are needed. Keep young plants moist and weed free.

Pests and diseases: Has few pest or disease problems. In some areas, a virus called spinach blight can cause yellowing of the leaves and stunted plant growth. It is possible to buy virus-resistant seed. Occasional bacterial (e.g. soft rot, leaf spot) and fungal (e.g. anthracnose, leaf spot, damping off, root rot) diseases can occur. Modern varieties, such as 'Upright F1', have been developed to be resistant to downy mildews. Few pests attack the plants, but they can be attacked by the spinach leaf miner.

Stachys affinis (syn. S. sieboldii, S. tubifera)

Chinese artichoke (Japanese artichoke, knotroot, crosne, crosnes, chorogi, kam-lu)

LAMIACEAE (LABIATAE)

Relatives: mints, rosemary, thyme, sage

Although called artichoke, it is not related to Jerusalem or globe artichokes, but is instead, closely related to the many mint herbs and to many wild herb plants such as betony and woundwort. Chinese artichoke is thought to originate from Southeast Asia, where it has been cultivated and used in Chinese, Japanese and Korean cuisine for thousands of years as a winter root vegetable. It was introduced into Europe and Britain in the early 1800s and became quite popular, particularly in France, where it is commonly known as crosne, and is still occasionally found for sale in local markets. However, it is now less often grown in Europe, which is a shame, as it is very easy to cultivate, needs very little care, and produces tasty, though small, tubers. It is occasionally grown as a vegetable in New Zealand, Australia and North America.

DESCRIPTION

Plants are shrubby perennials, growing only to ~0.5 m tall, but with upright, sprightly stems. There are two main varieties: 'Old Red' and 'Common White'.

Leaves: The stems and leaves are typical of this family, with distinctive four-sided stems and leaves arranged in opposite pairs, alternately up the stem. The leaves are oval with pointed tips and have a densely crinkled, coarse texture, are grey-green in colour, and have typical mint-like leaf veination. Larger veins and stems are often mauvish in colour.

Flowers: Small, white/pinkish mauve, pretty when looked at closely. They are borne mid- to late summer and have both male and female parts within each flower. However, they are reported to not always flower in colder areas. Pollination is by bees and insects.

Roots: Each plant has many knobbly, segmented tan- to white-coloured tubers, with a very thin outer skin. The inner storage flesh is white. They are small (only 2–5 cm long, and 0.5–1 cm wide) and come in 'strings'. The tubers grow mingled amongst its fibrous roots, and emanate out from a basal crown.

Harvest/storage: Plants take at least ~6 months to form their tubers. Each plant produces many tubers, but these are small, so several plants are needed to get good yields. The strings of small tubers, found not far below the soil surface, are dug up at the end of the season once the stem top and leaves begin to turn brown and die back. Once harvested, they can be stored in a polythene bag in a fridge for several weeks, but they tend to discolour and become yellowish in colour, and their flavour quality is reduced. They can be left in the soil to store until needed during the winter months. Any pieces of tuber left in the soil will readily form new plants in spring.

CULTIVATION

Easy.

Location: Can grow in full sun, but also in light shade.

Temperature: Can be grown in a range of climates from cool-temperate to tropical highlands, and can tolerate fairly high summer temperatures. Although frosts kill back the stems and leaves, the tubers are quite frost hardy, particularly if supplied with an organic mulch, which also helps retain moisture and adds nutrients. However, tubers

Food

Simply clean the soil off the small strings of tubers; their thin skin is fully edible. However, cleaning can be fiddly due to their small size. Remove any fibrous roots or harder tuber sections. They are best eaten soon after preparation as their flesh quickly discolours and flavour quality becomes reduced. Soak prepared tubers in water with a squeeze of lemon juice to reduce discolouration. They can be steamed for 10–15 minutes and served with a knob of butter and black pepper, or they can be sautéed with chopped bacon and chives to make a delicious dish. In France, they are often lightly fried with lemon. They can be grated or finely chopped and used raw in salads, perhaps with eggs and ham. In Asia, particularly China, they are often pickled or are added to stir-fries, with other vegetables, tofu, etc. The tender tubers have a good, mild nutty flavour that has been compared to salsify and to Jerusalem artichokes, hence their common name, though quality of flavour seems to vary with cultivation techniques. Their crisp texture is similar to that of water chestnuts, so they are sometimes used as a substitute for these in Asian recipes. The leaves are said to be edible, though their flavour is not recommended.

Nutrition/medicinal

The tubers contain a little protein, with ~25% of its weight being starch and sugars and they are moderately rich in minerals. The whole plant has been used historically to treat colds and other chest complaints, including pneumonia, as well as to reduce anxiety and as an analgesic.

Ornamental

Can be grown as a groundcover, particularly flourishing in wetter areas.

---

are damaged by severe cold, so are better dug up and stored in damp sand in a shed and replanted in spring.

Soil/water/nutrients: Plants need a friable loam or sand-based soil to form good tubers: they grow poorly in clays unless lots of organic matter and/or gypsum are incorporated. They also need regular moisture, so organic matter needs to be added to sandy soils. Periods of dryness result in shrivelled tubers, but they can tolerate periods of waterlogging or even flooded soils, particularly during their dormant winter months. They can grow in a range of soil pH, though prefer slightly acidic to neutral: 5.5–7. Some think their flavour becomes bland if grown in soils that are too nutrient rich, particularly if too rich in nitrogen.

Pot culture: Could be easily grown in deep pots if short of space. Provide good-quality compost and plenty of moisture.

Planting/propagation: *Seed:* Can be grown from seed, if available. Sow in spring and cover with ~0.5–1 cm of fine soil. Keep moist and relatively warm for germination. Plant seedlings out when they are a reasonable size, which may not be until the following spring. It can take 2–4 years until reasonable crops of tubers from seed-grown plants are achieved, so it is good to make successive plantings each year. *Cuttings:* Easy. The very easily divided tubers can be inserted into ~5 cm depth of soil, ~30–40 cm apart. A mulch around the plants helps retain moisture and suppresses weed growth.

Pests and diseases: Few problems reported, though likely to suffer the same pests and diseases as the mints, e.g. rusts.

Syzygium aromaticum (syn. *Eugenia caryophyllata*)
Clove (Zanzibar redhead)
MYRTACEAE
Relatives: Malabar plum, myrtle, feijoa, guava

From the large *Syzygium* genus, with more than 1000 species, and closely related to the *Eugenia*, *Syzygium* is now classified as being from the 'Old World', whereas *Eugenia* species have been reclassified to just originate from the 'New World'. Cloves are the unopened flower buds of a small tree that was originally native to the North Moluccas in Indonesia. They have long been used for their aromatic, and particularly their medicinal, properties. Using clove oil to reduce the pain of toothache is especially well known. Cloves were transported and spread from Indonesia long ago, with remains being found in a Syrian ship ~3800 years old. They were known to the Chinese about 2300 years ago, where, it is reported, officers of the Court were required to chew cloves to sweeten their breath before addressing the Emperor. Later they were popular with the Romans. Later still, the Portuguese, and then the Dutch, established this species in the Indian Ocean islands of Pemba, Zanzibar, Madagascar and Réunion. Most of the world's crop is still grown on these islands, particularly on Pemba, which is said to be almost covered with clove plantations. Cloves are also grown in Indonesia, India and Sri Lanka. Historically, including during the formation and exploitation of the spice routes, cloves (as well as several other spices) were often sold for large amounts. They were sometimes worth more than their weight in gold and many colonists and explorers made their fortunes along the way. The name 'clove' is from the French 'clou', meaning a nail, probably because the flower bud resembles a nail in shape.

Food

Cloves have a strong, warm to hot taste, with a distinctive flavour: only a small amount is needed to flavour foods. Cloves are either used whole or are ground and used as a powder, with the latter obviously not having to be removed after cooking. A clove or two are commonly added to fruit pies, particularly with apple, and are cooked with the fruit to impart their warm, spicy, distinctive flavour. Whole cloves are then discarded before eating. They are also used in cakes and desserts to give a spicy flavour, and are one of the ingredients in many pickling spices. Cloves are a popular ingredient in the cuisine of northern India, being added to most dishes, and they are added to biryani in southern India. Clove oil contains vanillin and is often used as replacement for vanilla, due to its lower cost. The fragrant fruits, though they do not have much flesh, are said to be pleasant to eat and are used to flavour desserts.

Nutrition/medicinal

Cloves have good amounts of fibre, fairly good amounts of vitamins C and K. They contain magnesium, manganese, iron and calcium. The cloves are rich in essential oil (~15%), which is a greater percentage than most plants. This contains mostly eugenol (~80%), but also caryophyllene. It is obtained by distilling the crushed leaves and unripe fruit.

The oil is used medicinally, particularly as an analgesic and anaesthetic for toothache and other oral problems, and is still recommended by professionals as a short-term remedy until visiting a dentist. The oil has been shown to have one of the highest synergistic rates when given with antimicrobial drugs to treat *Staphylococcus aureus*. Its oil has been found to be one of the strongest inhibitors against a wide range of pathogenic bacteria (both Gram-negative and Gram-positive), yeasts and moulds, including *S. aureus*, *Bacillus cereus*, *Enterococcus faecalis*, *Listeria monocytogenes*, *Escherichia coli*, *Yersinia enterocolitica*, *Salmonella choleraesuis*, *Candida albicans*, *Penicillium*

islandicum and *Aspergillus flavus*. It reduces the growth and activity of the *Herpes* virus and may have some activity against the hepatitis C virus. The oil has been shown to have antioxidant and anticarcinogenic properties against several cancer types: its compounds can dramatically reduce the mutagenic potential of several carcinogens tested. However, another trial found that eugenol is a weak tumour-promoter: so use the oil with great caution.

Historically, it was used by the Chinese and Persians as a stimulant, to ease digestive problems and to reduce flatulence. It has been used to expel internal parasites and has been proven to be 100% repellent (2–4 h) against three tested species of mosquito. This was higher than any of the other 37 plant oils tested. Historically, clove oil has been used as an aphrodisiac, with recent experiments showing that it does indeed lead to a significant and sustained increase in the sexual activity of normal male rats, without any adverse effects. ***Warning:*** Like all essential oils, clove oil should be treated with great respect and caution as, in larger amounts, its effects may be adversely unpredictable.

Ornamental

Makes an attractive, small, densely leaved shade tree, with pretty flowers. It can be grown outside in a frost-free environment or in a pot inside in colder regions.

Other uses

The buds are used in perfumery, and have long been used inserted into oranges to make a fragrant pomander. They are also an ingredient in incense in China and Japan. In the days of open sewers, cloves were extensively used by the aristocracy in London, who held them to the nose in handkerchiefs, when they were forced to traverse the streets of the poor. In Indonesia, they are popular in a type of cigarette known as *kretek* and they are sometimes mixed with marijuana.

DESCRIPTION

A smallish, slow-growing, neatly shaped, conical tree, growing to 7–9 m tall. Its branches form a dense structure. Its trunk can become buttressed as it ages and it has coarse grey, finely ridged bark.

Leaves: This evergreen species has a dense leaf covering, so forms a good shade tree. Leaves are dark green and are aromatic when crushed. They are opposite,

composite flowerheads have two sets of bracts around the base, which are not sepals. The inner layer is upright initially, protecting the flowerhead, and only droops at the time of seed release. Several flower stalks grow off the main stem and are borne from early spring to late autumn, though mostly open in late spring. Each flower lasts for several days, opening in early morning, and often closing again by afternoon or in cloudy, wet conditions. After a few days, they close and shed their outer petals, to form feathery seed heads which are dispersed in the wind. Pollination is by bees and insects, though many flowers are self-fertilised. Male and female structures occur within the same flower.

Harvest/storage: Has a long season, taking 18–20 weeks from seed sowing until the roots can be harvested, which is usually by autumn. Carefully lift the roots with a fork and cut off the older leaves. Damaging or cutting the root causes it to bleed and reduces its storage time. The roots can be left to 'store' in the soil over winter until they are needed; in colder regions, placing straw over them gives extra protection. Or they can be harvested and stored in cool, damp sand. The first frosts are said to sweeten the roots' flavour. Young leaves can be harvested during the summer for salads, etc.

Roots: A long (20–30 cm), white or pinkish skinned, thin taproot (~2.5 cm diameter), parsnip-like, fleshy, with white sap when mature.

CULTIVATION

Location: Can be grown in full sun or with a little shade. Fairly wind hardy and can be grown in coastal locations.

Temperature: Prefer cool- to moderately warm-temperate climates, though *T. prarensis* tolerates more cold and frosts. In hotter regions, plant salsify with some shade, as too much heat causes plants to bolt. Cooler weather gives slower, better root growth.

Soil/water/nutrients: Because of its taproot, it grows better in lighter soils and loams; although, it can grow in heavy soils, these are likely to impede root growth. It can grow in poorer soils, but grows best in soil that includes well-rotted organic-matter and is moderately nutrient rich. Do not use fresh manure as this can burn the roots and cause them to fork. Loosen soil to ~30 cm depth before sowing the seed or planting seedlings. Regular moisture gives the best growth, though plants can tolerate short periods of drought.

Planting/propagation: Because it takes at least 18 weeks until the roots can be harvested, the seed should be sown early in spring. Cover seeds with 1–2 cm of fine soil. The seeds germinate well in moist, warm compost; indeed, if allowed to flower, volunteer seedlings often appear the following spring. Best to use fresh seed, as viability becomes much reduced after 12 months. Usually sown *in situ* in rows, for flower beds, start seedlings off in trays or pots before planting out. Transplant with care to avoid damaging the taproot. The leaves of salsify are grass-like, so take care when weeding young plants. Thin plants to 8–12 cm apart, using removed seedlings in soups, salads, etc.

Pests and diseases: Has few problems.

Food

The seeds can be sprouted and used in salads. Young roots can be sliced or grated and eaten raw in salads. Older roots may be sliced and added to stir-fries or are roasted with other vegetables. Salsify has a fleshy consistency and its flavour has been likened to oysters. The roots can be boiled and served with black pepper and butter, or with cheese; or can be parboiled and then deep fried; or they can be cut into chunks and roasted. They can also be mashed. Lemon juice added to the water when boiling prevents oxidation and discolouration. Salsify roots can be cooked in milk, or made into a soup. In France, the fried root is sweetened before serving. The roots can also be dried and ground to make a coffee substitute, in the same way as chicory (to which it is related). The young leaves are cut finely and added to salads, and older leaves can be added to soups, stews, etc. or simply lightly steamed and eaten like spinach. They have an asparagus/mild oyster-like flavour.

Nutrition/medicinal

Both uncooked and boiled, the root has good quantities of protein (8–10%) and a very low GI (6). Contains virtually no fat. Contains some vitamin C (~11 mg/100 g), and has good levels of the B vitamins, particularly riboflavin and B6, with some folate, pantothenic acid and thiamine. Good amounts of the minerals.

Like other members of this family, salsify contains inulin as its main carbohydrate type. Inulin increases the population of 'good' gut bacteria, may improve the effectiveness of the immune system and increases the absorption of calcium. It prevents constipation and, consequently, is likely to reduce the incidence of bowel cancer. It binds with chemicals that are involved with the production of cholesterol, and so may indirectly help to lower cholesterol levels. Inulin is not digested, instead it is fermented in the large intestines, so does have the side effect of causing flatulence, though this is not as noticeable as with Jerusalem artichokes. As the inulin is not absorbed, salsify is an excellent alternative carbohydrate for diabetics and for those worried about weight gain. Historically, this plant has been used to treat liver and gallbladder disorders, and was thought to have detoxifying properties. It was also used as a diuretic, to treat coughs and bronchitis, and for stomach ailments.

Ornamental

Could be grown in a flowerbed for its pretty flowers.

uses

Trapa spp.
Water chestnuts
TRAPACEAE

Jesuit nut, water caltrop (*Trapa natans*); devil's pod, bat nut, ling kio, ling chio, bull nut, buffalo-head nut (*Trapa bicornis* (syn. *T. quadrispinosa* [four spined], *T. bispinosa* [two-spined]))

The only genus within Trapaceae, these water chestnuts should not be confused with the unrelated Chinese water chestnuts (*Eleocharis dulci*). There is confusion over the naming of these species, but *T. natans* is native to wetlands mostly confined to Europe and North Africa, and has four-spined fruits; *T. bicornis* is native to Asia, particularly Indonesia and China, but is also abundant in Kashmir where it is sometimes used as a staple crop. These are very similar species, with some considering them to be varieties of one common species. The strangely shaped fruits of these wetland species have long been harvested as a food. The Chinese are thought to have harvested the fruits of *Trapa bicornis* for at least 3000 years. They were used as food but were also in important ceremonies, and they are still seen for sale in markets. *T. natans* has a long history of usage as a food in Germany, and may have been a main food source at certain times of year; it was also a popular food in northern Italy. Chestnut describes the flavour of the edible seeds. Caltrop (*T. natans*) describes the shape of the four-spined fruits, with caltrop referring to an ancient, medieval weapon that had four points used to lame the enemy's horses (caltrops were also laid on roads, in World War II, to destroy enemy vehicle tyres). The two-spined fruit of *T. bicornis*, aptly named bat nut, is very like that of a bat's head. Unfortunately, *T. natans* is now a rare plant in much of Europe and other regions where it used to grow wild; however, it was introduced into the United States and has now become invasive in some eastern states and is considered a noxious weed in Australia. In some locations, it can crowd out native species. These are unusual and ornamental species to grow in a pond or in a container. They give good yields of seeds and make attractive wetland species.

DESCRIPTION

Fast-growing, wetland annuals that form long stems and floating leaves and flowers from their submerged, fibrous root systems. Long, slender stems grow upwards with leaves and flowers branching off the apex to float on the water surface, not unlike the growth of water lilies. Stems can grow upwards ~3 m, though plants grow better in shallower water (0.5–1 m depth). The stems carry oxygen down to the roots, but also become partially filled with air, increasing their buoyancy and helping keep the leaves above water. Its seeds are harvested in autumn. If allowed to self-seed over several years, in the right conditions, the dense foliage on the water surface restricts light to plants below; thus, it can become invasive and detrimental to the ecology of the water system.

Leaves: Has two types of leaves: fine, thin, feathery leaves within the water column from the slender stems, and undivided fan-shaped, hemispherical- to triangular-shaped floating leaves at the water surface. These latter leaves are mid-green, often tinged red, are 2–6 cm long and have saw-toothed margins. The floating leaves become arranged radially outwards to form a geometrically aesthetic pattern.

Flowers: Simple, white, small, four-petalled, plus four sepals that later develop into the fruit's spines. Flowers have both male and female parts and are borne from early to mid summer. Pollination is by insects.

Fruit/seeds: Once fertilised, the flower stalks curve downwards resulting in the fruit developing upside down, under water. The fruits have an unusual shape, and contain a single, large starchy seed. The fruit is usually brown or black in colour, though some varieties, e.g. 'Su Zhou', are an attractive rose-red colour. The fleshy outer pericarp covers a large 2- or 4-horned, hard endocarp. The knobbly, hat-shaped fruits of *Trapa natans* have four-pointed spiny projections, while those of *T. bicornis* have either two or four. In the wild, when the fruits mature and become detached from the plant in autumn, their spines can adhere to birds, animals and floating vegetation, thus hitching a free ride to other areas. Otherwise, they sink to the mud below, where they can remain dormant for many years. They are painful if they are stood on when swimming in waterways. Alternately, the fruits sometimes float down rivers, and can be found on the shorelines of coasts far away from their origins.

Harvest/storage: The fruits are harvested from autumn into winter from the water surface. Fruits ripen over a period of several weeks. Each seedling can produce 15–30 stems, each with rosettes of floating leaves. Each rosette can produce up to 15 to 20 seeds, so each plant has high yields of fruits.

Roots: Fibrous, adventitious, anchoring the stem and leaves to the substrate. Some botanists consider the stem's lower leaves to be roots rather than leaves.

CULTIVATION

Location: Prefers a site in full sun or in light shade.

Temperature: Plants of *T. natans* are quite cold hardy: their above-ground parts die back in winter and the storage rhizomes over-winter under water in mud. Severe

flour or white pasta, etc. Therefore mostly only the starchy endosperm (i.e. the storage material for the germinating embryo) remains to be used.

Harvest/storage: The grains are ripe when the leaves start to turn brown and the seeds have swollen, are just losing their inner milkiness and begin to become brittle within the ears. For small-scale harvesting, the wheat is easier to cut when just starting to turn brown and it can be cut with a scythe. The grain then needs to be removed by threshing. The stems are usually gathered into bunches and left to dry for a couple of weeks, during which time the grain fully ripens. This can be done outside in dry areas, or they can be placed in a barn. To remove the grain, wrap the bundles in sacking or similar, and beat them with a stick; this process is easier with wheat than many cereals. By shaking the grain in trays, much of the chaff is easy to remove. Store wheat in dry, rodent-proof containers, preferably with some diatomaceous earth. Weevils can be a problem in grain stored for longer periods; grain can be heated up to ~60°C to kill these.

CULTIVATION

Location: Grows best in full sun, sheltered from strong winds.

Temperature: A cool-temperate species, though not quite as cold hardy as rye or oats.

Soil/water/nutrients: Grows well in moderately nutrient-rich lighter soils, in which well-rotted manure or organic matter has been incorporated. Is quite drought hardy when established; does not tolerate waterlogging. Needs a neutral to slightly alkaline soil and grows poorly in acidic soils. Needs some nutrients, and a higher-nutrient soil than oats or rye. Nitrogen should be added as nitrate rather than urea, though too much nitrogen causes sappier growth and plants are more likely to be knocked over in winds, etc. Adequate potassium helps strengthen plants against lodging.

Pot culture: Could sow a selection of cereal grains in pots or a tray for interest or school projects.

Planting/propagation: Varieties of wheat have been developed that can be sown in autumn for a spring crop, can be sown in early spring for a summer crop, or can be sown in later spring for an autumn crop, with the latter being the traditional form. Spring-sown wheat grows quickly and the longer days of summer induce flowering. Winter wheat has been selected to have slower growth, with leaves and stored materials forming during the winter months. Flowering is induced by winter cold followed by the warmer, longer days of spring. Its extra storage materials give these types better-quality grains. Its longer growth period means that these plants produce more tillers, which are extra stems produced from usually dormant lateral buds at the base of the plant. Only a few of these buds in spring-sown wheat are activated during its fast growth. More tillers mean greater vegetative growth and, if conditions are right, a greater number of seedheads, but these may produce smaller seeds. In considering which wheat type should be planted, note that winter wheat does not grow well in cold-temperate regions. Commercially, much of the seed for sale is derived from hybrids; therefore, consider this if collecting seed

to re-sow. The seed can be broadcast, and then lightly raked to cover them, or they can be sown in rows or grids. Sowing the seed somewhat deeper (~2–3 cm) induces more tillering, but if sown too deeply, the shoots will fail to reach the soil surface. As long as the soil is weed free, there is little else that needs to be done until harvest. It is easy to plant up a small area to supply some grain plus straw. Rotation of cereals with species such as legumes or corn is beneficial to the soil and reduces the number of soil-borne diseases specific to wheat.

Pests and diseases: Small-scale growers are unlikely to encounter serious problems. Fungal diseases such as rusts, smuts and blights are the most serious, and used to do considerable damage to commercial crops. However, nowadays many disease-resistant varieties have been developed.

SIMILAR SPECIES

Palmer's grass (nipa grass), *Distichlis palmeri.* This remarkable species, which looks similar to wheat, can grow in very saline soils. It can even utilise seawater, making it a potentially very useful crop for the many saline soils of the world. It can grow in desert conditions, originating from the Sonoran Desert in western Mexico. As would be expected, it has very deep roots, to obtain moisture from depth, and is able to exude excess salts through pores in its leaves. It was used by indigenous peoples, but its cultivation then became very rare. However, it has been 'rediscovered' and plant trials are now ongoing in Australia and the United States, with new seed lines often patented. Its grain is palatable and has a good amino-acid profile. It is also gluten free.

Tropaeolum majus (T. minus)
Nasturtium (Indian cress)
TRAPAEOLACEAE
Relatives: mashua, anu

The several species within the plant family *Tropaeolum* are both annuals and perennials. In this family, nasturtium (*T. majus*) is particularly well known and valued. Its origins are thought to be South American, and from there it was taken to Europe and elsewhere by the Spanish. It is a very familiar sprawling/climbing garden plant, is very easy and quick to grow, is nutritious, and all its parts are edible. The leaves and flowers are great in salads, and the seeds are caper-like in flavour and make a good addition to Italian-style recipes. The seeds germinate readily, so much so that it often becomes a garden escape, growing on the tops of walls or on steep, poor soils where little else survives. However, it rarely becomes a problem plant, and can be easily controlled. It deserves to be grown more widely for its food value and nutritional benefits as it is so easy to cultivate, it is adaptable to a wide range of soils and conditions, plus makes a useful groundcover to semi-climbing plant that produces numerous cheerful, large, bright orange flowers.

DESCRIPTION
A fast-growing, sprawling/climbing annual. Individual stems can spread/scramble 4–5 m in a season, though, unsupported only grow to ~30 cm tall. There are also dwarfing varieties that are more bush-like in form and are suitable for smaller gardens. *T. minus* is a similar, smaller, bushier species that is good for borders, etc. Plants have petioles that readily curl around any structures they contact, enabling it to scramble over other neighbouring plants.

Leaves: Distinctive, attractive, thin, light green, rounded, with ~8 main veins radiating outwards from the leaf centre. They vary from 5–15 cm across depending on growth conditions and variety and are often slightly concave (particularly when young) catching the morning dew. Some ornamental varieties have variegated leaves.

Flowers: Slightly fragrant. Usually bright orange. Can also be red, golden yellow, white, pink or even purplish black. Plants have a long flowering season, lasting most

uses

Food
Nasturtium leaves have a peppery, often hot flavour, similar to cress. They are great in salads, and are often mixed with other greens, as some find their flavour too hot on their own. The flowers are wonderful as a garnish, and are edible, with a milder flavour than the leaves. The seeds are spicy and have a similar flavour to capers, and can be used in the same ways.

Nutrition/medicinal
The leaves are rich in vitamin A and contain good quantities of vitamin C, as well as fibre, calcium, iron and phosphates. The plant has been used to purify the blood and as a tonic. Its taste is largely due to isothiocyanates, which are similar to those found in watercress and other brassicas. The indigenous South Americans used this plant to treat respiratory diseases, and it has been used more recently to treat coughs, flu, colds. These compounds seem to have natural antibiotic properties.

Ornamental
Most often grown as an annual in flower borders, banks, and hanging baskets, for its attractive leaves and bright cheerful flowers. Many varieties have been selected for their ornamental value, such as flower size, double flowers, dwarfing form, variegated leaves, etc.

Other uses
Nasturtiums are highly valued by organic gardeners, as their presence inhibits aphid infestations from nearby plants and, when their leaves, flowers, or stems are macerated in fluid, they can repel whitefly and other pests. They make a great, easy, rewarding plant for young children to grow.

Valerianella locusta (syn. *V. olitoria*)

Lamb's lettuce (corn salad, mâche, field lettuce, field salad, loblollie, rapunzel)

VALERIANACEAE

Relatives: valerian

Closely related to the herb/garden flower valerian, this is one of the few vegetables from this plant family. Lamb's lettuce is thought to originate from regions around middle Europe to western Asia. It is now naturalised in many countries, including North America, and is often found as a weed on waste-ground or around the perimeters of arable fields (hence its name corn salad). An easy-to-grow salad crop, this plant grows well in cooler-temperate regions, and can provide fresh leaves for much of the year. It was a popular crop and was often grown in middle European monasteries during the 17th century. It is still popular and cultivated in middle European countries, such as the Netherlands, Belgium, Germany and France, and can provide fresh salad greens when little else is available. It is cultivated as a salad crop year-round in plastic tunnels in the United States, Australia and New Zealand. It is likely that its common name, 'rapunzel', originates from the well-known fairytale in which the maiden in the tower lowers her long tresses so she can be rescued by the handsome prince, though quite how the plant and the tale are linked remains a mystery. The species *Valerianaceae eriocarpa* is a very similar species, but is more heat tolerant, and is often grown in countries around the Mediterranean.

Lamb's lettuce is no relation to lamb's quarters, which belongs to a completely different family (see p. 164).

DESCRIPTION

Smallish, low-growing to only ~20–30 cm tall, with the same width. A short-lived (particularly if planted in spring) annual plant. Initially forms a rosette of leaves before forming a flower stem.

Leaves: In a rosette from a basal crown; can form loose, open or compact heads, depending on variety. Leaves are delicate, soft, usually spoon shaped (though can be pointed), often somewhat concave in shape, with mostly smooth margins. The leaves clasp the stem with no true leaf stalk. Vary in colour from light to dark green, depending on variety. The young leaves are tender and have a mild flavour.

Flowers: Umbels of tiny white or bluish flowers in early summer. Flowers have both male and female structures and can be self-fertile. Pollinated by insects.

Seeds: Two main seed types: plant varieties that produce smaller seeds, which generally produce more cold-hardy plants; and varieties with larger seeds, which usually produce more heat-resistant plants. Small-seeded varieties include 'Verte de Cambrai', which is very cold tolerant, but slow (relatively) growing; 'Verte d'Etampes', which is very cold tolerant and has thicker, dark-green leaves that remain fresh for long periods; and 'Verte à Coeur Plein', which is very cold hardy and has short, very bright-green leaves arranged in a compact rosette. Large-seeded varieties include 'Grosse Graine', which has larger but still tender leaves, and is quick to mature.

Harvest/storage: The young leaves can be harvested over

uses

Food

The leaves can be picked throughout the season and used fresh in salads. They have a mild but nutty flavour. The young leaves are the tastiest, but older leaves can be used if they haven't started to yellow. Because of their mild flavour, they can be mixed with tangy, stronger-tasting leaves such as sorrel or watercress. They go well with a drizzle of olive oil and balsamic vinegar, sundried tomatoes and some tasty cheese. Can be lightly steamed as a vegetable or can be added to quiches, omelettes, soups, etc., though are best not over-cooked.

Nutrition/medicinal

The leaves are rich in vitamin C (20–38 mg/100 g) and in vitamin A (as carotene: ~4000 I.U., with one serving supplying ~80% of the RDA), with some of the B vitamins, particularly B6 and folate. Contains good amounts of potassium, manganese and iron. Related to valerian, which has proven sedative properties, ingestion of lamb's lettuce leaves is said to have a soothing and calming effect.

a few weeks in spring and early summer, or for a longer period during autumn/winter. Wait until the plant has formed about six leaves before beginning to harvest: this takes 6–10 weeks, depending on climate, etc. Because the leaves do not have a clear leaf stalk, they are best cut: tearing them can damage the plant. Best used when freshly picked; otherwise, can be kept in a polythene bag (or a crisper) in a fridge for a few days. Best washed just before use to avoid loss of vitamins, etc. The leaves are easily crushed, so are best stored on top of other produce.

Roots: Deep, fibrous.

CULTIVATION

Easy.

Location: Prefers a site in full sun, though some shade if the weather is hot.

Temperature: Prefers a cooler-temperate climate: hot weather makes leaves less sweet. Plants can keep growing through autumn into winter, even during frosts, though not in extreme cold. They can even grow through snowfalls, though an organic mulch helps protect the roots and crown of the plant. Cold is said to improve leaf flavour. However, some varieties (usually those with larger seeds), are able to tolerate more summer heat; the similar species *V. eriocarpa* is also more heat tolerant. For all plants, hot days will initiate flowering;

so, for heat-tolerant varieties, remove any forming flower stalks, and shade young plants to extend their leaf-growing period somewhat. In warmer regions, lamb's lettuce is best grown as an autumn or winter crop.

Soil/water/nutrients: Grows best in nutrient-rich lighter soils, with some moisture, but is fairly drought hardy once established. Likes a deep, free-draining soil: is not tolerant of waterlogging. Grows best at neutral pH.

Pot culture: Easily grown in pots on a window sill or a deck if short of garden space. Plants take up very little room, are fast growing and need little care. Start plants off with good-quality, but freely draining, gritty compost, then water fairly regularly.

Planting/propagation: Seed: Can be sown in trays, if just wanting a few plants, or, thinly, in rows outside. Barely cover the small seeds with fine compost or sand: germination takes 14–21 days. Too much heat during germination reduces germination rate. Thin plants to 10–15 cm apart as they grow; the thinnings can be used in salads. If transplanting, take care as the roots dislike disturbance. Sow seeds at regular intervals to ensure fresh young leaves over a long season. Some growers cover the soil around the emerging rosettes with sand to keep the leaves cleaner. Reduce competition from weeds to get the best growth.

Pests and diseases: Has few problems, though can be attacked by bacterial leaf spot.

Vanilla planifolia
Vanilla
ORCHIDACEAE

Vanilla is a member of the highly ornamental, unusual, exotic orchid family. The name vanilla is derived from the Spanish 'vainilla', from 'vaina', which is derived from the Latin word 'vagina', and may refer to the flower's morphology. Thought to be native to Mexico, the wonderful flavour of its fermented seedpods was discovered long ago. They were valued by the Aztecs, and have long been used with cocoa beans to make a flavoursome drink. Later, it was taken back to Europe by the Spanish, and from there its usage spread to other European regions. Nowadays, it is mostly grown in Madagascar, but also in many countries and islands across the Pacific and Indian Oceans, from the Caribbean (particularly Jamaica), to Tahiti and Fiji, but also in Mexico, Sri Lanka and the Seychelles. The exacting growth conditions and lengthy processing needed to cultivate the pods, plus only a small product-yield per plant, makes vanilla extract a highly valued commodity, with its cost being almost as great as that of saffron. At the end of the 1800s, synthetic methods to produce vanillin, the main active principle within vanilla, were developed, which put pressure on the commercial, labour-intensive production of natural vanilla. The first substitute products used eugenol (from cloves), while later substitute products use lignin derived from tar or wood, or use tonka beans. World trade in natural vanilla is volatile and costs can plummet and soar, often varying according to politics, big companies and the weather. However, more recently, the increasing interest in global cuisine and more eclectic menus has meant that natural vanilla products are now sought after again, with synthetic products considered inferior because they lack the spectrum and depth of flavour. Although the species described here is the most common commercial variety, *V. pompona* and *V. tahitiensis* are also sometimes grown commercially. Vanilla grows best in a tropical climate and needs shade, but a vanilla vine could be grown in a warm, shaded glasshouse in temperate regions, and would make an interesting addition to a plant collection.

DESCRIPTION

A large, creeping perennial vine that, if left on its own, grows high into the branches of trees, though then only produces a few flowers. It is fast growing in the right conditions. In the wild it forms only a few long, succulent stems (~30 m) with little branching, whereas commercially it is pruned to have a shorter, bushier shape. It has long trailing roots from leaf nodes which anchor the vine to tree branches, but also sometimes find their way down to soil. It has a different type of photosynthesis to most plants, known as Crassulacean acid metabolism. This operates in several succulent species and allows the plant to store photosynthetic energy during the day, needing only to open its stomata at night to take in carbon dioxide. In this way it avoids water loss during the heat of the day and gains an ecological advantage over other species.

Leaves: Evergreen, thick, succulent and fleshy, alternate, regularly spaced up the long trailing stems. Oval, long, with pointed tips, olive green.

Flowers: Orchid-like and exotic, though not as showy as some ornamental orchid species. Pale yellow fused petals form a trumpet that is lightly ridged internally, surrounded by five pale green sepals. The trumpet structure contains the anthers above, and the stigma below: these are separated by a membrane, which prevents self-fertilisation. Flowers have a faint, sweet scent and are ~5 cm in diameter. They are borne on long, drooping racemes, with about 20 flowers per stalk. Pollination is sometimes by bees and hummingbirds, however, like many orchids it has evolved a main fertilisation procedure with a specific bee species. Because this is not present outside regions where vanilla is indigenous, pollination is difficult, therefore flowers may need to be hand pollinated. This is best done early in the morning, while the stigma are still receptive and the pollen is fresh. Apparently, Edmond Albius, a 12-year-old slave on the island of Réunion, discovered an efficient pollination method. He inserted a sliver of bamboo into the flower, between the membrane separating the anthers and stigma: the anthers could then be pressed onto the viscid stigma. Commercially, only a few flowers per cluster are fertilised. Vines are only 'allowed' to bear 15–30 pods: if more pods are produced, plants can be weakened and yield quality reduced. Each flower only lasts a day, so daily manual pollination is needed.

Pods/seeds: Vanilla is derived from dried, cured long (~10–15 cm), thin green pods that contain numerous, small, black seeds (or beans, as they are sometimes called). If the pods are left to fully mature, they begin to peel open and scatter their seeds. The seeds and inner flesh of the pod carry much of the vanilla flavour.

Harvest/storage: Plants grown from cuttings may begin to produce flowers pods ~18 months after planting, and then the first crop may be collected about 9 months later (or longer). An acre of land can support ~600 plants, and together these yield ~50 kg of cured pods. The smooth pods are harvested while still green, but have just turned slightly yellow at their tips. To ferment and cure the pods, they are scalded in boiling water for ~25 seconds or are quick frozen to kill enzymes, etc. They are then placed in layers between sheets of wet sacking or similar to 'sweat' at ~50°C, before being dried in the sun. Drying prevents the enzymatic action from proceeding too fast and any rots from developing. This process is done daily for 1–3 weeks, until the pods become brown and pliable, and weigh about a third of their original weight. The more slowly vanilla is cured the better. When curing is complete, the best vanilla has accumulated a coating of fine crystals on the outer surface of the pods. The pods should not

Food

It adds a cream-yellow to light-tan colour to foods. The seeds and inner layer of the pod have the most flavour. Either finely crushed or as a liquid, vanilla adds a unique flavour to many desserts. It has long been added to ice-cream and custards, but is also added to many chocolate dishes, cakes and flans, and the pods can be gently cooked in sauces to impart their flavour. The whole pods can be soaked in milk, in fruit juice or in alcohol (e.g. rum) to release their flavour into the fluid, and this can then be added to various dishes. The tiny seeds can be added whole to recipes, and give a strong vanilla flavour. It is an ingredient within Coca-Cola. Many foods that say they contain vanilla, only use the less subtle, cheaper vanillin flavouring. However, like many foods, e.g. coffee, tea, olives and chocolate, once real vanilla is tasted, few return to using the synthetic product. By taste, connoisseurs are said to be able to determine the country of origin of the pod, with the Bourbon variety, grown in Réunion and Madagascar, considered to be the finest.

Nutrition/medicinal

The main flavouring ingredient within vanilla is vanillin; it also contains piperonal, plus small amounts of many other compounds. Historically, it was considered to be an aphrodisiac, though there is little evidence for this usage. It is believed to ease indigestion, relieve stress and tiredness, and act as a general mood lifter. **Warning:** A few are skin-sensitive to some of the compounds within this species.

Ornamental

Makes an interesting, exotic climbing plant for a shady spot outside if the climate is warm enough, or in a shady part of a glasshouse. It is grown at Kew Gardens in the fern house.

Other uses

It has been used in perfumes and to scent tobacco.

with long, severe winters, the corms can be dug up and stored over winter to be replanted in spring. *X. caracu* and *X. maffaffa* are much less cold tolerant.

Soil/water/nutrients: These species grow best in organic-matter-rich soils with plenty of moisture, and they may even tolerate growing in standing water for a period of time. Prefer medium-textured soils: sandy soils do not hold adequate moisture unless lots of organic matter has been incorporated, and heavy clay soils impede corm growth. Grow best at soil pH of 6–7.

Pot culture: Can be grown in pots in colder regions. Make a wonderful plant for a conservatory or deck, or similar. Best to choose one of the smaller species, though plants do only grow to fit the size of pot available. Give plants good-quality rich compost, feed often when actively growing and keep the compost moist.

Planting: Space plants according to their final size, with larger species needing to be ~1 m apart. Reduce weed competition, particularly when plants are young, to significantly increases yields.

Propagation: *Seed:* Any seed that is produced is almost always sterile. *Cuttings:* Mostly propagated from the plant's side shoots, which, when removed with a few roots or basal tissue, will readily root in moist, warm compost. The corms can be sectioned, with at least 2–3 healthy buds, and inserted ~4 cm deep in compost to root and form shoots before transplanting to their final positions. Ensure that the vegetative material used is disease free. Commercially, as ornamentals in the United States, they are often propagated by tissue culture to reduce the spread of viral disease.

Pests and diseases: Few problems, though can get occasional fungal and bacterial infections (particularly when young) which cause wilt and root rots, especially in poorly drained soils or if plants are crowded together. Also, melanga virus often damages plants in South America. The high oxalic crystal content may deter many larger leaf-browsers, though pests such as leaf hoppers have become a problem in Australia, and slugs and snails cause significant damage in some areas.

Zanthoxylum spp. (*Z. piperitum, Z. sancho, Z. simulans, Z. bungeanum, Z. schinifolium, Z. rhetsa, Z. acanthopodium*)
Sichuan pepper (szechuan pepper, prickly ash, Japanese pepper)
RUTACEAE
Relatives: rue, orange, lemon, grapefruit

A popular Asian spice, sichuan pepper is the outer skin and flesh of tiny fruits obtained from several similar species. A member of the large Rutaceae family, which contains the citrus, sichuan is related to orange, lemon and grapefruit, and is even more closely related to strongly aromatic rue. Sichuan consists of several species within the genus *Zanthoxylum*, which contains about 200 species. Similar species are natives of North America, e.g. *Zanthoxylum americanum* (northern prickly ash), the fruits of which have long been used medicinally, particularly to increase appetite and aid digestion, but also to treat toothache and to heal wounds. Sichuan fruits are used to flavour a wide range of Asian foods, and are particularly popular in Korean, Chinese, Bhutanese, Indonesian, Tibetan and Japanese cuisine. Their common name, Sichuan, is after a province in China. As most of these sichuan species can be grown in temperate climates, and they are quite easy to grow, as well as being wonderfully aromatic and ornamental, they would make an interesting addition to a herbaceous border or as small specimen trees.

DESCRIPTION
The small fruits are obtained from a plant that can grow to ~7 m tall, but is often smaller in colder regions. It is a moderately fast-growing tree or large shrub that has a spreading form with many branches. Like many citrus species, the stems and leaf midribs are covered with greenish short spines, ~0.5 cm long.

Leaves: Composed of between 7 and 11 small oval leaflets, each 3–5 cm long. Waxy shiny appearance, mid to dark green. Unlike most citrus, these species are mostly deciduous. They are richly aromatic when crushed.

Flowers: In small drooping clusters, each flower is only

Food

Not unsurprisingly, the fruit has a citrus-like aroma and flavour, which is often described as lemony. Some species have anise characteristics, e.g. *Z. chinifolium*. Although the flavour is strong, it is not hot like chillies. Instead, eaten by itself, it gives an almost lip- and tongue-numbing sensation. The fruits are often lightly roasted or toasted before adding to food, to bring out their flavour, and are usually added towards the end of cooking. They are often added to fish or poultry dishes, to soups, to different noodle dishes and go well with species such as ginger. Sichuan pepper is a traditional ingredient within Chinese five-spice mixtures. An oil can be extracted from the fruits, and is used as a flavouring. The young leaves can be used fresh as a flavouring or can be added to soups, etc.

Nutrition/medicinal

The fruits contain several compounds, amongst which the most common are alpha, beta and gamma sanshool; they also contain coumarins and quercetin. The roots are particularly rich in these compounds. Historically, these species have been used as a stimulant and for digestive ailments. The fruits have powerful antioxidant properties, and have strong inhibitory activity preventing platelet aggregation, and so may help reduce blood clots and reduce heart disease and strokes. Recent research has shown that sichuan fruits can help suppress the antibiotic resistance of MRSA (methicillin-resistant *Staphylococcus aureus*). Volatile extracts have shown some anticancer properties, and may be useful in therapy for liver cancer. The oil has been found to effectively repel several species of mosquitoes.

Ornamental

Often grown as an ornamental towards the back of a herbaceous border, or can be grown as a specimen plant. Has attractive foliage, fragrant flowers and eye-catching bunches of small fruits.

~0.5 cm wide and is yellowish green in colour. They are pleasantly fragrant. Flowers are borne in late spring to early summer on older wood, are either male or female, and plants produce either male or female flowers, so more than one plant is needed to set fruits. Pollination is by bees and insects.

Fruit/seeds: The small fruits are ~0.4 cm long, and ripen to a dark red-brown colour. Inside are usually two small, hard, black seeds. If left to fully ripen, the outer fruit splits open to release the seeds, and the fruit then resembles a ripe beech nut.

Harvest/storage: Plants can begin to produce harvests when only 2–3 years old, or some say sooner. The small fruits are picked when just ripe and are then dried. Often, the outer 'fruit' layer is removed and the seed discarded as many consider it to have a bitter, gritty flavour and consistency, although *Z. chinfolium* is said to be an exception, with more pleasant-tasting seeds. Remove pieces of stem and other plant structures, such as spines. Dried fruits should be stored in a dark, cool, airtight container.

CULTIVATION

Location: Can be grown in full sun or in light shade.

Temperature: They vary in cold hardiness, but can be grown in temperate climates, and are frost tolerant once established. *Z. schinifolium* and *Z. piperitum* can tolerate temperatures down to ~−16°C.

Soil/water/nutrients: Grow best in moderately nutrient-rich soils. Prefer lighter loamy soils, and do not grow well in heavy clays. Grow best in deep soils. Are not tolerant of waterlogging. Although they prefer a little regular moisture, rainfall can be fairly low. Prefer neutral to alkaline soils, pH 6.5–8. Do not grow well in acidic conditions.

Planting/propagation: *Seed:* The seed can be started off in autumn or spring. A period of cold vernalisation (several weeks outside in colder regions, or in a fridge) and soaking the hard seed in warm water for ~24 hours helps germination. Finely cover the seeds: germination then takes 7–21 days, though can take much longer (several months) if conditions are not right. Seedlings can be grown-on in well-drained soil in pots for a year before planting out. Space at 2–3 m apart, if growing to maturity, though commercially they are planted at only ~60 cm apart. Weed control is important while the plants are small. Commercially, the seed is often simply broadcast *in situ*, and then replanted at regular intervals. *Cuttings:* Cuttings can be taken from half-ripe wood in summer: strip off lower leaves and insert into gritty, moist compost to root. Any suckers that grow around the base of the plant can be removed in early spring, and potted up to root. Short root cuttings can be taken in early spring, and laid horizontally in pots to root. Give warmth, shade and moisture as these are said to work well. Male and female flowers are on separate plants; vegetative propagation can ascertain the sex of the plant as well as reducing the time until the first harvests.

Pruning: Little pruning is needed, just to remove any damaged, diseased or straggly branches. Avoid removing too much old wood as this is where the next season's flowers and fruits are formed.

Pests and diseases: Few problems, though can carry citrus canker disease, which can spread to nearby citrus plantings. For this reason, its importation was banned in the United States for several years, but has now recommenced as imported fruits are heated to destroy any contamination before importation.

Zea mays
Corn (maize)
POACEAE
Relatives: barley, wheat, rye, lemon grass, bamboo, rice, millet

Known as both corn and maize, though more often referred to as corn in Europe and the United Kingdom, and as maize in South and North America. The term maize tends to be used when referring to this crop when it is grown for animal fodder or oil. A monocotyledonous species, it has grass-like growth with long leaves forming sheaths around the main stem. This crop is native of Central America, and Mexico in particular, and is a staple crop to many. It and other similar *Zea* species, have been used by indigenous populations in these areas for thousands of years; archaeological evidence suggests that it was being cultivated 7000 years ago. It was unknown elsewhere in the world until Columbus's arrival, though is now one of the main crops grown around the world, with more weight of maize grown than any other crop. Many varieties have been selected for different uses; apart from sweet corn, it is cultivated for its oil, for corn meal and as a food for livestock. For the home gardener, growing a few corn plants for their juicy sweet cobs is easy; they are also ornamental. Most corn is grown in the United States (~40%, of which ~75% is used to feed livestock); it is also grown in many other regions of the world, including China, Europe and the Far East. A large proportion of corn, particularly in the United States, is now genetically engineered for factors such as disease resistance, yields, and to tolerate herbicide spray, e.g. so that spray will kill broad-leaved dicot weeds only.

DESCRIPTION

Tall annual plants, growing to 1.5–2.5 m, though there are much taller and shorter varieties. Consist of a single, fast-growing 'stem', with leaves arranged spirally up its length. Being a monocot, there are no lateral branches off the main stems. The main types of corn are the following:

Blue corn: This type has recently become more widely grown and is used in foods such as corn chips. However, it is an old variety from South America, and its amylase and soft starch content give it a unique flavour, while its colour gives it novelty value. It is less sweet than sweet corn.

Corn on the cob: Sweet, plump, yellow kernels. Contains more sugar than starch as, genetically, it lacks specific genes that convert the sugars to starch. Plants tend to be somewhat shorter than other types.

Dent corn: An older-style corn, commonly grown in the United States, usually to feed livestock and for industrial processing. Contains only a little soft starch, but more hard starch.

Flint corn: Another older type, flint corn is grown more in Europe, Central America and Asia. It matures quicker than dent corn and has more vigour.

Flour corn: Contains mostly soft starch, so the kernels are softer. It is popularly used to make cornflour.

Podcorn: An older type of corn, seldom grown commercially, but interesting for its kernels. These tend to be smaller, and are enclosed within their own individual husk, in addition to the husk that surrounds the whole cob.

Popcorn: A type of flint corn, selected for its anatomical features that enable it to be heated to high temperatures, and to then finally explode. It contains mostly hard starch.

Waxy corn: As its name suggests, its outer covering is waxy. Its endosperm is starchy, but lacks the starch amylose; instead, it contains mostly amylopectin. These types are often grown to produce corn starch.

Leaves: Long (can be 50 cm long), strap shaped, with all leaf veins running lengthways. Bright green, attractive, with their leaf bases sheathing the stem, and successively younger leaves emerging from the centre of the stem. It is one of the best known C4 plants. This enables it to use carbon dioxide more efficiently than most other plants (C3 plants) and, on hot days, it can continue to photosynthesise when most other plants have closed their stomata. They have rapid growth rates.

Flowers: Naturally tends to flower in late summer. Male and female flowers occur on the same plant, but male flowers, which produce copious pollen, occur as tassels at the top of the stem, whereas female 'flowers' form below in groups within the leaf/stalk junctions. The grouped female 'flowers' form rows on the cob, which is covered with a distinctive leafy husk. Between 2–4 cobs form on a single plant, though less if the plants are grown close together. Fine silky threads extend from the apex of the cobs extending down to within the leafy husk, to reach the individual 'flowers'. Pollen has to travel down this route to reach the 'flowers' to fertilise them. Pollination is by wind.

Rich in minerals	Alfalfa, amaranth, asafoetida, bamboos, barley, beets, benniseed, borage, buckwheat, burdock, capers, cassava, celosia, chamomile, chervil, chickpeas, chrysanthemums, cocoa beans, corn, dandelion, dill, endive, fat hen, fenugreek, field mustard, garden cress, garlic, globe artichokes, good King Henry, hyacinth bean, Jerusalem artichoke, kale, kangkong, karela, landcress, lentils, maca, Manchurian wild rice, marjoram and oregano, mauka, melokhia, millet, mints, mushrooms, mustards, nasturtium, nettle, oats, orach, parsley, peas, pumpkin (seeds), purslane, quinoa, radish, rat-tail radish, rice (bran and brown), rye, safflower, salsify, samphire, scorzonera, seakale, seaweeds, sesame seed, sorghum, sorrel, soybeans, spinach, spirulina, sweet potatoes, tannia, taro, teff, tomatoes, turmeric, Vicia beans, Vietnamese coriander, Vigna beans, wasabi, watercress, wheat (whole grain), wild rice, yacón, yams Selenium: barley, broccoli, garlic, radish, rat-tail radish, rice, rye, Vicia beans, wheat (whole grain)
Rich in protein	Alfalfa, amaranth, Andean lupin, asparagus pea, barley, beans, benniseed, buckwheat, chickpeas, chlorella spp., corn, fat hen, field mustard, groundnut, horseradish tree (seeds), hyacinth bean, job's tears, lentils, linseed, maca, Manchurian wild rice (grain), mashua, millet, nettle, oats, okra, orach (seeds), peas, perilla (seeds), pumpkin (seeds), purslane (seeds), quinoa, rice (brown), rye, safflower, salsify, scorzonera, sesame seed, sorghum, soybeans, spirulina, teff, ulluco, Vicia beans, Vigna beans, wheat (whole grain), wild rice
Rich in unsaturated fats and/or essential fatty acids	Amaranth seeds, Andean lupin, borage, capers, chia, chickpeas, chlorella spp., corn, cuphea, gold of pleasure, groundnut (seeds), horseradish tree (seeds), Job's tears, linseed, nigella, plantains, pumpkin (seeds), purslane (seeds), quinoa, rape, rosemary, safflower, samphire, sesame seed, spirulina
Rich in fibre	Alfalfa, asparagus pea, bamboos, barley, beans, beets, biscuit root, Brussels sprouts, buckwheat, burdock, cardoon, carrot, cauliflower, celery, chickpeas, chicory, corn, dandelion, eggplant, field mustard, ginger, globe artichokes, Hamburg parsley, Jerusalem artichoke, jicama, Job's tears, kohlrabi, lentils, maca, millet, mustards, nettle, oats, okra, parsnip, plantains, purslane, quinoa, radish, rice (bran and brown), rocket, rye, salad burnet, salsify, scorzonera, sorghum, Spanish thistles, sweet potatoes, teff, Vicia beans, Vigna beans, wasabi, wheat (whole grain), wild sarsaparilla, yacón, yams
Rich in starch	Arrowhead, arrowroot, breadroot, bulrush, canna, cassava, Chinese artichoke, Chinese water chestnut, dog's tooth violet, potatoes, quamash, rice (white), sorghum (white), tannia, taro, ulluco, water chestnut, zeodary
Antioxidants (flavonoids, betalains, etc.)	Ajowan, alexanders, allspice, amaranth, angelica, anise, asafoetida, balm, barley, basil, bay leaves, beets, boldo, broccoli, Brussels sprouts, buckwheat, calendula, capers, cardoon, carrot, cassava leaves, cauliflower, celeriac, celery, celtuce, chard, chayote, chervil, chia, chicory, chillies, chrysanthemums, cloves, cocoa beans, coriander, costmary, cumin, curry-leaf tree, dandelion, daylily, dill, endive, epazote, fennels, fenugreek, field mustard, galangal, garden cress, garlic, ginger, globe artichokes, horseradish, horseradish tree, hyssop, Japanese knotweed, job's tears, juniper berries, kale, landcress, lavender, leek, lemon verbena, lovage, luffa, mace and nutmeg, marjoram and oregano, maté tea, melokhia, Mexican coriander, milk thistle, mints, nettle, New Zealand spinach, nigella, oats, okra, onions, orach, parsley, peppercorns, perilla, plantains, purslane, radish, rape, rat-tailed radish, rocket, rosemary, rye, safflower, saffron, sage, samphire, sarsaparilla, savory, seakale, sesame seed, Sichuan pepper, sorghum, sorrel, soybeans, spinach, star anise, sweet pepper, sweet potatoes, tannia (leaves), tarragon, thyme, tomatoes, turmeric, ulluco, vanilla, vegetable fern, Vietnamese balm, Vietnamese coriander, wasabi, watercress, yacón, yams, zeodary **Isothiocyanates:** broccoli, Brussels sprouts, cabbage, capers, Chinese greens, cauliflower sprouts, collards, field mustard, garden cress, horseradish, horseradish tree, kale, kerguelen cabbage, kohlrabi, landcress, mashua, nasturtium, radish, rape, rat-tail radish, rocket, seakale, turnip, wasabi, watercress
Essential-oil-producing plants	Ajowan, allspice, Andean lupin, angelica, anise, asafoetida, balm, basil, bay leaves, boldo, borage, calamus, caraway, cardamom, chamomile, cicely, cinnamon, cloves, coriander, costmary, cumin, curry-leaf tree, curry plant, dill, fennels, fenugreek, galangal, ginger, hyssop, juniper berries, lavender, lemon verbena, lemongrass, lovage, mace and nutmeg, marjoram and oregano, Mexican coriander, mints, nigella, parsley, peppercorns, perilla, purslane, rosemary, saffron, sage, savory, Sichuan pepper, star anise, tarragon, thyme, vanilla, Vietnamese balm, Vietnamese coriander
Cosmetic/shampoo etc. uses	Allspice, anise, arrowroot, balm, basil, bay leaves, borage, burdock, calamus, calendula, caraway, cardamom, chamomile, chervil, cocoa beans, costmary, cumin, cuphea, curry-leaf tree, dandelion, dill, fennels, fenugreek, galangal, garden cress, ginger, horseradish tree, hyssop, Japanese knotweed, job's tears, juniper berries, lavender, lemon verbena, lemongrass, lovage, luffa, mace and nutmeg, marjoram and oregano, milk thistle, mints, nettle, oats, parsley, perilla, quinoa, rape oil, rosemary, safflower, saffron, sage, savory, seaweeds, sesame seed, soybeans, thyme, turmeric, watercress, zeodary

465

Ornamental features

Dye/colouring producing plants

Alfalfa, amaranth, annatto, beets, calendula, cardoon, carrot, chillies, Japanese knotweed, Malabar spinach, marjoram and oregano, nettle, onions, perilla, poppy, quinoa, safflower, saffron, sorrel, Spanish thistles, spinach, sweet potatoes, turmeric

Ornamental foliage/ form

Alexanders, angelica, amaranth (some varieties), arrowhead, arrowroot, asafoetida, balm, bamboos, beets (some varieties), bay trees, bulrush, cabbage (some varieties), calamus, canna, caper, caraway, cardamom, cardoon, cassava, chard (several varieties), cinnamon, corn, dill, endive, fennels, galangal, ginger, globe artichokes, horseradish tree, Japanese knotweed, job's tears, juniper berries, kale, lavender, leeks (some varieties), lemongrass, lettuce (some varieties), marjoram and oregano, mashua, Mexican coriander, mints, nasturtium, oca, okra, orach, parsley, peppercorns, perilla, radicchio, rosemary, sage, salad burnet, samphire, sarsaparilla, savory, seakale, Sichuan pepper, sorghum, sorrel, tannia, taro, thyme, turmeric, vanilla, vegetable fern, Vietnamese balm, Vietnamese coriander, water chestnut, wild rice, yams, zeodary

Attractive or unusual flowers or fruits

Allspice, amaranth, Andean lupin, annatto, arrowroot, asparagus pea, boldo, borage, breadroot, broccoli/cauliflower, bulrush, calendula, canna, cardoon, chamomile, chillies, chrysanthemums, cloves, cocoa beans, costmary, courgette, curry-leaf tree, curry plant, dandelion, horseradish tree, Jerusalem artichoke, kangkong, lavender, lemon verbena, luffa, martynia, mashua, mauka, milk thistle, nasturtium, ox-eye daisy, poppy, quamash, quinoa, safflower, rat-tail radish, romanesco, saffron, salsify, scorzonera, sesame seed, sweet pepper, sweet potatoes, thyme, tiger lily, tomatoes, turmeric, vanilla, Vietnamese balm, Vigna beans (some varieties), water chestnut, wild sarsaparilla, yams, zeodary

Aromatic flowers and/or leaves and/ or roots

Ajowan, allspice, angelica, anise, balm, boldo, bay leaves, calamus, calendula, canna, caraway, chamomile, chervil, chia, chrysanthemums, cicely, cinnamon, cloves, coriander, costmary, cumin, cuphea, curry-leaf tree, curry plant, dill, fennels, fenugreek, jicama, juniper berries, horseradish tree, hyssop, lavender, lemon verbena, lemongrass, lovage, mace and nutmeg, marjoram and oregano, martynia, Mexican coriander, mints, mitsuba, parsley, perilla, rosemary, sage, salad burnet, sarsaparilla, savory, Sichuan pepper, star anise, tarragon, thyme, truffles, turmeric, Vietnamese balm, Vietnamese coriander

Vines, hedges, screens, groundcover, etc.

Annatto, bamboos, chamomile, chayote, cucumber, horseradish tree, hyacinth bean, hyssop, Japanese knotweed, Jerusalem artichoke, juniper berries, lavender, luffa, Malabar spinach, marjoram and oregano, mints, nasturtium, peppercorns, plantains, purslane, rosemary, sage, sarsaparilla, savory, sweet potatoes, thyme, vanilla, Vigna beans (some varieties), yams

Attracting bees, wildlife, etc.

Alexanders, alfalfa, Andean lupin, arrowhead, balm, borage, calendula, cardoon, chrysanthemums, cloves, coriander, cuphea, dandelion, fennel, globe artichoke, horseradish tree, hyacinth bean, hyssop, juniper berries, lavender, mace and nutmeg, marjoram and oregano, martynia, milk thistle, mints, nettles, orach, parsley, perilla, plantains, rampion, rice, rosemary, sage, samphire, sarsaparilla, savory, sorrel, thyme, truffles, wild rice

GLOSSARY

Abscisic acid: a plant 'hormone' responsible for abscission (c.f.) of leaves in autumn and helps retain winter dormancy.

Abscission: the process whereby parts of a plant break off naturally, e.g. dead leaves.

Adventitious roots: lateral roots that form off stems or off the main root.

Air layering: a method of propagation. Regions of stems are wounded and encouraged to form roots. The rooted stem can then be later removed to form a new plant.

Angiosperms: true flowering plants that produce a range of flower types and seeds that are enclosed within a fruit of some sort. Includes both dicots and monocots.

Anion: a negatively charged mineral ion, e.g. sulphate, phosphate.

Anther: the tip of the male structure that produces and releases pollen grains.

Antioxidant: a compound that can react with destructive free radicals (charged oxygen molecules) and reactive metal cations (see below) to render them harmless before they are able to affect DNA.

Auxin: a plant 'hormone' responsible for apical dominance, but is also used as a rooting hormone.

Awns: the structures that extend from the outer layers of cereal grains, i.e. often long 'hairs'.

Bisexual: having both viable male and female structures within the same flower. The terms 'perfect' or 'hermaphrodite' are also often used.

C4 photosynthesis: a photosynthetic mechanism used by many monocot species that enables them to use carbon dioxide more efficiently, which leads, indirectly, to reduced moisture loss.

Calyx: the remnants of sepals from the flowers that are often seen at the base or apex of fruits.

Cambium: actively dividing tissue that produces xylem and phloem in stems and roots. Forms a layer (usually) in dicots and is scattered in monocots and conifers.

Carpel: a female structure, often containing a single ovule, or many carpels can be formed together and become fused. They are then often referred to as an ovary.

Cation: a positively charged mineral ion, of which there are several within the body: e.g. calcium, sodium, potassium, iron, magnesium.

Cauliflorous: the production of flowers and fruits directly from the main stem and branches.

Chlorophyll: green pigments found within leaves (and sometimes stems) that are able to trap the sun's energy in a process called photosynthesis.

Chloroplasts: structures that hold the photosynthetic pigment, chlorophyll.

Cold stratification: treatment of some seeds with a period of cold to simulate winter (i.e. placement within a fridge for a few weeks): seeds then germinate, 'believing' it is spring.

Cross pollinate: pollination between separate plants, which is crucial for dioecious species, but also often improves fruit-set and quality of bisexual and monoecious species.

Cultivar: a subgroup of a species. Is often used interchangeably with the term 'variety'. Cultivars may be formed naturally or can be selected for advantageous qualities. Cultivars can be crossed genetically with each other within a species.

Cv: abbreviation for cultivar.

Cytokinin: a plant 'hormone' responsible for cell division. It is sometimes used to initiate flowering.

Dehiscent: when seed structures, e.g. many pods, dry and then spring open to release their seeds.

Dicotyledons (or dicots): having two cotyledons, or first leaves. Are mostly broad-leaved species with net-like veining. Flower parts are in multiples of fours and fives.

Dioecious: having female and male flowers on different trees, so a female and a male plant are needed to ensure pollination.

Diploid: two sets of chromosomes, as occurs in almost all non-sexual animal and plant cells

Endocarp: the outer layer of the pericarp. It may be hard or often forms a skin in fleshy fruits.

Endosperm: a layer of storage tissue that forms around the seeds of some species and provides nutrients to the developing seedlings.

Endospermic: where the endosperm is not all used up and the seed is oily.

Epicarp: the inner layer of the pericarp. Often a hard layer that protects the inner kernel, e.g. the shells of almonds or macadamias, but not always, i.e. berries.

Ethylene: a gas, produced by many ripe fruits, which speeds up ripening of under-ripe fruits in their vicinity.

Family: a taxonomic group that contains genus and species as subgroups.

Fibrous roots: usually formed near the surface, these roots have a large surface area to absorb moisture and nutrients.

Filament: the stalk of the male structure, below the anther.

Gamete: sex cells, either female (egg) or male (sperm), which contain half the number of genes of the parent. These fuse with that of the opposite sex upon fertilisation.

Genus: a subgroup of a family, containing a varying number of species. All members have particular floral characteristics in common.

Gibberellin: a plant 'hormone' responsible for many reactions, including plant height. It can also be used to break seed dormancy.

Gymnosperms: primitive plants, formed before the advent of pericarp production. Plants are woody, perennial and usually evergreen. Their kernels are usually contained within cones (e.g. pines) or arils (e.g. bunya-bunya). Needles are usually needle-, scale- or fern-like.

Heavy metals: these elements (e.g. arsenic, lead, cadmium) can become toxic in industrial soils or in mine waste, and also become much more soluble and may reach toxic levels in ordinary soils if they become waterlogged for extensive periods.

HDL (high-density lipid): found in the blood; associated with cholesterol. Often termed 'good' cholesterol as it can decrease the risk of heart disease.

IAA (indole acetic acid): another term for auxin, a plant hormone.

Indehiscent fruits: seeds within structures (e.g. pods) that do not spring open to release their seeds.

Inferior ovary: where the ovary is formed below the sepals, petals and other structures. Fruits formed from these have an apical calyx (sepal remains).

IU (International Units): another measure of nutrient content (like mg or g). IU is usually used when the nutrient occurs at very low concentrations.

Kernel: the mature embryo: the seed.

Lanceolate: lance-shaped leaf, often found in monocotyledonous species, e.g. grasses.

Lateral branch: a branch that grows off a main branch. Once a stem tip is removed, a lateral branch will grow readily in the region below the cut.

Layering: the partial burial of stem tips or lightly injured sections of stem to encourage rooting. Once rooted, these sections can be removed to form new plants.

LDL (low-density lipid): found in the blood; associated with cholesterol. Often termed 'bad' cholesterol as it can increase the risk of heart disease.

Micronutrient: a nutrient needed by plants, but only in a small amount. There is often a fine line between deficiency and toxicity, and applications should be done with care.

Monocotyledons (or monocots): having only one cotyledon, or first leaf. Mostly grasses, palms, lilies, bromeliads are monocots. In general, have narrow leaves with parallel veins, flower parts in multiples of three.

Monoecious: having both female and male flowers on the same tree, although not necessarily bisexual.

Mycorrhizal association: a symbiotic relationship between fungal species and the roots of plants that enables plants to obtain extra nutrients, while the fungi obtains sugars from the plant.

Necrosis: the death of cells.

Non-endospermic: seeds where the endosperm is not developed; these tend to be non-oily. Often, future storage for the seedling is within cotyledons, within the seed, e.g. leguminous species, walnuts.

Obovate: an egg-shaped leaf, but being slightly wider near the apex.

Ovary: a female structure, usually containing several ovules. Consists of several carpels that have become fused together, often with the intervening walls broken down to form a vessel.

Ovules: female structures that, if fertilised, go on to form an embryo and then a kernel.

Pericarp: a layer around the kernel of most fruits and nuts. It is sometimes clearly divided into three layers: the endocarp, mesocarp and epicarp. Variations in its form determine many of the structural features of fruits and nuts.

Petiole: the stalk of a leaf that attaches the leaf blade to a stem.

pH: a logarithmic scale of the concentration of hydrogen ions. Acid soils (<pH 6) have more free hydrogen ions; alkaline soils (>pH 7) have fewer.

Phloem: conducting tissue within the stems and roots that transports sugars from the leaves, and carries sap upwards in spring.

Photosynthesis: the trapping of the sun's energy at specific wavelengths, which can then be used to bind carbon dioxide and water to make sugars.

Pollen grain: the male sex cells (sperm) that are released from the anthers.

Polyphenolic: a very large group of compounds, many of which are related to tannins, which often give fruits and flowers their bright colours as well as myriad, as yet, largely unknown properties, though many are proving to be very effective medicinally.

Receptacle: the structure around which the ovules or the ovary are formed.

Root hairs: fine, cellular projections from the main roots, particularly formed near root tips. They can squeeze in between soil particles to absorb water and nutrients much more efficiently than the main corky roots.

Rooting hormone: plant 'hormones', prepared usually as a fine powder, in which cuttings can be dipped to enhance rooting.

Rootstock: often a hardy seedling species upon which a selected scion is to be grafted. The rootstock is sometimes the same species as the scion and often reduces the time the grafted plant takes to begin producing fruits.

Scarification: the scratching or cutting of hard seedcoats to enable the entry of water and gases to speed up germination.

Scion: a section of stem from a plant with desired qualities that is to be grafted onto a rootstock.

Self-fertile: able to fertilise itself, i.e. a bisexual of monoecious species often does not need a further species for pollination (though there are also many examples of self-infertility within these groups).

Self-infertility: practised by a number of monoecious and bisexual plants to prevent self-fertilisation by, e.g. mechanical or timing mechanisms, ensuring that cross fertilisation is necessary and variability of offspring is assured.

Senescence: deterioration with age.

Sp. or spp.: abbreviations for one species and several species, respectively.

Species: a subgroup of a genus. All members within a species can cross fertilise each other. Members of different species, usually, cannot.

Spur: short, stubby lateral branches that grow from the branches of several fruiting species, e.g. apples, peaches, and produce fruits for 2–4 years.

Stamen: inclusive term for the anther and filament, the male structures that produce pollen.

Stigma: the outer, often sticky surface of the female structure on which pollen grains land and then grow downwards.

Stomata: pores through which carbon dioxide enters the leaf, and from which oxygen, as a waste product, and water are released. They are situated mostly on the underside of dicot and conifer leaves, but tend to be on both sides of monocot leaves.

Stratification: usually applied to cold stratification. A period of cold given to seeds (usually from temperate regions) to reduce the time and increase the rate of germination. It makes the plant 'think' it has been through a winter, which initiates biochemical changes within the seed.

Style: the tube down which the pollen grain(s) grows to reach the ovule below.

Superior ovary: where the ovary is formed above the sepals, petals and other structures. Fruits formed from these have a basal calyx (sepal remains).

Symbiotic relationships: a relationship between two organisms where both gain some benefit, e.g. nitrogen-fixing bacteria.

Taproots: one or more deep, main roots from which a few lateral roots branch off. They are able to access water and nutrients at depth, but are susceptible to damage during transplanting, etc.

Testa: the seedcoat. This is sometimes reduced to a very thin covering in drupes, etc., but is more substantial in seeds, and gives the kernel protection.

Thinning: removal of some fruits, just after fruit-set, from plants in years when they tend to overproduce, to balance out yields.

Umbel: a collection of small flowers on short flower stalks of equal length that are joined at a common point.

Variety (var.): a subgroup of a species. Is often used interchangeably with the term 'cultivar'. Varieties may be formed naturally or can be selected for advantageous qualities. Varieties can be cross pollinated within a species.

Winter chilling: a period of cold, of temperatures of 4–8°C, which many temperate species need to effectively come into flower and leaf in spring.

Xylem: water- and nutrient-conducting tissue within plants.

treatments used by patients with cancer in eastern Turkey. *Cancer Nurs*., 26(3):230–6, 2003.

Gulcin I, et al. Antioxidant, antimicrobial, antiulcer and analgesic activities of nettle (*Urtica dioica* L.). *J. Ethnopharmacol*., 90(2–3):205–15, 2004.

Konrad A, et al. Ameliorative effect of IDS 30, a stinging nettle leaf extract, on chronic colitis. *Int. J. Colorectal. Dis*., 20(1):9–17, 2005.

Lopatkin N, et al. Long-term efficacy and safety of a combination of sabal and urtica extract for lower urinary tract symptoms — a placebo-controlled, double-blind, multicenter trial. *World J. Urol*., 23(2):139–46, 2005.

Safarinejad MR. *Urtica dioica* for treatment of benign prostatic hyperplasia: a prospective, randomized, double-blind, placebo-controlled, crossover study. *J. Herb Pharmacother*., 5(4):1–11, 2005.

New Zealand spinach: Cambie RC, Ferguson LR. Potential functional foods in the traditional Maori diet. *Mutat. Res*., 523–4:109–17, 2003.

Nigella: Ali BH, Blunden G. Pharmacological and toxicological properties of *Nigella sativa*. *Phytother. Res*., 17(4):299–305, 2003.

Hajhashemi V, et al. Black cumin seed essential oil, as a potent analgesic and anti-inflammatory drug. *Phytother Res.,* 18(3):195-9, 2004.

Kalus U, et al. Effect of *Nigella sativa* (black seed) on subjective feeling in patients with allergic diseases. *Phytother. Res*., 17(10):1209–14, 2003.

Salim EI, Fukushima S. Chemopreventive potential of volatile oil from black cumin (*Nigella sativa* L.) seeds against rat colon carcinogenesis. *Nutr. Cancer*, 45(2):195–202, 2003.

Salman MT, et al. Antimicrobial activity of *Nigella sativa* oil against *Staphylococcus aureus* obtained from clinical specimens. In: 38th Annual Conference of Indial Pharmacological. Society, 28–30 Dec., 2005, Chennai, India, 2005.

Zaoui A, et al. Acute and chronic toxicity of *Nigella sativa* fixed oil. *Phytomedicine*, 9(1)69–74(6), 2002.

Nutmeg and mace: Bhamarapravati S, et al. Extracts of spice and food plants from Thai traditional medicine inhibit the growth of the human carcinogen *Helicobacter pylori*. *In Vivo*, 17(6):541–4, 2003.

Chung JY, et al. Anticariogenic activity of macelignan isolated from *Myristica fragrans* (nutmeg) against *Streptococcus mutans*. *Phytomedicine*, 13(4):261–6, 2006.

Hallstrom H, Thuvander A. Toxicological evaluation of myristicin. *Nat. Toxins*, 5(5):186–92, 1997.

Morita T, et al. Hepatoprotective effect of myristicin from nutmeg (*Myristica fragrans*) on lipopolysaccharide/D-galactosamine-induced liver injury. *J. Agric. Food Chem*., 51(6):1560–5, 2003.

Myristica fragrans: International Programme on Chemical Safety Poisons Information Monograph 355. At: http://www.inchem.org.

Narasimhan B, Dhake AS. Antibacterial principles from *Myristica fragrans* seeds. *J. Med. Food*, 9(3):395–9, 2006.

Parle M, et al. Improvement of mouse memory by *Myristica fragrans* seeds. *J. Med. Food*, 7(2):157–61, 2004.

Tajuddin M, et al. An experimental study of sexual function improving effect of *Myristica fragrans* Houtt. (nutmeg). *BMC Complement. Altern. Med*., 5:16, 2005.

Venables GS, et al. Nutmeg poisoning. *Br. Med. J.*, 1(6001):96, 1976.

Oats: Hara H, et al. Short-chain fatty acids suppress cholesterol synthesis in rat liver and intestine. *J. Nutr*., 129(5):942–8, 1999.

Mahoney CR, et al. Effect of breakfast composition on cognitive processes in elementary school children. *Physiol. Behav.*, 85(5):635–45, 2005.

Storsrud S, et al. Beneficial effects of oats in the gluten-free diet of adults with special reference to nutrient status, symptoms and subjective experiences. *Br. J. Nutr*., 90(1):101–7, 2003.

Suttie J. *Avena sativa* L. FOA, at their website at: http://www.fao.org/ag/AGP/AGPC/doc/GBASE/DATA/PF000466.HTM.

Tariq N, et al. Effect of soluble and insoluble fiber diets on serum prostate specific antigen in men. *J. Urol*., 163(1):114–8, 2000.

Thompson T. Do oats belong in a gluten-free diet?

J. Am. Diet. Assoc., 97(12):1413–16, 1997.

Oca: Albihn PB, Savage GP. The bioavailability of oxalate from oca (*Oxalis tuberosa*). *J. Urol*., 166(2):420–2, 2001.

Flores T, et al. Ocatin: a novel tuber storage protein from the andean tuber crop oca with antibacterial and antifungal activities,. *Plant Physiol*., 128(4):1291–302, 2002.

Okra: Ansari NM, et al. Antioxidant activity of five vegetables traditionally consumed by South-Asian migrants in Bradford, Yorkshire, UK. *Phytother. Res*., 19(10):907–11, 2005.

Lengsfeld C, et al. Glycosylated compounds from okra inhibit adhesion of *Helicobacter pylori* to human gastric mucosa. *J. Agric. Food Chem*., 52(6):1495–503, 2004.

Onions, leeks, etc.: Challier B, et al. Garlic, onion and cereal fibre as protective factors for breast cancer: a French case-control study. *Eur. J. Epidemiol*., 14(8):737–47, 1998.

Mayer B, et al. Effects of an onion-olive oil maceration product containing essential ingredients of the Mediterranean diet on blood pressure and blood fluidity. *Arzneimittelforschung*, 51(2):104–11, 2001.

Mennen LI, et al. Consumption of foods rich in flavonoids is related to a decreased cardiovascular risk in apparently healthy French women. *J. Nutr*., 134(4):923–6, 2004.

Rose P, et al. Bioactive S-alk(en)yl cysteine sulfoxide metabolites in the genus *Allium*: the chemistry of potential therapeutic agents. *Nat. Prod. Rep*., 22(3):351–68, 2005.

Orach: Wright KH, et al. Composition of *Atriplex hortensis*, sweet and bitter *Chenopodium quinoa* seeds. *J. Food Sci*., 67(4):1383–5, 2002.

Damrosch B. Spinachs brilliant cousin. *The Washington Post*, 6 April, p. H07, 2006.

Oregano and marjoram: Alma MH, et al. Screening chemical composition and in vitro antioxidant and antimicrobial activities of the essential oils from *Origanum syriacum* L. growing wild in Turkey. *Biol. Pharm. Bull*., 26(12):1725–9, 2003.

Goun E, et al. Antithrombin activity of some constituents from *Origanum vulgare*. *Fitoterapia*, 73(7–8):692–4, 2002.

Lemhadri A, et al. Anti-hyperglycaemic activity of the aqueous extract of *Origanum vulgare* growing wild in Tafilalet region. *J. Ethnopharmacol*., 92(2–3):251–6, 2004.

Lin YT, et al. Inhibition of *Helicobacter pylori* and associated urease by oregano and cranberry phytochemical synergies. *Appl. Environ. Microbiol*., 71(12):8558–64, 2005.

Lin YT, et al. Inhibition of *Listeria monocytogenes* in fish and meat systems by use of oregano and cranberry phytochemical synergies. *Appl. Environ. Microbiol*., 70(9):5672–8, 2004.

Pavela R. Insecticidal activity of certain medicinal plants. *Fitoterapia*, 75(7–8):745–9, 2004.

Tampieri MP, et al. The inhibition of *Candida albicans* by selected essential oils and their major components. *Mycopathologia*, 159(3):339–45, 2005.

Parsley: Adsersen A, et al. Screening of plants used in Danish folk medicine to treat memory dysfunction for acetylcholinesterase inhibitory activity. *J. Ethnopharmacol*., 104(3):418–22, 2006.

Brat P, et al. Daily polyphenol intake in France from fruit and vegetables. *J. Nutr*., 136(9):2368–73, 2006.

Kreydiyyeh SI, et al. The mechanism underlying the laxative properties of parsley extract. *Phytomedicine*, 8(5):382–8, 2001.

Kreydiyyeh SI, Usta J. Diuretic effect and mechanism of action of parsley. *J. Ethnopharmacol*., 79(3):353–7, 2002.

Ozsoy D, et al. Effects of parsley (*Petroselinum crispum*) extract versus glibornuride on the liver of streptozotocin-induced diabetic rats. *J. Ethnopharmacol*., 104(1–2):175–81, 2006.

Stransky L, Tsankov N. Contact dermatitis from parsley (Petroselinum). *Contact Dermatitis*, 6(3):233–4, 1980.

Parsnip: Zidorn C, et al. Polyacetylenes from the Apiaceae vegetables carrot, celery, fennel, parsley, and parsnip and their cytotoxic activities. *J. Agric. Food Chem*., 53(7):2518–23, 2005.

Peas: Blackberry I, et al. Legumes: the most important dietary predictor of survival in older people of different ethnicities. *Asia Pac. J. Clin. Nutr*., 13(Suppl):S126, 2004.

Oelke EA, et al. Dry field pea. *Alternative Field Crops Manual*. University of Wisconsin Cooperative Extension Service, the University of Minnesota Extension Service and the Center for Alternative Plant and Animal Products.

Sanchez D, et al. Vicilin and convicilin are potential major allergens from pea. *Clin. Exp. Allergy*, 34(11):1747–53, 2004.

Peppercorns: Chaudhry NM, Tariq P. Bactericidal activity of black pepper, bay leaf, aniseed and coriander against oral isolates. *Pak. J. Pharm. Sci*., 19(3):214–8, 2006.

Dorman HJD, Deans SG. Antimicrobial agents from plants: antibacterial activity of plant volatile oils. *J. Appl. Microbiol*., 88(2):308, 2000.

Mujumdar AM, et al. Anti-inflammatory activity of piperine. *Jpn J. Sci. Biol*., 43(3):95–100, 1990.

Rasheed M, et al. Phytochemical studies on the seed extract of *Piper nigrum* Linn. *Nat. Prod. Res*., 19(7):703–12, 2005.

Scott IM, et al. Efficacy of botanical insecticides from *Piper* species (Piperaceae) extracts for control of European chafer (Coleoptera: Scarabaeidae). *J. Econ. Entomol*., 98(3):845–55, 2005.

Vijayakumar RS, Nalini N. Piperine, an active principle from *Piper nigrum*, modulates hormonal and apo lipoprotein profiles in hyperlipidemic rats. *J. Basic Clin. Physiol. Pharmacol*., 17(2):71–86, 2006.

Peppers: Chile-man website provides a wealth of information about chillis, including providing a database of nearly 3600 varieties, at: http://www.thechileman.org/search.php.

Chu YF, et al. Antioxidant and antiproliferative activities of common vegetables. *J. Agric. Food Chem*., 50(3):6910–6, 2002.

Lim K, et al. Dietary red pepper ingestion increases carbohydrate oxidation at rest and during exercise in runners. *Med. Sci. Sports Exerc*., 29(3):355–61, 1997.

Macho A, et al. Non-pungent capsaicinoids from sweet pepper synthesis and evaluation of the chemopreventive and anticancer potential. *Eur. J. Nutr*., 42(1):2–9, 2003.

Mathew A, et al. Diet and stomach cancer: a case-control study in South India. *Eur. J. Cancer Prev*., 9(2):89–97, 2000.

Ramirez D, et al. Antimutagenic effect of one variety of green pepper (*Capsicum* spp.) and its possible interference with the nitrosation process. *Mutat. Res*., 496(1–2):39–45, 2001.

Simon JE, et al. Capsicum pepper. In: *Herbs: an indexed bibliography. 1971–1980. The scientific literature on selected herbs, and aromatic and medicinal plants of the temperate zone*. Archon Books. Hamden, CT, USA, 1984.

Surh YJ, Lee SS. Capsaicin in hot chili pepper: carcinogen, co-carcinogen or anticarcinogen? *Food Chem. Toxicol*., 34(3):313–6, 1996.

Yoshioka M, et al. Effects of red pepper on appetite and energy intake. *Br. J. Nutr*., 82(2):115–23, 1999.

Perilla: Banno N, et al. Triterpene acids from the leaves of *Perilla frutescens* and their anti-inflammatory and antitumor-promoting effects. *Biosci., Biotechnol., Biochem*., 68(1):85–90, 2004.

Brenner D. Perilla: botany, uses, and genetic resources. In: Janick, J. & Simon, J.E. (eds). *New Crops*. John Wiley & Sons, NY. pp. 322–8, 1993.

Makino T, et al. Anti-allergic effect of *Perilla frutescens* and its active constituents. *Phytother. Res*., 17(3):240–3, 2003.

Takano H, et al. Extract of *Perilla frutescens* enriched for rosmarinic acid, a polyphenolic phytochemical, inhibits seasonal allergic rhinoconjunctivitis in humans. *Exp. Biol. Med*., (Maywood), 229(3):247–54, 2004.

Plantains: Abraham ZD, Mehta T. Three-week psyllium husk supplementation: effect on plasma cholesterol concentrations, fecal steroid excretion, and carbohydrate absorption in men. *Am. J. Clin. Nutr*., 47(1):67–74, 1988.

Anderson JR, et al. Decomposition of wheat bran and isabgol husk in the stomach and small intestine of healthy men. *J. Nutr*., 118(3):326–31, 1988.

Fernandez D, et al. Randomized clinical trial of

Plantago ovata seeds (dietary fiber) as compared with mesalamine in maintaining remission in ulcerative colitis. *Am. J. Gastroenterol.*, 94(2):427–33, 1999.

Galvez M, et al. Cytotoxic effect of *Plantago* spp. on cancer cell lines. *J. Ethnopharmacol.*, 88(2–3):125–30, 2003.

Hannan JM, et al. Aqueous extracts of husks of *Plantago ovata* reduce hyperglycaemia in type 1 and type 2 diabetes by inhibition of intestinal glucose absorption. *Br. J. Nutr.*, 96(1):131–7, 2006.

Hanson CV, et al. Psyllium. *Alternative Field Crops Manual*. University of Wisconsin and University of Minesotta Extension Services at: http://www.hort.purdue.edu/newcrop/afcm/psyllium.html.

Samuelsen AB. The traditional uses, chemical constituents and biological activities of *Plantago major* L. A review. *J. Ethnopharmacol.*, 71(1–2):1–21, 2000.

Poppy: Geitmann A, et al. The self-incompatibility response in *Papaver rhoeas* pollen causes early and striking alterations to organelles. *Cell Death Differ.*, 11(8):812–22, 2004.

Potatoes: Centro Internacional de la Papa have a website filled with information about potatoes at: http://www.cipotato.org/news_index.asp.

Friedman M, et al. Anticarcinogenic effects of glycoalkaloids from potatoes against human cervical, liver, lymphoma, and stomach cancer cells. *J. Agric. Food Chem.*, 53(15):6162–9, 2005.

Kavvadias D, et al. Identification of benzodiazepines in *Artemisia dracunculus* and *Solanum tuberosum* rationalizing their endogenous formation in plant tissue. *Biochem. Biophys. Res. Commun.*, 269(1):290–5, 2000.

Leeman M, et al. Vinegar dressing and cold storage of potatoes lowers postprandial glycaemic and insulinaemic responses in healthy subjects. *Eur. J. Clin. Nutr.*, 59(11):1266–71, 2005.

Purslane: Chan K, et al. The analgesic and anti-inflammatory effects of *Portulaca oleracea* L. subsp. Sativa (Haw.) Celak. *J. Ethnopharmacol.*, 73(3):445–51, 2000.

Dweck AC. Purslane (*Portulaca oleracea*): the global panacea. *Personal Care Magazine*, 2(4):7–15, 2001: Comprehensive review on its medicinal benefits around the world.

Habtemariam S, et al. The muscle relaxant properties of *Portulaca oleracea* are associated with high concentrations of potassium ions. *J. Ethnopharmacol.*, 40(3):195–200, 1993.

Malek F, et al. Bronchodilatory effect of *Portulaca oleracea* in airways of asthmatic patients. *Phytother. Res.*, 18(6):484–7, 2004.

Rasheed AN, et al. Investigation of the active constituents of *Portulaca oleraceae* L. (Portulacaceae) growing in Jordan. *Pak. J. Pharm. Sci.*, 17(1):37–45, 2004.

Schelstraete M, Kennedy BM. Composition of miners lettuce (*Montia perfoliata*). *J. Am. Diet. Assoc.*, 77(1):21–5, 1980.

Simopoulos AP, et al. Common purslane: a source of omega-3 fatty acids and antioxidants. *J. Am. Coll. Nutr.*, 11(4):374–82, 1992.

Quamash: Candra E, et al. Two steroidal saponins from *Camassia cusickii* induce L1210 cell death through the apoptotic mechanism. *Can. J. Physiol. Pharmacol.*, 79(11):953–8, 2001.

Kuroda M, et al. Steroidal glycosides from the bulbs of *Camassia leichtlinii* and their cytotoxic activities. *Chem. Pharm. Bull.*, (Tokyo), 49(6):726–31, 2001.

Stevens ML, Dale DC. At: http://plant-materials.nrcs.usda.gov/pubs/orpmctn230999.pdf. Plant Materials Technical Note No. 23 (September 1999). US Department of Agriculture Natural Resources Conservation Service, Portland, Oregon, 1999.

Quinoa: Wright KH, et al. Composition of *Atriplex hortensis*, sweet and bitter *Chenopodium quinoa* seeds. *J. Food Sci.*, 67(4):1383–5, 2002.

Ogungbenle HN. Nutritional evaluation and functional properties of quinoa (*Chenopodium quinoa*) flour. *Int. J. Food Sci. Nutr.*, 54(2):153–8, 2003.

Ruales J, Nair BM. Nutritional quality of the protein in quinoa (*Chenopodium quinoa*, Willd) seeds.

Plant Foods Hum. Nutr., 42(1):1–11, 1992.

Johnson DL, Ward SM. Quinoa. In: Janick J. & Simon JE (eds). *New Crops*. Wiley, New York, pp. 219–21, 1993.

Johnson DL. New grains and pseudograins. In: Janick J. & Simon JE (eds). *Advances in New Crops*. Timber Press, Portland, OR, pp. 122–7, 1990.

Koziol MJ. Quinoa: a potential new oil crop. In: Janick J. & Simon JE (eds). *New Crops*. Wiley, New York, pp. 328–36, 1993.

Radish: Pedrero Z., et al. Selenium species bioaccessibility in enriched radish (*Raphanus sativus*): a potential dietary source of selenium. *J. Agric. Food Chem.*, 54(6):2412–7, 2006.

Takaya Y, et al. Antioxidant constituents of radish sprout (Kaiware-daikon), *Raphanus sativus* L. *J. Agric. Food Chem.*, 51(27):8061–6, 2003.

Rape: Bourre JM. Dietary omega-3 Fatty acids and psychiatry: mood, behaviour, stress, depression, dementia and aging. *J. Nutr. Health Aging*, 9(1):31–8, 2005.

Dupont J, et al. Food safety and health effects of canola oil. *J. Am. Coll. Nutr.*, 65(3):360–75, 1989.

IENICA (Interactive European Network for Industrial Crops and their Applications): summary report for the European Union 2000 at: http://www.ienica.net/crops/oilseedrapeandturniprape.pdf.

Rice: Amano Y, et al. Correlation between dietary glycemic index and cardiovascular disease risk factors among Japanese women. *Eur. J. Clin. Nutr.*, 58(11):1472–8, 2004.

Ardiansyah, et al. Rice bran fractions improve blood pressure, lipid profile, and glucose metabolism in stroke-prone spontaneously hypertensive rats. *J. Agric. Food Chem.*, 8;54(5):1914–20, 2006.

Kuno T, et al. Chemoprevention of mouse urinary bladder carcinogenesis by fermented brown rice and rice bran. *Oncol. Rep.*, 15(3):533–8, 2006.

Rocket: Barillari J, et al. Direct antioxidant activity of purified glucoerucin, the dietary secondary metabolite contained in rocket (*Eruca sativa* Mill.) seeds and sprouts. *J. Agric. Food Chem.*, 6;53(7):2475–82, 2005.

Vollmann JA, et al. Gold of pleasure: improvement of *Camelina sativa*, and under exploited oilseed. In Janick J. (ed.). *Progress in New Crops*. ASHS Press, Alexandria, VA, pp. 357–62, 1996.

Rosemary: Al D, et al. Pharmacology of rosemary (*Rosmarinus officinalis* Linn.) and its therapeutic potentials. *Indian J. Exp. Biol.*, 37(2):124–30, 1999.

Huang MT, et al. Inhibition of skin tumorigenesis by rosemary and its constituents carnosol and ursolic acid. *Cancer Res.*, 54(3):701–8, 1994.

Moreno S, et al. Antioxidant and antimicrobial activities of rosemary extracts linked to their polyphenol composition. *Free Radic. Res.*, 40(2):223–31, 2006.

Nolkemper S, et al. Antiviral effect of aqueous extracts from species of the Lamiaceae family against *Herpes simplex* virus Type 1 and Type 2 in vitro. *Planta Med.*, 72(15):1378–82, 2006.

Offord EA, et al. Rosemary components inhibit benzo[a]pyrene-induced genotoxicity in human bronchial cells. *Carcinogenesis*, 16(9):2057–62, 1995.

Petersen M, Simmonds MS. Rosmarinic acid. *Phytochemistry*, 62(2):121–5, 2003.

Prajapati V, et al. Insecticidal, repellent and oviposition-deterrent activity of selected essential oils against *Anopheles stephensi*, *Aedes aegypti* and *Culex quinquefasciatus*. *Bioresour. Technol.*, 96(16):1749–57, 2005.

Yamamoto J, et al. Testing various herbs for antithrombotic effect. *Nutrition*, 21(5):580–7, 2005.

Rye: Hallmans G, et al. Rye, lignans and human health. *Proc. Nutr. Soc.*, 62(1):193–9, 2003.

Juntunen KS, et al. Consumption of wholemeal rye bread increases serum concentrations and urinary excretion of enterolactone compared with consumption of white wheat bread in healthy Finnish men and women. *Br. J. Nutr.*, 84(6):839–6, 2000.

Laaksonen DE, et al. Dietary carbohydrate modification enhances insulin secretion in persons with the metabolic syndrome. *Am. J. Clin. Nutr.*, 82(6):1218–27, 2005.

Larsson SC, et al. Whole grain consumption and risk of colorectal cancer: a population-based cohort of 60,000 women. *Br. J. Cancer*, 92(9):1803–7, 2005.

Leinonen KS, et al. Rye bread decreases serum total and LDL cholesterol in men with moderately elevated serum cholesterol. *J. Nutr.*, 130(2):164–70, 2000.

Oelke EA, et al. Rye. *Alternate Field Crops Manual*, at: http://www.hort.purdue.edu/newcrop/afcm/rye.html.

Safflower: Koyama N, et al. Serotonin derivatives, major safflower (*Carthamus tinctorius* L.) seed antioxidants, inhibit low-density lipoprotein (LDL) oxidation and atherosclerosis in apolipoprotein E-deficient mice. *J. Agric. Food Chem.*, 54(14):4970–6, 2006.

Lee JY, et al. Antioxidative flavonoids from leaves of *Carthamus tinctorius*. *Arch. Pharm. Res.*, 25(3):313–9, 2002.

Oelke EA, et al. Safflower. University of Wisconsin. *Alternative Field Crops Manual*, at: http://www.hort.purdue.edu/newcrop/afcm/safflower.html.

Yoo HH, et al. An anti-estrogenic lignan glycoside, tracheloside, from seeds of *Carthamus tinctorius*. *Biosci., Biotechnol., Biochem.*, 70(11):2783–5, 2006.

Zhang HL, et al. Antioxidative compounds isolated from safflower (*Carthamus tinctorius* L.) oil cake. *Chem. Pharm. Bull.*, (Tokyo), 45(12):1910–4, 1997.

Saffron: Abe K, Saito H. Effects of saffron extract and its constituent crocin on learning behaviour and long-term potentiation. *Phytother. Res*, 14(3):149–52, 2000.

Escribano J, et al. Crocin, safranal and picocrocin from saffron (*Crocus sativus* L.) inhibit the growth of human cancer cells in vitro. *Cancer Lett.*, 100(1–2):23–30, 1996.

Giaccio M. Crocetin from saffron: an active component of an ancient spice. *Crit. Rev. Food Sci. Nutr.*, 44(3):155–72, 2004.

Nair SC, et al. Saffron chemoprevention in biology and medicine: a review. *Cancer Biother.*, 10(4):257–64, 1995.

Noorbala AA, et al. Hydro-alcoholic extract of *Crocus sativus* L. versus fluoxetine in the treatment of mild to moderate depression: a double-blind, randomized pilot trial. *J. Ethnopharmacol.*, 97(2):281–4, 2005.

Verma SK, Bordia A. Antioxidant property of saffron in man. *Indian J. Med. Sci.*, 52(5):205–7, 1998.

Sagittaria spp.: Stevens M. Plant guide. Wapato: *Sagittaria cuneata* E. Sheldon. USDA NRCS National Plant Data Center, at: http://plants.nrcs.usda.gov/plantguide/pdf/cs_sacu.pdf.

Salad burnet: Janot MM, et al. Antibiotic activity of a tannin-tormentol complex extracted from the salad burnet (*Poterium sanguisorba* L.) [in French]. *Ann. Pharm.*, 13(3):167–8, 1955.

Salvia: Akhondzadeh S, et al. *Salvia officinalis* extract in the treatment of patients with mild to moderate Alzheimers disease: a double blind, randomized and placebo-controlled trial. *J. Clin. Pharm. Ther.*, 28(1):53–9, 2003.

Baricevic D, et al. Topical anti-inflammatory activity of *Salvia officinalis* L. leaves: the relevance of ursolic acid. *J. Ethnopharmacol.*, 75(2–3):125–32, 2001.

Feres M, et al. In vitro antimicrobial activity of plant extracts and propolis in saliva samples of healthy and periodontally-involved subjects. *J. Int. Acad. Periodontol.*, 7(3):90–6, 2005.

Imanshahidi M, Hosseinzadeh H. The pharmacological effects of *Salvia* species on the central nervous system. *Phytother. Res.*, 20(6):427–37, 2006.

Nolkemper S, et al. Antiviral effect of aqueous extracts from species of the Lamiaceae family against *Herpes simplex* virus Type 1 and Type 2 in vitro. *Planta Med.*, 72(15):1378–82, 2006.

Petersen M, Simmonds MS. Rosmarinic acid. *Phytochemistry*, 62(2):121–5, 2003.

Salvia divinorum users guide at: http://www.sagewisdom.org/ has lots of information on all aspects of this species.

Samphire: Salicornia, oil-yielding plant for coastal belts. Sci Tech Section. *The Hindu*, 5 September, 2003.

Sarsaparilla: Chu KT, et al. Smilaxin, a novel protein

with immunostimulatory, antiproliferative, and HIV-1-reverse transcriptase inhibitory activities from fresh *Smilax glabra* rhizomes. *Biochem. Biophys. Res. Commun.*, 340(1):118–24, 2006.

Humpert F. The effect of a sarsaparilla preparation (renotrat) in chronic nephritis, with particular reference to the uric acid content of the blood and urine;. *Klin. Wochschr*, 12:1696, 1933.

Iddamaldeniya SS, et al. A long-term investigation of the anti-hepatocarcinogenic potential of an indigenous medicine comprised of *Nigella sativa*, *Hemidesmus indicus* and *Smilax glabra*. *J. Carcinogen*, 5:11, 2006.

Rafatullah S, et al. Hepatoprotective and safety evaluation studies on sarsaparilla. *Int J. Pharmacognosy*, 29:296–301, 1991.

Sautour M, et al. Bioactive steroidal saponins from *Smilax medica*. *Planta Med.*, 72(7):667–70, 2006.

Shu XS, et al. Anti-inflammatory and anti-nociceptive activities of *Smilax china* L. aqueous extract. *J. Ethnopharmacol.*, 103(3):327–32, 2006.

Thurman FM. The treatment of psoriasis with sarsaparilla compound. *New Engl. J. Med.*, 337:128–33, 1942.

Trouillas P, et al. Structure-function relationship for saponin effects on cell cycle arrest and apoptosis in the human 1547 osteosarcoma cells: a molecular modelling approach of natural molecules structurally close to diosgenin. *Bio-org Med. Chem*, 13(4):1141–9, 2005.

Savory: Chorianopoulos N, et al. Characterization of the essential oil volatiles of *Satureja thymbra* and *Satureja parnassica*: influence of harvesting time and antimicrobial activity. *J. Agric. Food Chem.*, 54(8):3139–45, 2006.

Gulluce M, et al. In vitro antibacterial, antifungal, and antioxidant activities of the essential oil and methanol extracts of herbal parts and callus cultures of *Satureja hortensis* L. *J. Agric. Food Chem.*, 51(14):3958–65, 2003.

Hajhashemi V, et al. Antinociceptive and anti-inflammatory effects of *Satureja hortensis* L. extracts and essential oil. *J. Ethnopharmacol.*, 82(2–3):83–7, 2002.

Lampronti I, et al. Antiproliferative activity of essential oils derived from plants belonging to the Magnoliophyta division. *Int. J. Oncol.*, 29(4):989–95, 2006.

Skocibusic M, Bezic N. Phytochemical analysis and in vitro antimicrobial activity of two *Satureja* species essential oils. *Phytother Res.*, 18(12):967–70, 2004.

The Local Food Nutraceuticals Consortium (Corporate Author). Understanding local Mediterranean diets: a multidisciplinary pharmacological and ethnobotanical approach. *Pharmacol. Res.*, 52(4):353–66, 2005.

Yamasaki K, et al. Anti-HIV-1 activity of herbs in Labiatae. *Biol. Pharm. Bull.*, 21(8):829–33, 1998.

Scorzonera: Douglas J. *Scorzonera hispanica*: a European vegetable. New Zealand Institute for Food and Crop Research Ltd, at: www.crop.cri.nz/home/products-services/publications/broadsheets/028scorzonera.pdf

Seakale: Péron JY. Seakale: a new vegetable produced as etiolated sprouts. In: Janick J. & Simon JE (eds). *Advances in New Crops*. Timber Press, Portland, OR, pp. 419–22, 1990.

Seaweeds: Guiry MD. A website all about different aspects of seaweeds at: www.seaweed.ie.

Maeda H, et al. Fucoxanthin from edible seaweed, *Undaria pinnatifida*, shows antiobesity effect through UCP1 expression in white adipose tissues. *Biochem. Biophys. Res. Commun.*, 332(2):392–7, 2005.

Round FE. *The Biology of the Algae*. Edward Arnold Ltd., London, 1962.

Skibola CF. The effect of *Fucus vesiculosus*, an edible brown seaweed, upon menstrual cycle length and hormonal status in three pre-menopausal women: a case report. *BMC Complement. Altern. Med.*, 4:10, 2004.

Uses of different seaweeds, see the useful website at: http://www.innvista.com/HEALTH/foods/vegetables/seaveg.htm.

Sesame: Liyana-Pathirana CM, et al. Antioxidant properties of sesame (*Sesamum indicum*) fractions. Paper presented at the 2003 Institute of

Food Technologists Annual Meeting in Chicago, USA.

Oshodia A, et al. Chemical composition, nutritionally valuable minerals and functional properties of benniseed (*Sesamum radiatum*), pearl millet (*Pennisetum typhoides*) and quinoa (*Chenopodium quinoa*) flours. *Int. J. Food Sci. Nutr.*, 50(5):325–31, 1999.

Sichuan pepper: Cho EJ, et al. The inhibitory effects of 12 medicinal plants and their component compounds on lipid peroxidation. *Am. J. Chin. Med.*, 31(6):907–17, 2003.

Hatano T, et al. Effects of tannins and related polyphenols on methicillin-resistant *Staphylococcus aureus*. *Phytochemistry*, 66(17):2047–55, 2005.

Kamsuk K, et al. Effectiveness of *Zanthoxylum piperitum*-derived essential oil as an alternative repellent under laboratory and field applications. *Parasitol. Res.*, 100(2):339–45, 2007.

Paik SY, et al. The essential oils from *Zanthoxylum schinifolium* pericarp induce apoptosis of HepG2 human hepatoma cells through increased production of reactive oxygen species. *Biol. Pharm. Bull.*, 28(5):802–7, 2005.

Skirret: Larhsini M, et al. Investigation of antifungal and analgesic activities of extracts from *Sium nodiflorum*. *J. Ethnopharmacol.*, 53(2):105–10, 1996.

Larhsini M, et al. Screening of antibacterial and antiparasitic activities of six Moroccan medicinal plants. *Therapie*, 54(6):763–5, 1999.

Leclerc J, Peron JY. Mineral, sugar and vitamin contents of skirret (*Sium sisarum* L.). *Acta Hort.* (ISHS), 242:325–8, 1989.

Sorghum: Awika JM, et al. Decorticating sorghum to concentrate healthy phytochemicals. *J. Agric. Food Chem.*, 10;53(16):6230–4, 2005.

Awika JM, Rooney LW. Sorghum phytochemicals and their potential impact on human health. *Phytochemistry*, 65(9):1199–221, 2004.

FAO. Sorghum and millets in human nutrition. FAO Food and Nutrition Series, No. 27, Rome, Italy, 1995.

Varady C, et al. Role of policosanols in the prevention and treatment of cardiovascular disease. *Nutr. Rev.*, 61(11):376–83, 2003.

Sorrel/spinach: Duke JA. *Rumex crispus* L.. In: *Handbook of medicinal herbs*. CRC Press, Boca Raton, FL, pp. 414–5, 1985.

Fairbairn JW, Muhtadi FJ. Chemotaxonomy of anthraquinones in *Rumex*. *Phytochemistry*, 11:263–8, 1972.

Soybean: Berk Z. Technology of production of edible flours and protein products from soybeans. Ch. 9: Tofu, tempeh, soysauce and miso. FAO Agricultural Services Bulletin no. 97. Food and Agriculture Organization of the United Nations, Rome, 1992.

Branca F, Lorenzetti S. Health effects of phytoestrogens. *Forum Nutr.*, (57):100–1, 2005.

Brezinski A, Debi A. Phytoestrogens: the "natural" selective estrogen receptor modulators?. *Eur. J. Obstet. Gynecol. Reprod. Biol.*, 85(1):47–51, 1999.

Cassidy A. Potential risks and benefits of phytoestrogen-rich diets. *Int. J. Vitam. Nutr. Res.*, 73(2):120–6, 2003.

Cheng SY, et al. The hypoglycemic effects of soy isoflavones on postmenopausal women. *J. Womens Health* (Larchmt), 13(10):1080–6, 2004.

Choi MS, Rhee KC. Production and processing of soybeans and nutrition and safety of isoflavone and other soy products for human health. *J. Med. Food*, 9(1):1–10, 2006.

Clair RS, Anthony M. Soy, isoflavones and atherosclerosis. *Handbk Exp.*, (170):301–23, 2005.

Humfrey CD. Phytoestrogens and human health effects: weighing up the current evidence. *Nat. Toxins*, 6(2):51–9, 1998.

Kataoka S. Functional effects of Japanese style fermented soy sauce (shoyu) and its components. *J. Biosci. Bioeng.*, 100(3):227–34, 2005.

Petri Nahas E, et al. Benefits of soy germ isoflavones in postmenopausal women with contra-indication for conventional hormone replacement therapy. *Maturitas*, 20;48(4):372–80, 2004.

Setchell KD. Soy isoflavones — benefits and

risks from natures selective estrogen receptor modulators (SERMs). *J. Am. Coll. Nutr.*, 20(5 Suppl):354S–62S; discussion 381S–83S, 2001.

UK Food Standards Agency. Some soy sauce products to be removed. Ref: 2001/0120, 2001. At: http://www.food.gov.uk/news/pressreleases/2001/jun/soysaucerecall.

Spinach: Joseph JA, et al. Long-term dietary strawberry, spinach, or vitamin E supplementation retards the onset of age-related neuronal signal-transduction and cognitive behavioral deficits. *J. Neurosci.*, 18(19):8047–55, 1998.

Rutzke CJ, et al. Bioavailability of iron from spinach using an in vitro/human Caco-2 cell bioassay model. *Habitation* (Elmsford), 10(1):7–14, 2004.

Spirulina: Ayehunie S, et al. Inhibition of HIV-1 replication by an aqueous extract of *Spirulina platensis* (*Arthrospira platensis*). *J. Acquir. Immune Defic. Syndr. Hum. Retrovirol.*, 18(1):7–12, 1998.

Gemma C, et al. Diets enriched in foods with high antioxidant activity reverse age-induced decreases in cerebellar beta-adrenergic function and increases in proinflammatory cytokines. *Exp. Neurol.*, 22(14):6114–20, 2002.

Hayashi K, et al. A natural sulfated polysaccharide, calcium spirulan, isolated from *Spirulina platensis*: in vitro and ex vivo evaluation of anti-herpes simplex virus and anti-human immunodeficiency virus activities. *AIDS Res. Hum. Retroviruses*, 12(15):1463–71, 1996.

Mao TK, et al. Effects of a Spirulina-based dietary supplement on cytokine production from allergic rhinitis patients. *J. Med. Food*, 8(1):27-30, Spring 2005.

Sánchez M, et al. *Spirulina* (*Arthrospira*): an edible microorganism: a review. At: http://www.spirulina.org.nz.

Singh S, et al. Bioactive compounds from cyanobacteria and microalgae: an overview. *Crit. Rev. Biotechnol.*, 25(3):73–95, 2005.

Wang Y, et al. Dietary supplementation with blueberries, spinach, or spirulina reduces ischemic brain damage. *Exp. Neurol.*, 193(1):75–84, 2005.

Star anise: De M, et al. Antimicrobial properties of star anise (*Illicium verum* Hook f). *Phytother. Res.*, 16(1):94–5, 2002.

Star of Bethlehem: Goetz RJ, et al. Star of Bethlehem. In: Indiana plants poisonous to livestock and pets. Cooperative Extension Service, Purdue University, Indiana, USA at: http://www.vet.purdue.edu/depts/addl/toxic/plant39.htm.

Summer savory: Gulluce M, et al. In vitro antibacterial, antifungal, and antioxidant activities of the essential oil and methanol extracts of herbal parts and callus cultures of *Satureja hortensis* L. *J. Agric. Food Chem.*, 51(14):3958–65, 2003.

Hajhashemi V, et al. Antinociceptive and anti-inflammatory effects of *Satureja hortensis* L. extracts and essential oil. *J. Ethnopharmacol.*, 82(2–3):83–7, 2002.

Mosaffa F, et al. Antigenotoxic effects of *Satureja hortensis* L. on rat lymphocytes exposed to oxidative stress. *Arch. Pharm. Res.*, 29(2):159–64, 2006.

Sahin F, et al. Evaluation of antimicrobial activities of *Satureja hortensis* L. *J. Ethnopharmacol.*, 87(1):61–5, 2003.

Swede: Undersander DJ, et al. Rutabaga. In: *Alternate Field Crops Manual*. University of Wisconsin Cooperative Extension Service, University of Minnesota Extension Service and the Center for Alternative Plant and Animal Products, online at: http://www.hort.purdue.edu/newcrop/afcm/rutabaga.html.

Sweet potato: CGIAR (Consultative Group on International Agricultural Research). Sweet potato, at: http://www.cgiar.org/impact/research/sweetpotato.html.

Collins WC. Sweetpotato. *NewCrop Fact Sheet*. Purdue University, Center for New Crops and Plant Products.

Islam MS, et al. Anthocyanin compositions in sweetpotato (*Ipomoea batatas* L.) leaves. *Biosci. Biotechnol. Biochem.*, 66(11):2483–6, 2002.

Philpott M, et al. In situ and in vitro antioxidant

477